Art in the Lives of Immigrant Communities in the United States

Rutgers Series on the Public Life of the Arts

A series edited by

Ruth Ann Stewart
Margaret Jane Wyszomirski
Joni Maya Cherbo

Joni Maya Cherbo, Ruth Ann Stewart, and Margaret Jane Wyszomirski, eds., *Understanding the Arts and Creative Sector in the United States*

Joni M. Cherbo and Margaret J. Wyszomirski, eds., *The Public Life of the Arts in America*

Jan Cohen-Cruz, *Local Acts: Community-Based Performance in the United States*

Paul DiMaggio and Patricia Fernández-Kelly, eds., *Art in the Lives of Immigrant Communities in the United States*

Kate Fitz Gibbon, ed., *Who Owns the Past? Cultural Policy, Cultural Property, and the Law*

Diane Grams and Betty Farrell, eds., *Entering Cultural Communities: Diversity and Change in the Nonprofit Arts*

Lawrence Rothfield, ed., *Unsettling "Sensation": Arts Policy Lessons from the Brooklyn Museum of Art Controversy*

Susan Scafidi, *Who Owns Culture? Appropriation and Authenticity in American Law*

Art in the Lives of Immigrant Communities in the United States

EDITED BY
PAUL DIMAGGIO
AND
PATRICIA FERNÁNDEZ-KELLY

RUTGERS UNIVERSITY PRESS
NEW BRUNSWICK, NEW JERSEY, AND LONDON

Library of Congress Cataloging-in-Publication Data

Art in the lives of immigrant communities in the United States / edited by Paul DiMaggio and Patricia Fernández-Kelly.

p. cm. — (The public life of the arts)

Includes bibliographical references and index.

ISBN 978-0-8135-4757-2 (hardcover : alk. paper)

ISBN 978-0-8135-4758-9 (pbk : alk. paper)

1. Arts and society—United States—History—20th century. 2. Arts and society—United States—History—21st century. 3. Immigrants—United States—Social life and customs—20th century. 4. Immigrants—United States—Social life and customs—21st century. 5. United States—Social life and customs—20th century. 6. United States—Social life and customs—21st century. I. DiMaggio, Paul. II. Fernández-Kelly, María Patricia

NX180.S6A73 2010

700.86′9120973—dc22

2009043148

A British Cataloging-in-Publication data for this book is available from the British Library.

Visit our Web site: http://rutgerspress.rutgers.edu

Manufactured in the United States of America

Contents

Acknowledgments

We are deeply grateful to the Rockefeller Foundation, whose grant made possible the conference upon which this volume is based, and to the Andrew W. Mellon Foundation and the Pew Charitable Trusts, for their support for the Center for Arts and Cultural Policy Studies, directed by Stanley Katz, and cosponsorship of this conference. Thanks also to the Princeton University Center for Migration and Development, directed by Alejandro Portes, for its cosponsorship. The conference would not have materialized without the remarkable ability and collaboration of Nancy Doolan, associate director of the Center for Migration and Development.

Art in the Lives of Immigrant Communities in the United States

CHAPTER 1

Introduction

THE DIVERSITY AND MOBILITY OF IMMIGRANT ARTS

Paul DiMaggio and Patricia Fernández-Kelly

Over the past three decades, the dramatic rise in immigration from Asia, Latin America, and the Caribbean has greatly expanded the palette of cultural practices and styles to which people in the United States have access. Once considered exotic, the foods of Japan, India, and Mexico have become as American as the hamburger. Salsa music and reggae are now as familiar in many parts of the United States as they are in the Dominican Republic or Jamaica. And even as immigrants are changing mainstream tastes, the nation is altering the artistic expressions of immigrants. Hip-hop music and graffiti art now join second-generation Cuban, Arab, Mexican, and Vietnamese youngsters in places as near and far away as Brooklyn, Miami, Chicago, and San Diego. Immigration and art have thus become key elements to understanding life, culture, and creativity in contemporary America.

Given the richness of artistic expressions in immigrant communities and their impact on the larger culture, it is surprising how little has been written about the relationship between art and immigration to the United States. Although much about the new immigrant communities has been studied and documented in exquisite detail, there is virtually no research on their aesthetic practices or their contributions to American art and culture more broadly. The absence of research on this topic has been costly to both students of immigration and students of art and cultural policy. Research on the former has focused on economic and political institutions and social relations, paying less attention to the cultural life of new immigrants. Writings on immigrant art, by contrast, emphasize aesthetic and cultural details from countries of provenance, often at the expense of economic, political, and social factors in areas of destination. This book takes stock of and brings together those two divergent trends—one focusing on immigration, the other centering on aesthetics—in order to provide the first comprehensive analysis of the role of art in the life of immigrant communities in the United States. It comprises nine original papers first presented at the Conference on Migration and the Arts, sponsored by the Princeton Center for Art and Cultural Policy Studies and the Center for Migration and Development, on June 1–2, 2006, and two papers prepared shortly thereafter.

The title of this introduction refers to diversity of several kinds. First, there is the diversity of the United States' new immigrant communities themselves, most visible perhaps in New York's Queens Borough or in East Oakland, where various permutations of halal butchers, Chinese fishmongers, Mexican taquerias, Kosher delicatessens, and Cambodian sandwich shops spill one onto the other, making it possible to traverse vast ranges of social and cultural space in just a few city blocks. Then there is the *diversity within* immigrant communities, structured by point of origin (rural *vs.* urban and/or region of provenance), social class, and generation. Moreover, the arts serve a variety of functions for the migrant men and women who create and consume them: they provide the comfort of familiarity, helping them to interpret personal experience; they communicate about the old world to the young; and they serve as foci of rituals of solidarity and communion that bring immigrants together. The arts also enable immigrants to *represent themselves* to the host country, affirming public as well as private identities, for purposes both commercial and political. A final dimension of diversity, especially crucial for members of the immigrant second generation, spans the space between pursuit of traditional cultural forms to wholesale adoption of host-country genres—or, more often, the production and consumption of hybrid forms, reworking traditional ones to express new realities and inflecting host-country styles toward the shared migrant experience.

This last point begins to address the second theme evident in our title, that of mobility. By "mobility" we refer to the difficulty of keeping artistic genres confined and intact when the people who bear those traditions enter a new society and come into contact with previously unknown art and broader networks. In much of the twentieth century, it was conventional to describe the relationship between immigrant culture and mobility in terms of loss: immigrants, so the story went, sacrificed their culture of origin at the altar of assimilation, taking on the new world's culture as restitution for the old. Today, as our understanding of both the arts and immigration is influenced by work in anthropology and cultural studies on globalization, it seems more appropriate to understand the transformation of culture through migration in such terms as hybridity, multivocality, and translation. Immigrants move across forms of art, music, fashion, and cuisine, but art forms migrate as well, from immigrant communities to the mainstream and back. Such mobility involves not substitution, but accretion. Rather than abandon their old cultures, immigrants develop attachments to new styles while retaining their ties to the old, deploying both as sources of intrinsic satisfaction and as signals of identity. For example, Italian American families in Philadelphia in the 1980s served

American food to celebrate their shared mobility when their daughters married men of Italian descent, but offered Italian dinners to render ethnic boundaries clear when their daughters married Anglos (Goode, Curtis, and Theophano 1984). And when the Chinese-British young people that Wei (1994) studied spoke with their parents, they marked disagreements over adherence to traditional Chinese behavioral norms by using English phrases to emphasize their distance from their parents' world.

Cultural forms likewise change as they cross boundaries, incorporating elements of host-country genres (for example, substituting available for traditional ingredients in Old Country recipes) or creating true hybrids (as in the rai/rap fusion styles of France's Algerian young people). To be sure, cultural boundary crossings associated with immigration are nothing new: German immigrants to Mexico in the 1860s introduced the accordion, which became central to Mexican popular music, and conjunto bands in Texas were one of the sources that flowed together into Western swing, an indigenous jazz form whose conjunto roots gave it natural appeal to the children of Czech and German immigrants in Texas's plains (Peña 1985b). Perhaps the biggest difference today is the global context within which such borrowings and adaptations occur: Robert Rodriguez, a brilliant second-generation Mexican American writer/director from Texas in *Sin City* perfected the evolution of the graphic novel, a visual/literary form borrowed from Japan, into feature film.

In other words, both in past and more recent immigration waves, expressive behaviors, including art, have constituted a potent instrument to maintain distinct identities, salvage integrity, and negotiate inclusion into the host society. Because collective self-definitions related to nationality, race, and ethnicity are not static, aesthetic production remains fluid as well, often giving voice to existential realities that are difficult to pinpoint through quotidian language. Art allows for a kind of freedom not found in other forms of communication. And, because the immigrant condition is often restrictive and fraught with danger in receiving areas, art enables immigrants to break across boundaries through the use of their imagination.

Three questions concerning the diversity and mobility of immigrant arts unify the contributions to this volume. First, what is the role of the arts in the adaptation and assimilation processes of immigrant communities in the United States? For nearly 35,000 years, the capacity to communicate through art has supplemented and enhanced spoken and written language. The universal ability to convey information through music, dance, line, and color has been used to neutralize the potential for chaos and misunderstanding derived from linguistic diversity. As ancient as humanity is the anxiety that led the Hebrews to conceive of a Tower of Babel. Almost equally old are the high-relief drawings in the staircases of Persepolis commissioned by Darius I to broadcast his mission among people who spoke wildly different languages in his vast empire.

In areas of destination modern immigrants face linguistic barriers similar to those that plagued the Persians of antiquity. By resorting to artistic forms, often derived from tastes acquired in their countries of origin, immigrants strengthen bonds with other members of their own national and ethnic communities while using art as a bridge to connect with older, more established groups. Artistic expression thus plays a significant role in immigrant adaptation—it humanizes strangers, making them comprehensible and even appealing in their adopted country. The essays in this collection eloquently speak to this point, explaining how various immigrant communities use art to interact with and interpret the receiving society.

Second, how do aesthetic expressions contribute simultaneously to affirming cultural or national distinctiveness while enabling immigrants to integrate into the host society? Newcomers typically arrive in the United States hoping to fulfill dreams of prosperity and freedom. The majority, however, face language and cultural differences that force them to rethink who they are and how they are understood in their adopted country. Immigrant lives are, by definition, self-scrutinized lives. The gaze of established residents and citizens magnifies differences that immigrants are asked to account for. People with strong national identities are suddenly immersed into pan-ethnic classifications unknown in their countries of origin. "Asian," "Hispanic," and even "African American" are categories that erase the national distinctiveness of Chinese, Mexicans, and Haitians. Immigrants are thus torn between two poles, one connecting them to historical memory and national pride and one that beckons to a new form of American identity. In the case of exiles and refugees, whose departure from home countries tends to be characterized by extreme forms of dislocation, the pressure to retain national self-definitions while at the same time assimilating reaches dramatic proportions. This is the stuff out of which art is made. One way to make sense of such contradictory experiences is by recasting them in aesthetic ways that touch the heart as well as the mind. The chapters in this book weave together an integrated narrative in which art anchors the unique character of experience of various immigrant groups even as they open new channels for integration into the United States.

Third, what are the main differences and similarities in the artistic production of various immigrant communities and between first- and second-generation immigrants? This book takes a comparative approach by pinpointing commonalities and disparities in the aesthetic creations and lives of immigrants. It focuses on elements that transcend ethnic, national, and even generational boundaries. For instance, regardless of their provenance, immigrants tend to use art as a form of cultural capital that strengthens intragroup cohesiveness while at the same time making their groups visible to the larger society. On the other hand, specific historical trajectories and political and economic experiences give each community a unique flavor. An example of this is the strong connection between art and religion found among Haitians in Miami, as described by Rey and Stepick in this volume. Such levels of piety are less pronounced in many other immigrant communities. Originally from Mexico, *ranchera* music acquires a new meaning when adapted to the experience of Central American immigrants in the United States, as eloquently illustrated in the chapters by Cecilia Menjívar and Clifford Murphy.

Several of the chapters shine light on intergenerational differences among first-generation immigrants and their offspring. Older immigrants, exiles, and refugees tend to rely on known national forms and styles as they produce an art infused with nostalgia for the countries left behind. Their aesthetic expressions—as described by Fernández-Kelly, Maira, and Espiritu—are decisively centered on national traditions that forcefully denote cultural and class distinctiveness. In the imagination of first-generation immigrants, mores learned before arrival in the United States are often recast as a fountainhead of aspiration, honor, and cultural superiority. Their children, in contrast, tend to adopt pictorial and musical styles common in the United States but use them to communicate experiences derived from the immigrant condition. Such eclectic fusions become cornerstones of innovation and creativity not just in immigrant communities but also in the society at large.

Generational differences structure the way that immigrant families interact with artistic expression. First-generation adults, especially those with less command of English, may adhere to traditional forms from their country of origin. Frequently, they consume or exhibit artistic objects at home or in communal religious institutions. Buddhist temples, for example, are primarily responsible for preserving and passing down the classical traditions of Thai music and dance in the United States (Cadge and Sangdhanoo 2005).

By contrast, their children are more likely to seek independence by affiliating with host-country forms. In this volume, Stern and his associates provide a lovely illustration in their description of arts night at a Southeast Asian church in a working-class neighborhood of West Philadelphia. A performance of traditional Southeast Asian dances by children under their first-generation parents' influence was followed by presentations by college-educated second-generation members focusing on how to build careers in the commercial arts, and then a talent show by the community's young people—the latter devoted entirely to performance of rap, disco, and reggae.

Art also provides second-generation immigrants with the tools to circumvent the limitations of labor markets. In the age of globalization, when high educational levels necessary to secure desirable jobs are not available to many youngsters, artistic expression provides a means to succeed through self-employment, innovation, and creativity. Even immigrant children in prosperous and educated families now see art as a channel not only to prosper but to instill life with meaning. Immigrant parents toil and sacrifice, opening up paths for economic and social mobility; their children take a measure of prosperity for granted while yearning for something more than survival—prominence, pleasure, and even fame. The result is expressive entrepreneurship—that is, a type of self-employment that relies on artistic inventiveness to produce or disseminate goods and services. Through poetry, graffiti art, dancing, and music, immigrant children seek independence from the strictures and conventions of nine-to-five jobs. A multiplicity of new aesthetic forms in cities like Miami, Los Angeles, New York, and Chicago are the visible manifestation of those adaptations.

Immigration Past and Present

Immigration to the United States has a long history associated with that country's development and emergence as a world power. There are many countries throughout the world with large immigrant populations, but the United States is singular in the extent to which immigration is viewed as central to its national identity. The words of Emma Lazarus at the foundation of the Statue of Liberty are but one example of the way in which this country views itself. Yet the normative narrative of oppressed or destitute foreigners arriving on American shores to the embrace of freedom and opportunity carries a less sanguine subtext—that of exploitation, vilification, and exclusion. Perhaps with the exception of America's founders, every other group arriving in this country has experienced discrimination. It is, in fact, the vulnerability of immigrants that makes them ideal workers at times of economic expansion.

Throughout the second half of the nineteenth century, immigrants arriving mainly from various points in Europe filled the manufacturing jobs that turned the United States into a mighty exporter of durable goods. During that period and well into the twentieth century, immigrant workers and their descendents forged the American Dream—a predominantly white working class whose accomplishments were the fruit of hard work, effective mobilization, and a belief in individualism. And throughout the same period art provided respite, dignity, and humor to people whose main function was to increase economic power for investors and entrepreneurs. Irish, Italian, and Polish developed extraordinary repertories of color and diversity in their cuisines and religious practices, all of which blended elements of aesthetic significance. Eastern European Jews—among the most discriminated against of immigrants—not only took *Vaudeville* to previously unknown heights but also forged fundamental elements in the industry that became Hollywood. It is impossible to forget that the iconic images of cowboys, saloons, and shootouts in Wild West towns that made American cinema distinctive were patterned after shtetls and pogroms that Jews had witnessed in their countries of origin (Buhle 2004; Gabler 1989).

It was the jarring experience of bodily relocation that led Robert Park (1928) to note in a foundational article the marginal character of immigrants. Imbued with the culture left behind, they beheld an alien culture ahead. Between and betwixt, they were precariously positioned between two worlds but also ideally endowed to engage in decision-making processes that reconfigured who they were and who they might become. Acculturation, the term used by Park and his followers, thus entailed multidimensional choices that recast national background and identity in places of destination. Class, race, and gender were implicated in this progression. Immigrants' delicate negotiations to preserve personal and group identity have been a consistent aspect of American history.

Although immigration has been a constant in U.S. development, the economic and political conditions surrounding immigrants have changed over time. The most dramatic transformations have occurred since the 1960s, first with the passage of the Family Reunification Act that enabled larger numbers of people from Asia and Latin America to migrate to the United States; and then with the increasing momentum of globalization and industrial restructuring that altered the number and quality of economic opportunities available to those new immigrants. While European arrivals in the nineteenth and early twentieth centuries stepped into environments where manufacturing jobs were plentiful, their successors in the 1970s and beyond found employment mostly in low end services.

In addition to the changing character of the U.S. economy, political factors have further reconfigured the context of migration. Starting in 1986, after the passage of the Immigration Reform and Control Act (IRCA), and accelerating in the wake of the brutal 9/11 attack on New York and Washington, new forms of hostility and organized repression against immigrants took shape. The newly formed Department of Homeland Security redefined immigration from a labor management affair into a strict foreign and domestic security concern. Hundreds of new detention centers emerged throughout the nation to hold large numbers of people captured in homes and places of employment. Pundits and media personalities successfully reframed unauthorized immigration as a crime even as much of the public rallied against those who violated immigration laws. The emphasis was upon the transgressions of new arrivals, mostly from Mexico and Central America, not on the failings of an obsolete immigration policy.

As shown in this volume by Menjívar and by Durand and Massey, the dramatic changes in the political and economic climate surrounding modern-day immigrants have given way to distinct forms of artistic expression. Together with religion, art constitutes the most effective means to address transcendent questions, articulate political discourses, and shape personal and collective identities. Mexicans and Guatemalans languishing in detention centers turn to piety and drawing to express a condition fraught with suffering. In art and prayer they find a repertory of symbols to impose meaning upon a degraded existence.

Furthermore, in the wake of neoliberal economic policies and the temporary triumph of markets, art and religion are among the very few refuges to which impoverished, dislocated, and marginal peoples can turn in the search for respect. In other words, a major effect of religious and artistic expression is to enable individuals and groups to (a) imprint alien or destabilizing experiences with meaning; (b) facilitate new forms of sociability that bring immigrants into contact with material and human resources; and (c) reconfigure personal and collective identities in manners that reconcile cultural predicates learned in countries of origin with those prevailing in the adopted land.

Among the children of immigrants, the part that religion and art play in adaptation becomes even more complex. Having been raised in the United States, the New Second Generation has a thinner understanding of the cultural tenets that framed morality and aesthetic expression among their elders. For many, however, personal and collective identity requires the appropriation of symbols and points of view learned from parents imbued with national pride. This can produce dense ideational repertories that comfortably mesh images originally meant to contest one another in countries of origin. In a thought-provoking narrative, Ron Kelley, Jonathan Frielander, and Anita Colby (1993) describe the rooms of second-generation Iranian youths in Los Angeles, where posters of the Ayatollah Khomeini coexist with images honoring the memory of Mohammad Reza Shah Pahlavi. In life the two men were once at the two extremes of a political continuum; now they stand as fragments of a reconstructed self-definition made possible by temporal and spatial distance. In the mind of Iranian youngsters, national self-respect—a precondition for adaptation in a pluralistic nation like the United States—overcomes now-forgotten divisions.

A divided self may be part of the condition of modernity, but it acquires momentous proportions among the children of immigrants responding to pressures that pull them in various directions. Many immigrant children thus recompose cultural legacies to make sense of existence in their new country. Others wield art as a defensive tool to achieve vindication or reclaim honor. Still others choose styles that may allow them to reposition themselves vis-à-vis their elders. The chapters by Jamal and Maira in this volume illustrate such complex processes among second-generation Muslims and Indians in the United States.

Facets of Art in Migration

Culture is never more salient than in unsettled times (Swidler 1986). And few experiences are more unsettling than immigration, especially when associated with economic and linguistic dislocation. The arts, along with religion (Portes et al. 2006), are the principal cultural forms to which migrants appeal. Indeed, in the variety of roles they play for men and women adapting to a new life, the arts are the Swiss army knife of immigrant culture, suitable for many purposes.

Art as a Source of Comfort

The arts—music, cuisine, visual images—have always been a source of comfort to sojourners. The sounds, tastes, or images of home can provide solace and sustenance to an immigrant forging a life in a new and strange environment. The emphasis on home and family extends not just to the arts that immigrants pursue, but also to where they pursue them. The predominantly Latino immigrants who Stern and his colleagues interviewed (chapter 2) were significantly more likely to experience the arts at home and in church than their neighbors, and less likely to encounter the arts in nonprofit venues or public spaces. Indeed, for many immigrants, the arts and theodicy are closely linked. Devotional themes are common in visual expressions, for example, in the Haitian communities about which Terry Rey and Alex Stepick write. The *retablos* from which Jorge Durand and Douglas Massey derive so much insight about the history of Mexican migration to the United States owe their very existence to the devotional impulse, as they were produced by migrants and their families to give thanks for successful journeys.

Art as a Way to Interpret the New World

In his chapter, Gilberto Cárdenas describes the work of Mexican visual artists and photographers who documented and interpreted immigrant life, at first incidentally and, in recent years, by making the immigrant experience an explicit focus of their artwork. The task of interpretation is never solitary. Enduring productions in the visual arts are often sponsored by institutions, and their character is shaped by the needs of their sponsors. The artists Cárdenas describes produce their work for galleries and other public spaces, with an audience in mind. Cárdenas also describes a large depiction of Mexican migration in the stained glass of a Chicago church, where thirty-six murals illustrate the midcentury migrant experience, but in a stylized way that minimizes conflict and magnifies Catholic conventions.

Cecilia Menjívar's chapter explores the way in which the arts of Guatemalan and Salvadoran immigrants reflect their efforts to grapple with a critical aspect of their experience of migration, the liminal legal status in which many of them reside. She uses the arts to open "a window into immigrant worlds and meanings that often elude our analytic gaze, worlds that often remain clandestine." Especially striking in her account is the way the first generation's preoccupation with legality shapes not just their own art, but extends into the creative expressions of their children as well.

The Vietnamese artists, poets, and novelists who constitute the subject of Yen Le Espiritu's contribution do more than interpret or reflect upon their group's experience: They also attempt to repair and recover a collective memory of the historical events that drove their migration. They give voice to populations otherwise silenced by the burden of history. The public reconstruction of the past through literary works represents a peculiar fusion of private reflection and public witness, articulating the feelings of fellow immigrants while representing the group to the host society. We see the same dynamic in Patricia Fernández-Kelly's description of the work of Cuban-American painter Xavier Cortada, whose works bear transfigured witness to Cuba's struggles and to the experience of migration itself. But witness is not only the province of cosmopolitan, professional creative artists. We see a quieter, more personal form of witness in the *retablos* that Durand and Massey describe—votive paintings depicting challenges that immigrants faced in passage or giving thanks for a successful journey.

Arts consumers, as well as artists, employ music and images as opportunities for reflection. For example, popular music and dance are means by which the Indian American young people Sunaina Maira studied "grapple with ideologies of ethnic authenticity, national allegiance, and transnational affiliation."

Art as a Means of Extension to the New World

Immigrant artists look outward as well as inward, creating work for publics beyond their own community. There are many reasons for this. In some cases, when work is community focused, their social network may share a neighborhood with others who, by virtue of their presence, see a mural or listen to a band as it plays in a local park. Other artists craft messages for broadly political reasons—to help build coalitions across group boundaries or to tell their story to the host society in a compelling way. Still others reach out for the same reasons that most artists seek a public: To build careers that will grant them autonomy and support their creative expression.

Doing this is never easy. First, as Stern and his colleagues note, artists, especially those operating in traditions that seek critical as well as popular acclaim, find it especially difficult to break into the established framework of nonprofit presenters and exhibitors. Their work may be unfamiliar; they usually lack connections or the pedigree of prominent teachers; and because their only opportunities for sponsorship often come from community-based nonprofits, critics and impresarios may for that reason assume that their work is "educational," or "social," rather than "real art."

Second, once artworks cross ethnic boundaries, they are almost certain to be reappropriated, and not always in the ways that the artist would choose. Moreover, artists who seek mainstream success often will need to modify aesthetic traditions to match the tastes or training of their new publics. In the 1950s and 1960s, for example, musical artists from Latin America often adopted mysterious (Yma Sumac) or comic (Desi Arnaz) personae (Hayward 1999) to usher in new elements without alienating mainstream Americans.

Perhaps the most vivid examples of creative reappropriation come from cuisine, where the imperatives of the market render symbolic boundaries vulnerable once immigrant entrepreneurs reach out to host-country nationals. New York baby boomers grew up accustomed to dining at Cuban/Chinese restaurants—culinary hybrids run by Chinese Cuban restaurateurs transplanted to Chelsea after the revolution—just as their parents went to Chinatown for what menus termed "wonton [kreplach] soup" and moo goo gai pan. Today, one can find Ecuadorian/Italian cuisine in Trenton, Peruvian/Italian in New Brunswick, and Brazilian/Portuguese in Newark, all in neighborhoods where Latin American immigrants have succeeded older generations of European Americans.

At the same time, it is important to recognize the difference between hybridity and assimilation. Stern, Seifert, and Vitiello point out that "as migrants learn to adapt to the ways of their hosts, the hosts themselves inevitably change as well." Cilantro, lemon grass, and habanero peppers are available, unmarked as to origin, in suburban supermarket vegetable sections; *Slumdog Millionaire* introduced millions of non-Indian Americans to *desi* music; and salsa has become a staple of mainstream tables *and* dance clubs. Stern and his colleagues raise the possibility that immigrant artists may influence not just the content and style of art and music, but also the way in which arts institutions are organized: If Philadelphia is typical, artists from new immigrant communities are eschewing the grant-supported nonprofit organizations that for the past century have been the primary way serious artists have reached their publics, in favor of new arrangements, often rooted in commercial enterprise.

Art as a Form of Mobility

Fernández-Kelly calls attention to a phenomenon in the Cuban American community that is echoed in many chapters in this volume: expressive entrepreneurship, or the attraction of immigrant and second-generation young people to careers in the media and the arts. Maira's *desi*-club DJs, Wong's Chinese American and Jamal's Arab American rap artists, Espiritu's Vietnamese American poets and artists, Murphy's mariachi bands, and many others depicted in this volume exemplify this phenomenon. Expressive entrepreneurship appeals to young immigrants, especially working-class youth, for many reasons. When mobility into many mainstream professions may be blocked, the arts offer the possibility of economic success without extensive investment in formal education. The arts also provide a means of separating from the family and the more constraining aspects of immigrant culture while sustaining a deep, if selective, connection to that culture as expressed through aesthetic work. By espousing expressive entrepreneurship, the children of immigrants and immigrant children subvert normative expectations about labor in a capitalist society. The demands of the commercial marketplace may ease these young people either toward mainstream pop culture or, alternatively, as in the case of the Boston area's mariachi bands, toward pan-ethnic inclusivity. Not every form of artistic career is equally autonomous, of course. As Maira points out, many young people who do not go into artistic careers may be supported indirectly by the cultural economy—for example, by working in neighborhood groceries that sell music tapes or rent DVDs from their country of origin or by serving as guards in local cinemas.

Art as a Mode of Political Action

Immigrant artists have often sought to give voice to the political aspirations of their community and, in so doing, have often used a mix of indigenous and host-country cultural forms. Many, like the norteña band Los Jornaleros del Norte (described by Cecilia Menjívar), produce hard-hitting material for an audience of their compatriots. Others, by contrast, have one foot in the community and one in the larger art world. Nothing illustrates this better than Cesar Chavez's collaboration with Luis Valdez to use theatrical pieces to animate striking farm workers in California's Central Valley (see Cárdenas, this volume): Although his work was rooted in Mexican traditions, Valdez was a sophisticated and cosmopolitan director whose El Teatro Campesino evolved into a central player in Bay Area theater, influencing subsequent art within and outside the Mexican American community.

Such intellectual cosmopolitanism is common among immigrant artists who address political themes. As Cárdenas points out, Chicano artists, speaking at once to their own people and to larger publics, were aware of and influenced by Beat and Dadaist artists before them. It is perhaps typical of political artists to at once address their own communities and to extend beyond them. Cárdenas describes how the Centro Cultural de la Raza of San Diego reached out to Native American communities in the early 1970s. Immigrant artists working in conventional high-culture forms—for example, visual artists dependent on the dealer/gallery system for their success—may face additional boundary-spanning challenges when they wish to speak both to their own communities (only the relatively elite of whom may feel at ease in downtown arts centers) and the host-country public (for whom the work may require interpretation or translation, lest it be misunderstood or even misappropriated). Clifford Murphy, for example, describes the ways in which audiences at Boston area folk festivals code profoundly and subtly multiethnic Latino working-class ensembles as "Mexican" or, more damagingly (though more rarely), perceive them as illegal immigrants.

Art as a Means of Cultivating Understanding and Repairing Stereotypes

If immigrant artworks can be a means of representing a group to itself, they can also serve to provide an alternative narrative to those featured in the mainstream media and to repair negative attributions imposed upon the group by host-country nationals. Cecilia Menjívar notes that many first-generation Central American authors choose to express themselves in English: like Salvadoran American poet Jessica Grande, they tell their stories outside the community of Spanish speakers. Because of linguistic diversity, second-generation Asian Americans *must* communicate in English if they wish to be understood widely outside their own national-origin group, a condition that leads them, in effect, to address both Asian American and non-Asian publics by default: Filmmaker Justin Lin speaks simultaneously to other Asian American youth and to a broader non-Asian public. More broadly, elements of the AZN youth culture that Wong depicts aim to counteract the "model minority" image under which many Asian American young people labor. For the Haitian immigrants whom Rey and Stepick describe, visual art transcends linguistic difference as a means to improve and elevate an image tarnished by racism, AIDs, and negative depictions of the homeland.

As Amaney Jamal notes, no group faces a greater burden than do Arab American artists to address pejorative representations of their group in the larger culture. Jamal notes the complexity of this process when Arab American artists speak both to outsiders and to fellow Arab Americans, describing a "*dialectic* relationship between identity representations that emerge from within an ethnic group and the complementary identifications that preexist in the mainstream." While many Arab American artists actively reject the stereotypes imposed by the mainstream media, those who wish to reach a broader public face a singular challenge: feeling that they can only reach beyond their own community with work that perpetuates negative stereotypes of Arab Americans.

Art as a Means of Incorporation by the Majority

Just as immigrants can use art to interpret their own experience to themselves and their communities, so can institutions in the host society use art to interpret the immigrant experience to itself. Gilberto Cárdenas's chapter breaks ground in this little-explored topic with its discussion of the depiction of Mexican immigration to the United States by host country artists and photographers (men and women as prominent as Ansel Adams and Georgia O'Keeffe) throughout the twentieth century. As always, sponsorship shaped the record that remains, in both the simple sense (work sponsored by institutions is more likely to survive than the paintings or photographs of unaffiliated individuals) and in more complex ways. Thus, artworks sponsored by *National Geographic* took a historic view, focusing on group life more than on individuals, and emphasizing themes of cooperation, whereas photographs sponsored by the New Deal's Works Progress Administration employed realist conventions and included more portraits depicting a larger number of men and women at work.

As Cárdenas points out, even works produced by immigrant artists may, in effect, be reappropriated and their meaning transformed when they are placed in a museum setting. In her chapter, Espiritu calls attention to a more radical form of appropriation, when host-society monuments, like the Vietnam War Memorial or the Alamo, interpret events central to immigrant groups' own national histories from the vantage point of the host society. And, argues Sunaina Maira, incorporation also may occur when the host culture prescribes culturally mandated forms of difference. In a consumer society, she argues, "multicultural citizenship is performed through the consumption of distinct products that mark racial or ethnic identification."

Immigrant and Ethnic Identity

A central theme in the sociology of culture is that culture is connected intimately to individual and group identity. As a branch of culture that is produced with forethought, often by networks of specialized creators, art is especially important in this regard. Art, and culture more generally, can build fences or bridges, as Mary Douglas put it (Douglas and Isherwood 1979). The arts serve as a source of within-group solidarity and as a means to reach out and establish common cause with members of other groups as well. Max Weber ([1925] 1946) initiated this line of thinking with his seminal work on status groups—collectivities that share a common identity (which, he argued, could be based on any similarity no matter how modest) and a common sense of honor, often connected to a distinctive status culture. Such status cultures entailed characteristic modes of expression, conventions of propriety, and forms of taste. Significantly, the passages in *Economy and Society* on ethnic groups echo those on status groups. Weber viewed ethnic groups as a specific form of status group, for which membership is rooted in a shared construction of common nativity or descent ([1925] Weber 1978). Art, especially performing art, holds special value as a means of ratifying a shared status because it enables in-group members to assemble in ritual settings in which their shared identities are interpreted and affirmed in ways that produce heightened identification (Collins 2004). This dynamic is most marked in art annexed to religion but exists in secular art scenes as well. Similarly, cultural goods, or talk about in-group culture, can produce solidarity at the dyadic level: Even bitter political foes can find common ground over a bowl of congee or a dish of fried plantains.

Weber's ideas were developed further by Pierre Bourdieu, who emphasized the use of culture as a source of distinction, a means of separating in-group constituents from outsiders. Although Bourdieu emphasized the manner in which elites use familiarity with prestigious art forms as a means of cultural domination, he also noted that members of dominated groups espouse aesthetic standards (austerity and minimalism for the well educated but impecunious; simplicity and unpretentiousness for the working class) that make a virtue out of economic necessity. In a similar way, members of immigrant groups can use indigenous forms of artistic expression to distinguish themselves from outsiders in ways that honor values such as piety, domesticity, or spontaneity that they regard as distinctive sources of collective honor.

The arts also represent a forum in which artists and audiences can work out questions of identity and of the relationship of the group to the larger society. This more deliberative, reflective use of art is ordinarily in the realm of cultural specialists, often those associated with artistic forms or traditions (literature, modernist art, or theater, for example) favored by a group's elite. Yet songwriters and rappers may also do such identity work for a broader audience.

Art and Cultural Distinctions

To say that the arts sustain immigrant identities is true enough, but it is also too simple, because it presumes that there is only one identity to sustain. That is rarely the case. Groups connected by national origin are often divided by region, class, or ethnicity. Where numbers are few, immigrant communities may form around broad identities alien to most people in their countries of origin. Tammy Smith (2007), for example, has described the way in which Italians and Croatians from Istria—a region divided between Italy and Yugoslavia after World War II and characterized by years of ethnic strife—define themselves as "Istrians" in the Brooklyn neighborhood they share. Jamal highlights the ways that organizers of Arab art exhibits and traveling performing artists use shared symbols and common values to promote an "Arab" identity that transcends differences of national origin, class, and even religion. As Jamal notes, nonprofit organizations are especially committed to conflict-free identity presentations, discouraging Arab American artists from addressing political topics, especially when their work will be exhibited beyond the ethnic community, and highlighting the contributions of mostly well-educated and assimilated members of the Arab American community to mainstream America. Yet even the best-intended can find this difficult when stakeholders divided by politics, nationality, or class pressure institutions to foster conflicting representations of the group.

In her contribution to this volume, Deborah Wong identifies a division between Asian American kids who embrace an "Amerasian" self-definition that combines Asian American pan-ethnicity with youth culture from Japan and elsewhere on the Pacific Rim, on the one hand, and, on the other, those who adopt an Asian American version of hip-hop. Although the styles are loosely related to social class, both permit young people to celebrate an Asian American identity (albeit very different versions) while distancing themselves from the culture of the first and, in some cases, the second generations. A defining aspect of Asian immigration to the United States is that spoken languages vary from country of origin to country of origin, so that English becomes the lingua franca and mastery of English (ordinarily associated with exposure to and knowledge of U.S. pop culture) is the sine qua non for participation in pan-ethnic settings. The cultural, economic, and linguistic diversity of Asian American national-origin groups poses a special dilemma for cultural institutions that seek to represent (and to constitute by representing) the "Asian American community" (Fred and Farrell 2008).

Clifford Murphy describes a different kind of pan-ethnicity at work in the Boston area's mariachi and norteña music clubs. Musicians, even within a band, come from different countries and must transcend their individual national identities to create an audience. In the working-class city of Chelsea, the focus of his study, musical pan-ethnicity comes out of a history of conflict, as Latinos from many countries joined for many years in "a multiethnic resistance to Latino solidarity." In this context, the bands and music clubs do not simply reflect pan-ethnicity but also actively contribute to its construction, eliding ethnic difference by emphasizing commonalities of social class. Rather than developing explicitly pan-ethnic personae, Chelsea's mariachi bands and clubs invoke the national symbols and *charro* dress and cuisine of Mexico, the dominant culture in the Latin American diaspora. They signal their broader identity musically through a use of accordion and incorporation of norteña and conjunto styles attractive to working-class immigrants from throughout Latin America.

Contemporary African immigrants share a particularly complex relation to native-born African Americans whose families were taken to the Americas through the slave trade. As Stern and colleagues note, black Philadelphians old enough to remember the cultural nationalism of the 1960s retain an interest in African art, despite some suspicion of African immigrant artists; whereas black youth of the hip-hop generation have little interest in African culture. Adding to the complications are class distinctions (African immigrants tend to be well educated, if not prosperous) and resource scarcity, with straitened African American institutions reluctant to share funds or funders with African newcomers.

The Arts as Bridges

The arts are not only a way to represent difference, however. They are also tools with which immigrants can build bridges to host-country nationals. In some instances, this takes place when immigrant artists inflect their own forms of expression to the tastes and needs of the broader public. In others it involves affiliating with host-country cultural forms.

Reaching Out through Traditional Art. The viability of this strategy requires that there be some fit between immigrant art forms and genres familiar to members of other groups. Thus Philadelphia's Latin American immigrant artists contribute to the production of murals—a distinguished tradition in Mexican art—but with themes tailored to realities of the multiracial communities in which they reside. Bridging efforts are often directed not to the public at large but to members of other immigrant collectivities and may take the form of collaborations, as in the case of Philadelphia's "Chino Latino" exhibitions of Asian influences on Latin American art. In other cases, mainstream media may arouse interest among host-country nationals in aspects of immigrant culture: In parts of the United States, new age enthusiasm for Eastern religion attracts locals to traditional dance classes in Thai Buddhist temples, where they study alongside of, if not in precisely the same way as, first-generation Southeast Asian immigrants (Cadge and Sangdhanoo 2005).

The Second Generation and Hip-Hop. The affinity between many in the immigrant second generation and hip-hop, the culture of black urban America and, increasingly, of white suburban middle-schoolers as well, emerges clearly from several of the chapters in this volume. Hip hop culture, especially rap music, has been America's most successful cultural export in the last twenty years. Forms of artistic expression developed within U.S. African American communities and first employed by black Americans as means of resistance and emblems of identity quickly spread beyond urban ghettoes to middle-class African Americans and from there to the white middle class. By 2005, nearly every nation on earth, from the Netherlands to Turkmenistan to Japan, had its own rap music or rap-inflected version of indigenous pop.

It should be no surprise then that hip hop has appealed to immigrant youth, nor that immigrant youth have adopted forms of expression that hip-hop made popular, given that many first-generation immigrants encountered such forms before migration. Jamal counterposes the way that established nonprofit institutions project Arab American identity as mainstream and unthreatening to the more radical posture of many Arab American youth. It is significant that rather than embracing cultural expressions from their countries of origin, these young people, many of whose families have moved to the United States relatively recently, have adopted hip-hop as a mode of expression, identifying symbolically not with their countries of origin, but with the dispossessed of their new country. From the standpoint of identity, hip-hop elides differences based on nationality and permits Arab American youngsters to express an affirmative and confrontational identity while remaining selective in their embrace of "traditional" Middle Eastern practices and values.

At the same time, there is an important distinction to be made between those who consume hip-hop culture and those who produce it. For the former—Jamal's young Arab Americans or the Cuban Americans youth of whom Fernández-Kelly writes—hip-hop music and fashion represent a generational signal of independence, a way to distance themselves from home and parents and to align symbolically with outsiders. At the same time, identification does not imply association: Cuban immigrant youth, for example, and poor or working-class African American kids occupy different worlds, dancing at different clubs and hanging out on different corners; the identification is purely symbolic. And Indian American *desi* youth can flirt with hip-hop styles, but only if they socialize within the group (Maira, this volume).

For the creators, by contrast, embracing hip-hop often requires involvement with businesses in which African Americans are dominant, and immersion in African American social worlds. For the poets Bao Phi or Suheir Hammad, or the rap artists Jin or Iron Sheikh, success has meant the creation of tangible bridges between immigrant and black communities and, in some cases, mentor relations with senior African American entrepreneurs and artists.

What is perhaps most striking in the chapters of this book is the subtlety with which second-generation youth deploy traditional and host-country forms to construct cultural identities. Maira describes a performance by an Ivy League South Asian student group that mixed "kathak, an Indian classical dance, with flamenco, and a very energetic hip hop fusion ensemble," noting that the working-class South Asian girls she brought to the performance enjoyed such hybrid numbers more than either traditional or "American" alternatives. Immigrant youth are thus attracted to hybrid forms that keep identities fluid, open, and a little ambiguous, preserving many opportunities and foreclosing none.[1]

Similarities and Differences in Immigrant Art

Thus far we have emphasized the existential conditions that most migrants share: the experience of entering a new society—usually with limited or insecure material resources and frequently in the face of adverse, even tragic, conditions in one's place of origin—and needing to find a footing and make a life in the adopted land. Barriers to communication with the host-country population, active discrimination, or both add to the economic challenges. All immigrants use the cultures that they bring with them to some degree, often finding in indigenous forms a degree of comfort, a ratification of personhood, and a means of expression available from few other cultural resources.

That said, men and women from different countries of origin enter the immigrant experience with vastly different aesthetic resources and orientations, and they face very different pressures and constraints. Social class, education, and language all shape the role of the arts in different immigrant communities at both the collective and individual levels. The circumstances surrounding migration—whether voluntary and gradual or traumatic and disruptive—also shape the use of the arts. So do the ways in which the arts are connected to other institutions.

Artworlds, Resources, and Incentives

Howard Becker (1974) used the term "artworld" to refer to the integrated network of actors who together produce a work of art. Becker's point was that, whatever conventions define authorship in a particular culture and art form, it always takes, if not a village, at least a creative community and a set of shared conventions to generate art. We expand the notion of "artworld" slightly to include engaged audiences, those who, in interacting with one another and with artists themselves to define and evaluate artworks and performances, become, in effect, participants in the creative process. In emphasizing connections, Becker taught us to examine the context in which art is produced and consumed, and the ways in which producers depend upon institutions to provide the resources they need and to help them reach a public. Multiple institutions—mass media, small commercial establishments, nonprofit presenters, churches, political parties, and so on—impose different constraints on the creative process and filter the access of publics to the arts in various ways. In so far as artists in different immigrant communities have different relationships to institutions, their work and the way their work enters into their communities' life is likely to vary.

The chapters in this volume describe a vast range of institutional linkages, some pertaining to forms of art (visual artists need places to exhibit their work; actors need venues in which to perform; authors need publishers) and others related to the exigencies of particular communities. Many of the connections the authors describe are commercial: Sunaina Maira, for example, describes nightclubs that sustain *desi* culture for middle-class Indian youth, and Clifford Murphy introduces the Boston area nightspots within which mariachi and norteña music flourish. Not all such linkages are commercial, however: Terry Rey and Alex Stepick emphasize the role of the church in Miami's Haitian communities, and Amaney Jamal discusses the role of the arts among Arab Americans for whom culture can never be entirely separate from the political struggles that shape the experience of many, and among whom the most politically oriented are also those who view the arts as most important to their identities. Because different institutions select artists and artworks for support and presentation on the basis of differing principles, and also impose dissimilar constraints on the artists who work within them, such institutional variation is an important source of distinction among immigrant communities.

Access to Institutions, Artistic Traditions, and Differences among Immigrant Groups

As Stern and his colleagues note, new immigrants tend to pursue artistic activities without benefit of the nonprofit organizations that have sustained the arts in the United States for almost a century. And though some of the Central American artists, writers, and musicians about whom Menjívar writes work through established institutions, many others record their own CDs, publish their own poetry and novels, and paint or write for themselves and their friends, employing a form of do-it-yourself production more often associated with highly educated, technologically sophisticated mainstream youth.

At the same time, there are some differences on this dimension, primarily related to the number of generations in which groups have been present in large numbers and to the extent to which their members pursue high-culture art forms conventionally organized by nonprofit entities. Some of these differences have to do with the number of years group members have lived in the United States.

It takes many years for informal artistic activities to evolve first into organizations and then into institutions. Other differences are associated with class position. Fernández-Kelly describes the distinguished history of Cuban ballet, a genre that has long been sponsored by wealthy patrons and nonprofit institutions. Maira notes that Indian classical arts have long been embraced by U.S. (as well as Indian) elites, finding a place in museum galleries and prestigious venues like Carnegie Hall. And Haitian visual artists have developed relationships to U.S. galleries that facilitate access for immigrant painters. By contrast, groups whose art lacks a classical tradition (or whose classical tradition has not been embraced by host-country elites) are far more likely to work through informal or commercial organizations.

If immigrant artists have limited access to nonprofit institutions, their ability to penetrate the mainstream media is even more restricted. Despite the popularity of a few Latin superstars like Ricky Martin and the occasional success of immigrant or second-generation comedians (e.g., Carlos Mencia, Russell Peters, Margaret Cho, and the Axis of Evil) on nonnetwork cable, little programming reflects immigrant cultures, and that which does largely translates those cultures for the host-country population. Latinos should have an edge, because they are a large language group. Spanish-language television is a sizable and successful business throughout Latin America, and even in the United States two Spanish-language television networks have competed for the immigrant audience (Mora 2011). Yet relatively few Latinos are employed in mainstream network television, and little programming addresses their interests. Baynes (2009) contends that immigrant Internet use is depressed (even in households with computers) by the relative paucity of major Spanish-language resources online. For other groups, the situation is even worse. Efforts to create Asian American networks have foundered on issues of language and generation—programming for the English-speaking second generation illustrates the problem of linguistic diversity and raises new issues of audience size. And whereas earlier immigrant waves had access to block-purchased radio time on small, locally owned stations or published their own newspapers, the rise of national radio chains and the crisis of the newspaper industry have reduced the availability of these options.

As a result, immigrant groups' relation to popular culture that reflects their own national origin or immigrant experience is partial and depends on characteristics of home-country media. Univision and Telemundo have provided access to Mexican or Venezuelan *telenovelas* to immigrants from Latin American in recent decades. Thriving media industries, sustained by middle-class publics, in Japan, Korea, and Hong Kong provide youth culture to the middle-class GenerAsians, about whom Deborah Wong writes. And India's vital film and pop music industries, combined with American club culture, sustains *desi* culture in the United States. For other groups—Central American, Haitian, Arab-American—access is more limited and, in so far as the Internet is the best source (for music, at least), constrained by economic factors. Yet for those who do have Internet access, like the South Asian high-schoolers whom Maira studied, the Web facilitates participation in a transnational community, shaping identities and patterns of culture consumption that are more focused with respect to subnational identities at the same time that they are diffuse and global with respect to space. The Internet does not dictate such global patterns, of course. These are most likely to be pursued by immigrants relatively less integrated into their new communities. For those with proper incentives, the Internet can be an avenue to broader, pan-ethnic identities, as with the GenerAsian youth described by Wong or in the case of Dennis Martinez, the young Cuban American described by Fernández-Kelly who learned hip-hop online because blacks and Latinos in his school did not interact.

The Political Context of Migration

Relationships to the arts are also shaped by the political context of migration both directly, when artists feel compelled to address disruptive historical events, and indirectly, by influencing the kinds of persons who migrate. The Cuban immigration that Fernández-Kelly describes was a product (in large part) of the Cuban Revolution, and the first wave of immigrants were highly educated. The disruptiveness of the change, and the ban on travel to Cuba, created an art embedded in what Fernández-Kelly calls a "culture of nostalgia," and the prominence of Cuban elites among the founders of Miami's Cuban American community ensured that Cuban high culture would figure prominently in Cuban life. Similarly, as Espiritu points out, the chaotic and traumatic war that led to Vietnamese migration to the United States left scars that artists are still addressing. And for many in the Arab American community, politics is either central to their identities, as in the case of many Palestinian Americans, or has been thrust upon them by discrimination and scapegoating after 9/11.

Class Differences within Immigrant Communities

Class does not only differentiate between groups, it works within them as well. "To study ballet in Miami," Fernández-Kelly tell us, "is more than a hobby, it is also a class entitlement, a way to mark superior breeding." Appreciation of opera, another genre in which Cuban artists historically excelled, is also associated with high class standing.

One's prospects in the host society and the resources at one's command determine the value of investments in U.S. or traditional home-country cultural forms, producing different strategies even within national-origin groups. We see this clearly among the Indian American young people about whom Maira writes. The predominantly middle-class and Hindu New Jersey youth became artistically bilingual, with command of both traditional Indian high culture *and* U.S.-Indian hybrid pop forms. Just as parents define authentic Indian high culture as the classical traditions of music and dance, so their children have the power to define fashionable authenticity in popular culture. By contrast, the working-class and in many cases Muslim youth she studied relied more heavily on Indian and Pakistani popular culture, rented from South Asian video shops, gleaned from the Internet, and consumed in private. With fewer prospects for upward mobility, and often outsiders by religion as well as national origin and class, their consumption patterns were more similar to those of peers in South Asia than to those of upper-middle-class immigrant youngsters.

The influence of class is often complicated by its association with other factors that divide immigrant communities. In the South Asian case, for example, working-class immigrants are more likely than their middle-class counterparts to be Muslim, to come from rural areas, and to have arrived recently. Class is closely associated with time of arrival among Cuban Americans, as well, where the first large cohort came from society's top ranks, while later cohorts, especially the Mariel émigrés of 1980, were mostly unskilled and semiskilled workers.

Art as a Window into the Immigrant Experience, Immigration as a Window into the Arts

We have written primarily about the art and artists that the authors of this volume's chapters have studied and described. If this book does nothing more than tell their stories, it will achieve a great deal. But we believe that this work has broader implications for scholars interested in both immigration and the arts.

With respect to the first, the arts provide windows into the immigrant experience through which scholars of immigration would do well to peek. These windows are never transparent: As Wendy Griswold (1987) has explained, the relationship between a community and its artists entails many levels of mediation and selection. Nonetheless, despite interpretive ambiguity, analyzing artworks that immigrants produce and consume can provide information about the immigrant experience unavailable from other sources.

There are two reasons for this. First, artworks are rich in meaning, both intended and unintended: They give the analyst access both to textured accounts of feelings and motives *and* to the preconscious of the artists who produce them. To be sure, one can also study meaning through fieldwork and ethnography, but analyzing art provides a wider and somewhat different focus. In this regard it is worth distinguishing, as historians do, between the typical and the exemplary. Durand and Massey focus on the typical—they have amassed a large collection of immigrant *retablos* and have analyzed it as a way to understand the challenges that immigrants faced across several decades of Mexican migration to the United States. By contrast, Espiritu and Wong focus more on exemplary figures, successful professional artists whose work is compelling for transcending local boundaries or articulating collective themes more forcefully or clearly than could less gifted creators. Cárdenas covers both the typical and the exemplary, exploring the value of photography in documenting immigrant life and the capacity of murals to capture the political intentions of immigrant artists.

Second, some immigrant groups have produced a visual or musical record for periods in which written sources are scarce. The men and women who left *retablos* throughout the Southwest produced no memoirs, and if they kept diaries they did not survive. We can learn about the dreams and fears of contemporary Central American immigrants from the poems and *corridos* that Cecelia Menjívar describes and from the words of the mariachi and norteña tunes that Clifford Murphy has studied. In this way, the arts produce a kind of bread-crumb trail where lettered signposts are absent, providing vital if imperfect insight into lives that would otherwise be opaque to later generations.

Research of the kind presented here is as critical for understanding the arts in America as it is for understanding immigration. Without appreciating both the art forms that the United States' newest residents have contributed and the ways in which immigrants adapt and transform art forms they encounter here, we can only reach a stylized and imperfect understanding. The tools that social scientists and policy analysts have ordinarily used to characterize the arts in the United States are ill equipped to apprehend the aesthetic expressions of the newest Americans and their influence on the broader society. National surveys, by their nature, must ask questions that most respondents can understand: Listing the dozens of musical genres, literary forms, types of traditional dance, craft arts, and visual genres of the new immigrants on a national sample survey would exhaust respondents' patience to no avail. Statistical studies of cultural organizations ordinarily focus upon those that are easiest to find—those in well-established genres, with their own trade or service organizations, which can provide membership lists (and whose members have staff to complete complex surveys). When there are just a few organizations of a given kind and no one has enumerated them, or where artists or curators work in community groups that are not themselves "arts organizations," or where creative people work outside of formal organizations altogether, their arts have been invisible to most researchers (DiMaggio 2006).

The contributors to this volume have not tried to map the arts synoptically at the national level. Many, such as Fernández-Kelly, Maira, Menjívar, and Murphy, employ ethnographic methods to gain a deep understanding of the art of a particular community or of a specific set of creators or performers. Some focus on the artworks themselves, using critical methods to describe distinct bodies of creative work. Still others combine interpretive and statistical methods to understand a concrete art form (Durand and Massey's study of *retablos*) or a set of artists and organizations in a single metropolitan area (Stern et al.'s study of Philadelphia). Such efforts complement the results of national surveys by unveiling hidden substrata of the arts in the United States. Such aesthetic expressions may be too new to the United States or too marginal or insufficiently institutionalized to have a high profile at present. But they mean a lot to many Americans; and some of them will, like other forms brought by earlier waves of immigration, shape mainstream U.S. culture, both high and popular, in decades to come.

NOTE

1. Sociologists refer to behaviors that preserve multiple options in this way as "robust action" (Padgett and Ansell 1993). One can extract from the accounts we have discussed here an analogous concept of "robust culture."

CHAPTER 2

Migrants and the Transformation of Philadelphia's Cultural Economy

Mark J. Stern, Susan C. Seifert, and Domenic Vitiello

Assimilation is the problem of the twenty-first century. The number of international migrations has nearly doubled in the past quarter century from 99 million in 1980 to 190 million in 2005 (United Nations 2006). The issue of how to bridge the chasms that separate the world's peoples in general and those that separate migrant from host populations confronts an ever-expanding share of the world's nations.

Assimilation is often conceptualized as a one-way process: "to make like," according to the simplest dictionary definition. Certainly, there is a long history of efforts to do that to migrant populations. The efforts to Americanize the immigrants of the early twentieth century sought to encourage or coerce them into giving up their cuisine, religion, and child-rearing patterns so they could be "made like" earlier generations of Americans (Mink 1995). Yet, these efforts rarely succeed because assimilation typically is a two-way process. As migrants learn to adapt to the ways of their hosts, the hosts themselves inevitably change as well.

This chapter examines the two-way process of assimilation in the case of immigrant involvement in the arts and cultural world of Philadelphia, whose immigrants have adapted to their new home by incorporating some American cultural practices while retaining some of their own. At the same time, however, immigrant cultural practice is changing the social organization of the arts and culture in the United States. In particular, the presence of immigrant artists and cultural participants has strained the American system of nonprofit arts. Although the status of nonprofit cultural organizations has already been challenged by other changes in the cultural world and its audiences, immigrants' cultural engagement appears to be accelerating this trend.

While not a gateway city, Philadelphia is representative of a large number of American metropolitan areas with a relatively recent and moderate increase in the foreign-born population. Indeed, if Philadelphia's modest immigrant presence has had a significant impact on the region's cultural sector, immigrants are likely to have even more influence in gateway metropolitan areas.

Data from a variety of sources developed by the Social Impact of the Arts Project (SIAP) at the University of Pennsylvania demonstrate that immigrants are relatively disengaged from the mainstream cultural institutions of metropolitan Philadelphia. Yet migrants are engaged in informal and commercial culture in levels comparable to those of the U.S.-born population. The expansion of immigrant cultural engagement has given a push to trends that were already well under way in the arts world, specifically the shift in the division of labor among nonprofit, commercial, and informal arts.

The Social Structure and Ecology of Immigrant Communities

Immigrants represented a larger share of Philadelphia's population at the beginning of the twenty-first century than at any time since the 1950s. As recently as 1990, only 6.6 percent of the city's population was foreign-born, and by 2006, according to the American Community Survey, the proportion had reached 11.3 percent. In addition to their sheer growth, immigrant communities have influenced the cultural sector in two ways. First, the immigrant population displays a distinctive class structure as a result of broader changes in the economy and in immigration policy and enforcement practices. Second, the immigrant generation and the second generation have reacted in distinctive ways to different sectors of the cultural world.

More than nine million immigrants entered the United States between 1991 and 2000, the largest influx in American history (U.S. Department of Homeland Security 2008). As a result, the proportion of the nation's population that was foreign-born reached 12 percent in 2005. When this immigrant wave started to swell in the 1970s and 1980s, the vast majority of immigrants settled in a small set of gateway centers: New York, California, Texas, and Florida, in particular. But by the end of the century, immigrants and their influence on the nation's social, economic, and cultural life had spread to secondary cities and nonmetropolitan areas (Portes et al. 2006).

Philadelphia reflected this pattern. Between 1945 and 1990, internal migration—by African Americans and Puerto Ricans—had been the defining feature of the city's demographic history. As late as 1990, Puerto Ricans had swelled the size of the city's Latin American population to 7 percent, while the relatively small Russian, Korean, and Southeast Asian communities were the major immigrant presence.

By the early twenty-first century, this situation had changed markedly. Puerto Ricans had been joined by 129,000 foreign-born Latin Americans. Meanwhile, by 2005, 184,000 Asians lived in the metropolitan area. Although fewer in number, the

42,000 African immigrants living in metropolitan Philadelphia made a visible impact on the economic and cultural life of the city. Of the nearly half million foreign-born persons in the metropolitan area in 2005, more than one-quarter had entered the United States since 2000.[1]

Within the city, a distinctive urban ecology had emerged (fig. 2.1). African and Caribbean immigrants found homes within the sprawling African American neighborhoods of West Philadelphia. Southeast Asians in Southwest Philadelphia, by contrast, entered a buffer zone between black West Philadelphia and the predominantly white neighborhoods of the far Southwest. For two decades, Asians replaced Italians and other groups in South Philadelphia, even as a smaller Mexican community began to take a foothold. In the Pennsylvania suburbs, Asians—particularly Koreans and South Asians—were the most significant immigrant groups.

North Philadelphia presented the greatest diversity. By 2000 a number of former white working-class neighborhoods—Olney, Juniata Park, and Oxford Circle—became home to a mix of Asian and Latin American immigrants, Puerto Ricans, and African Americans. In place of an ethnic map defined by homogeneous black and white enclaves, North Philadelphia became a complex mixture of diverse neighborhoods.

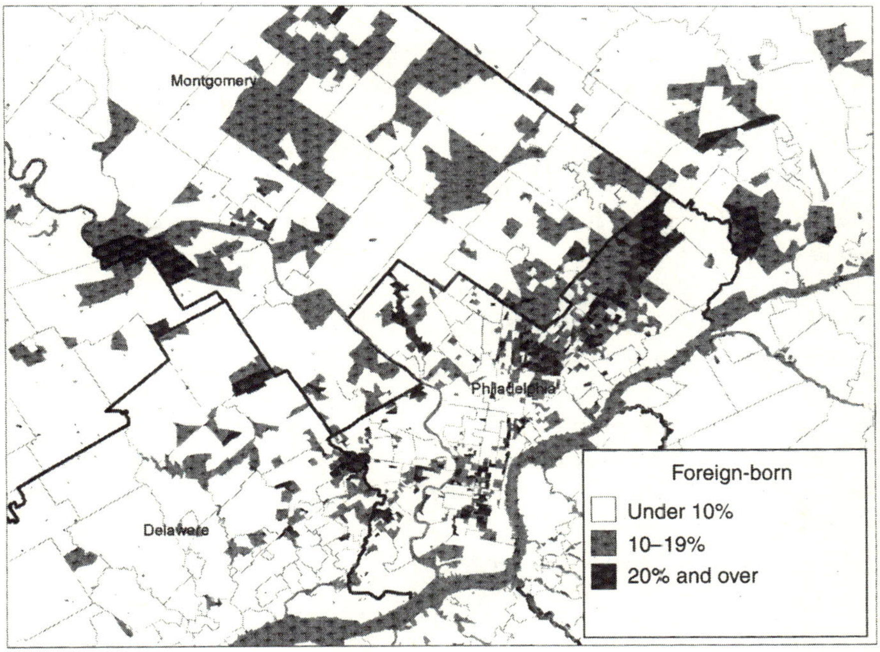

Figure 2.1. Block groups with a concentration of foreign-born population in five Pennsylvania counties in metropolitan Philadelphia, 2000. *Source*: U.S. Bureau of the Census 2000, SF3.

Immigrants have never held a single class position. The labor flows of the late twentieth century, however, widened class divisions within and between immigrant groups. The vast majority of immigrants—both legal and undocumented—have entered the low-wage sectors of the American economy, including service occupations, unskilled factory employment, and domestic work. Although a majority of immigrant workers enter the bottom of the labor market, a substantial proportion of immigrants arrive in the United States with college degrees. These workers have tended to concentrate in some of the most robust sectors of the economy, including information technology and pharmaceuticals. As with the rest of American society, immigrants have developed a two-tier occupational structure comprising an affluent minority and a low-wage majority.

Frequently, social class mirrors differences *between* nationality groups. Asian immigrants—especially those from India, Korea, and Hong Kong—were likely to arrive in the United States with college degrees that allowed them to enter white-collar work, while Western Hemisphere immigrants were more concentrated in low-skilled work. For example, in 2000, 42 percent of foreign-born Asians in Philadelphia were college graduates, but only 6 percent of Puerto Rican–born residents and 11 percent of foreign-born Hispanics had a college education.

Yet, *within* nationality groups, there remained considerable differences in education and income. The occupational structure of immigrant communities also exhibited a two-tier structure. In 2005, foreign-born blacks, whites, and Asians were more concentrated in professional and technical work than the population as a whole, while at the same time they were overrepresented in service employment. Although the Hispanic population lagged behind other foreign-born groups in income and educational attainment, U.S.-born Hispanics were more likely than U.S.-born African Americans to be professional or technical workers. A significant share of Puerto Rican–born residents had professional or technical occupations, even though the group was overrepresented at the bottom of the occupational ladder as well (table 2.1).

Migrants' incomes were less equally distributed than those of the U.S.-born population. Hispanics born outside the fifty states, foreign-born blacks, and foreign-born Asians were all underrepresented among middle-income households. Forty-nine percent of all households in the region had adjusted incomes between 50 and 150 percent of the metropolitan average, but only 37 percent of foreign-born Hispanics, 43 percent of foreign-born blacks, and 45 percent of foreign-born Asians did. All foreign-born groups were overrepresented among those with adjusted incomes less than half the regional average.

The social stratification of immigrant groups had a spatial dimension as well, with Center City and suburban immigrants having significantly higher incomes (table 2.2, columns 1 and 3) than those in Philadelphia neighborhoods (column 2).[2] Immigrant average incomes in Philadelphia neighborhoods outside of Center City were less than two-thirds of the metropolitan area average, ranging from 36 percent among Puerto Rican–born households to 63 percent among

TABLE 2.1

OCCUPATIONAL CLASSIFICATION BY ETHNICITY AND NATIVITY, METROPOLITAN PHILADELPHIA LABOR FORCE, 2005

Ethnicity and nativity	*Professional and technical (%)*	*Agricultural and extractive (%)*	*Managers and proprietors (%)*	*Clerical (%)*	*Craft (%)*	*Operative (%)*	*Service (%)*	*Laborer (%)*	*Nonoccupational responses (%)*	*Total (%)*
U.S.-born, non-Hispanic white	28.1	0.3	16.4	25.3	9.7	6.6	9.8	3.4	0.3	100.0
U.S.-born, non-Hispanic black	19.8	0.0	8.5	25.7	5.1	8.2	26.2	3.6	2.9	100.0
U.S.-born Hispanic	22.3	0.6	8.6	28.2	7.8	8.0	18.1	3.6	2.9	100.0
U.S.-born Asian	45.8	0.0	22.0	16.9	0.8	7.6	6.8	0.0	0.0	100.0
Puerto Rican– born Hispanic	17.2	0.4	3.9	19.0	12.9	15.5	24.6	5.6	0.9	100.0
Foreign-born Hispanic	8.1	3.8	5.3	13.4	10.0	19.6	23.9	15.3	0.5	100.0
Foreign-born black	26.8	1.0	5.2	21.1	3.7	9.2	29.5	2.0	1.5	100.0
Foreign-born Asian	37.3	0.2	8.3	14.4	5.5	13.0	19.8	1.1	0.5	100.0
Foreign-born white	27.1	0.4	15.0	18.1	9.9	9.6	14.1	5.2	0.5	100.0
Other	21.3	1.0	14.9	22.8	5.3	12.9	16.3	4.3	1.2	100.0
All members of labor force	26.8	0.3	14.5	24.5	8.8	7.5	13.3	3.5	0.8	100.0

Source: Ruggles et al. 2008.

TABLE 2.2

HOUSEHOLD INCOME AS PERCENTAGE OF AREA AVERAGE, BY ETHNICITY/NATIVITY AND LOCATION, METROPOLITAN PHILADELPHIA, 2005

Ethnicity/nativity	*Center City*	*Rest of Philadelphia*	*Rest of metropolitan Philadelphia*	*Entire metropolitan area*
U.S.-born non-Hispanic white	171	91	112	111
U.S.-born non-Hispanic black	70	57	75	65
U.S.-born Hispanic	153	39	106	84
U.S.-born Asian	149	81	123	117
Puerto Rican–born Hispanic	74	36	70	51
Foreign-born Hispanic	138	50	60	59
Foreign-born black	89	59	66	62
Foreign-born Asian	78	59	106	92
Foreign-born white	177	63	114	103
Other	140	72	87	86
Total	148	69	107	100

Source: Based on Ruggles et al. 2008.

Note: Household incomes adjusted to total household income divided by number of persons in household.

foreign-born whites. Average foreign-born household incomes in Center City and the Philadelphia suburbs were considerably higher.

Immigrants with college educations were also concentrated in Center City. Fifty-eight percent of foreign-born persons over the age of twenty-five living in Center City were college graduates. The comparable figures for the rest of Philadelphia and the suburbs were 26 and 40 percent respectively.

The demography of the foreign-born population of metropolitan Philadelphia has a number of implications for its cultural engagement. First, the immigrant community is, by and large, a recent immigrant population. In 2005, about half the foreign-born had lived in the United States for fewer than fourteen years, and a majority of this population were relatively new to Philadelphia. Second, the immigrant population was sharply divided by class and geography. Center City and, to a lesser extent, the suburbs were home to college-educated, relatively affluent immigrants; while Philadelphia neighborhoods were dominated by lower-income, less-well-educated immigrants. These social and economic realities have framed the ways in which Philadelphia's immigrant communities have engaged in local arts and culture.

The Cultural Engagement of Foreign-Born Philadelphians

As the immigrant population of Philadelphia grew and diversified during the last years of the twentieth century, the cultural economy of American cities like Philadelphia was also experiencing significant changes. The nonprofit sector that had been central to the expansion of the arts during the middle of the twentieth century was challenged both by declines in philanthropic and government support, and by a vigorous expansion of for-profit culture (McCarthy et al. 2001).

By the early twenty-first century, Philadelphia's cultural economy was composed of a mix of established nonprofit organizations, commercial cultural firms, and an informal arts sector composed of unchartered participatory groups, guilds, and associations. DiMaggio (2006) conceptualizes the world of noncommercial arts activity as three concentric zones. At its center is a core of established, free-standing cultural organizations recognized by the IRS as tax-exempt organizations. Around this core are two rings—one consisting of embedded programs associated with a church, a university, or another more established nonprofit organization and one consisting of minimalist arts groups like participatory associations and artists' collectives.

Establishing the relative sizes of these different zones is no easy task. A SIAP study of cultural providers in the five-county Philadelphia region (Southeastern Pennsylvania) in 2003 suggested that the entire noncommercial sector consisted of roughly 1,500 entities (Stern and Seifert 2005a). A 2006 report by the Greater Philadelphia Cultural Alliance, in contrast, identified in the five-county region 218 established nonprofit organizations, a figure that could be taken as a first approximation of the nonprofit core (Greater Philadelphia Cultural Alliance 2006).

Estimating the commercial cultural sector, too, is an imprecise exercise. Using 2003 data, SIAP estimated that more than two thousand for-profit cultural firms are located in Philadelphia and its four suburban Pennsylvania counties (Stern and Seifert 2005b). A 2008 metropolitan study of the for-profit creative economy—which includes eleven counties in southeastern Pennsylvania, southern New Jersey, northern Delaware, and a number of sectors beyond the arts and culture—estimated that Greater Philadelphia hosts nearly ten times as many firms with employees in creative industries (Innovation Philadelphia 2008).

The size of the informal sector—cultural and creative activity that is associated with neither an established nonprofit nor a commercial cultural firm—is much more difficult to estimate. A significant portion of the 1,500 entities identified by SIAP in 2003 would fit into this definition, as would a range of activities not detected by any of these sources. A survey of metropolitan Philadelphia artists, for example, concluded that about a quarter of all reported professional projects or positions undertaken during the previous year were either in informal or private unincorporated settings (Stern, Seifert, and Zaman 2005).

Participation Patterns in Immigrant Neighborhoods

Immigrants are less involved in the region's nonprofit cultural programs than U.S.-born residents of Philadelphia. Yet this relative underengagement in nonprofit culture does not carry over to their participation in informal cultural activities or in commercial culture. Several possibilities might explain this divergence. To the extent that the centrality of nonprofit organizations in cultural production and consumption in the United States is exceptional, immigrants' low involvement in the sector may simply reflect a lack of familiarity with the rules of the game. Alternatively, low immigrant involvement may result from particular historical circumstances; the recent immigrant wave coincided with a period of significant retrenchment within the nonprofit arts sector as public and philanthropic funding stagnated or contracted. Finally, low rates of immigrant involvement in the nonprofit sector might derive from a form of social exclusion, in particular, from the social networks that bind cultural producers, patrons, and funders.

Our findings about immigrant cultural engagement are based on evidence from three sources. First, we use a regional geographic database to examine the relationship of cultural engagement to the concentration of immigrants. Although this database is our most comprehensive source, it suffers from its ecological structure; that is, we know that cultural engagement is lower in immigrant neighborhoods, but we cannot tie these low rates to individual immigrants. Second, in order to make that connection, we turn to a 2004 survey of residents of North Philadelphia and Camden, New Jersey (a small city directly across the Delaware River from Philadelphia). This survey suggests that foreign-born residents are as involved in informal cultural practices as U.S.-born residents but are much less likely to attend institutional cultural events. Finally, we use a 2004 survey of artists in metropolitan Philadelphia to estimate in which sectors foreign-born artists are more likely to work.

As we have seen earlier, immigrants—although only a small share of metropolitan Philadelphia residents—concentrate in particular neighborhoods. Overall, 23 percent of the metropolitan area's block groups had a foreign-born population that composed more than 10 percent of their population. As a result, we can use evidence on the cultural engagement of residents of these block groups to gauge the behavior of foreign-born residents.

The regional geographic database developed by SIAP compiles data from a variety of public and organizational sources. We gathered information on cultural participants by compiling the participation databases of over seventy-five regional and community-based cultural organizations.[3] An inventory of nonprofit cultural providers was developed by SIAP from a variety of sources, including the IRS master list of exempt organizations, grant applications, and a search of relevant media and Internet sites. Data on commercial cultural firms were acquired from a search of digital yellow pages. The concentration of resident artists posed the greatest challenge. Here the Pew Fellowships for the Arts kindly allowed us to use its mailing list, which represents area artists who made inquiries or were otherwise identified by the organization. We consider this list, although far from comprehensive, the best single source for estimating the concentrations of artists across metropolitan Philadelphia.

Each of these databases was geo-coded and then aggregated to a census block group file. As a result, we are able to estimate four dimensions of cultural

TABLE 2.3

CULTURAL ENGAGEMENT INDEXES BY FOREIGN-BORN CONCENTRATION, METROPOLITAN PHILADELPHIA BLOCK GROUPS, 2003–2004

Foreign-born concentration	*Cultural participation rate*	*Nonprofit cultural providers*	*Commercial cultural firms*	*Resident artists*
Under 10%	126.0	4.62	4.1	3.41
10% or higher	160.3	11.69	7.65	6.79
Total	133.8	6.24	4.91	4.18

Source: SIAP 2008.

Note: Cultural participation rate is participation per 1,000 residents in block group. Other indexes are average number within one-half mile of block group.

engagement: rates of participation in metropolitan-area cultural programs, nonprofit cultural providers, commercial cultural firms, and resident artists for every block group in the five Pennsylvania counties of the metropolitan area.[4]

The four cultural engagement indices are, in fact, higher in immigrant neighborhoods than in the rest of the metropolitan area, a finding that seems to contradict our major claim. Take the example of participation rates, calculated as the number of cultural participants per 1,000 residents. In block groups in which over 10 percent of the residents were foreign-born, the cultural participation rate was 160 per 1,000 residents, while in other parts of the metropolitan area the rate was only 126 per 1,000, a difference of 27 percent. The differences for nonprofit, commercial, and artist concentration all favor immigrant neighborhoods as well (table 2.3).

If we use a finer measure of foreign-born concentration, the picture gets a bit more complicated. Cultural engagement and immigrant presence have a curvilinear relationship, rising until the foreign-born percentage of a block group reaches 20 percent and then falling. Still, overall, areas with higher numbers of immigrants appear to have higher rates of engagement.

This apparent contradiction is the result of other confounding characteristics of high-immigrant block groups. Most important, the immigrant block groups with the highest concentration of cultural participation are those located in or near Center City. In addition to locational advantage, these sections of the metropolitan area happen to have the highest concentration of college graduates. These two variables—metropolitan location and educational attainment—complicate our ability to identify the unique impact of immigrant concentration on cultural engagement.

Areas of metropolitan Philadelphia with high numbers of college graduates, for example, in 2004, had more than twice the average rate of regional cultural participation, while those with low educational attainment had only a quarter of the

TABLE 2.4

CULTURAL ENGAGEMENT INDEXES IN METROPOLITAN PHILADELPHIA BLOCK GROUPS, 2003–2004

Metro location	*Cultural participation rate*	*Nonprofit cultural providers*	*Commercial cultural firms*	*Resident artists*
Center City	635.0	98.5	50.3	41.3
Rest of Philadelphia	100.3	8.2	3.1	6.3
Suburban counties (Bucks, Chester, Delaware, and Montgomery)	140.4	2.4	4.7	1.8
Total	133.8	6.2	4.9	4.2

Source: SIAP 2008.

TABLE 2.5

CULTURAL PARTICIPATION RATE, BY FOREIGN-BORN CONCENTRATION, METROPOLITAN PHILADELPHIA BLOCK GROUPS, 2003–2004

Metropolitan area	*Less than 10%*	*10% or greater*	*Total*
Center City	1000.0	634.8	635.0
Rest of Philadelphia	107.2	83.5	100.3
Suburban counties (Bucks, Chester, Delaware, Montgomery)	136.0	162.4	140.4
Total	126.0	160.3	133.8

Source: SIAP 2008.

regional rate. The correlation of the cultural indices with metropolitan location was even sharper. Center City and its immediate surroundings had a rate of cultural participation that was nearly five times the regional average. Likewise, the concentrations of nonprofit cultural providers, commercial cultural firms, and resident artists in Center City were sixteen, ten, and ten times the regional average, respectively (table 2.4). When we estimated the relationship of immigrant concentration to cultural engagement for different metropolitan locations, for example, we found that regional cultural participation rates in high immigrant sections were only about 60 percent those of low immigrant areas. Only in the suburbs were the cultural participation rate of immigrant concentrations higher than areas with few immigrants (table 2.5).

TABLE 2.6

CULTURAL ENGAGEMENT INDEXES BY FOREIGN-BORN CONCENTRATION, METROPOLITAN PHILADELPHIA BLOCK GROUPS, 2003–2004

Foreign-born concentration	*Cultural participation rate*	*Nonprofit cultural providers*	*Commercial cultural firms*	*Resident artists*
Less than 10%	246.0	36.8	19.0	15.6
10% or greater	231.6	35.5	19.0	14.6

Source: SIAP 2008.

Note: Results of general linear model analyses, estimates of marginal means controlled for educational attainment and metropolitan location.

To gain a clearer portrait of the unique influence of the concentration of foreign-born residents on cultural engagement, we produced a set of estimates of the four indices corrected for the influence of metropolitan location and the concentration of college graduates in block groups.[5] When corrected for metropolitan location and college graduation rates, the relationship between the concentration of immigrants and the cultural indices of block groups was nearly reversed. For three of the four indices, the corrected estimate for high-immigrant neighborhoods was now *lower* than that of other block groups. For example, the cultural participation rate for high immigrant neighborhoods was 6 percent lower than for other block groups, while the differences for nonprofit providers and artists were 4 and 7 percent respectively. All three of these differences were statistically significant at the .01 level (table 2.6).

The one exception to this pattern is instructive. Commercial cultural firms were as likely to be present in high immigrant neighborhoods as in the rest of the metropolitan area, even after controlling for metropolitan location and educational attainment. Commercial culture appears to be the sole sector in which the concentration of immigrants is not associated with a weaker presence in a block group.

Using a slightly different method of correcting for the influence of metropolitan location and educational attainment, we examined immigrant neighborhoods where this correction had an impact (figs. 2.2 and 2.3).[6] As a comparison of the maps suggests, correcting for these factors had little effect on the cultural participation rates of high immigrant sections in Center City and the sections of Montgomery County near the Philadelphia city line. However, the estimated participation rates were reduced in the more affluent sections of Montgomery County farther from the city and the high-immigrant neighborhoods of Northeast Philadelphia. At the same time, high immigrant block groups in North Philadelphia—including the neighborhoods of Olney and Juniata Park—saw their corrected cultural participation rates increase.

As we noted earlier, the immigrant community of Philadelphia is divided between affluent and well-educated newcomers, who are more likely to live in

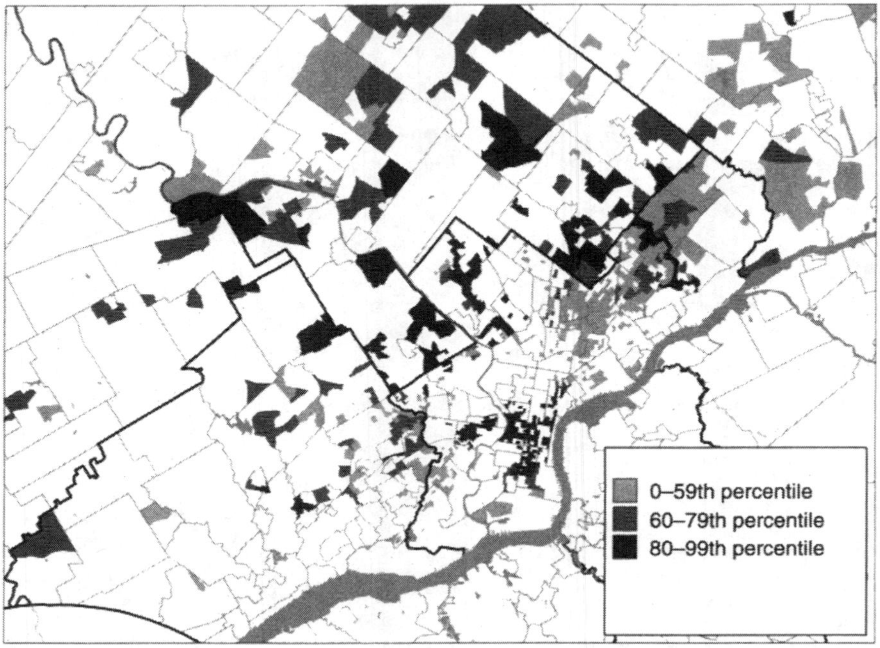

Figure 2.2. Cultural participation index for block groups with foreign-born concentration in five Pennsylvania counties in metropolitan Philadelphia, 2000.

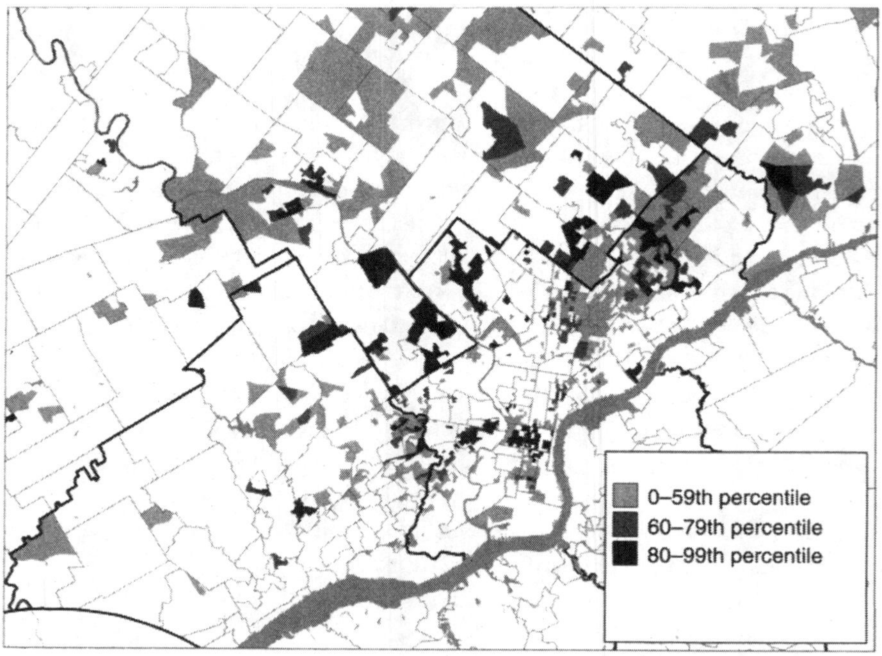

Figure 2.3. Cultural participation index, corrected for metropolitan location and college-graduation rate, for block groups with foreign-born concentration in five Pennsylvania counties in metropolitan Philadelphia, 2000.

Center City and the suburbs, and moderate-income immigrants, who tend to reside in the neighborhoods of the city. Although we can control for these influences in the interest of statistical analysis, social class and geography play important roles in structuring the cultural experience of immigrant communities.

To summarize, the analysis of regional Philadelphia cultural-asset data leads to two conclusions. First, when corrected for other neighborhood characteristics, block groups with high concentrations of immigrants are less likely to have the key elements of the established nonprofit cultural system—high rates of regional participation, presence of nonprofit organizations, and presence of artists. Second, commercial cultural firms are as likely to be present in high immigrant neighborhoods as in the rest of the metropolitan area.

Individual Cultural Participation of New Philadelphians

The geographic analysis demonstrates that, at the aggregate level, concentrations of immigrants are associated with lower levels of mainstream nonprofit cultural engagement. In this section, we use results of a 2004 survey of residents of low-wealth neighborhoods in North Philadelphia and Camden to examine individual cultural participation patterns among immigrants.[7] This survey of approximately six hundred respondents between the ages of eighteen and eighty-three was intended to examine the connections between residents' involvement in informal social and cultural activities (for example, singing alone or socially) and their participation in institutional cultural programs (for example, attending musicals or plays). Overall, the research identified a significant gap between the two. Respondents had active social and cultural lives that were focused on private homes and commercial cultural venues like bars and nightclubs but relatively little involvement in the cultural programs of formal nonprofits. The survey also solicited open-ended information on what residents consider their creative outlets. These data included a very broad set of activities, such as holiday decorating and automobile detailing, as well as more conventional creative activities like ceramics, needlecraft, and creative writing (Stern and Seifert 2005c).

Among the 602 respondents, 44 identified themselves as foreign-born and 35 as U.S.-born with foreign-born parents. Forty-three of the foreign-born and 25 of the second-generation respondents identified themselves as Latino or Hispanic. As a result, the survey provides little evidence on the arts and cultural engagement of Asian, European, or African immigrants.

Immigrants and U.S.-born residents with foreign-born parents were significantly less engaged in established cultural activities than other U.S.-born residents. They attended music concerts, plays, musicals, dance performances, and live theater less often than residents from nonimmigrant families. For example, more than half of U.S.-born respondents reported attending a music concert during the previous year compared to only 25 percent of immigrant respondents. Along the same lines, 35 percent of U.S.-born residents with U.S.-born parents had attended a community arts program during the previous year, but only 12 percent of immigrants and 24 percent of U.S.-born respondents with foreign-born parents had done so (table 2.7).

TABLE 2.7

NORTH PHILADELPHIA AND CAMDEN, NEW JERSEY, RESIDENTS INVOLVED IN SELECTED CULTURAL AND CREATIVE ACTIVITIES, BY NATIVITY, 2004

	Foreign-born n = 44 (%)	*Foreign-born parent n = 35 (%)*	*Other n = 523 (%)*	*Total N = 603 (%)*	*F*	*Sig.*
Cultural Involvement						
Arts education	15.9	14.3	7.6	8.6	2.51	0.082
Music concert	25.0	57.1	55.4	53.3	7.83	0.000
Music concert in neighborhood	20.5	54.3	48.2	46.5	6.84	0.001
Play or musical	22.7	34.3	48.0	45.3	6.24	0.002
Play or musical in neighborhood	20.5	34.3	40.9	39.0	3.78	0.023
Music, dance, theater	40.9	65.7	66.7	64.8	6.03	0.003
Attended community arts program	11.6	23.5	34.9	32.5	5.64	0.004
Play musical instrument informally	4.5	2.9	4.4	4.3	0.10	0.908
Sing informally	11.4	20.0	21.6	20.8	1.30	0.273
Play musical instrument privately	11.4	11.4	6.1	6.8	1.50	0.223
Sing privately	38.6	65.7	32.1	34.6	8.56	0.000
Total activities	2.1	3.6	3.3	3.2	5.86	0.003
Total institutional activities	1.5	2.6	2.7	2.6	6.73	0.001
Any activity	0.77	0.83	0.79	0.79	0.2	0.823
Any institutional activity	0.50	0.66	0.68	0.66	2.86	0.058
	Foreign- born	*Foreign-born parent*	*Other*	*Total*	*F*	*Sig.*
Creative Activities						
Art with kids	34.1	40.0	20.8	22.9	5.14	0.006
Auto detailing	6.8	14.3	6.9	7.3	1.33	0.264
Calligraphy	0.0	0.0	0.8	0.7	0.30	0.739
Ceramics	6.8	5.7	5.2	5.3	0.12	0.891
Clothing design	18.2	14.3	16.6	16.6	0.11	0.898
Decoration, holiday, etc.	31.8	34.3	13.0	15.6	10.68	0.000

TABLE 2.7

CONTINUED

	Foreign- born	Foreign-born parent	Other	Total	F	Sig.
Doll making	0.0	2.9	0.0	0.2	8.30	0.000
Graffiti	6.8	5.7	3.3	3.7	0.96	0.385
Graphic design	2.3	5.7	2.5	2.7	0.67	0.511
Illustration	4.5	2.9	1.7	2.0	0.90	0.408
Jewelry	2.3	2.9	1.3	1.5	0.35	0.703
Knitting	18.2	17.1	11.7	12.5	1.16	0.313
Needlepoint	9.1	0.0	3.4	3.7	2.55	0.079
Painting	13.6	25.7	7.3	8.8	7.80	0.000
Photography	9.1	14.3	9.0	9.3	0.55	0.580
Printmaking	2.3	0.0	0.2	0.3	2.73	0.066
Quilting	6.8	8.6	3.1	3.7	2.09	0.124
Rug hooking	0.0	0.0	0.4	0.3	0.15	0.860
Sculpture	0.0	0.0	0.2	0.2	0.08	0.927
Sewing	13.6	17.1	16.1	15.9	0.11	0.897
Weaving	0.0	0.0	1.0	0.8	0.38	0.684
Woodworking	4.5	5.7	3.6	3.8	0.23	0.798
Fiction	4.5	14.3	10.3	10.1	1.09	0.335
Nonfiction	2.3	11.4	9.8	9.3	1.44	0.237
Letters	22.7	28.6	17.2	18.3	1.73	0.177
Diary	15.9	20.0	10.5	11.5	1.92	0.148
Poetry, rap	9.1	25.7	24.3	23.3	2.70	0.068
Plays	2.3	2.9	2.1	2.2	0.05	0.956
School or business	4.5	8.6	4.6	4.8	0.57	0.566
Creative writing	34.1	54.3	38.0	38.7	2.04	0.131
Creative writing last year	27.3	51.4	31.2	32.1	3.36	0.035
Social dance	2.3	8.6	2.3	2.7	2.52	0.081
Total creative activities	3.16	4.43	2.78	2.91	5.26	0.005

Source: Based on Benchmark Project resident survey (Stern and Seifert 2005c).

Note: Foreign-born status is based on response to a question asking if the resident was born in the United States. It appears that some respondents answered negatively because they were born in Puerto Rico.

By contrast, immigrants and U.S.-born respondents with foreign-born parents were involved in informal cultural activities at least as often as the U.S.-born respondents. For example, immigrants and their children were as likely as nonimmigrants to play musical instruments or to sing at home or when alone. Moreover, immigrants and the children of immigrants reported participating in as many creative pursuits as the rest of the population.

Nativity was associated with *where* respondents reported they participated. The survey asked about the venue for a series of neighborhood activities (including live music concerts, social dancing, dance performances, plays and musicals, and art exhibits). Overall, the most frequently cited venues were community centers (cited 370 times), home (cited 416 times), and nightclubs (cited 291 times).

Immigrants were much more likely to report that they engaged in activities at home (39 percent of all venues) compared to 36 percent among U.S.-born respondents with foreign-born parents and 27 percent among U.S.-born respondents. Immigrants were somewhat more likely to attend events at churches (11 percent) than U.S.-born respondents (6 percent). They were much less likely to participate in cultural activities in parks and other outdoor venues (4 percent compared to 14 percent) and community centers (16 percent versus 28 percent) (table 2.8).

The portrait of immigrant cultural participation that emerges from the resident survey is consistent with our claims about immigrant engagement generally. There

TABLE 2.8

VENUE OF NEIGHBORHOOD CULTURAL PURSUITS, BY NATIVITY, OF NORTH PHILADELPHIA AND CAMDEN, NEW JERSEY, RESIDENTS, 2004.

Venue	*Foreign-born (%)*	*Foreign-born parent (%)*	*Other (%)*	*Total (%)*
Home	38.5	35.7	27.3	28.7
School	9.2	9.2	4.9	5.5
Church	11.0	7.1	5.9	6.4
Park or other public space	3.7	16.3	14.4	13.7
Community center	15.6	8.2	27.8	25.6
Nightclub	22.0	23.5	19.7	20.1
Total	100.0	100.0	100.0	100.0
N	44	35	523	602
Venues cited	109	98	1,241	1,448

Source: Based on Benchmark Project resident survey (Stern and Seifert 2005c).

Note: Information on venue at five types of events (live music concerts, social dancing, dance performances, plays and musicals, and art exhibits) held in the respondent's neighborhood.

is no underlying lack of cultural engagement by the foreign-born survey respondents, but the types of participation in which they engage are less oriented to the programs and venues that are the focus of official nonprofits. Instead, the data suggest that immigrants are more likely than others to participate in the commercial or informal cultural sectors.

The data also suggest that generational differences are an important dimension of ethnic cultural experience. Among Latinos, the shift from first to second or third (or later) generations is associated with changes in the character of cultural involvement. For example, two of the most common creative pursuits identified by respondents were poetry or rap writing (23 percent of all respondents) and creative writing (39 percent). Among foreign-born respondents, however, the participation rate for poetry and rap writing was quite low. Only 9 percent identified poetry or rap as an activity they had undertaken. Among *second-generation* respondents (U.S.-born with foreign-born parents), however, the proportion identifying these pursuits was higher than that of other U.S.-born respondents. Fully 26 percent of second-generation respondents reported that they wrote poetry or rap, and 54 percent reported any type of creative writing.

Among young adults, the differences were even stronger. Thirty percent of all respondents between the ages of eighteen and thirty-four reported that they wrote poetry or rap. The figure for foreign-born respondents was less than half of this (14 percent), while fully 37 percent of second-generation respondents (U.S.-born with foreign-born parents) reported doing so. Controlling for gender did not alter these differences.

Where the resident survey gives us insight into the cultural participation of foreign-born residents, a survey of artists in the Philadelphia metropolitan area gives us a glimpse into the world of cultural producers. Although the survey included relatively few foreign-born artists, data from those who did respond support the theory that immigrant artists are more likely to be involved in the informal cultural sector than artists born in the United States. The survey included questions on the different projects or positions (paid or unpaid) in which the respondents had worked as an artist during the previous year. Overall, the survey collected information on over one thousand projects and positions, of which forty were undertaken by foreign-born artists. Yet, while only 11 percent of the projects undertaken by U.S.-born artists were located in the informal settings, fully one-quarter of those undertaken by immigrant artists were situated in the informal sector. This difference was statistically significant at the .02 level. Because of the small sample size, we should treat this finding as no more than suggestive (Stern, Seifert, and Zaman 2005).

Data on the individual behavior of cultural participants and artists reinforce our portrait of immigrant cultural engagement. Immigrants are engaged in informal cultural activities in private and social settings. Immigrant artists, too, are more likely than U.S.-born artists to produce professional work in informal settings.

One additional factor that emerges from this analysis, however, is generation. The children of immigrants, when they reach adulthood, appear to move away from the cultural patterns of their parents—for example, by embracing cultural forms like rap that their parents have eschewed. Generation, like social class, adds complexity to the story of immigrant involvement in Philadelphia's cultural economy.

The Trajectories of Immigrant Cultural Engagement

Here we explore how social structure and cultural organization interact to influence cultural engagement in three Philadelphia immigrant communities—Latin Americans, African Americans, and Asian Americans. As we have seen, the story of immigrant involvement in "American" arts and culture is complicated by generation and social class. Latinos, Africans, and Asians born overseas often come into conflict with those who came earlier to the United States. In the case of African Americans, in fact, the experience of African immigrants is influenced by the development of black cultural consciousness among African Americans who have lived in the United States for generations.

Latin Americans

The coincidence of broad cultural engagement and narrow institutional connections is well illustrated in Philadelphia's Latin American community. The city's Latino community has been predominantly Puerto Rican since World War II. According to the 2000 census, for example, 91,527 (71 percent) of the city's 128,928 Latin Americans identified themselves as Puerto Rican.[8] After 2000, however, Philadelphia's Latin American community became more diverse. Between 2000 and 2005, the Mexican population doubled from six to twelve thousand, using official figures; the actual increase may have been considerably larger. A growing number of newcomers have arrived from other parts of Central and South America.

For Puerto Ricans, the main destination in Philadelphia has long been an area of old metal-working and textile mill districts along North Fifth Street, where they found affordable housing in the wake of factory closings and the flight of German and Jewish families to the suburbs (Vitiello 2000; Whalen 2001). To the west are the African American neighborhoods of North Central Philadelphia; to the east are the working class Irish neighborhoods of Fishtown and Kensington.

The concentration of the Puerto Rican community along North Fifth Street has created the opportunity for a distinctive form of Latino cultural expression, the transformation of public space. One element of this transformation has been the use of murals to beautify the built environment. The City of Philadelphia's Murals Arts Program has produced more than two thousand murals citywide over the past two decades, many of which are located in the barrio. Mural-making in Philadelphia's Latin American neighborhoods, however, has spilled out from the narrow confines of the city program. First, murals have continued to play a role as political protest, like *Liberty Forsaken*, a mural created by a team of graffiti artists from North Philadelphia, Europe, and the Caribbean to critique the treatment of immigrants, people of color, and graffiti artists.[9] At the same time, a booming commercial mural industry has sprouted up in the neighborhood, largely in response to requests for murals that memorialize young men killed in gang and drug violence.

The use of the arts as a means of transforming public space is just one indicator of how the cultural life of the Latin American community does not fit neatly within the existing structure of Philadelphia's cultural sector. The same can be said for Latin American cultural organizations. As a result, Latino cultural groups often find themselves disadvantaged in explaining their missions to funding agencies and the wider community.

Even the most established of these nonprofits, Taller Puertorriqueño, defies easy classification. Taller Puertorriqueño (Puerto Rican Workshop) was founded in 1974 by artists and activists as part of the then emerging expression of Puerto Rican cultural identity. Since its beginning, however, Taller has evolved into a multidisciplinary and multicultural program. Taller offers the standard fare of a community arts center, including children's and youths' arts classes, summer camp, and amateur performances. Yet, with its art gallery, bilingual bookstore, and theater, Taller has also become an intellectual and cultural center for the region's Latino community. Its annual symposium on race and class in the Latin American community and its sponsorship of a variety of mind-bending avant-garde events (like a Spanish-language performance of the Sufi classic, *The Conference of Birds*, or its Chino-Latino exhibition of Latin American arts influenced by Asian cultural forms) take it well beyond identity politics. Taller has also been central to the life of its community by serving as a conduit for a variety of embedded cultural groups and artists that could not receive funding on their own. The diversity of Taller's program is one reason why it draws participants from throughout the metropolitan area, with more than three-fourths coming from outside its immediate neighborhood. Its expansive view of the community arts center extends to governance as well (Stern and Seifert 2005c). At a foundation-sponsored seminar on building nonprofit boards of trustees, a representative from Taller explained how the orthodox view of boards (that they should raise funds and contribute business acumen) was not useful to an organization expected to represent the diverse views of a low-income, immigrant community.

The merging of official, commercial, and informal approaches to murals characterizes Latin American cultural expression generally. The experience of Grupo Motivos, a program of the Norris Square Neighborhood Project in the West Kensington neighborhood of North Philadelphia, is typical of this lack of fit between migrants' modes of cultural expression and existing cultural institutions in Philadelphia. The women leaders of Grupo Motivos enlisted the help of the Pennsylvania Horticultural Society to establish community gardens growing chilies, yucca, and pigeon peas. Some of the garden plots are perennially adorned with signs calling for peace in Palestine, Kosovo, and Iraq. The group has collaborated with the City's Mural Arts Program to commission murals for the walls adjoining the gardens with Puerto Rican landscapes and narratives and portraits of community residents. To educate the second and third generations about their

Puerto Rican and African heritage, Grupo Motivos runs environmental education and cooking classes. In one garden, they have built a replica of a rural home (casita) from 1940s Puerto Rico, furnished with objects from that era—a museum of cultural heritage. In another garden, they have built a symbolic African village with stucco huts, an outdoor kitchen, rows of vegetables native to Africa, and a storytelling room. Despite international recognition by environmental and women's groups, Grupo Motivos remains a grassroots organization for which issues of women's rights, cultural preservation, and social justice remain painfully relevant. Their integration of culture with gardening, antidrug campaigns, and political action makes the group difficult to classify by the standard categories of nonprofit organizations. Indeed, in spite of the centrality of the arts and culture to its program, the group has generally been overlooked by arts funders (Norris Square Neighborhood Project 2008).

This crossing of established cultural-sector boundaries is a defining characteristic of the Latin American cultural community. It has led to some striking public-private partnerships, as in a case described by an artist employed by a local community development corporation. Commenting on the lack of local galleries to support plans for a monthly community arts open house, he noted:

> So, we have been setting up exhibits within the businesses themselves. For example, in [a] Gym, a beautiful old factory space, they put art on the walls and along the perimeters of the gym. In the same building on the first floor, where we used to have a bakery, the sitting area was turned into a gallery. We generally have good cooperation with businesses. Even [a local politician] has turned his reception area into a venue for exhibition. Now a new neighbor, [a] Health Clinic, has physically designed its lobby area to be a host, sponsor, and community partner for [the event].[10]

Thus, Latin American residents' conception of culture has complicated their relationship to Philadelphia's larger cultural community. On the one hand, because a significant share of community-based cultural activity does not fit comfortably into a nonprofit model, local arts foundations are often wary about funding immigrant-serving programs. At the same time, whether it is mural-making, the transformation of public space, or the creation of arts venues, Latin Americans have found ways of bringing their culture to the work of community building in ways that challenge convention as well as outsiders' expectations of disadvantaged communities.

African and Caribbean Immigrants and African Americans

The experience of the emerging African and Caribbean immigrant cultural community has been complicated by the presence of Philadelphia's large African American community. On the one hand, the recent cultural history of Philadelphia's established black community created a fertile ground for black immigrant artists. Yet, at the same time, the influx of African and Caribbean immigrants into African American communities has created a new set of tensions.

Although older African Americans—who have been interested in their African roots for three decades—are eager consumers of African-centered cultural practices, a younger generation of less-well-off urban youth are more often indifferent to African culture and see recent Africans and Caribbeans as rivals and competitors.

Had the current wave of black immigration commenced several decades earlier, new arrivals to Philadelphia would have found scant evidence of an African legacy. Certainly, jazz and other black musical forms owed much to African musical traditions, but the link between Africa and the U.S.-born black community of the postwar years was barely acknowledged. In the wake of the civil rights movement, however, a dominant theme in black cultural life became the rediscovery of black Americans' African roots. In Philadelphia, two artists—Robert Crowder and Arthur Hall—were particularly noteworthy in this movement.[11]

Drummer Robert Crowder, born in West Virginia in 1930, relocated with his family later that decade to North Philadelphia. Drawn to the rhythms of the African Diaspora, Crowder began, in his words, "searching for our lost heritage." From the 1940s to the 1960s, he studied Haitian, Brazilian, and African drumming. In the early 1970s, he founded the Kulu Mele African Dance Ensemble, whose current members represent several generations of artists. Their performances "are authentically costumed and choreographed to convey . . . the meanings of dancing and drumming in the African societies from which these traditions come." Philadelphia's leading African American practitioners of African arts have generally followed this pattern of apprenticeship with West African, Brazilian, and Caribbean artists—from the vanguard of Afro-Cuban jazz in Havana and New York to traditional folk artists in West Africa (Philadelphia Folklore Project 2008).

Arthur Hall, a colleague of Robert Crowder, has been called "the father of the black arts movement in Philadelphia." In 1953, as a young dancer training in Philadelphia, Hall met Ghanaian exchange student and artist Saka Acquaye, who introduced him to West African cultural and performance traditions. "Keeping this lore in America" became Hall's life's work. "Our people are not aware of their culture and heritage. I saw in the dances a chance to bring grandeur back into blackness." In 1958 Hall recruited the group of dancers who became known as the Afro-American Dance Ensemble. In 1969, with funding from the Model Cities program, Hall founded the Ile Ife Center in the North Philadelphia black community on Germantown Avenue, where the ensemble "became the elite company of a thriving cultural center and school" (Ngozi-Brown 1997). Hall offered classes for local children, youths, and adults in dance, percussion, and stilt walking and established a touring company that performed across the United States, Europe, and Africa, giving African Americans access to worlds far beyond their segregated neighborhoods. In the early 1980s Hall and his colleagues developed a plan for an African village: a grassroots community and economic development agenda. As a grassroots organization of artists who practiced African religious traditions, Ile Ife was viewed with suspicion by civic leaders who controlled the city's community development funding. Financial distress and a deteriorating neighborhood, compounded by Hall's personal troubles, forced the center to close in 1985.[12]

The most visible continuity of Philadelphia's Africanists is the annual June ODUNDE festival, which celebrates the Yoruba New Year. Founded in 1975 by South Philadelphian Lois Fernandez, with the help of Arthur Hall, ODUNDE starts with a procession to the Schuylkill River, where a Yoruba-initiated priest makes an offering of flowers and fruit to the river goddess Oshun. This ceremony is followed by a street festival with music, dance, and vendors from West Africa, the Caribbean, and Brazil that attracts many thousands of people each year (Philadelphia Folklore Project 2006).

The ODUNDE festival, where many African artists now perform, has served as a bridge between African Americans and artists who have arrived during the major migrations of West Africans to Philadelphia in the 1990s. The Philadelphia Folklore Project has also played a significant role in forging connections between foreign-born and U.S.-born artists and between immigrant artists and local communities by sponsoring programs and advocacy initiatives like Philly Dance Africa performances, Artists in Exile exhibitions, and an African refugee oral history project (Morton 2006).

Indeed, class and generational differences have complicated the relationship of U.S.- and foreign-born black Americans. While middle-class, middle-aged African Americans sustain the interest in African cultural forms that Hall and others nurtured from the 1960s, hip-hop culture represents a different sensibility. Like an earlier generation, hip-hop captures the separation between black America and mainstream culture, but its practitioners are more likely to look to the street than to a lost diaspora for inspiration. By the same token, African immigrants devoted to more traditional cultural forms see hip-hop as a debased, commercial form of cultural expression. Voffee Jabateh, CEO of the African Cultural Alliance of North America (ACANA), views some popular cultural expression, including most rap music and much of what he sees on television, as demeaning to African Americans, even promoting a "minstrel mentality."[13]

While an older generation might look to African immigrants as bearers of a treasured cultural legacy, tensions and violence between African American and African immigrant youths represent a major problem in Philadelphia. In a well-publicized 2005 incident, a Liberian teenager named Jacob Gray was brutally beaten by African American boys on his way home from school. Many African Americans resent the African newcomers for the special services and advantages they perceive are afforded to immigrants and refugees. In these neighborhoods, where factories closed decades ago, some African Americans accuse immigrants of taking their jobs and undermining their position in the labor market.

Beyond these social and economic tensions, cultural and identity politics among African and African Americans youths are likewise fraught with tension. In spite of a generation of conscious efforts to develop a positive image of African and African American history, black youths often accept mainstream views of Africa. "Africa is looked at as a destitute continent, where people are not supposed to know anything," explains South African artist Mogauwane Mahloe. "People assume that you are primitive" (Morton 2006).

The differences in social class and cultural orientation that have sparked tensions between U.S.- and foreign-born African Americans have also created problems for Philadelphia's established African American cultural organizations. The African legacy and the story of enslavement, endurance, and liberation were the mainstays of Philadelphia's major African American performing arts groups and museums. New generations of middle-class African Americans, many of whom have moved to the suburbs, are less likely to support city-based institutions. As a result, the city's major black institutions have found themselves struggling for audiences and for a solid financial footing. Both the African American Museum in Philadelphia and the New Freedom Theatre have had to close for periods during the last decade because of financial difficulties.

The influx of a significant number of Caribbean and African immigrants to Philadelphia neighborhoods has set off a complicated dynamic among segments of the black community. A three-decade-long interest in African culture among many U.S.-born blacks has created a market for immigrant artists and facilitated immigrant integration into the African American community. The rise of hip-hop culture, on the other hand, has increased tensions between U.S.-born and immigrant youths. At the same time, many black cultural institutions—and those employed by them—have struggled with declining markets and a more precarious future.

Asian Americans

The story of immigrant incorporation and cultural expression among Asian Americans differs from the African American and Latin American experiences in several ways. First, Asian immigrants, for the most part, have entered the United States with greater economic assets than the other groups. Second, although they have historically faced discrimination, the racialization of Asian Americans has declined, especially in the past two decades—a conclusion supported by increasing rates of intermarriage between Asian and white Americans (Bean and Lee 2007).

The diverse history and heritage of immigrants from Asia have added complexity to the process of engagement between foreign-born and U.S.-born Asian Americans. Although Latin American, African, and Caribbean labels often obscure the considerable diversity within these immigrant populations, other conditions have mitigated these differences. Puerto Ricans until quite recently have been such a dominant part of Philadelphia's Latin American community that intergroup differences have been less apparent. Among African Americans, the artificiality of many national boundaries in Africa and the template provided by the Africanist legacy have tended to obscure rather than highlight differences among immigrants from Africa's numerous regions and countries.

In contrast, Asian immigrants of different national origins rarely see themselves as part of a single ethnic group. Of the 166,000 foreign-born Asians and Pacific Islanders living in metropolitan Philadelphia in 2006, for example, no single nationality made up more than one-quarter. The strength of national identities has made it less likely that immigrants born in Asia would identify themselves as Asians.

As a result, through the past several decades distinct cultural organizations formed within the Chinese, Cambodian, Filipino, Korean, and South Asian communities. Some of these nationality groups developed nonprofit organizations—such as the Cambodian Association of Greater Philadelphia—that integrate the arts and culture into a wide variety of services. Some Asian immigrant cultural institutions have thrived as embedded or minimalist entities—like St. Augustine's Church in Old City Philadelphia, which has become a center for the Filipino community, whether its members were born abroad or have long resided in the United States. Some Asian immigrant groups tend to be oriented toward commercial culture—for example, a framing shop in Philadelphia's Olney neighborhood that has used its proximity to the Korean business district to develop a thriving business in imported Korean art (Broder et al. 2008).

The generational differences among Asians are as great as among any of Philadelphia's new immigrant groups. The combination of assimilation, educational attainment, and economic success created a second-generation Asian American community that is predominantly college educated (Portes et al. 2006). Among this cohort, while individual national identities remain, a pan-Asian identity has grown in importance. In Philadelphia, the Asian Arts Initiative (AAI), based near Chinatown but incorporating members from a variety of ethnic backgrounds, has emerged as the chief forum for creative expression of this emergent Asian American identity and "as one of the very few Asian American community arts centers in the country." In contrast to many nationality-focused organizations, AAI is less likely to focus on cultural preservation and more likely to fuse old and new cultural forms in programs that explore the contradictions of the model minority status enjoyed by many Asian Americans (Asian Arts Initiative 2008).

For many Asian Americans, however, model minority status is indeed a myth. The Southeast Asian community of Southwest Philadelphia, for example, finds itself wedged between African American and white communities. For this community, the class and generational tensions of immigrant cultural life are fully on display. One example may illuminate how these tensions enter the cultural world of Asian Americans. As part of a foundation-funded community arts initiative, an Asian American cultural organization based in Center City entered a partnership with a small, church-based organization located in this community. The intent of the collaboration was to provide trained artists for the church-based program and to open opportunities for local youths to connect to a more cosmopolitan cultural milieu in Center City.

The emergence of an Asian American identity among second- and third-generation young adults is one of the major stories of ethnicity in recent years. Yet, the second-generation Southeast Asian kids served by the church-based organization did not fit easily into either the evolving Pan-Asian identity or the narrower ethnic identities of the immigrant generation.[14]

These differences in cultural identity between immigrant parents, second-generation working-class youths, and middle-class Asian Americans were fully visible at the Appreciation Night sponsored by the church-based group one night in June 1998. The event, held in the church basement, consisted of four parts: an awards ceremony for those involved in the program, a cultural dance program that presented traditional Southeast Asian dances (a hat dance and a ribbon dance), a contemporary cultural program sponsored by the Center City organization, and a talent show organized by the teenagers involved in the program.

The cultural dance program was clearly an effort on the part of adults to transmit their heritage to the younger generation. The brief dances were well organized, accompanied by recorded music, and greeted with polite, if muted, applause. The contemporary cultural program, in contrast, suggested that the chasm of social class might be greater than the gap between the generations. The two representatives of the Center City organization—both college educated—brought their own cultural perspectives to the neighborhood. One ran a graphic arts workshop to help the teens create a portfolio to support their applications to arts school. The other taught a creative writing class that developed a presentation called "Heroes and Heroines."

If the cultural dances represented the voice of the parents' generation and the contemporary program that of the assimilated, middle-class second-generation, the talent show appeared to be exclusively the work of the working-class kids associated with the church. The show consisted of three acts: a group of fifteen young men performing a hip-hop routine, a lip-syncing young woman performing disco hits, and a group of young women dancing to reggae music. If anyone had missed the strains of social class and generation, the food served at the reception made them clear—fried rice, cheese curls, sandwich cookies, coke, and orange soda.

Conclusion

We do not yet know exactly why the nonprofit arts sector is marginal to immigrant culture. While this chapter has presented evidence on the cultural preferences of immigrants, we do not yet have the depth of knowledge about how immigrant arts operate or how relationships between producers and consumers in this sector are structured. In classical theories of the nonprofit arts, the cost disease of the cultural sector has been a major impetus for the development of the nonprofit form (Baumol and Bowen 1966). We know from studies of labor economics that immigrant workers are likely to evaluate employment opportunities not only on the basis of American opportunities, but in light of opportunities in their country of origin (Waldinger and Lichter 2003). It may be that—as with other low-wage work—immigrant artists are willing to produce for the American cultural market in return for less remuneration than U.S.-born artists.

Alternatively, the connection between immigrant arts and the informal and commercial sectors may derive from institutional barriers that reduce the opportunities for immigrant artists and arts organizations to access the existing nonprofit system. There are many studies of the hurdles faced by immigrant professionals (Chiswick, Lee, and Miller 2003; Portes et al. 2006). For example, immigrant health care workers often find it difficult to gain the licensure necessary to practice their vocations in the United States. While one does not need a license to practice art, the rapid institutionalization of the nonprofit arts during the postwar years led to the elaboration of a variety of requirements—including academic credentials, the ability to develop a reputation, the expertise to establish a 501c3 (tax-exempt) organization, and (on a more mundane level) skills in writing grant proposals. Arts philanthropy, although rationalized to some extent, remains at its core built upon patron-client relationships, whereby nonprofit organizations develop and sustain connections with grant-makers. Because migration patterns coincided with a period of retrenchment in the nonprofit arts field, it may be that immigrant cultural groups found themselves in an unequal competition with more experienced organizations. Along similar lines, migrant-serving groups often mount cultural programs embedded in a multiple-service organization, which makes it more difficult to gain recognition for their artistic achievements. For example, as noted earlier, Grupo Motivos, despite its commitment to incorporating the arts and culture into neighborhood revitalization, has not been recognized as a cultural provider by local or national funders and has been passed over repeatedly in efforts to promote the arts in North Philadelphia.

Ultimately, the importance of informal and commercial arts for contemporary immigrants may simply be a result of the particular historical period in which the migration has occurred. Immigrants began to influence the social and cultural life of Philadelphia just as the balance was shifting among the nonprofit, commercial, and informal cultural sectors. The diversification of cultural tastes, the increasing educational attainment of the population, and the impact of digital technologies on the production and dissemination of art—all created new markets for culture just as the nonprofit sector faced diminishing prospects (DiMaggio 2006).

Although we cannot answer the question of why immigrants have been attracted to the commercial and informal arts, there is no question about their impact on those sectors. By developing apart from the nonprofit sector, immigrant cultural engagement has given a significant boost to alternative organizational forms. It has provided new impetus to a drift that was already under way and by so doing has changed the underlying reality. Over time, immigrant culture may come to seem more American, but the structure of that American culture has already changed significantly as a result of immigrant presence.

One of the great paradoxes of social structure is that it is created through the behavior of agents who feel that their agency is constrained by social structure, a dilemma that social theorist Anthony Giddens has called the "double hermeneutic" (Giddens 1976). In the case of immigrant arts, this paradox plays out in that existing institutions channel cultural expression even as those institutions experience change. As we have seen, Latin American, African American, and Asian immigrants and U.S.-born residents have incorporated nonprofit, commercial, and informal cultural forms in developing their collective cultural lives. Yet in making their choices, immigrant groups have changed the balance among these organizational forms. Indeed, the most profound expression of the interaction between immigrants and existing cultural institutions is the expanding role during the past several decades of informal culture in American urban communities.

The emergence of the informal cultural sector parallels larger forces in the political economy. As the state has expanded its efforts to regulate economic and social behavior, a gap has opened up between activities that are fully legal and those that defy regulation. Labor law, environmental regulations, and tax policy all have the potential to generate types of economic and social behavior that, while not strictly legal, are able to flourish. The rebirth of the sweatshop in American cities during the 1990s, for example, came about through the explosion of undocumented immigration and the decrease in labor-law enforcement initiated by conservative politicians (Sassen 2006).

The history of the cultural sector between World War II and the 1980s was essentially a story of institutionalization. Led by philanthropic foundations and followed by government action, an increasing share of cultural activity occurred in formal institutions, with official nonprofits comprising an ever larger proportion of that activity. A significant share of funding went to subsidizing workers in this sector, which kept average wages high relative to market rates and made nonprofits a desirable venue for all but the most popular artists (DiMaggio 1991; Kreidler 1996). One aspect of the unraveling of government support for the arts in the 1990s was the loss of this wage edge. As nonprofit funding for the arts stagnated and as a "winner-take-all" logic entered the nonprofit sector, a gap opened between the limited opportunities for average artists in the commercial sector and the meager wages provided by most nonprofit jobs. It is this gap that has driven the informal cultural sector. While the most visible manifestation is an increase in street musicians and performers, its scope encompasses the development of live/work spaces in defiance of zoning and fire laws and entrepreneurial pursuits to bring artists' work to audiences on the street, in urban neighborhoods, or on the Internet (Zukin 1982, 1995).

While the informal cultural sector first received scholarly attention during the 1970s and 1980s, the 1997 publication of the American Assembly's report, *Art and the Public Purpose*, gave the concept new prominence (American Assembly 1997; DiMaggio 1987). That report characterized a range of "citizen arts—community, avocational, traditional, or folk arts, the indigenous arts in their many manifestations"—as the "unincorporated" sector and sought ways of integrating it into the existing nonprofit structure. Subsequently, a number of researchers suggested that the term "informal" is more appropriate than "unincorporated" because it captures not only those activities that might one day become integrated into formal culture but also cultural practices and artistic work undertaken in the private sphere (like home or church), the voluntary sector, and the informal economy.

Two sets of ethnographic studies that document the informal sectors in Chicago and Silicon Valley, respectively, have made another point: that immigrant cultural practices—which are often seen as marginal to formal culture—are central to the informal cultural sector (Moriarty 2004; Wali, Severson, and Longoni 2002; and Wali, Contractor, and Severson 2007). Taken together, this work demonstrated the relational role of the informal sector and the key role of immigrant arts within the sector. The 2002 Chicago study posited an arts continuum in which the informal sector serves a bridging role between the private world of culture within the home and the formal cultural sector. The Silicon Valley study noted the importance of participatory arts to community capacity-building in immigrant communities. It argued that informal culture contributed both to developing community self-identity and to linking immigrant communities to the wider social structure. The 2007 Chicago study found that the artistic and cultural activities and networking assets of Mexican immigrants contribute to neighborhood social and economic vitality and stimulate the local economy—in particular, the music industry and service sector. In the Chicago and Silicon Valley studies, immigrants not only made use of the informal cultural sector but were critical to its expansion.

In this chapter, we have used evidence to explore how immigrant cultural expression has developed outside of Philadelphia's established world of nonprofit arts and how, in response, immigrant groups have explored new avenues for self-organization. In so doing, newcomers to the region have contributed to a much wider redefinition of the cultural economy. Because informal arts are not marginal but are intimately connected to the rest of the cultural sector, immigrant cultural practices—even in the informal sector—have a ripple effect felt throughout the art worlds of the twenty-first-century city.

NOTES

1. One notable feature of Philadelphia's immigrant geography was its distinctive suburban profile. Generally, more prosperous Asian groups—including the Koreans, South Asians, and Chinese—were more likely to concentrate in the suburbs. Eastern Europeans, who had originally settled in Northeast Philadelphia, had by 2000 become a significant presence in the adjacent suburbs as well.

2. Center City statistics were estimated using public use microdata area (PUMA) 4109, which includes Center City and several neighborhoods north and south of it. See Ruggles et al. (2008).

3. Cultural participation rates were calculated by adding the total number of participants for all organizations and dividing by the number of residents in each census block group in 2000. If an individual appeared on more than one list, he or she was counted more than once. Rates are expressed per one thousand residents.

4. Counts were calculated for the number of organizations or artists within one-half mile of each block group. The one-half-mile buffers were used to estimate the availability of these assets for residents and to correct for the lack of commercial or work sites in many block groups. The four New Jersey counties of the Philadelphia metropolitan area are excluded from this analysis. A more detailed description of methods can be found in Stern and Seifert (2005a, 2005b) and Stern, Seifert, and Zaman (2005).

5. These estimates are based on a general linear model analysis in which metropolitan location, percentage of college graduates, and percentage of foreign-born were entered as fixed factors. The figures in table 2.6 are the estimates of the population marginal means corrected for the distribution of the other factors and can be interpreted as the cultural index adjusted for the influence of its metro location and college graduate rate.

6. For this analysis, we conducted a general linear analysis model with only metropolitan location and percentage of college graduates entered as factors. The map for "corrected" participation is the predicted residual—that is, the difference between the predicted and actual cultural participation rate for each block group.

7. The resident survey of North Philadelphia and Camden, New Jersey, was based on in-person interviews conducted during the summer and fall of 2004. Households were selected using a two-stage cluster sample. We selected a random sample of block-faces within the two areas and then selected dwellings from each block-face. Canvassers were given a list of addresses for each block-face and instructed to move down the list until they completed the number of interviews expected from the block-face (typically three or four). Canvassers were instructed to interview any adult in the household. A bilingual (Spanish-English) canvasser was included in each team.

8. The term "Latin American" refers to all persons whose ethnic identity is Hispanic, whether they are foreign- or U.S.-born.

9. The mural depicts a hostile Statue of Liberty holding back the huddled masses that emerge from a wave of water, representing waves of human migration from Africa, Asia, and Latin America. In the statue's arms is a boy with a distressed look on his face reaching for his lost can of spray paint, while someone in the crowd holds a sign reading "How would you feel?" Swaths of stylized city blocks wrap around either side of the image. Other images show a U.S. government satellite watching the earth and, at the far right, a dark, postapocalyptic urban scene from a Japanese animé story in which a repressive government brings about the downfall of society.

10. SIAP interview with Juan Gutierrez, August 23, 2006.

11. Much of this section is indebted to documentation by the Philadelphia Folklore Project and its director, Debora Kodish.

12. Ile Ife's African village plan was partially implemented by Chinese American artist Lily Yeh, whom Hall invited to North Philadelphia in 1986 to develop a garden on Germantown Avenue. From 1986 to 2004, Yeh served as executive director and leading artist of Ile Ife's successor, the Village of Arts and Humanities, which has produced murals and sculpture gardens and continues to use the center for arts, educational, and community programs.

13. Jabateh wants the African Americans in his Southwest Philadelphia neighborhood to know "pure African arts." ACANA's cultural programs employ Ile Ife alumni as well as African immigrant artists. The group holds a fashion show at the Pennsylvania Convention Center during Black History Month. Its annual summer street festival, called "From Africa to America: A Millennium of Music and Dance," frames the African and African American experiences as part of the same diaspora.

14. An additional feature of the story is the ecology of the Southeast Asian community in Southwest Philadelphia, which is located in a slender salient between the bulk of black West Philadelphia and a strongly defended white area of Southwest Philadelphia. This neighborhood has been the site of a number of notorious hate crimes over the years. Thus, the Southeast Asian community serves as a kind of buffer between two neighborhoods linked by their mutual animosity.

CHAPTER 3

A Howl to the Heavens

ART IN THE LIFE OF FIRST- AND SECOND-GENERATION CUBAN AMERICANS

Patricia Fernández-Kelly

In a review of Phillip Roth's prolific contribution to American literature, the critic Claudia Roth Pierpont observes about the central character in Roth's most notorious book that Alexander Portnoy's onanistic hold to the flesh is "literally, in rebellion against the life that is being forced upon him . . . a fiercely comic shtick that is also a howl to the heavens" (Pierpont 2006, 82). The same may be said about much of art, including the art of Cuban Americans in the United States.

This chapter focuses on the relationship between aesthetic expression and immigrant incorporation. What is the role of art in the adaptation of newcomers often facing harsh environments? How do music, dance, and the figurative arts define, and how are they defined by, the quest for national and ethnic distinctiveness? How does immigrant art differ in terms of class, and what do those differences reveal about modes of incorporation, types of reception, and structures of opportunity in the host country?

Although the importance of these questions is obvious as soon as they are formulated, mine is among the first attempts to address them. Omissions are especially puzzling given the enduring significance of art as an element of the human experience and the richness of artistic manifestations in immigrant communities. It may be a testimony to the supremacy of market-economics thinking that there are many more treatises about immigrant employment and exploitation than about the way immigrants use art to combat punishing conditions in the labor market.

This chapter is partly based on information collected through the Children of Immigrants Longitudinal Survey (CILS).[1] For more than a decade CILS has followed a national sample of immigrants from early adolescence to young adulthood.

By combining survey and ethnographic research, it has amassed the largest data base available for the understanding of immigrant incorporation in the United States in the latter part of the twentieth century. Although CILS did not focus directly on artistic expression, that subject spontaneously emerged in interviews with members of the original sample. I rely on them, my own ethnographic research, and a profuse literature on the arts to develop an interpretive framework.

Overview

Artistic expression among older and more educated Cuban Americans draws from historical and cultural traditions in the country of origin to affirm national pride in places of destination. It also depends on shared agreements about the value of creativity to connect with the receiving society. In the case of Cubans, the majority of whom first arrived in the United States as exiles, artistic production entails a reinvention of the ancestral land and the forging of a *culture of nostalgia* that strengthens coethnic bonds, separating insiders from outsiders. In other words, artistic tastes among the members of early Cuban waves—like equivalent manifestations by recent immigrants from other places—assert distinctiveness even as they uses aesthetic empathy to establish roots in the adopted country. It is in this sense that art, especially music, becomes a universal language forging bridges between newcomers and their host environment.

The children of immigrants face circumstances dissimilar from those confronted by their forebears and, as a result, their artistic tastes diverge from those cultivated by the first generation. Having grown up in America they do not possess their parents' close connection to or deep understanding of the country of origin. Some feel an impulse to relearn traditions as a way to preserve or recast cultural identity. Others embrace the mores and art of youth subcultures in the new nation. The two trends are not mutually exclusive—they often merge, giving way to innovative manifestations. Those tendencies can also vary in terms of class, with more affluent and educated populations seeking elements of authenticity and cultural purity in the art of sending countries and more humble groups resorting to forms that mix ethnic and American modalities or adopting distinctly American forms. Especially informative in that respect is the popularity of hip-hop among young Cubans, especially those living in the City of Hialeah, a working-class district in Miami-Dade County. When they appropriate art forms originally created by African Americans to voice opposition and reclaim power, Cuban youngsters symbolically join hands with multitudes sharing comparable experiences throughout the world. Immigrant art thus becomes an instrument for vindicating tarnished identities and rejecting the homogenizing pressures of the market.

At the beginning of the new millennium a new relationship is being forged between changing structures of opportunity and aesthetic expression. In an article written with Lisa Konczal (Fernández-Kelly and Konczal 2005), I introduced the concept of expressive entrepreneurship to designate the propensity of second-generation immigrants to use art and artlike ventures as instruments to circumvent formal labor markets. Whether they are affluent or not, immigrant children take for granted a measure of prosperity. This is true for all national groups but especially for Cubans youngsters, given the rapid ascent of their group in the United States. Their parents toiled hard to provide them with more than basic survival—they, in turn, measure success in accordance with the normative standards of the host society. Independence, wealth, and even fame feature prominently in the dreams of immigrant children. Their aim is to craft a meaningful life where employment is but a means to an end. Expressive entrepreneurship is part of that quest. Although it is present among well-off youngsters, it becomes urgent among working-class immigrants who face limited opportunities in the postindustrial age. At a time when desirable jobs require high levels of education and formal skills that many do not have or cannot afford, immigrant youngsters are turning to the arts as a path to success

Sociology and Art: A Minimalist Perspective

Clifford Geertz (1973) notes in his most famous article that we are beings suspended in "webs of significance." To be human is to be irretrievably dependent on signs, symbols, and metaphors without which social interaction would be impossible. Geertz's semiotic approach has inspired abundant work by anthropologists, sociologists, and historians, but most of them have not focused on art (Howard Becker is a striking exception [Becker 1984; Becker, Faulkner, and Kirshenblatt 2006]. Yet it is in aesthetic manifestations that meaning-making, the core of Geertz's formulation, is anchored. The invention of music, dance, sculpture, and painting signals the debut of humankind—that is, its differentiation from other species. Like language, art is embedded in the human attempt to make sense of natural and constructed environments.

Two intellectual traditions are relevant to the understanding of aesthetic production. The first one, derived from authors like Immanuel Kant and Sigmund Freud, yields a vision of art as a tool to assuage anxieties and reestablish psychic balance. The second, originating in Karl Marx, centers on the relationship between expressiveness and labor.

Leaving aside the lasting contributions of Greek philosophers like Aristotle (who understood art as the ultimate manifestation of moral sense) or Cato (for whom art was inseparable from politics), the first modern of consequence to have written extensively about art was the founder of the liberal tradition in aesthetics, Immanuel Kant ([1790] 1987). He adopted an evolutionary approach, characterizing art first as a correlate of magic and then as a progressively independent phenomenon buttressed by new notions of freedom, refinement, and genius (Kemal 1991). In that perspective, the creation and enjoyment of art require cultural conditions associated with class privilege (an insight developed by Pierre Bourdieu [1984] nearly two centuries later). Gradually, Kant argues, artistic expression ceases to be a guard against cosmic chaos to become a source of satisfaction for those with refined faculties. Such ideas resonate in the modern world of immigrants, many of whom use aesthetic tastes and production to uphold their identity as cultivated people. Educated Cubans, for example, affirm a superior class position through their taste for the opera, ballet, and theater.

Like other people throughout the world, immigrants use art to distinguish between mundane and out-of-the-ordinary experiences. Relevant in that respect is the work of Mircea Eliade (1987), the Rumanian scholar who became best known for his work on the history of religions. Borrowing from Kant ([1790] 1987) and Max Otto ([1917] 1958), he drew a distinction between the sacred and the profane. That demarcation, central to religious practice, is also useful with respect to art. In its most exalted form, aesthetic creation is bereft of ordinary intent; it divides prosaic needs from expression solely for the sake of expression. That separation is vital among immigrants and exiles who must divide work for survival from activities that make them visibly human in places of destination. The capacity for aesthetic enjoyment heightens their membership in the host society, reducing their alien character.

Also written in the Kantian tradition, Sigmund Freud's *Civilization and Its Discontents* (1930) brought together old philosophical ideas and the new science of psychology. Culture, argued Freud, is a response to finitude. Lost in an indifferent universe and aware of their own mortality, humans transform anguish into transcendence. Fear leads to neurosis, the basis of civilized living. In this perspective, art is a privileged form of neurosis (Glover 2005). It is also a manifestation rooted in social context. Freud's contribution sheds light on the irrational elements of the creative process. A Freudian approach also permits a fuller comprehension of immigrant art, which usually emerges in response to pressing needs for self-identification under anxiety-producing conditions.

A different tradition encompasses the work of materialist thinkers. Karl Marx's *Economic and Philosophical Manuscripts* ([1844] 1959) and *The German Ideology* ([1845] 1998) lay down the foundations for an understanding of art as a superior form of labor. Through cooperation to ensure collective survival, people enter into specific relations of production, which once established cannot be easily undone. Social development gives way to multiple versions of inequality that hinge on the exercise of power. Under capitalism, the realization of profit requires the subjugation of workers but also the expansion of markets and therefore an uninterrupted increase in the scale and complexity of labor exploitation. Transformed into cogs in a depersonalizing machinery, workers are ripped apart from their own creation. Alienated labor becomes the trademark of modern society.

Yet Marx envisions a higher state of being where labor would recover its integrity. This is a vision of labor as the fulfillment of the human capacity to create. In a nonexploitative society, work would fuse with art and pleasure; aesthetics would replace the debased products of exploitation. Art, in fact, would be coterminous with existence. This utopian rendition, infrequently included in Marxian exegeses, opens up a fertile ground for the understanding of artistic manifestations in populations, like those formed by youth groups, whose aim is to circumvent the deadening effects of low-skill employment. As will be discussed, many children of immigrants emblazon a tendency to overcome market constraints through the production of art.

The Marxist tradition inspired a multitude of authors, including Walter Benjamin ([1936] 1969), who explored the relation between technology, commodity production, and creativity, and John Berger (1990), the novelist, painter, and critic who examines art as both an embodiment of exchange value and a reflection of social yearnings for emancipation. Even more recently, Pierre Bourdieu (1984) draws from Max Weber and critiques Marxian ideas to explain how aesthetic preferences influence and *are* influenced by class advantage. Yet it was Herbert Marcuse who most thoroughly theorized the relationship between productive work and art by joining the insights of Freud and Marx. In *Eros and Civilization* ([1958] 1974) he too describes an ideal society buttressed by beauty, sensuality, and play, in contrast to modern social arrangements founded on reason, production, and repression.

From Kant to Freud and from Marx to Marcuse, a framework anchored by two central ideas enables a better comprehension of immigrant art. First, aesthetic expressions concretize and diffuse existential uncertainties and anxieties common among those who cross real and imaginary borders. Second, art may be helpfully conceived as a form of labor in ambivalent relationship with market production. In that respect, immigrants and their art constitute what Robert K. Merton would have called a "strategic research site"—they vividly reveal elements of life less apparent in more settled populations, thus enabling the observation and evaluation of creative processes that have general interest.

Even under auspicious circumstances, immigrants and exiles face dislocation, loss of personal and collective identities, and occasional hostility from those with whom they come in contact in adopted countries. Unable to communicate for lack of linguistic skills or familiarity with cultural mores, many fall back on symbolic repertories to palliate anxiety and restore comfort. One of those reserves is religion; the other one is art, and the connection between the two is not haphazard. Faith and aesthetic expression rely on universal means that transcend language barriers and insular practices. They entail the promise of connection beyond temporal divides. In that sense, they are as visceral as a howl or a prayer.

Leaving behind familiar customs and environments, immigrants are thrust into milieus where they confront new challenges. Dislocation is followed by the need to comprehend or at least manage elusive cultural norms. "Learning the ropes" entails a potential for anomie. The need to survive through employment or business formation limits the capacity for idle enjoyment. Practical ends threaten to overwhelm romantic ideals. It is perhaps because of those tensions that art is so rich in immigrant communities.

Art and Diaspora in the First Generation

Generational divisions are closely related to class differences among South Florida Cubans. The first waves to arrive in Miami in the 1960s included a substantial number of educated and professional families. After that, growing numbers of working-class people arrived and settled in districts like Hialeah. The 1980 Mariel Boatlift further contributed to the expansion of the Cuban working class. Throughout their life in the United States, Cubans of all class backgrounds have been engaged in the production of art. Here I focus on two kinds of expressions: those favored mostly by older Cuban exiles carving a distinct position of economic and social superiority and those that cross class lines, especially music.

Among the most popular ballads in Cuban Miami is "Contigo en la Distancia," written by César Portillo de la Luz, who was born in Havana in 1922. Perhaps the most distinguished lyricist of his generation, Portillo de la Luz is responsible for a trove of melodic jewels. Like many others, "Contigo en la Distancia" is a love song, but it may also be read as an expression of longing for a country lost to Fidel Castro's revolution. Castro's victory coincided with the abrupt departure of nearly one million Cubans, most of whom found refuge in Miami. Later waves have replenished the vibrant community right up to the present. More than forty years after the first arrivals, Cubans in the United States still see Castro as the cause of their expulsion from paradise. "Not a moment goes by when I can bear to be away from you," wrote Portillo de la Luz, "the world seems strange without you by my side. Far beyond . . . the sun and the stars, in spite of distance, I am always with you, my beloved."[2] Those are fitting words to describe the feelings not only of long-distance sweethearts but also of exiles whose success in the adopted country has never alleviated the yearnings of their soul.

The story of Cubans in exile has been aptly recounted before (Portes and Stepick 1994; Rieff 1994), and therefore only a bare sketch is needed here to situate the artistic tastes and expressions of the first generation.

Cubans are responsible for the speediest success story in the history of immigration to the United States. It took the Irish three generations to take control of Tammany Hall. In less than a generation, Cubans placed a heavily accented Xavier Suárez in Miami's mayoral seat and three other compatriots in the U.S. Senate and the House of Representatives. In roughly thirty years they transformed Miami from a provincial resort town into the gateway to the Americas, invigorating its economy and taking over its political structure. Such a precipitous ascent was the result of several factors. One entailed cultural norms that prioritized determination, achievement, and family loyalty. Another one related to sound U.S. government policies. As "freedom fighters" escaping a Communist regime, Cubans promptly received naturalized status as well as educational and economic incentives that eased their incorporation into the receiving society. Between 1961 and 1973, nearly 50 percent of all loans issued by the Small Business Administration in the state of Florida went to Cubans (Light and Rosenstein 1995).

Another factor in the Cuban success story is the class composition of early émigrés. Most Cubans in Miami are skilled and semiskilled workers. Nevertheless, among those arriving in the 1960s was a significant concentration of professionals and entrepreneurs whose expertise and high socioeconomic status on the island translated into the formation of a successful business enclave in South Florida

(Portes and Zhou 1996). Even today the Cuban community continues to exhibit a rate of entrepreneurship and business formation that surpasses the national average. Once in the United States, those older Cubans set the tone for cultural production. They shared many tastes with coethnics of lesser status but some of their aesthetic preferences were distinctive of their class position.

Cuban success was also buttressed by narratives that focused on solidarity brought about by the common experience of exile. A ferocious denunciation of Fidel Castro and his perceived betrayal of the nation shaped a hegemonic discourse repeated without cessation by a few Cuban-owned radio stations. For more than four decades, La Cubanísima (WQBA), La Poderosa (WWFE), and, more recently, Radio Mambí, also known as La Grande (WAQI), have transmitted and given shape to a totalizing worldview shared by almost every Cuban in South Florida, regardless of class background. Most powerful has been the influence of Armando Pérez Roura, Radio Mambí's executive director, whose voice is heard daily recounting Castro's real and imagined crimes. According to that station's mission statement, Pérez Roura regularly writes or participates in newscasts, commentaries, open microphone programs, and radio editorials meant to "remember on a daily basis the names of victims who have disappeared or been murdered by Fidel Castro's dictatorship." Comparatively young and vigorous, Pérez Roura reigns supreme at the Spanish-speaking station with the largest listening audience in South Florida. He is the proud representative of Cuban *intransigencia*—in his worldview, as in that of his compatriots, intolerance and rancor are virtues that keep unifying memories alive.

When Pérez Roura is not expatiating against Castro and Communism, he is introducing the songs of his beloved country. Other radio stations, newspapers, and TV channels do the same. Fervid political commentary alternates with poetic and musical offerings plucked from Cuba's rich tradition. Although the island is but a speck in the ocean, its contributions to the world of art are legion. Before and after the Revolution, personalities like Alicia Alonso, Ernesto Lecuona, Bola de Nieve, Benny More, Celia Cruz, and Olga Guillot acquired international reputations. In today's Miami, they are invoked as the representatives of a classical era defined by romance, chivalry, and grace. Forgotten, for the most part, are the gross inequalities, authoritarian politics, and racial discord that first led Castro to the Sierra Maestra in the spirit of insurrection. The old Cuba is remembered as an idealized country whose capital city, Havana, rivaled Paris in architectural beauty and whose level of civilized living was unmatched.

The daily repetition of tales of cruelty perpetrated by Fidel Castro and his supporters as well as the remembrance of the stolen nation have created strong ties among Cuban exiles—regardless of class background—and between them and their children, cementing what Portes and Sensenbrenner (1993) call "bounded solidarity." That process has also frozen time. Like Sleeping Beauty, the Cuban community lives suspended between a reimagined past and a future that awaits realization (Rieff 1994). It is as part of the culture of nostalgia that rich artistic production thrives in Miami. Its most important feature is continuity. The artistic preferences of older Cubans—whether professional or working class—are marked by cultural linearity.

It is perhaps in comedy and drama that the continuous, linear character of Cuban culture is best manifested. Banter, especially the kind that gives way to self-deprecation and loud laughter, has always been a quality of interaction on the island and in Miami. In both places levity is highly valued. The term *pesado* (bore or stiff) carries a strong pejorative connotation. The thinking is that by laughing at oneself or at one's situation, hurt can be muted. To use humor when pointing to personal misfortune is thus considered a brand of nobility, whereas self-pity betrays weakness.

As with its Jewish counterpart, Cuban humor is a way to assuage grief or disappointment—from a Kantian perspective, it is an ironic vehicle for restoring order. For that reason humor flourishes in South Florida, where the voices of the two greats of Cuban comedy, the late Leopoldo Fernández (better known as Trespatines) and Guillermo Álvarez-Guedes can still be heard every day in radio broadcasts. Trespatines is to Cuban folk art what Cantinflas was to Mexico and Charlie Chaplin to the United States, an *everyman* confronting adversity through endurance and wit. Famous throughout Latin America, Fernández and Álvarez-Guedes have defined more than half a century of Cuban American *burla* and *choteo*, terms akin to "mockery" and "ridicule." In their image, lesser figures continue to entertain the children of exiles. Among them are Salvador Ugarte and Alfonso Cremata, best known for theater work poking fun at all aspects of life in exile. There are also actors like Salvador Blanco, Armando Roblán, Aleida Leal, Marta Picanes, Eddie Calderón, and Carmen Peláez, who regularly give life to comedic characters whose roots go back to sixteenth-century Spanish literature.

Away from the judgmental gazes of American society, educated and working-class Cubans still frequent theaters like Las Máscaras, located in Little Havana, where comedies or *zainetes* are performed. With a long history and reminiscent of genres begotten by other national groups, the *zainete* is a theatrical play that builds upon confusion and double entendre to make audiences laugh. It bears a likeness to vaudeville but also to Shakespeare. Hapless patriarchs, devious wives, and wise homosexuals are often featured in scripts that build on the news of the day. In Miami, plots often involve an upturning of the grievous realities that caused Cubans to leave their country. Fidel Castro is the butt of many jokes, but so are the newly arrived refugees escaping his hold and even older Cubans living in Miami. The theater is about the only place in which self-parody is possible for the benefit of a group that approaches political matters with deadening gravity. Always written and performed in Spanish, such productions are homegrown, created by grassroots playwrights and featuring local actors. Although the genre is fading, it attests to the power of Cuban endurance and wit.

Also a mark of cultural linearity—primarily but not exclusively in the educated classes—is the Cuban predilection for classic ballet, whose iconic figure is Alicia Alonso. Born in 1920, Alonso is still considered the nation's premier dancer. As a girl growing up in Havana she was impressed with Isadora Duncan's innovative motions (Siegel 1979; Terry 1981). She wanted to have long hair to see it float when her body stretched and leaped. Her father, a prominent military man, took Alicia to Spain so that she was exposed to the art of the motherland, whose traditions had so significantly influenced Cuba. Alonso grew up to become a world-class dancer. She also became an entrepreneur, founding the Ballet Alicia Alonso in Havana in 1948 and then renaming it the National Ballet of Cuba in 1959 when it received official state backing. Alonso was also a key player in what would become the American Ballet Theatre. She starred in Broadway musicals with Ethel Merman, learned *Les Sylphides* from Mikhail Fokine himself, and was the inspiration for masterpieces by George Balanchine and Antony Tudor. She was extensively praised for her performance of Giselle. Followed by fame and fortune, Alonso and her company traveled widely with the acquiescence of the Castro regime. Throughout most of her life, New York was as much of a home as Havana. Even in Miami, where she faced hostility for her bonds with the Cuban government, Alonso represents some of the values that unite Cubans despite political divisions: achievement, sophistication, and creativity.

Beyond its contributions to classical dance, Alonso's troupe is important for another reason—throughout the years it has been a steady source of defections. Interviewed by critic Octavio Roca (2003), Alonso dismissed his probes on the subject by saying about the latest absconders, "I don't think it is worth commenting on them." Her response was disingenuous. The escapes sucking talent away from her company have been numerous and continuous. In 2003, twenty Cuban ballet dancers fled while performing in New York. Some of Alonso's students and former associates have opened lucrative schools in Miami, where children are taught the basics of an art cultivated, now as in the past, by Cuban families, especially those of means. To learn ballet in Miami is more than a hobby; it is also a class entitlement, a way to mark superior breeding. In fashionable districts, like Coral Gables and South Beach, passersby can often steal a glimpse, through studio windows, of little girls in tights and tutus reproducing the pliés and pirouettes of classical ballet, an inheritance made partly possible by Alicia Alonso.

Classical ballet is not the only genre anchoring class supremacy in Miami. The success of operatic figures like Blanca Varela, Marta Pérez, and Miguel Le Grande attest to the presence of a public willing to support refined musical expressions. Their repertory transcends popular offerings from Europe to include the works of conationals like Ernesto Lecuona (1895–1963), perhaps the island's greatest musician of all time. Known as the "Cuban Gershwin" he was a child prodigy who grew up to become a piano virtuoso and composer (Sublette 2004). His most famous work, "Malagueña," is part of a Spanish suite played throughout the world. *Maria La O*, Lecuona's *zarzuela* (operetta) is often produced in Miami. Like other works by Lecuona, it is central to the identity of Miami Cubans regardless of social class or generation. His music operates in two ways: it conveys a clear message of accomplishment, given its international reach, and it reminds Cubans of their common historical roots. *Maria La O*, for example, blends elements derived from

African and Spanish traditions into remarkable melodic innovations to tell the story of a humble woman rising above adversity.

Because Cuba was occupied by the Spanish in 1511, and later allowed the importation of African slaves, class and race were always points of contention in Cuba. A small white minority ruled over a vast population formed by blacks and mulattos, most of them concentrated in rural locations punctuated by *ingenios* (sugar mills) and *bohios* (peasant huts). Afro-Cuban art and culture flourished in a contested environment where all things European were regarded as superior. Those evaluative modes are still present in Miami, but they are also transformed. It is worth observing that the overwhelming majority of Miami Cubans are of a fair complexion and Spanish descent, but that does not prevent them from enjoying distinctly Afro-Caribbean forms and expressions. The Spanish conquerors may have subjugated the bodies of African slaves, but they in turn colonized the minds of their masters, whose descendants brought to the United States a vibrant and syncretic musical art.

This style of art is evident in the singspiel *Cecilia Valdés*, written by Gonzalo Roig in 1932, whose popularity has not faded in Miami. Set in 1830, it tells the story of a beautiful mulatto woman in love with an aristocratic white student unaware that he is her half-brother. Cecilia, in turn, is loved by a black musician. The tragic triangle is mainly a vehicle to expose racial and sexual contradictions born out of the colonial past. Seduced and betrayed, Cecilia is a thinly veiled metaphor of the Cuban *pueblo* (the people), always infatuated with Europe and ambivalent about its mixed heritage. Although the story ends badly, it stands in the Cuban imaginary as a hybrid representation of African and Spanish traditions. In Miami it is also a link to the past and an expression of cultural continuity.

Cuba has a long history of musical accomplishments (Carpentier and Brennan 2002; Moore 2006), and many of those jewels have been transposed to South Florida by the émigré community. Among the works that have survived revolution and exile are those of Esteban Salas, a Baroque composer active in the late eighteenth century who gained esteem beyond the island's borders. The same is true of Robredo Manuel (1817–1870), an innovator who transformed the *contradanza* into a modern genre in the nineteenth century; Laureano Fuentes Matons (1825–1898), who wrote the opera *Selia*; Gaspar Villete (1851–1891), who had three operas play first in Europe; and José Silvestre White (1835–1918), a mulatto of half-Haitian origin who became a violinist and composer of renown. It was Ignacio Cervantes (1847–1905), however, who advanced a musical sense of Cuban nationalism that still persists in Miami. He studied at the Paris Conservatoire under Antoine François Marmontel, Ruiz Espadero, and Louis Moreau Gottschalk (Brozensky, Cabrera, and Collins 1999). His compositions incorporated Afro-Cuban and *guajiro* (peasant) sounds and led Aaron Copland to describe him as the Cuban Chopin. Other exponents of *Afrocubanismo* included Alejandro Caturla (1906–1940) and Amadeo Roldán (1900–1939), whose works continue to be produced in the United States. Roldán's operetta *La Rebambaramba* is one of the finest examples of Afro-Cuban classicism. Based on a scenario by Alejo Carpentier, it depicts Havana's lowlife on the Day of Epiphany in 1830. Roldán was the leading musical figure of his day. As a composer, he was the first to bring Afro-Cuban music to the concert hall and among the first to create works for percussion only.

After the Cuban Revolution a new wave of classical musicians emerged, the most important of whom may be Leo Brouwer, the director of the Havana Symphonic Orchestra whose significant innovations in classical guitar influenced and consolidated the Nueva Trova movement (Moore 2006). Pablo Milanés, the best-known figure in that highly regarded trend, uses classical melodies to recast folk and political themes. Hybridity of all kinds marks Cuban art both on the island and in the United States.

Although most Miami exiles would be hard pressed to agree, the Cuban Revolution brought about a new era of respect for popular education on the island. Together with the development of a topnotch health system, education—including artistic training—has been a high priority under Castro's regime. Such advances have had unintended consequences. Most significant has been not only the emergence of a new generation endowed with superior abilities but also the ambition to use them in the pursuit of prosperity and success. The lack of individual freedoms and economic opportunity has driven many young artists to defect. Ironically, they are at once Cuba's "brain drain" and living evidence of Castro's revolutionary success. Cuba's loss has been South Florida's gain. For several decades, Miami has been flooded by classical and popular musicians who, having received superior instruction in their home country, now perform in local nightclubs and theaters. The most famous of those performers is Albita Rodriguez, whose personal story tells much about the invisible bridges that unite the island and its American counterpart.

The daughter of well-known Cuban performers, Albita was born into music in 1965. By the age of nineteen she was a personality on Cuba's national television. In 1991 she was offered a major recording contract to work in Colombia and received permission from Castro's government to travel to South America. After several junkets through the continent, she finally escaped by walking casually across the bridge separating Ciudad Juárez, Mexico, and El Paso, Texas. Her action was described by a Miami journalist as a bucket of ice water falling on Fidel Castro's head.[3] A political renegade in tailored suits and slicked-back hair, Albita became an instant sensation as soon as she arrived in Miami in 1993, rekindling the passion of the exile community with music steeped in the rhythms of the Afro-Cuban tradition. On stage, she projects an androgynous image, and her contemporary twist on *guajiras* and *sones* is credited for reviving musical styles that went out of fashion before she was born.

Albita's persona is emblematic of a new Miami current. She simultaneously represents cultural linearity and fracture. Her credibility among exiles is bolstered by her political defection and her loving rendition of the music of the past. She is, in that sense, part of the culture of nostalgia. On the other hand, her sexualized profile and homoerotic insinuations place her in a new postmodern terrain. She transforms the expectations of audiences by dispensing with the familiar features of Caribbean exoticism and folkloric banality, offering instead an ambiguous portrayal that is as Cuban as it is American, and yet neither of the two. Her kind of fusion dissolves national boundaries while affirming them. It is no wonder, therefore, that Albita's packed performances at Little Havana's Centro Vasco have attracted a sophisticated following that includes jet-setters, Hollywood celebrities, and international couturiers. As shown by the striking images on her Web page, Albita has become an icon within and outside the Cuban community.

Albita's dazzling success is connected to another South Florida phenomenon: In 1994, shortly after her arrival in the United States, she signed a contract for the Epic-distributed Crescent Moon label created by Emilio and Gloria Estefan, the entrepreneurs whose mission is to turn Miami into the Motown of Latin Sound. A five-time Grammy award winner for singing and songwriting, Gloria Estefan was born in Havana in 1957 and grew up in Miami. She began her career in 1975 as lead vocalist for the Miami Sound Machine, a band she created with her future husband and manager, Emilio. Aptly named for its comprehensive artistic approach, which blends dance, music, and singing, the Miami Sound Machine produces a total immersion in feeling. From the beginning, it set out to attract Hispanic and non-Hispanic audiences. Its performances blend Spanish and English in a combined expression of broad appeal.

By the 1980s the Estefans had developed a potent international emporium with hit singles like "Dr. Beat" (1984) and "Conga" (1986). The highly popular Afro-Cuban rhythms of "Conga" represent both the capacity of Cubans to communicate beyond ethnic or national boundaries and the receptive capacity of American society, whose culture continues to be replenished by immigrant inventiveness.

Cuban Americans have also made a contribution to the figurative arts (Bosch 2004; Libby and Martinez 2006). Sponsored by the Sociedad Pro Arte Grateli—a well-endowed foundation whose mission is to foment aesthetic expression—notable masters have regularly exhibited their work in Miami galleries. Among them are Eduardo Abela, Amelia Peláez, Cervando Cabrera Moreno, Victor Manuel, and the internationally recognized Wilfredo Lam. But perhaps the best-known painter of the Cuban diaspora is Humberto Calzada, whose melancholy depictions of architectural structures—columns, pediments, lintels, stained-glass windows, and doors opening up to bodies of water leading nowhere—have attracted wide interest. He was born in Havana in 1944, and it was there that he began his education. Leaving the island with his family in 1960, he completed high school in Miami. He studied industrial engineering and finance at the University of Miami and became a full-time artist in 1976. His taste gravitates toward pastel-colored interiors and exteriors bathed in even lighting that imparts an impression of classic stability. None of his paintings feature people or animals. His spaces are dormant, expectant, unfilled. Typical of Calzada's style is *La Espera*, an idyllic rendition depicting the portal of a typical Cuban home. Elegant, empty, and silent, it is the evocation of a vanished world that perhaps exists only in the mind of exiles.

In their aesthetic preferences and production, older educated Cubans perpetuate cultural and, in some cases, class-based ideals. The anxieties of dislocation are given shape in works that affirm a cultivated spirit. They embody the yearning for refinement and civilization that Kant and his followers would have predicted. A taste for the opera and ballet, distinctive among educated professionals, coexists with musical forms that cut across class lines with their African and *guajiro* cadences. In both cases, first-generation Cuban art connects with the past even as it communicates with and becomes part of the American experience.

Art among Working-Class Cubans

Figurative artists Dennis Martinez, from Hialeah, and Xavier Cortada, from Little Havana, illustrate a common phenomenon among working-class Cubans reared in the United States.[4] Both artists are members of the second generation, and in their separate styles and degree of success they represent expressive entrepreneurship, an attempt to circumvent the limitations of nine-to-five jobs, and a way to imprint with meaning an otherwise uncertain existence. While Martinez is in the early stages of his quest, experimenting with graffiti and attempting to transform the streets into a canvas, Cortada has already become a muralist of international repute. One has a high school education and is trying to complete his studies in graphic arts at a Fort Lauderdale institute; the other holds two professional degrees, one in the field of law.

Through his art, Martinez seeks to evade the common fate of young people with limited means and education. Cortada uses his talent to achieve more than a prosperous life already accessible through advanced degrees. In both cases the yearning is for not only financial independence but also significance and transcendence. Their creative work salvages elements familiar to the utopian longings of Walter Benjamin and Herbert Marcuse. By turning aesthetic expression into a superior form of labor they reject common expectations even as they seek to surpass them. In both cases, racial and ethnic self-definitions find a way into their paintings.

In the United States, race and ethnicity play a salient role as vectors shaping the collective identity of second-generation immigrants. With the singular exceptions discussed later in this section, Cubans in Miami have a fuzzy notion of discrimination and its leveling effects. For many of them, discrimination is unthinkable given their economic success and social mobility—Cubans display high rates of intermarriage with members of other ethnic groups, including Anglo Americans. In Miami, they also benefit from the "Cuban bubble effect" that protects most exiles and their children from external hostility. More than a million strong, the Cuban community in Miami stands like a fortress shielding insiders often oblivious to the prejudice of outsiders. It is hard for Cubans to feel socially excluded by Americans when most of the people they interact with are members of their own group.

Exempt from that generalization are Cubans who entered the United States after 1980, the year of the Mariel Boatlift. The cleavage between pre- and post-Mariel arrivals is deeply rooted in local culture, with older Cubans self-defining as politically untainted and those in more recent waves being tagged as economic opportunists unfairly partaking of the success forged by earlier members of the diaspora. Urban space divides along those lines, with the City of Hialeah, a residential district in Miami-Dade County, emerging in the collective mind as the redoubt of politically suspect refugees, or "refs" as they are designated in popular parlance.

Dennis Martinez's mother, Adelia, whose husband spent several years in a Cuban prison for his political dissidence, said, "I came to Miami after being raped—yes! Fidel [Castro] violated me and my family. I am now living a second exile in Hialeah." Almost universal is the perception that Cubans who grew up under Castro are less hard working and prone to feelings of entitlement. Ironically, people like Adelia Martínez agree, although they are part of the same population vilified by more educated Cubans. Hialeah exposes the contradictions and underbelly of the Cuban success story.

Unlike other Cubans in South Florida, young people in Hialeah say they experience discrimination almost every day. Dennis Martinez, who is twenty-five years old and lives with his parents on 45th Street, has a father who migrated from Cuba to the United States in 1981 after serving an eight-year sentence for opposing Fidel Castro. Since then his father has worked mostly in construction and now owns his own business. The house where the Martinez family lives is vintage Hialeah—a one-story brick structure with windows protected by iron bars. The Star-Spangled Banner is prominently displayed at the entrance as a testimony of devotion to the adopted country. The front door opens directly into a living room dotted with chairs in golden armatures and upholstered in red brocade. On a console is a sculpture of Santa Bárbara Bendita, or Changó as the Catholic saint is known among the practitioners of Santería, the Afro-Cuban religion favored by working-class Cubans, many of whom are of fair complexion and undiluted Spanish ancestry. Martinez is one of those votaries.

Martinez's parents illustrate a distinctive Hialeah experience—that of people who have overcome daunting troubles on behalf of their children but who face isolation in their adopted country.[5] Spatially concentrated, most of them do not interact with non-Cubans outside of workplaces or with more educated coethnics in private and working environments. There is a vast distance between Martinez's experience and that of his mother and father, but his parents do not know it. "Me and my brother," said Martinez, "we wanted to make it in this country, but we didn't have a lot of guidance. We had to invent new ways to adapt." He seeks to emulate his father in only one way: to succeed through self-employment. "I've learned a lot from my dad and his business," Martinez remarked, "but I want more, a lot more—I want to revolutionize everything I touch."

Growing up, Martinez moved repeatedly, always into low-income neighborhoods. As a result, he attended a string of "really bad" schools. By the sixth grade he knew kids already "out mugging people." But it was the following year that he began to fully appreciate the "dark side of . . . public school." On the first day of classes he was appalled by the cagelike windows, security guards on every corner, and doors locked and "barricaded." He saw kids getting their "chains" snatched, found knives hidden in benches, and stepped over syringes while walking in the yard. It was also during that time that Martinez had his first taste of racial discord; he saw blacks and Hispanics (mostly Cubans but also Nicaraguans and members of other Latin American groups) confronting one another. His memories are laden with regret: "going to school meant that you were always afraid—even your sneakers, you had to defend." Studying came second to worrying about rival gangs. He persisted, however, and graduated with a grade-point average good enough to be admitted at a Fort Lauderdale graphic design school.

Most of Martinez's friends were not so lucky; they dropped out and were stuck "holding their ground" on the street in a futile search for respect. They survived by hustling—that is, "flipping anything you can into money." Martinez seldom hustles, but he still sees beauty in the ways of the street. His friends are the lone rangers of urban survival. For that reason, he despairs that outsiders (Cubans and non-Cubans) have turned street culture into a fashion. "There's rich boys out there," he noted, "who have their lives covered and still are fronting *golds* and claiming gangs . . . Those automatically have beef with inner cities and kids who don't have the money." According to Martinez, "fakers and posers" make hollow what was intended to be solid.

Fair complexioned with light brown eyes, Martinez says that he feels hostility every day because of the way he dresses and speaks. When he was twenty-one, he tried to get a job and was interviewed by a Cuban American in his thirties. The experience left him smarting:

> I say to the guy, "yo, wassup!" He took that as disrespect [and] degraded me saying, "what kinda way is that for a first impression?" He mocked me. So what does it matter if I don't speak like you? I can probably do the job better than you ever could! So I walked out [because] I wanna be hired for what I do, not the way I look.

For almost three years Martinez worked at Security Mart, a store in the Westland Shopping Mall where the managers are Anglo. There he created commercial signs because, as he put it, "I have graphic art in my blood." Although the job paid a paltry hourly wage, it allowed him to support himself while pursuing his real passion: graffiti art. Martinez hopes to turn creativity into a business. In 2002 he and six of his crewmembers (one female) set out to paint walls with a colorful representation of their ideal world. They wanted to take aesthetics to a new level. "Graffiti," said Martinez, "is a way to, how should I put it? Murder the alphabet, bringing about a new order where people are valued for who they are not just what they do." He aims to take signs and symbols "off the wall, where we'll have our own way to make words out of noises." Reinventing language is part of that mission. In Martinez's view, African Americans may have created hip-hop, but that genre has now broken across racial and national boundaries. Hip-hop, he explained, is mostly about artistic phrasing. It entails the reshaping of terms and meanings in the interest of self-distinction.

Authenticity is Martinez's paramount concern. He and his crew resent the stigma that mainstream people impose upon their expressive lexicon. In discussing Tupac Shakur, one of the tragic figures in gangsta music, Martinez observed:

> He's someone [kids] look up to, a role model, meaning, "look, you don't have to wear a tie and suit to work because, look at him [Shakur], he made it and he's representing us." My goal is to push my culture, to help it roll in my own community so I don't see it die. Where I am, Hip-Hop and graffiti is part of Cuban culture. We have Cuban graffiti writers, Cuban MCs, Cuban break-dancers. The baddest break-dancer around is Speedy Legs [Richard Hernandez]. He was born in Cuba and grew up in Hialeah.

In other words, to mute the sting of disrespect and redeem local ways of life are the goals of Dennis Martinez and his friends. They see themselves as inner-city casualties, neglected and held in contempt by outsiders. With rhetorical flare he asked, "If I don't give honor to my neighborhood and culture, who will?" The answer is obvious—he and those like him will recast working-class Cuban identity.

It is for that reason that, in their pursuits, Hialeah youngsters like Martinez are shunning the rich artistic legacy of their Cuban ancestors and turning instead to hip-hop, with its potent alternation between disc jockeying, break-dancing, rap music, and graffiti painting. That choice has multiple implications: First, it abjures dominant Cuban culture with its evocations of control and superiority. Second, it upholds expressions created by urban blacks as instruments of confrontation and racial validation. The effects of that appropriation, however, are not the same. Because hip-hop has become part of mainstream America, it offers Cuban youths like Martinez a way to express dissent without danger, resistance without risk. To the extent that it is an international phenomenon, it also promises membership in youth networks that transcend borders. Dennis Martinez learned much of what he knows about hip-hop not from interaction with African Americans—with respect to whom there were sharp divisions in the schools that he attended—but from the World Wide Web. The Internet has opened new channels for communication and contact between people in disparate locations and social groups, and by going online Martinez has learned about artistic innovators. Reverently he noted the pilgrimages of people who travel long distances to visit graffiti shrines in Miami or Los Angeles.

By emulating styles invented by vulnerable but heroic segments of American society, working-class Cubans are claiming a common status with "the wretched of the earth," while at the same time making more distinct their identity vis-à-vis educated Cubans. Their goal is to succeed on their own terms. The reality is that they cannot succeed in any other way.

Adherence to hip-hop culture allows young people like Martinez to see themselves as part of a larger community without "selling out." The aim is success without surrendering the authentic self. In their early twenties working-class Cubans, with a limited education, face dire options: either small business drudgery or menial employment. Music and art pose limitless possibilities to achieve wealth and recognition "through the back door." The aim of young men like Martinez is not to abdicate wealth and status but to reach them by utilizing the best resources available in the surrounding context. They take inspiration from media figures who have become wealthy and famous without altering their mode of speech or the way they dress. Expressive entrepreneurship is the term that best characterizes their intent—they seek to use artistic expression to escape the restrictions of the formal labor market. Yet they are as interested in aesthetics as they are in financial success.

Martinez's fear is that people like him will be ignored, blotted out, and erased both by the larger society and by more accomplished members of his national group. It is in that sense that he aims at "murdering the alphabet." By reconfiguring language and communicating through art, he and those like him will heighten their profile, making it visible and howling "I am!"

What Martinez dreams about has already been accomplished by Xavier Cortada. He was born in New York in 1970, the son of Cuban refugees, but grew up close to Miami's South West 8th Street, or Calle Ocho en la Sauecera, as local Cubans call the area. When he was a child, his grandmother told him stories about Cuba from her rocking chair. It was the only way for her to introduce family members on the island to her U.S.-born grandson. She succeeded. Xavier knew them all by name. Xavier also learned from his grandmother to abhor Fidel Castro's revolution:

> [She taught me] how it executed opponents, proscribed civil liberties, denied due process, appropriated private property. In my head, I saw how she pleaded for the militants to spare the lives of her detained sons. I saw how my Dad boarded an airplane and was forced to flee his beloved homeland. Growing up in Cuban Miami—attending Los Municipios, praying in La Ermita [de la Caridad del Cobre], or listening to Cuban radio—I experienced first hand how the regime had destroyed so many other lives. Every time another exile landed, I relived the stories.[6]

In his late thirties, Cortada is one of the most distinguished Cuban painters of his generation. He is best known for his collaborative public art, including murals in Switzerland, South Africa, Northern Ireland, and Cyprus. In 1998 "Cubaba," his first solo show in Miami, focused on identity, which Cortada interprets as "being Cuban, being American, being both [while] being neither." Three years later, the "No Tengan Miedo" exhibit allowed him to explore the impact of the pope's visit to the island. In 2002 he tackled his most ambitious project yet, the installation of a monument to freedom in Miami, the city that has become the mecca of Cuban creativity. As he put it,

> I tackle the tragedy of the Cuban Revolution by appropriating one of its airplanes. I am literally painting vibrant images on one half of the actual Russian Antonov-2 Colt airplane that brought a family from Cuba to the United States.

> The other half I am leaving intact—bare, neglected, dilapidated—a metaphor for the state of Cuba after 45 years of oppression. As part of the installation, I am also presenting 45 pieces of luggage numbered sequentially from 1959 to 2004, representing each year the Cuban community has been in exile.

Cortada speaks eloquently about the cultural erosion created by the diaspora. He sees erosion in the absence of Cuba's children from the island, the many that never saw their homeland again and are buried in foreign lands. He is especially moved by what he sees as the plight of Cubans still living under Castro's regime: "The many Cubans who live daily lies, who eat a piece of their own soul day in and day out, so that in the end they are mere husks. But saddest of all are the empty rafts that have washed up on the beaches of Florida." In Cortada's mind, erosion is mainly represented by the vast graveyard of water that separates Cuba and Florida—no one knows how many bodies lie in its bottom of people who sought a new life abroad. Yet Cortada is certain one thing will not erode: "an enduring awareness of all that has happened under Cuba's repressive regime." The original pain of the older exiles lives on in the recovered memory of second-generation Cubans.

Xavier Cortada and his color-splashed murals depicting a yearning for freedom that for being Cuban is all the more universal bring this chapter full circle. Some years ago it was possible to anticipate the fading of passion over the lost country among youth growing up in Miami. They were to be *los pinos nuevos*, the new pine shoots that José Martí—Cuba's topmost hero—had evoked almost a century before as the hope for the nation. Instead, growing up in Miami, a new generation of talented Cubans clings to the memories of their parents as a mark of identity and as a testimony of their devotion to the dislocating experience of their elders. Their art—filled with images of a story heard but not lived—is now part of American culture.

Conclusion

In one of his most celebrated movies, *All about My Mother* (1999), Spanish filmmaker Pedro Almodóvar introduces the remarkable character of Agrado, whose name literally means "delight." Agrado is a transsexual prostitute with an open heart and a penchant for survival who has spent a good amount of money on plastic surgery. Forced in an emergency to face a hostile theater audience, Agrado demurs that authenticity is never more aptly achieved than when re-creating the body in the image of the ideal self. The quip is not only meant to be humorous—it is also a serious reflection about the nature of social realities. In the case of Miami Cubans, the vanished island that the heart pines for has become an idea inscribed in the walls of the collective mind, an imagined nation for that very reason more real than the one described through factual accounts in history books, a country made visible through the reenactment of dance, theater, painting, and music.

Among older Cubans, regardless of class distinctions, aesthetic expressions and tastes denote cultural linearity—they are a bridge to the familiar forms of the past. In some cases, however, they also constitute a means to assert superior breeding and class status in an adopted country known for its propensity to discriminate. A taste for the opera, ballet, and classical music signals to the host society some of the reasons why Cubans are entitled to belong in America. Beyond linguistic barriers, art emerges as a universal means of communication. Those capable of aesthetic enjoyment are members of the same community despite temporal or geographic divides. Aesthetic empathy is also one of the elements of bounded solidarity (Portes and Sensenbrenner 1993). Shared tastes and styles unite people into a cohesive whole. The music of Lecuona, the dancing of Alicia Alonso, Albita's smoldering performances, and Gloria Estefan's crossover appeal are all part of a process by which the Cuban culture of nostalgia merges with and is absorbed by American society.

Among the children of immigrants the tendency is toward fracture and innovation. Yet the story is more complex than suggested by those words. Expressive entrepreneurship is a means to attain financial independence and social recognition through aesthetic creation. Immigrant children and the children of immigrants take survival for granted but yearn for autonomy and lives filled with meaning. To turn artistic expression into a means to achieve economic success and social prominence is part of their outlook. Artistic expressions among the children of the Cuban diaspora continue to give voice to the anguish that resulted from expulsion and relocation. The imaginary country forged in the mind of exiles is now the legacy of the youth who grew up in the United States. It is also the subject of their art.

For young Cubans in the United States, artistic possibilities are not limited to the forms derived from the rich history of the ancestral country. They are now Americans and as such a broad spectrum of new cultural manifestations is available to them. Hip-hop has become a source of inspiration for youngsters in this country, including the children of immigrants. The black experience of suffering and endurance has now been embraced by youth groups throughout the world as a marker of identity and sometimes rebellion. Hip-hop stands as a symbol of resistance against the homogenizing effects of the market and the oppressive effects of formal employment. It is in that sense that the descendants of slaves and the children of exiles have become one community. In the world of art almost anything is possible.

NOTES

1. Led by Alejandro Portes (Princeton University) and Ruben Rumbaut (University of California, Irvine), the CILS began in 1993 and continues to the present. A sample formed by more than 6,000 young people evenly divided between San Diego and Miami-Dade Counties were repeatedly interviewed over the years on matters of education, immigrant background, family composition, work-related aspirations, ethnic identity, and related issues. The survey has been complemented by a series of ethnographic modules, several of which I have conducted in collaboration with Liza Konczal (Barry University) and William Haller (Clemson University).

2. No existe un momento del dia en que pueda apartarte de mi. El mundo parece distinto cuando no estás junto a mi. Más allá . . . del sol y las estrellas, contigo en la distancia, amada mia estoy.

3. See http://www.yuca.com/albita.htm.

4. Part of this section was previously published in Fernández-Kelly and Konczal (2006).

5. I use the real name of Dennis Martinez with his permission.

6. Cortada's quotations are taken from http://www.cubanmonumenttofreedom.com/pages/artist.html.

CHAPTER 4

Inside and Outside the Box

THE POLITICS OF ARAB AMERICAN IDENTITY AND ARTISTIC REPRESENTATIONS

Amaney Jamal

Arab American identity is strongly rooted in the political realities and social identity constructions of the homeland. For decades homeland attachments have shaped Arab American identity; thus, it is not surprising that Arab American arts have traditionally relied on the cultural and folkloric elements of social ties and other relationships to the homeland. As with other ethnic groups, however, an additional dimension also shapes Arab—and Arab American—identity. The long history of political conflicts in the Arab world has played an equally significant role in structuring Arab American identity and its artistic expressions. The politically contentious realities of the Middle East—from multiple U.S. involvements in the region, to the Arab Israeli conflict, to the newly constructed War on Terror—are all at the heart of Arab and Arab American identity.

Yet when we examine predominant representations of Arab identity in Arab American arts, an overarching theme becomes all too clear. The transmission of an Arab identity into mainstream American discourses is contingent not only on what Arabs think of themselves but also on the ways the mainstream has historically defined Arabs. This dialectic relationship between identity representations that emerge from within an ethnic group and the complementary identifications that preexist in the mainstream define the nature of Arab American arts today. The politics surrounding representation very much dictate not only the content but also the medium through which Arab American arts are disseminated. This ongoing, sometimes fluid, sometimes static relationship between competing articulations of identity has resulted in what we can today broadly categorize as the Arab American arts. The debates over representation are influenced by important facets of art dissemination like resources (money) and audiences (mainstream vs. Arab). This interaction between ethnic and mainstream identity representations has also led to new forms of artistic expression like Arab hip-hop music, which is a direct result of the ongoing tensions involved in defining an Arab identity in the West.

Since 9/11 two forms of responses have emerged from the Arab American community. Mainstream Arab American organizations like the Arab Community Center for Economic and Social Services (ACCESS) in Dearborn, Michigan, have now institutionalized the Arab American National Museum as a key source of Arab American representation. Such forums seek to define and exhibit the Americanness of Arabs in America. There are also new forms of artistic expression adopted by the second generation that highlight the Arabness of their identities while simultaneously exposing mainstream intolerance. These two forms of artistic expression address the stereotyping within mainstream society and appeal differently to each generation. The first generation is far more likely to want to showcase its positive attributes to mainstream society. The second generation, however, is more adamant about asserting its own identity and pointing out the discrimination and intolerance of the surrounding culture.

Overview of the Arab American Community

About 1.2 million of the total 281.4 million U.S. population reported Arab ancestry, according to the 2000 census (de la Cruz and Brittingham 2003).[1] This population grew by 41 percent in the 1980s and 38 percent in the 1990s. About half of the Arab population is concentrated in five states: California, Florida, Michigan, New Jersey, and New York. Michigan has the highest concentration of any state (1.2 percent of the total state population), growing by 51 percent in the 1990s.

Before World War II Arab immigrants (first and second waves) were predominantly Christian, coming from the Mount Lebanon part of Greater Syria; most were men who took jobs as unskilled laborers, peddlers, and factory or mine workers. Many in this cohort saw themselves as sojourners. Yet this group of immigrants was almost completely cut off from the homeland as a result of World War I and the imposition of strict immigration quota laws in the 1920s. While the Arab American community felt increasingly separated, two alternative patterns emerged simultaneously within the community: strong ethnic solidarity and a more assimilationist worldview. Arabs realized they were in the United States for the long haul.

After World War II, Arab immigration continued with a much more diverse population coming to the United States than before. This third wave of Arab immigrants included those escaping political turmoil, like Palestinians and Iraqis; those escaping civil war, like Lebanese and Yemenis; and those looking for better economic opportunities and constituting the brain drain of the Arab world, like Egyptians and Syrians. These new arrivals were better educated and more affluent than those in the earlier flows. Furthermore, many in this new wave were also Muslim. While earlier immigrants did not necessarily see themselves as part of the American fabric—their children, rather than they, assimilated—post–World War II immigrants tended to appreciate the democratic process; they were politically galvanized, especially around issues pertaining to the homeland (Suleiman 1999).

Both previous immigrant waves came to the United States with strong nationalistic sentiments, although they were not as strong as the sentiments of the third wave. The first and second wave of Arab immigration in the early 1900s coincided with the weakening of the Ottoman Empire in the Arab world, as the Ottomans began to be seen by Arabs (especially Christian Arabs) more as foreign occupiers than as indigenous Muslim rulers. The third wave of immigrants, however, is most inspired by a growing national Arab consciousness because of its direct relationship to political unrest linked to the colonial period. With the creation of the state of Israel and numerous Arab Israeli wars, this new wave was the most devoutly nationalistic in sentiment and identity. During the 1970s, 1980s, and 1990s, as political conflict after political conflict erupted across the Arab world, third-wave Arab immigrants continued to trickle into the U.S. Arab national identity—an identity that would come with Arabs to America—is rooted in the political upheavals of the Arab world.

Arab American Identity and the Arts

Arab American identity is normally bound up with the social, cultural, and political realities of the homeland. The Detroit Arab American Study (DAAS) found that key identity indicators include attachment to the homeland, speaking the Arabic language, supporting Palestine, and participating in Arab arts and cultural activities.[2] Through various institutions, social networks, and the arts, Arab Americans continue to reproduce these identity characteristics and attachments in the United States.[3] Religious institutions, social service organizations, antidiscrimination groups, and Arab and Islamic schools have all become key sites where Arab American identity is promoted and preserved. Family networks are no less important. Marrying within the community and socializing with other Arabs are also important features of identity sustenance. Further, political allegiances and discourses remain paramount in describing and linking one's self to a broader Arab nation abroad. Since most Arab immigration patterns to the United States have resulted directly from political upheavals in the Arab world, the world of politics is an underlying denominator of Arab American identity today (see Howell 2000; Naff 1993; Suleiman 1999).

Historically, then, Arab American arts have promoted intertwined symbols of cultural traditions, class and religious experiences, and homeland identities. It is curiously difficult to separate the cultural or social elements of Arab identity from the political. Arab arts tend to encompass these multiple self-definitions. Since Arab American identity is in fact a conglomeration of the political and the cultural, Arab American arts have simultaneously featured these dual expressions. Arab art exhibits, for example, have historically showcased traditional Middle Eastern garb. Long robes with detailed embroidery, headscarves, and jewelry signify a cultural heritage that underscores both the religious traditions of the region and their peasant origins. One might assume that dress on its own is apolitically cultural in nature; however, for Arab Americans, the traditional dress is not only culturally but also politically salient. The *fellah* (peasant) looms large in the mind-set of Arab Americans. Before colonization, Arabs enjoyed an intimate relationship with their lands, which symbolized not only nationalist pride but also the means of subsistence before the onset of globalization. Various agricultural tools and hand-woven items used to collect wheat and vegetables, items like trays and bowls, are often on display, projecting a deep sense of attachment to Arab lands. Furthermore, the traditional dress also demonstrates what many will consider a rejection of Westernization altogether.

On the musical scene, belly dancing, the traditional Arab *debke* (troop dance), and other instrumental performances—which include music performed on the drum, *shababe* (short flute), and windpipes—all epitomize expressions of Arab identity. These forms of music are often considered nationalist in origin, and they dominate Arab American cultural festivals, weddings, social gatherings, and the like. To rally an Arab American crowd, one needs only to begin a *debke*; it assures full and animated audience involvement. In a typical *debke*, dancers hold hands in large circles and move counterclockwise, coordinating the movement with foot tapping and stomping. These *debkes* are normally accompanied with lyrics that either explicate social and cultural norms and ties (like kinship, attachments to family and friends, patriarchal relations, and so on) or focus on political national phenomena. The *debke* is a folkloric mode of identity expression passed on from generation to generation. The themes of displacement, living in the diaspora, occupation, and foreign intervention are topics that *debke* songs capture in eloquent, poetic fashion. These various cultural forms are so integral to and expressive of Arab identity that any Arab arts display must include them.

Performances across the United States capture the connection between the arts and the political aspects of Arab identity. When the famous Lebanese artist Fairooz visited the United States, her fans—mostly Arabic—crowded the aisles and seats of New York's Carnegie Hall, their distinct dialects clearly audible. At the end of her concert, the audience asked for an encore of the song "Jerusalem" and began chanting in one voice: "*Al Quds, Al Quds*" (Jerusalem). The year was 1971, and the 1967 war was very much on the Arab mind (Bushnaq 2002). As Inea Bushnaq reminds the United States, "The [arts] are a means for Arabs to convey to an audience beyond their own community their view of events in the Arab world" (2002). In Carnegie Hall, the Arab audience was communicating their deep attachment to Jerusalem.

Representations and Counterrepresentations

In the United States the package of Arab American arts has been segmented into two dichotomous categories. For decades, the American mainstream has been fascinated by Orientalist representations of Arab culture (Lockman 2004; McAlister 2005; Said 1979; Shaheen 2002). Dating back from the early days of Hollywood, portrayals of Arabs in predominant media circles have often emphasized the "backward" elements of the heritage. Susan Akram discovers this process in the "deliberate mythmaking" tactics of film and media, in the polemical stereotyping strategies of "experts" on the Middle East, "in the selling of foreign policy agendas, and in a public susceptible to images identifying the unwelcome 'other' in its midst" (Akram 2002, 61). A long history of misrepresentation and the promotion of violent stereotypes mark the popular American media; Arab and Muslim Americans were portrayed as terrorists long before 9/11 (see Gerges 2003; Mandel 2001; Shaheen 2003; Suleiman 2002; Tessler and Corstange 2002). Muslims and Arabs are consistently absent from that desirable group of "ordinary people, families with social interactions, or outstanding members of communities such as scholars or writers or scientists." "This process of demonization," Akram goes on to say, "has been so complete and so successful that film critics, most Americans and social commentators have barely noticed" (Akram 2002, 66). Not only do popular images do little justice to Arab representations, they often shape policies vis-à-vis the Arab American community. Says Jack Shaheen, a leading expert on Arab American popular representations:

> Hateful words and images have their impact on public opinion and policies. There is a dangerous and cumulative effect when repulsive screen images remain unchallenged as *real* portrayals of Muslim culture, which come back to afflict Americans of Arab heritage as well as non-Arab Muslims in their dealing with law enforcement or judicial officials. For example, in January 1997 a judge in Dearborn, Michigan, was asked to rule whether an attorney could show *Not Without My Daughter* to a jury deciding on a child-custody case between an Arab-American father and a European American mother. Incredibly, the judge allowed this defamatory film portraying an Iranian man as a child abuser and child kidnapper to be introduced in court, influencing the judicial proceeding.
>
> (Shaheen 2002, 207)

Not only is Arab culture portrayed as "backward," but it is also depicted as violent, savage, and inhumane. The traditional Arab dress, which for many Arabs signifies cultural and political pride, has become in the United States the lens through which Arab men oppress and their women become victims. Female forms of Arab dance, which include belly dancing, are seen in the mainstream as purely exotic and erotic. More often than not, women in mainstream depictions, especially on television, are portrayed either as exotic sexual beings and/or submissive and abused objects. Because of geopolitical strategic reasons, the relationship between the United States and the Arab world is one that erects, highlights, and reinforces difference between "us" and "them." Thus, it is difficult for average Americans to understand what Arab American cultural expressions are all about. The audience is quite tainted.

Not only has the ongoing conflict-based relationship between the United States and the Arab world hampered efforts to create better cultural understanding, but in many cases there are deliberate attempts to downplay or ignore important elements of the Arab identity altogether. To be more precise, much resistance meets Arab Americans who desire to display artistic expressions that have political undertones—and, as documented above, Arab identity in general is highly political (Howell 2000). Arab nationalist consciousness was born of the political upheavals in the region, and the modern nation-state system in the region is a result of World War II. In the United States, however, Arab artists and exhibitors are often told to "tone down" their political identities. Artistic expressions about foreign intervention, Palestine, the Occupation, and war are vetoed out of Arab art exhibits. Lyrics, songs, and images that document political Arab experiences are excised from display lists, brochures, and handouts. Arab American art forms are censored by non-Arab exhibit owners, and often the non-Arab funders, too, show similar intolerance toward Arab political identity. Funding organizations are much more comfortable providing grants to promote "social" rather than "political" expressions of the culture, often asking grant writers to remove any mention of politics. This intolerance is most visible when any art forms thematically relate to Palestine or the Occupation, resulting in a segmented representation of Arab American identity within the arts. The mainstream American public is more privy to the image of an Arab woman as a belly dancer or abused wife than as a woman wearing a traditional embroidered dress that carries a potent political message of homeland attachments. Why? Because layers of censorship have reduced Arab American identity to just that. Thus, the existing social image of the "Arab" is one that the U.S. mainstream is comfortable with. It is exotic, mysterious, and represents mystical, Orientalist fascinations with the Arab world.

Micromanaging this apparent disconnect between the reality and representation of Arabs in the arts is mind-boggling for any organizer of an Arab American arts exhibit. Sally Howell, a former arts director at the Arab Community Center for Economic and Social Services in Dearborn Michigan (ACCESS), captures this dilemma when she describes her attempt to organize an arts display in the 1990s that would showcase Arab American arts to the mainstream. According to Howell:

> The only artists the American art establishment would fund were those who specialized in the folkloric, home-oriented art forms. . . . ACCESS was compelled to present the most traditional forms of Arab expressive culture to a larger society that already considered Arabs backward or worse. We were trapped between an identity politics that demands public representation of "ethnic heritage" and a political discourse that stigmatizes all things Arab in America. (Howell 2000, 62)

At numerous junctures Howell felt her efforts to promote Arab American arts to a larger mainstream constituency was stifled because of political considerations. "Some program officers from national granting agencies asked me to remove the word 'Arab' from my grant applications because they thought it 'too pejorative.'" She added:

> They preferred that I refer to immigrants by their national affiliations. I was advised to substitute the word "Israel" for "Palestine" and to describe Palestinian needlework traditions by village name rather than by national or ethnic titles such as "Palestinian" or "Arab." This was the advice of staffers who were friendly to ACCESS; they were trying to soften the negative connotations of Arabness our applications would carry for some members of folk arts and humanities panels in Washington and elsewhere. (Howell 2000, 69)

When we look at the ways in which various artistic expressions about Arab Americans emanate from the mainstream, we are in reality only witnessing glimpses of the actual dynamics of Arab American identity behind these images. For mainstream society, acceptable images of Arabs are those that depict a backward culture, fascinating in its very backwardness. For Arab American artists this has posed a serious dilemma as they find themselves in the troubling situation of reproducing a distorted identity of themselves. While the political aspects of their identities are being defined by the mainstream as irrational and inhumane, their social identity has been reduced to stereotypical representations that capture neither Arab identity abroad nor Arab American identity in the United States (Howell 2000).

This phenomenon has created much unease among Arab American artists and community members. In fact, it creates a paradox. On the one hand, Arab American artists feel that the only way they can obtain a mainstream audience is to conform to the existing understandings of Arab identity. On the other hand, artists may choose only to perform for and/or display their work to more understanding Arab American audiences, thus keeping their works of marginal significance in terms of the larger issues surrounding the mainstream. Either mechanism reproduces Arab American marginalization. Only being able to perform or display artistic qualities to one's own group normalizes an inward-looking rather than outward-looking endeavor. Furthermore, if one can only exhibit arts to an audience that has already predetermined the subordinate qualities of the ethnic group, then conforming to those expectations reinforces one's own subordinate status as well. Arab American identity has been subordinated and marginalized in artistic expressions.

In an era where outreach is needed to improve cultural understanding and incorporation of Arab Americans into the larger society, these conundrums infuriate many Arab Americans who want mainstream society to see Arabs outside this tainted box. Arab Americans who are more wealthy and better off often register disgust with the ways Arabs are portrayed in these folkloric types of artistic exhibits. They are sick and tired of "traditional" images of Arabs showcased as the only images. Sally Howell captures these critiques of existing art displays by the Arab Dearborn elite:

> When we [ACCESS] represented Yemeni musicians we were accused by the Lebanese of making Arabs look primitive and backward, dark-skinned, even black. . . . Traditional art projects in general were frowned on by urban

> professionals, who thought they made Arabs look like peasants. . . . Bourgeois Arabs resented being represented by art forms associated so obviously with the past and the foreign (needlework, calligraphy, weaving) at the expense of more modern and elite art forms (painting, sculpture, classical music) (Howell 2000, 71).[4]

Yet, these modern and elite "high" art forms are heavily influenced by class location and social hierarchy. Embracing one form of art over others that are more pan-nationalistic, encompassing identities across classes would not lessen the marginalization of Arab identities. Furthermore, the transition to forms of artistic expression that are already part of the mainstream and do not necessarily emanate from the homeland means that the identity of the artist gives the music its ethnic quality and not the music itself. A handful of Arabs, including Simon Shaheen, perform using modern instruments and attract a wide audience. But if one listens to Shaheen's music on its own, it is hard to notice a distinctive Arab quality. His music has African, Asian, and European elements as well (Bushnaq 2002; Howell 2000). There is little about it that is distinctly Arabic.

The Importance of Art to Arab Americans in Detroit

Artistic expression remains a key mode for the expression of Arab American identity. In the DAAS, Arab Americans were asked whether participating in Arab arts and cultural events was important to "being" Arab; 54 percent of the Detroit Arab population agreed that it was. Often, it is assumed that Muslims are less open to the arts because Islam is much stricter about music, and the depiction of humans in paintings and portraits is shunned as part of theological interpretations (Denny 1984). Nevertheless, we found that Muslim and Christian Arabs are almost equally likely to believe that arts and cultural events are important to their Arab identity—55 percent of Christian Arabs believe in the importance of the arts, compared to 51 percent of Muslim Arabs. Fifty-seven percent of Arab women and 49 percent of Arab men hold this view as well. We also found that among the various nationalities significant variations emerge. Palestinians are far more likely than other nationalities to embrace the arts as part of their identity. Sixty-three percent of Palestinians believe the arts are important, compared to 56 percent of the Lebanese and Syrians, 51 percent of Iraqis—who are predominantly Chaldean—and 42 percent of Yemenis. It appears that proximity to the central issue of Palestine is directly related to positive appreciation of the arts as a means to assert identity. In fact, of those Arabs who believe the arts are important for their identity, 77 percent also said that supporting Palestine was important for their Arab identity—compared to 39 percent of those who do not believe the arts are important.

Identifications with Arabness extend beyond Palestine. Arab Americans in the DAAS were asked about the importance of the following three questions for their overall identity: Is it important for others to know you are Arab? Is socializing with other Arabs important for your sense of Arab identity? Do you identify with other

Arabs? Eighty-seven percent of those Arabs who believe that Arab arts and cultural events are important for their identity more strongly identified as Arab.

Not only are the arts a means for Arabs to assert their identity; it also appears those who embrace the arts are more likely to fear discrimination and perceive unfair treatment. Sixty percent of those who value arts for their identity are likely to worry about their futures in the United States, compared to 43 percent who are not that attached to the arts. Only 44 percent of those who value the arts believe Arabs and Muslims can get a fair trial in the United States, compared to 58 percent of those who do not believe the arts are important for their identity. Further, those who embrace the arts are also significantly more likely to believe the media is biased against Muslims and Arabs. And while only 10 percent of the entire Arab American population has participated in protests, of those who believe the arts are important to their identity 16 percent have protested compared to 6 percent who do not believe the arts are important to sustain their identities. All in all, it appears that those who embrace the arts are more likely to assert their identity while simultaneously responding to mainstream forms of discrimination.[5]

Within and Outside the Box

Two different aesthetic modes have captured the ways Arab Americans have embraced their identities, especially in the post-9/11 period. On the one hand, there has been an overwhelming commitment from community members to assert the "Americanness" of the community and to illustrate the many and multifaceted contributions of the Arab American community. On the other hand, and especially among the second generation, there also emerges a tendency to highlight Arab American identity as distinct from the mainstream population. The dominant tone here is also about discrimination and unfair treatment.

The Arab American Museum in Dearborn, Michigan

In May of 2005 the $16 million Arab American National Museum in Dearborn, Michigan, opened its doors as a hallmark of the Arab American community. For decades Arab Americans have had to rely on other spaces both to provide them forums and to represent their communities. The museum is the first institutionalized American venue representing the Arab community. It received ample funding from both Arabs and non-Arab donors, but large mainstream corporations played a significant role in funding too. It appears that post-9/11 many non-Arab organizations attempted to embrace Arabs as American partners. For example, corporations like Chrysler, Ford, and GM donated over $4 million toward the museum. Today it operates on a $2.5 million annual budget, with the bulk of that funding coming from non-Arab donations.

Anan Ameri, director of the Arab American National Museum, highlights its significance for the Arab American community. As a longtime member and respected leader of the Arab community in Dearborn, Ameri felt that Arab Americans had been excluded from mainstream representations of themselves. In order to ameliorate the image of Arabs, the community needed its own space to "document the presence [of] and be able to present Arab Americans to the mainstream public" (pers. comm. 2006). According to Ameri, the museum is an enormous asset, providing not only a forum for the mainstream to learn about Arab Americans—local public schools and members of the community visit—but also a space for aspiring Arab American artists. Many of the debates that Howell documents above about the ability to find space and funding for Arab artists can be directly addressed with the newly created museum. In the spring of 2007, the museum hosted a Diwan conference, which brought together various Arab American artists to discuss their work. A central theme of the conference focused on identity. These artists, however, were addressing issues on their own turf; hence, candid discussion of identity was possible. These themes included youth identity, hyphenated identities, misrepresentations of identity, and female identifications.

The museum has also organized an Arab American artist exhibit and is already in the process of sponsoring two edited volumes on Arab American arts. In many ways, the Arab American National Museum provides a space for Arab artists to showcase their work while simultaneously packaging these artistic expressions to a larger mainstream audience, without the interference of mainstream biases. Ameri, hoping that similar museums will emerge in other key American cities, believes that the museum in Dearborn can serve as a model for other Arab American community organizations.

The themes of the museum highlight the ordinary Americanness of the Arab American experience. This strategy is seen as vital in terms of countering decades-old and mounting stereotypes against the community. The museum has three permanent exhibits: "Coming to America," "Living in America," and "Making an Impact." While the first two exhibits highlight the specifics of the Arab American immigrant experience, they also draw strong parallels to the immigrant experience more generally. Thus, although one is able to appreciate the uniqueness of Arab Americans, one is also able to see Arabs as part of a larger immigrant category, one that at its very essence is an American experience.

The exhibit "Making an Impact" showcases the many contributions of Arabs to the mainstream and reveals the Arab identities of several icons—including presidential candidate Ralph Nader, White House journalist Helen Thomas, auto racing legend Bobby Rahal, and opera singer Rosalind Elias—demonstrating that not all Arabs are potential threats. In fact, one Arab American featured in the exhibit has worked with every presidential administration for fifty years—as the White House Santa. Statements such as "Numerous Arab-Americans have made it their lives' work in improving the lives of all Americans" and "All areas of government and politics have been well-served by the hard work and commitment of Arab-Americans" are found across the exhibits. Such statements demonstrate ACCESS's goal: to package Arab Americans as pertinent, constructive, law-abiding citizens who have given back to the United States.

The strategy of showcasing similarities and American commitments, however, is one that the mainstream still has problems fathoming. Even in its effort to create understanding, the museum still encounters resistance from the mainstream. Take, for example, the coverage of the museum by *New York Times* reporter Edward Rothstein. In his review he states, "One exhibit . . . shows a collage of images of Arab terrorists on television, and asks why a more accurate image of Arabs is not broadcast—one more closely resembling another collage, of smiling children and families." But the reason is not necessarily a reflection of prejudice, he says: "Islamic-motivated terror has compelled a rethinking of everything from airport design to foreign policy; smiling families have not" (Rothstein 2005, 51). It is these types of responses that the second generation, like its artists, seems less likely to tolerate. Rather than package their Americanness to a mainstream audience that is more or less suspicious and weary of Arab Americans, these activists directly address the bigotry associated with statements like Rothstein's through their various artistic expressions.

The Hip-Hop Genre

An oppositional mode of artistic expression can be juxtaposed with the aesthetic mode described above, the goal of which is to create understanding of Arabs through the arts. Hip-hop artists in various media seek less to create understanding and more to point out that American society is bigoted toward Arabs and Muslims.[6] In the last decade, young Arab American artists have begun to reject the predominantly folkloric ways in which Arabs are represented in the arts. To an extent, they also reject Arab American artists complicit in this process. A new, mostly second-generation group of performers attempting to break into submainstream forms of artistic media have emerged. Abandoning everything "Arab"—all the traditionally defined signifiers of Arab identity—these Arab American artists are becoming visible with a vengeance.

For these second-generation artists, the "political" becomes an overtly visible and structuring component of their art. Rather than using "traditional or folkloric" expressions, they use mainstream forms that include poetry, hip-hop, and comedy to step outside the essentialized box of Arab identity. Adopting the discourse of the oppressed and marginalized in the United States, especially that of African Americans, these new artists see themselves and their identities as a minority subjected to racial discrimination. Their plight, they claim, is due to an inherent prejudice against Arabs. These artists do not see Arabs as white, nor do they support U.S. policies in the Arab world. As American citizens, this class of Arabs is an oppressed minority.

Take Suheir Hammad, the widely celebrated Palestinian American poet, for example. Her first book of poems, published in 1996, is entitled *Born Palestinian, Born Black*. Not only does she boldly use the word "Palestinian," but she also links it directly to the U.S. black experience. Her collection has gained widespread recognition among similar second-generation Arab Americans and other groups dedicated to human rights, gender equality, gay rights, and other coalitions of color—groups that Arab Americans do not generally support. New artists, seeking a larger audience, tend to form alliances with segments of the population not traditionally Arab. This strategy seeks to tackle the issue of Arab misrepresentation through the establishment of alliances with other minority groups rather than from within the dominant mainstream audience. Instead of trying to change the mainstream perception of Arabs from within, by showing Arab American sympathy with the status quo, these new artists also critique that mode of Arab artistic expression as complicit. By forming alliances with nontraditional segments of the mainstream population, second-generation Arab hip-hop artists are attempting both to expand their audience base and to emphasize continuities of oppression. The vast majority of the first-generation Arab immigrant community would neither recognize Hammad's contributions nor understand her poetry. Hammad's audience, like that of her second-generation cohort, is a broader coalition of individuals that includes other minority groups. Her poetry resonates well with those who have been affected by injustice in the context of American racial clashes and social conservatism. Her poetry is both overtly political and what many would consider radical (Shalal-Esa 2003).

In "Exotic," Hammad distances herself from mainstream portrayals of "Arabness" and takes on the essentializing, exoticizing portrayal of women. She speaks generally about women of color, but her primary focus is on Arab women. Nor is Hammad timid or lukewarm about her support for the Palestinian cause. Palestine looms large as a theme in many of her poems, and she often ties the Palestinian issue to other pertinent daily events that ordinary Americans can identify with. "Of Refuge and Language," her poem about Hurricane Katrina, directly draws on the Palestinian discourse and has found support within Arab and non-Arab circles alike:

> I do not wish
> To place words in living mouths
> Or bury the dead dishonorably
> I am not deaf to cries escaping shelters
> That citizens are not refugees
> Refugees are not Americans
> I will not use language
> One way or another
> To accommodate my comfort
> I will not look away
> All I know is this
> No peoples ever choose to claim status of dispossessed
> No peoples want pity above compassion
> No enslaved peoples ever called themselves slaves

While Hammad never explicitly refers to Hurricane Katrina, her language of "shelters," "refugees," "dispossess[ion]," and the "dead" clearly evokes the traumatic event. Similarly, while she never explicitly refers to the Palestinian experience, such language equally signifies occupation, diaspora, and camp life. By tying the devastated New Orleans to Palestine, Hammad links the identities of

Arab and "dispossessed" American. Yet Hammad goes even further, rejecting an uncritical association or an association denuded of action, "pity" without "compassion." Adopting the lyrical, yet stark qualities of hip hop, she vocally takes up the work that poetry can do. "Language" should not "accommodate . . . comfort." Rather, it should help us "not look away" from the truth, the truth that "No peoples ever choose to claim status of dispossessed / No peoples want pity above compassion / No enslaved peoples ever called themselves slaves." Hammad's poetry is clearly political in form as well as content. Unlike an attempt to win over mainstream society, Hammad, like other second-generation artists, is committed to illustrate the reckless insensitivities commonly understood as mainstream consensus.

The Iron Sheikh

These newly emergent artistic images, like Hammad's poetry above, resonate powerfully within Arab American youth culture. Hammad has many fans within Arab hip-hop forums. Since 2000, Arab American hip-hop has really become more of a trend than a fad. This second generation hip-hop phenomenon is represented in the experiences of other minority groups, like Cuban Americans and Asian Americans (see chapters 2 and 7 in this volume). Like the poetry that Hammad constructs, Arab hip-hop addresses similar issues, directly linking Arab hip-hop artists to the politics of the homeland. Their lyrics prioritize antiwar and anti-occupation themes. In the words of "Narcy of the Euphrates," an Iraqi Canadian hip-hop crew, hip-hop is "the voice that felt oppressed speaking out." In many ways these young hip-hop artists want to reclaim their identity, an identity that has been distorted in popular media and the arts. Their songs also address salient issues of race relations and discrimination in the United States. These hip-hop artists are critical of "assimilationists" in the Arab American community. The Iron Sheikh, one of the most well known of new Arab hip-hop artists, sings about the injustices inflicted on the Arab world, his disgust with U.S. policies vis-à-vis the region, and growing up Arab in America. He also raps about surveillance, monitoring, suspicion, and discrimination. In "Growing Up," the Iron Sheikh asserts that Arab Americans are here to stay, and it is not up to the U.S. government to "take away our rights without a fight." In the "Tale of the Three Mohammads," the theme of Arab American persecution is repeated: "But we are all Arab at the Heart. / Please Don't Hate Us from the Start. / We'll keep living and never depart. / It's the Tale of the Three Mohammads." In my summer 2006 interview with the Iron Sheikh, he was adamantly critical of those in the Arab American community who believe that in order to assimilate Arab Americans should refrain from criticizing government. The point of hip-hop, he argues, "is to empower people who already feel alienated." Empowerment for the Iron Sheikh should be part of any assimilation script. While the audiences for artists like Narcy of the Euphrates and the Sheikh are predominantly Arab, the themes in their work draw from and extend to the oppression of other minority groups—especially African Americans.

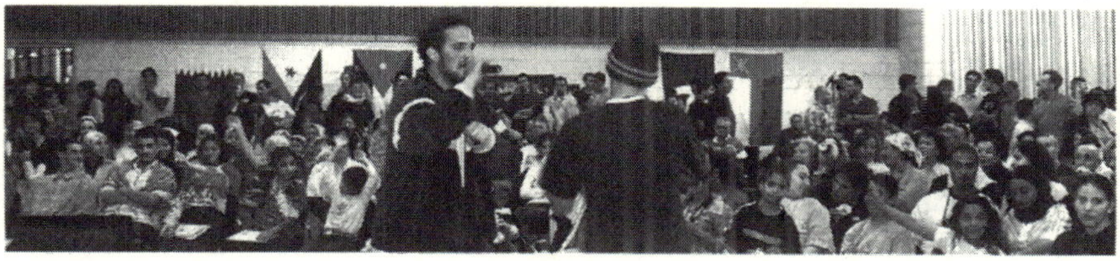

Figure 4.1. The Iron Sheikh in concert at the Arab Cultural and Community Center in San Francisco. Photo by Amaney Jamal.

Discussing the creation of his crew and the formation of his aesthetic, the Iron Sheikh describes the origin of his name:

> The Iron Sheikh was a professional wrestling character who served as the stereotypical Middle Eastern villain. He wore a headdress, flowing robes, and the curly *Arabian Nights* shoes. Growing up, he was a powerful icon that taught me that Middle Easterners are the bad guys, and to be Arab is to be evil. . . . Now I want to reclaim that moniker and redefine it in an empowering way. In short, my name is in itself political commentary on the misrepresentation of Arabs in the popular media, and what Arab-Americans can do about it through performance arts. (Saada 2005)

Although the Iron Sheikh has been a huge hit among Arab American youth, his overtly political lyrics have drawn criticism from larger segments of mainstream society. In 2003 three of his shows were canceled because of the political content of his raps as they pertain to the Arab world.

The new hip-hop generation attempts to forge new ties and illuminate existent links to other youth cultures that understand the history of racial conflicts in this country. They are drawn to the hip-hop world because they also find the music appealing in ways that allow them to identify with other American youth, forging new aesthetic and political alliances. In the older generation of Arab Americans, some find these trends disturbing. Not only is hip-hop considered a form of cultural expression that stands against all things Arab and that is too "American," but it also forges ties with other "colored" communities. For Arabs, this poses a direct challenge to their own "white" identity in the United States. The DAAS found that close to 65 percent of Arabs see themselves as "white" and not "Other," with the older generation more likely to identify as white. Further, Arab Americans are one of the most affluent ethnic communities in the United States. The land of opportunity, at least on the economic side of the story, has been kind to them. Identifying as black, even if it is at the expense of romanticizing the black experience, many will say, would be a further subordination of their status. Older generation Arabs simply do not identify as a colored minority. Hence the generational struggle between first and second generation Arabs is not about recognizing misrepresentation, but about how Arabs should be represented.

The Axis of Evil

Taking Muslim and Arab American (especially second-generation) audiences by storm are comedy groups, including the famous Axis of Evil, which critique the ways in which Arabs and Muslims are essentialized as terrorists in the media and news organizations. In reference to the anthrax scare right after 9/11, the Axis of Evil ironically proclaimed that Arabs and Muslims do not take the time to put a stamp on an envelope and mail anthrax. "No, no, no, no," Maz Jobrani, a comedian of the group says, Muslims would strap the anthrax to their bodies and charge into a group of people. By using the imagery of Arab suicide bombers, the Axis of Evil draws sharp attention to common mainstream stereotypes.

The comedy group features Middle Eastern comedians Ahmed Ahmed, Aron Kader, and Maz Jobrani, with a special guest Dean Obeidallah. The tour, named after President Bush's State of the Union reference to Iraq, Iran, and North Korea as the "Axis of Evil," began in November 2005. In March of 2007, they were given their own Comedy Central special. The group's goal is to point out the hysteria surrounding the war on terror and illustrate its impact on the Arab American community. They do this through laughter, as a means of striking back, asserting their identity, and also drawing an audience of support around their cause. The group sees its tour as a means of defining the Arab American community rather than having terrorists define them. "We don't want to be defined any longer by the worst examples in our community, and it's a very small amount of people. There are a few terrorists and they define all of us" (Dougherty 2007). Not only does the Axis of Evil break down stereotypes and win the laughter of Arabs and non-Arabs, but like the Iron Sheikh and Hammad, the comedy troupe sees itself as part of this new identity marker that is nonwhite. On stage Dean Obeidallah says, "Before 9/11 I was white . . . Arabs are now the new blacks . . . Oh, my God. We're cool!" (Poniewozik 2007).

Yet the identification with the black experience is one that galvanizes an identity that stands against bigotry toward Muslims and Middle Easterners. Even our political elite are not immune from such bigotry, as recently highlighted with the mainstream attack on Barrack Obama for his alleged Muslim connections. Insinuations about Obama's Muslim father, rumors that he attended a *madrasah*, jokes about his middle name (Hussein), and the confusion of his surname with "Osama" are but a few of the instances that showcase the reach of hostility toward Islam. It is these types of portrayals that the Axis of Evil, Hammad, the Iron Sheikh, and many others hope to counter.

Conclusion

The existing artistic articulations of Arab American identity are neither complete nor all-encompassing. Historically, exhibits and performances by Arab American artists have bolstered the social and cultural elements of the heritage. Because these artistic depictions are often packaged for a mainstream audience, they also tend to reinforce stereotypical representations of Arabs as backward and traditional. Arab portrayals of themselves through such media as the Arab American museum are a step toward addressing the ways in which the mainstream has defined the Arab, empowering Arab artists to represent themselves on their own terms. Time will tell if the mainstream is receptive to these types of portrayals, and whether Arab portrayals of themselves will be consistently structured to appease a skeptical mainstream audience. The embrace of alternate forms of artistic expression like hip-hop and poetry with a target audience that is neither mainstream nor white may reify Arab American marginalization in the mainstream. Not only do these forms enter the aesthetic realm from the perspective of the oppressed, but the alliances they forge with other colored communities create a cleavage within the Arab community itself.

The politics of representation of Arab Americans in the arts is multifaceted and nuanced. This chapter offers a glimpse of the multiple layers that structure negotiations among Arab Americans and the mainstream, and among Arab Americans themselves, about their representation in the realm of the arts. These representations are influenced by debates that have emerged between immigrants and their children, among various sectors of the mainstream—whether to embrace or not to embrace Arab Americans, and among those with varying political loyalties in the United States, and they are directly influenced by war and tragedy in the Middle East. To understand Arab American arts it is vital to fully comprehend the politics surrounding their representation.

NOTES

1. Any mention of an Arab country constituted Arab ancestry.

2. The DAAS was produced through an intensive collaboration between the University of Michigan, the University of Michigan–Dearborn, and an advisory panel of community representatives from over twenty secular, religious, and social service organizations. Research team members are Wayne Baker, Sally Howell, Amaney Jamal, Ann Chih Lin, Ron Stockton, and Mark Tessler. The DAAS is a representative survey of all adults of Arab or Chaldean descent eighteen years and older who resided in households in Wayne, Oakland, and Macomb counties from July to December of 2003. Between July and November of 2003, 1,016 face-to-face interviews were conducted. Seventy-three percent of those asked to participate in the survey did so. In addition, 508 members of the general population, age eighteen and over, in these three counties were interviewed during roughly the same period through the Detroit Area Study. About 85 percent of the questionnaire items are common to both surveys, permitting extensive comparison of the two populations.

3. These included organizations like the Michigan Council for the Arts and the National Endowment for the Arts (see Howell 2000).

4. Yemenis in Dearborn are more recent arrivals. The Lebanese in Dearborn have now been there for over four generations.

5. These findings substantiate what other scholars have learned while studying the tendencies among the second generation. Portes and Rumbaut argue that "segmented assimilation" represents many of the trajectories shaping the incorporation of the second generation in the United States. "Unequal modes of incorporation," they maintain, shape the extent to which immigrants may enrich society or find that their aspirations are blocked, becoming therefore more poised to experience downward mobility. In a subsequent study, Portes and Rumbaut further examine the sources of downward mobility among second-generation immigrants. They find that there are elements of dissonant acculturation linked to these experiences. They

label this process, drawing on Irving Child's "Reactive Ethnic Formation." Groups that experience "extreme discrimination and derogation of their national origins are likely to embrace them ever more fiercely; those received more favorably shift to American identities with greater speed and less pain" (Portes and Rumbaut 2001, 187). Thus, how the second generation is received determines the extent to which the second generation adopts oppositional attitudes toward the mainstream. This has consequences for social mobility more generally. Portes and Rumbaut find that Mexican Americans in California (while intense debates about immigration reform ensued in the 1990s) developed many of the reactive ethnic formation attributes. Fernández-Kelly and Schauffler (1994) also find this pattern applicable to the Nicaraguan American experience as well.

6. For a more elaborate discussion of hip-hop culture and ethnic identity, see Stolick (2000), Smith (1997), and Szwed (2005).

CHAPTER 5

Desis in and out of the House

SOUTH ASIAN YOUTH CULTURE IN THE UNITED STATES BEFORE AND AFTER 9/11

Sunaina Maira

South Asian immigrants in the United States are generally associated with popular culture and artistic expressions that are considered exotic, colorful, and traditional. There has long been a particular market in the United States for elite forms of South Asian culture, such as classical music and dance, performed by maestros at "high culture" venues and favored by world music aficionados as well as upper-middle-class South Asian Americans. But there has also been a growing interest in more popular forms of South Asian cultural production, such as folk dance and Bollywood film and music, culminating in the fashionability of all things Indian since the mid-1990s (Maira 2000). The emergence of "trendy" South Asian popular culture, echoing the fascination with Indian aesthetics and spirituality in the 1960s and 1970s, draws attention to the ways that certain cultural productions of immigrant communities are labeled "art" and others "popular culture," highlighting distinctions of cultural capital that rest on class hierarchies within these communities and the society at large (Bourdieu 1984), as well as American policies in South Asia at a particular historical moment.

The surge in commodified "Indo-chic" in the 1990s coincided with an increasing diversification of South Asian immigrant communities in the United States. The Immigration Act of 1965 opened the door to the second major wave of immigration from South Asia since the early twentieth-century migration of agricultural laborers and railroad workers from the subcontinent. The revised immigration laws gave preference to highly qualified, technically skilled immigrants, so the South Asians who migrated in the 1960s and 1970s were largely affluent, highly educated professionals. The "model minority" image of South Asians, particularly Indian Americans, shifted after a third wave of less affluent and educated immigrants began arriving in the 1980s and working as taxi drivers, convenience store owners, and restaurant workers.

In this chapter I examine the popular culture practices of the children of these two major waves of South Asian immigration, first touching briefly on findings from a previous study of second-generation youth culture in the mid-1990s and then turning to a more detailed exploration of my new research on South Asian Muslim immigrant youth after September 11, 2001. I will only present a thumbnail sketch of my previous research on Indian American youth culture (Maira 2002) and will dwell more on my study of South Asian Muslim youth in the United States, a group that has not been adequately studied. I juxtapose the findings from this new research with those from my earlier work to draw out a comparative analysis of cultural consumption and production by middle-class, second-generation college students in New York, on the one hand, and working-class, high-school youth in the New England area, on the other. In addition, these observations are shaped by the historical moment in which they emerged, for my research on South Asian Muslim youth was conducted in 2001–2003 and was significantly shaped by the post-9/11 climate and the heightened scrutiny of Muslim, South Asian, and Arab Americans. The Indian American youth I studied in New York were largely Hindu, with a few from Christian and Jain backgrounds, and while non-Hindus certainly felt marginalized within Indian and South Asian immigrant communities, anti-Muslim sentiments were visibly heightened during the War on Terror. While both groups of youth displayed some common patterns in cultural consumption, such as the interest in Bollywood music and films and the growing affiliation with hip-hop, there were also several important differences that reveal the impact of class, in particular, and the state's relationship to specific ethnic or religious groups at a particular historical moment.

I want to note that this analysis does not emerge from a comparative study designed as such. For that reason, this chapter is solely a reflection on these two different groups of youth that highlights some important questions of the meanings of popular culture in relation to ethnic identification, racialization, nationalism, multiculturalism, and citizenship. What becomes clear is that cultural consumption and production are important sites in which ideas of national, subcultural, and ethnic belonging are produced and contested, and in which young people grapple with ideologies of ethnic authenticity, national allegiance, and transnational affiliation.

"Desi Parties" in New York

From 1996 to 1998 I did an ethnographic study of second-generation Indian American youth in New York, home to the largest concentration of Indians in the United States. These youth were the children of post-1965 immigrants and were generally from middle-class backgrounds, studying at colleges in Manhattan and from families living in the other boroughs of New York and, in some cases, the larger region. While exploring their ethnic and national identifications it was very apparent that the major site for producing and performing ethnic identity for Indian American youth were the "desi" (or South Asian) dance parties held at clubs, restaurants, and college campuses. Every weekend several "Indian parties," as they are also called (although they include Pakistani, Bangladeshi, and Indo-Caribbean youth), are organized by young desi party promoters. Deejays, generally young desi men, spin the latest remix of Hindi film music or bhangra—a Punjabi folk genre fused with dance music in the 1980s by pioneering British-born South Asian musicians—layering the "Indian beats" with techno, hip hop, reggae, and drum and bass. The bhangra party scene exploded in New York in the mid-1990s, initially drawing an almost exclusively South Asian youth audience but later becoming mainstream and trendy for urban hipsters. Droves of desi youth continued to attend these parties in the city and other venues, paying sometimes twenty dollars at the door. Desi parties became the major context in which social networks were created among youth and ethnic as well as racial and gender identities were produced and refashioned.

In *Desis in the House: Indian American Youth Culture in New York* (Maira 2002), I argue that this desi party subculture helped produce a notion of what it means to be "cool" for second-generation Indian Americans that draws on local codes of style and music, including hip hop, and that collides with notions of who or what is "truly" Indian. I found that for many of these second-generation Indian Americans, authenticity was tied to a vision of Indian culture based on classical arts, conservative gender ideals, religious orthodoxy, and a largely static image of Indian society based on notions selectively imported by their middle- and upper-middle class immigrant parents (Prashad 1996). Remix music and culture became emblematic of a "diluted" ethnic identity, contaminated by "Western" influences and flirting with seductive and corrupting "American culture" (Maira 1999). I argue that although this remix youth culture exhibits a hybrid aesthetic that is uniquely second-generation, it is absorbed into the dichotomy of "cool" and "authentic" that these youth grapple with in their everyday lives and that permeates community, as well as larger public, discourses about second-generation identity.

The notion of "cool" draws on hip-hop culture, in style if not in musical preference, for most youth and especially males, who were dressed in hip-hop gear even if they were not fans of rap music. Yet Indian American women who dressed in hip-hop style, or who hung out with African American youth, were chastised for being too "hoody" and not immersing themselves in the desi youth subculture. Those who did not socialize exclusively with other desi youth, who dated non-desis, or who had a multiracial background were seen as not "authentically" Indian. In addition, South Asian student organizations tended to be largely Hindu in leadership and focus, if only implicitly and symbolically, and tensions existed around whether Muslims or Christians were as authentically "Indian," reflecting debates in the larger community tied to the growth of Hindu nationalist movements in India and in the diaspora.

These middle-class college students struggled with their parent's expectations of them to become professionals, especially young men, who keenly felt the pressure for class mobility and viewed hip-hop culture as a defiance of these expectations of integration into the techno-managerial class, if only while in college. At the same time, these desi youth generally did not feel they had shared experiences as "youth of color," and for most of them hip-hop was simply a marker of being "cool" in New York's cultural landscape, rather than a sign of common racial politics. As such, I argue that remix youth culture's sampling of hip-hop allowed these desi youth to hold the two impulses, of ethnicization and of racialization, in a delicate balance. It deferred the question of "black or white" posed by the U.S. racial binary through the ambiguity of adopting black style but in an ethnically exclusive space (Maira 2002, 69).

Muslim Immigrant Youth in Wellford

The South Asian immigrant youth in the New England town I call Wellford represent the most recent wave of migration from South Asia to the United States.[1] They are predominantly working- to lower-middle class, with minimal to moderate fluency in English, and have lived in the United States generally between one and five years. Most Indian immigrant youth in the public high school in Wellford belong to Muslim families from small towns or villages in Gujarat in western India. Most had migrated within the last five to seven years, though some had fathers or relatives who had come to the United States much earlier. Several of the South Asian students are actually related to one another because their families have sponsored relatives as part of an ongoing process of chain migration. The parents of these youth generally work in low-income jobs in the service sector, and the students work after school, up to thirty hours a week, in fast food restaurants, gas stations, retail stores, and as security guards. The families of these South Asian (Sunni) Muslim youth tend to socialize mainly with people from their own ethnic community, but they do not seem to affiliate with the Indian American or Pakistani American community organizations, which tend to involve mainly middle- to upper-middle class suburban families.

The town of Wellford is a small, predominantly white city that was transformed in the 1990s by the abolition of rent control and accelerated gentrification, and by increasing immigration.[2] The year I was doing my fieldwork there were about sixty students of South Asian origin in the high school who were almost evenly split between immigrant students and second-generation youth.[3] Reflecting more or less the national immigration trends for South Asians in the United States, the largest South Asian group in the high school was from India, followed by Pakistan, Bangladesh, Nepal, Tibet, and Afghanistan. Students from India, Pakistan, Bangladesh, and Afghanistan constituted the largest Muslim population in the school, followed by youth from Ethiopia, Somalia, and Morocco.

The ethnographic study I began in September 2001 was based on interviews with South Asian Muslim immigrant students, second-generation South Asian youth and other Muslim immigrant students, parents of immigrant and nonimmigrant students, teachers, staff, youth program organizers, community and religious leaders, and activists working on immigrant and civil rights. I did fieldwork in the school and at a range of sites in Wellford, including homes, workplaces, social gatherings, and cultural and political events. While doing this research, I was also working as a volunteer with the South Asian Mentoring and Tutoring Association (SAMTA), a support program for South Asian immigrant students in the high school's bilingual program. I helped to organize biweekly workshops in coordination with the International Student Center at the school for South Asian students on social, cultural, and academic issues and hung out with these youth in a variety of spaces, at school, with their families, and on trips to films and cultural events.

Popular Culture: Private and Public Spaces

The most striking aspect of the relationship of these South Asian immigrant youth to popular culture is that they actually participated very little in the public consumption of popular culture. As working-class youth, they had very limited disposable income and most were struggling to find jobs to help support their families, so unlike the more affluent youth I studied in New York, they could not afford to go to the cinema often or attend dance parties. For example, one Gujarati boy, Farid, told me that he had wanted to attend a party celebrating Navratri (Gujarati festival) at a local college campus, but when he and another Gujarati immigrant student from the school arrived at the door, they found out that the tickets cost fifteen dollars and so they left. Since they were only in high school, these youth were also generally too young to attend clubs, but even those who were older were not connected to the circuit of South Asian parties frequented by college students, because they were relatively recent immigrants and because these parties attracted a specific class segment of the community. Their public consumption of popular culture was generally limited to occasionally going to a cinema in a nearby suburb that showed Indian movies or to a mall where they browsed with friends.

So on the surface, it may appear that these youngsters were not as actively engaged with popular culture, and this was not as central to their identification as the second-generation college students in New York. Over time, however, I realized that cultural consumption was, in fact, an important component of their lives and shaped their understandings of "local" and urban, "regional" (for example, Gujarati or Punjabi), and "national" (such as Pakistani or Bangladeshi) identities, but in different sites than for second-generation, middle- and upper-middle class youth. For these working-class immigrant youth, the consumption of popular culture happened most often in private spaces—they watched Hindi movies and listened to music at home or surfed the Internet for Bollywood or Pakistani cultural Web sites. In many of the apartments where they lived, a large-screen television with a VCR was prominently displayed in the living room for watching Bollywood movies and Hindi television serials on videocassette. Some families also subscribed to the satellite link with the South Asian Zee-TV channel that had recently become available, beaming Hindi soap operas and regional cultural performances into their homes and allowing them to participate in a transnational "mediascape," or globalized popular culture realm (Appadurai 1996).

The Internet is a site of popular culture consumption and production that plays an important role in connecting immigrant, as well as second-generation, youth to various forms of popular culture and that allows for private access to virtual "public" culture and experimentations with online identities, as work on cyberculture and racialized minorities demonstrates (Kolko, Nakamura, and Rodman 2000; Lee and Wong 2003; Nelson and Tu 2001). For example, Muslim American high school students increasingly have access to sites such as MySpace that allow them to create electronic portraits and links to popular culture sites, including those for bhangra and hip-hop, creating virtual public identities (Sattar 2006). Although these online identifications may be experienced as more private than those in "real life," they are still subject to online public surveillance, especially so for Muslim Americans after 9/11.

While surfing the Internet may be a less costly form of popular culture to engage in than clubbing, it is not a utopian space that levels all economic distinctions (Sterne 2000). Many of these high school students did not have a computer at home and accessed the Web on computers at school, often while they were hanging out at the International Student Center between or after classes. While I was there, I noticed that many of the South Asian boys regularly surfed the Internet for Hindi film and music Web sites, and a couple of Pakistani boys proudly told me that they had created their own Web sites, complete with links to Indian and Pakistani film sites. Walid, a Pakistani boy, said that he got most of his music from the Internet, for a friend of his downloaded Bollywood music for him at home. Jamila, a Bangladeshi girl, said she visited Internet chat rooms to connect with Bangladeshi youth in other countries as well as youth in Bangladesh, suggesting that she was part of a transnational Bangladeshi youth cyberculture. Jamila found an affinity with these other Bangladeshi youth living in the diaspora, saying that "in London, they're like, they're almost the same as me."

These South Asian immigrant youth relied on films, music, and Internet sites to bolster their transnational South Asian identification. These forms of popular culture connected the private space of their home to other local and national sites of affiliation, to old and new "homelands." Some of the girls regularly watched episodes of Hindi television serials on DVD, videotape, or cable television. For example, Sara, a Gujarati Indian girl, was a fan of *Kusum*, a Hindi serial, and knew all the details of the intricate family and social relationships of the extended families in the show. She and other youth were themselves living in extended or "joint" families reconstituted in the United States, though these were now spread across apartment buildings and city blocks in Wellford. These serials provide a link to a South Asian cultural imaginary to which these youth continue to feel attached, but they also have very different meanings for working-class immigrant youth in the United States who are living lives that were not "imaginable" to them while in South Asia. At the same time, the serials offer images and fantasies of a cultural life conjured up by processes of globalization and economic liberalization policies that drive migration from South Asia.

One evening I went to Sara's house to watch episodes of Kusum, which was her favorite Hindi television series. Sara regularly brought home videotapes of the show from her uncle's Indian grocery store, and since I had never seen the show before, she took on the role of introducing it to me. Sara took me inside her family bedroom, where there was a television and VCR, smaller than the giant-screen television in the living room. *Kusum* is ostensibly about an Indian woman who marries a rich man and lives with his extended family, and about the conflicts and dramas that emerge between family members, but it also highlights issues of work, class aspirations, and globalization. One episode was about an affluent couple that had returned to India from London and were arguing because the woman worked for a multinational company whose products were competing with those of her husband's Indian-owned corporation. Another episode portrayed a highly successful Indian businesswoman talking about financially "selling out" her husband. It seemed that most of the female characters in the series who were successful career women were depicted as being excessively devious, callous, and scheming; as Sara put it, they were simply "kharab" (bad). The morality of the series seemed to have a clearly gendered message: financially successful and powerful women are morally questionable. But the episodes I watched could also be a commentary on the paradoxes and social shifts produced by globalization in general, and by the neoliberal economic policies in India after 1991 in particular, that have resulted in increasingly acute inequity between the cosmopolitan upper classes and everybody else in India. Sara did not comment on this class inequity while watching the series with me, but it was undoubtedly an economic factor motivating her family's migration, and that of most of her friends.

Sara was adept at following the complex chain of events in the TV series and knew the intimate details of the intricate web of relationships among the characters. There was both a nearness and distance between the show and Sara's own life in Wellford that was striking to me. While watching a scene where Kusum's brother is sitting in his plush office and talking to a woman with whom he is having an affair, I asked Sara if she wanted to work in an office. She said that she didn't know. Sara's sister, Rukshana, was working in the family store till eleven that night but Sara was not going to work there anymore. While I initially assumed she was happy about this situation, she later told me she was at home because her family already had four members working in the store and there was simply not enough work for her. Sara was looking for a job at Dunkin Donuts and going to the school employment office, but she had had no luck so far.

Working at Popular Culture

My experience of viewing a few episodes of *Kusum* with Sara could not fully reveal how she made sense of all the gender and class issues in the intricate TV series, but it raised some interesting questions in thinking about the relation of the series, and popular culture more generally, to her everyday life. One of the issues that became apparent to me after getting to know Sara, as well as some of the other youth, was that they were not just consumers of popular culture but also had jobs relating to the production or dissemination of popular culture. Sara worked part time at an Indian grocery store that, like many other all-purpose immigrant stores, also had videos for rent. Walid worked as a security guard at a multiplex cinema downtown, but mentioned that he could not watch films while on duty and had only seen a couple of movies himself that semester. Though he enjoyed seeing his friends occasionally when they came to the theater, he also sometimes had to deal with stressful situations caused by difficult customers. For instance, he once had to call the police because a drunk customer was being disruptive and other theatergoers complained. At nine dollars an hour, with occasional seventeen-hour shifts at different locations on weekends, Walid wanted to find a better job; but without fluent English speaking skills, it was not easy for him or other immigrant youth.

Some of these youth were actually part of the economy of popular culture because of their after-school jobs, and they were exposed to different aspects of the entertainment industry, other than consumption, in their role as low-wage service workers. They were not just viewing movies or TV shows but renting them to customers or managing audiences viewing them in cinemas. Middle-class South Asian youth in New York sometimes worked in the clubbing industry, as party producers or deejays, but they generally took these jobs by choice, hoping for an entry into this exciting world. There is an aura of glamour that surrounds deejaying and producing dance parties that being a guard at a cinema or a clerk at a video store simply does not have; these youth were probably acutely aware of that, but their primary concern was helping their families financially.

The jobs held by these working-class youngsters cast another angle on the relationship of immigrant youth or communities to cultural production, drawing attention to the ways that some relate to popular culture as labor. This is a wider phenomenon involving youth similarly positioned in the labor market due to their marginalized socioeconomic status (Tannock 2001) and echoes Robin Kelley's analysis of how "black youth put culture to work for them," as deejays, graffiti artists, or MCs in the hip-hop culture industry (Kelley 1997; see also Forman 2002; Kitwana 2002). Fernández-Kelly (2006) also finds that Cuban American youth in Miami use popular culture as a form of "expressive entrepreneurship," or an economic avenue to circumvent the mainstream labor market. The case of working-class youth in these part-time jobs related to entertainment is somewhat different, however, for they are not working in artistic production but as low-wage, part-time service workers in the distribution of popular culture. Their experiences, however, contribute to the larger discussion of how immigrant or second-generation youth are not just consuming but also working at popular culture, so their relationship to cultural production has multiple dimensions.

While these youth did not explicitly comment on how their entertainment-related jobs shaped their views of the culture industry, they were very vocal in pointing out how their work limited their access to popular culture. Walid, for example, wanted to go to clubs on "under twenty-one" nights, but he lamented, "I don't have too much time. The club night is Friday night, I work Friday night till midnight. Come home one o'clock, wake up seven o'clock, so I don't have that much time." He added, "And the other thing is, if you want to go meet someone, like your friend, you have a job and he has a different day off. Sometimes on Eid [Muslim festival], we get together and we go and chill out." For both boys and girls, festivals and weddings were the settings where they enjoyed music, dance, food, and collective celebration, depending on the occasion.

Samira, a Gujarati Indian girl who worked at her family's convenience store in the evenings and on weekends, said, "It's not right that we don't go anywhere, we just go to school and to work." Samira made this comment to me one evening when I took her and Sara to see a South Asian culture show performed by college students at a local campus. SAMTA organized field trips with the students to watch movies about South Asian youth in the diaspora and to culture shows at the local universities, events that the students may otherwise have not attended. The South Asian culture shows also highlighted issues of cultural capital and class difference, however, as they were held at elite universities and staged by South Asian youth, generally second-generation, who occupied a very different world from these working-class high school students. While passing by the ivy-covered classroom buildings, I wondered if taking the students to these performances at elite universities was a good idea: was it reinforcing class distinctions and reminding them how difficult it would be to get admission into a four-year college, let alone an Ivy League school, or was it simply one more place in a web of social and class hierarchies that they were already well aware of as working-class immigrant youth? These culture shows were bound up with issues of class and cultural capital, but perhaps they created more unease for me than for the girls, who seemed to take great pleasure in watching the performances and the college students milling about them in the auditorium. In fact, Samira remarked to me that this university was not the "only great school," pointing out that there are "others that are good to go to." After graduating from high school, Samira went to a two-year college, attended by many of the immigrant students at the high school, with the hopes of eventually transferring to a four-year college.

Performing Authenticity and Hybridity

The expeditions I took with students to attend South Asian culture shows and films in Wellford highlighted questions of distinctions of taste, cultural aesthetics, and regional and national identities constructed through popular culture. The culture shows featured both classical dance and music performances and more hybridized performances mixing South Asian regional, folk, or classical styles with American or European music and movements. For example, Samira's favorite performances at the show that night was a dance mixing kathak, an Indian classical dance, with flamenco, and a very energetic hip-hop fusion ensemble. Tasmeena, another Gujarati immigrant girl, loved the fusion dance performance at another South

Asian culture show I attended on the campus with a group of South Asian girls from the school. It was striking that the girls generally seemed drawn to these hybridized performances more than to the classical numbers or generic Bollywood dance sequences reproduced from Hindi movies, rejecting, at least in this arena, the primacy of cultural authenticity. This issue of cultural aesthetics could just be a matter of personal and idiosyncratic preference, but there is a larger politics of ethnic authenticity in which these seemingly individualized preferences are embedded and which makes these girls' responses meaningful.

As I found in my research on second-generation youth and South Asian culture shows at college campuses in New York, there is a contestation, often quite intense, related to representations of South Asian culture. Certain aesthetic expressions, such as classical dance and music, are considered culturally "pure" and so culturally superior to hybridized performances that are seen as "diluted" by other aesthetic and cultural influences. These definitions of what is "authentic" national culture are partly shaped by the preferences of elite immigrants, who often decide what cultural representations should be staged for consumption within the community and by other audiences (Bhattacharjee 1992). They are also influenced by existing notions of "South Asian culture" in the United States that are generally somewhat Orientalist, stressing the "exotic" and "ancient" (Prashad 2000). While the popularization of "Indo-chic" in mainstream fashion and the heightened interest in "Indian remix" music beginning in the mid-1990s may have changed the receptivity to hybrid aesthetics, I think the contestation of cultural authenticity persists as an ongoing discourse reflective of deeper anxieties about ethnic identity in the second generation. In my earlier work, I showed that the hierarchy of "authentic" culture and contaminated remixes in cultural performance is a reflection of the desire for "pure" ethnic identities, presumably free of (selected) sullying elements of "Western" culture, that was pervasive among second-generation youth and also in the immigrant community at large. I argued that the cultural nostalgia of the immigrant generation constructed a yardstick of ethnic authenticity that was to some extent absorbed, and widely espoused, by the second generation, even if it was contradicted by their own everyday actions and social relations, that often challenged these norms, and by the hybrid aesthetic of desi dance parties.

The immigrant youth in Wellford did not seem as preoccupied with the discourse of cultural authenticity as second-generation South Asian college students. They sometimes made comments about wanting to "hold on" to their culture and expressed in various ways their negotiations of "national" traditions and local aesthetics, such as through experimentations with style and music. Nevertheless, apart from the fact that their concerns with finding a job or getting into college were uppermost, I think they were simply less obsessed with the notion of cultural authenticity and, as recently arrived immigrants, had not been in the United States long enough to express "nostalgia" for their home countries. Even if they missed their hometowns and villages intensely and often expressed feelings of sorrow and loss at being uprooted from their previous lives, they did not view their "homelands" through the diasporic filter of an idealized culture of origin, uncontaminated by "Western" influences. If anything, these youth generally struggled more with their disillusionment with "American culture," for their views of the United States were shaped in part by stories of relatives living overseas and also by Hollywood movies. After arriving in the United States, many were surprised to find that it was not as "clean" or "beautiful" as they had imagined, and that American society was not as it was portrayed by Hollywood, which they associated with a world that was far less ethnically and racially diverse than their school and community in Wellford.

Subcultural Citizenship

For many of these immigrant youth, arriving in Wellford meant being suddenly immersed in a racially and ethnically diverse high school where students of color were actually the majority and where urban youth culture represented, in many ways, what it meant to be "American." It was not hard to notice this with Farid, an Indian immigrant boy who dressed in hip-hop style and always had a pair of earphones draped around his neck so he could listen to rap music. Farid had come to Wellford at a much younger age than the other South Asian immigrant boys and so was much more embedded in the local urban culture of the high school, where the largest minority group was African American. His friend, Tawfiq, was also increasingly drawn to hip-hop, which was interesting because he and his sister, Zeenat, had arrived only in 2001, and the other immigrant boys generally had not adopted hip-hop music or stylistic codes as yet. As with many other youth who join subcultures because of friends, Tawfiq had begun to dress and talk like Farid as the two hung out together frequently. Many of the second-generation South Asian youth who had grown up in Wellford generally identified with hip-hop through music, style, or language, and the immigrant students were largely immersed in Bollywood films and music, with a few exceptions such as Faisal, a Pakistani boy who was a rock fan, and Sohail, who identified as punk. Yet the situation of South Asian immigrant youth in Wellford was different from that of the college students I studied in New York, who were generally distanced from African American youth or other youth of color in their everyday social lives, unlike the students in the Wellford high school, which had a very large and visible African American and Latino student population. As working-class immigrant youth living in a multiethnic, urban landscape, their experiences of cross-ethnic affiliation were probably closer to those of working-class desi youth growing up in Queens, New York.

In a larger framework, the turn to hip-hop by South Asian immigrant youth has to be placed in the context of the appropriation and mainstreaming of hip-hop in the United States, and its growth as a global youth culture with local and national inflections (Perkins 1996). Hip-hop has become the marker of "cool" not just for urban or minority youth in the United States, but also for an entire generation of youth across the nation, regardless of class or racial background. In the high school in Wellford, in particular, belonging to the dominant subculture meant belonging via hip-hop. A Salvadoran teacher, himself a refugee and former student at the high school, commented insightfully that the high school's youth subcultures seemed to provide "pockets of culture" within the larger American society that allowed immigrant youth to "cross over in the new culture" and to combat isolation and marginalization as newcomers. The teacher, Mr. Vasquez, also pointed to the deeply gendered contours of the adoption of hip-hop by immigrant youth, noting that "some South Asian youth are adopting what it means to be a young man of color in this society, their body language . . . young people from other groups also adopt that, for they seem to think that's what it means to be a young person in this society, the gangsta-ghetto look—what seems to provide the window into this culture is black role models." A few of the South Asian girls, who like Farid had come to the United States at an early age, also identified with hip-hop or more broadly, with the style of black and Latina girls. Even in the time I knew the students, I witnessed the gravitation of some of the girls, such as Zeenat, to the style of their peers in the high school rather than the salwar kameez (traditional dress) of the immigrant girls. So for many of these youth, integrating into the high school culture, which is a proxy for the larger society, is integrating into local, urban youth culture. Furthermore, some of these young South Asian Muslims felt a greater affiliation with other youth of color after the anti-Muslim backlash and expressed a deeper understanding of the exclusion from national belonging experienced by other minoritized communities, particularly African Americans, the largest minority group in the school.

This affinity with local subcultures could be considered an instance of the "segmented assimilation" of second-generation youth (Portes and Zhou 1993; Rumbaut 1994), the process whereby the children of immigrants enter into different economic sectors and subcultures in American society. This model counters the earlier sociological emphasis on assimilation into middle-class white American culture as the most desirable outcome (Suárez-Orozco and Suárez-Orozco 2001). However, it is also important not to assume that the affiliation with youth of color is necessarily maladaptive, and will lead to academic failure or delinquency; this shared affiliation is often due to common experiences of racism and can provide a source of political resonance and support. But one cannot also idealize hip-hop as an intrinsically antiestablishment movement and assume that all youth drawn to hip-hop are asserting their rebellion and resistance against the dominant social order in the United States. There is a strand of hip hop that remains progressive—"message" or "conscious" rap—but there are also "ghetto fabulous," gangsta, or "hyphee" incarnations that glamorize conspicuous consumption and "bling bling" (Allen 1996; George 1998).

It is useful to think about the affiliation with hip-hop through the lens of youth subculture theory, understanding that young people are drawn to certain subcultures because of social and economic contradictions in their lives (Gelder 1997; Thornton 1996). Subcultures provide youngsters with a set of "social rituals" associated with a "collective identity," in response to the personal, political, and economic questions that they confront on the brink of adulthood (Clarke et al. 1976, 47). But these subcultures do not express dichotomous choices of conformity or dissent. I argue that subcultures provide a microcultural realm for *subcultural citizenship*, a space where youth learn codes of belonging based on style, body language, cultural interests, adopting different orientations to the adult world and larger society. Second-generation youth in the high school were generally more involved in subcultures that connected them to local and national youth cultures in the United States, but immigrant youth also formed their own subcultures within the school based on common national or regional identities, such as Pakistani, South Asian, Haitian, Central American, Latino, or Brazilian.

For most of these immigrant youth, it was also important to emphasize that they had friendships that crossed ethnic and racial boundaries, as Walid did in commenting on his black, Egyptian, Moroccan, and Gujarati Indian friends. In their daily lives, these students did, in fact, hang out with Latino, Caribbean, African American, and Asian students and, especially, with Muslim Africans who were from Somalia, Ethiopia, or Egypt, forming an incipient pan-Islamic identity. Immigrant youth in this study could be said to form a subcultural connection with one another based on their shared identification as immigrant, South Asian, and Muslim, which flowed into a sense of belonging in transnational, South Asian, or pan-Islamic communities. I found, however, that if they affiliated with one another as "Muslim youth" it was generally based on a common minority identity, rather than through a common understanding of "Islam" or what it meant to be "Muslim." The young immigrants seemed to be crafting an immigrant subculture that was not defined solely by being Muslim, South Asian, urban, working-class, or immigrant, but rather on a combination of *all* these elements as understood differently by each of these youth, who still collectively identified and socialized with one another. It is a subculture based on a hybrid notion of cultural belonging that challenges the dichotomy of "tradition" and "modernity," but in ways perhaps more subtle and less obviously commercialized than the cultural rituals of middle-class or affluent South Asian immigrant youth (Maira 2002).

Subcultures can also promote the notion of individual freedom to "choose" an identity based on style, through purchasing certain kinds of fashion, music, or other commodities. Young people, like adults, practice a form of "consumer citizenship" where turn-of-the-millennium American neoliberal nationalism is closely tied to a culture of consumption (Cohen 2003; Ong 1996). The notion of "youth" itself, as a set of generational groupings that has particular social interests and consumption patterns is, after all, a marketing category created by the cultural industries to target young consumers (Clarke et al. 1976). South Asian immigrant youth did share similar interests in South Asian films and music and common experiences of negotiating their relationships with new cultural institutions, such as the school, and their immigrant families. Yet theirs was not a subculture formed out of choice but rather born of their cultural displacement, and it was not centered primarily on cultural consumption, but rather on managing their precarious economic position and cultural and political alienation from post-9/11 America.

Much of the mainstream media discourse about Muslim youth in the United States, after 9/11 but also well before, has tended to dwell on the image of fanatical, militant Muslim boys and girls wearing *hijab* (the headscarf), generally producing an Orientalist notion of Muslim youth bound by an unchanging religion and completely outside of "modern" (Western or American) youth culture. Yet only one of the South Asian Muslim girls in the high school that I interviewed wore a headscarf—whose meaning itself is more complex than that of Orientalist frameworks about Islam (see Ahmed 1992; Mernissi 1991), as is the notion of modernity. Furthermore, these girls' engagement with U.S. popular culture and also with work outside the home contradicted the perception of Muslim immigrant youth as alienated from mainstream American culture, a belief that is outdated given the global penetration of U.S. popular culture.

South Asian immigrant girls engaged with popular culture in ways that defied stereotypical assumptions about the cultural tastes of "traditional" Muslim females and the expectations that immigrant youth are either fully "Americanized" or "ethnicized" in their cultural consumption. A vivid example of this was one evening when I was in a car with a group of South Asian girls from the high school, driving them to a South Asian culture show at a local university. Tasmeena brought her own CD of Hindi remix music and requested that I put it on and turn it up very loud. We drove through the streets of Wellford blaring Indian film music, the girls piled on top of one another, laughing and chattering in Gujarati, Hindi, and English. Driving around with music pumping into city streets is something one might associate with teenage boys, but it was clear that the girls got immense pleasure from blasting Hindi music into the night (and I must confess, so did I!). These girls rarely got a chance to drive around the city, and it was by no means common to hear Bollywood music in public spaces in Wellford. Tasmeena's small, sonic gesture seemed to be claiming the city for her own, if only for a few minutes while in motion through its streets.

Multicultural Belonging

Teachers and students in the high school had varying perceptions of the South Asian Muslim students and their newly formed youth subculture. The high school is known to be politically progressive, and the teachers, especially the staff of the bilingual program that housed nearly all these students, were generally very supportive of Muslim immigrant youth and sympathetic to their plight, especially after 9/11. The director of the program organized talks about racial profiling and the War on Terror and was quick to help any Muslim students who experienced harassment or threats after 9/11, intervening on behalf of some boys targeted in a couple of incidents in the school (see Maira 2005). Yet the larger cultural discourse about Muslim immigrant youth that is often espoused by liberal observers opposes racial profiling and Islamophobia while still highlighting the cultural alienness and social alienation of Muslim youth. There is a perception in U.S. mainstream media and even implicitly in some academic research that what binds immigrant youth together is the presumed "culture clash" between "traditional" family values and "American" public culture, suggesting that intergenerational conflict is a key element of immigrant youth subcultures, a theme that is greatly emphasized in discourse about Muslim immigrant youth. Much has already been written about Muslim immigrant youth straddling "two worlds," a trope that is pervasive in the academic literature on immigrant and second-generation youth and also within the community and in general public discourse, which views "Muslim" and "American" identities in opposition (Ajrouch 1999; Eisenlohr 1996; Sarroub 2001).

This discourse about Muslim American youth extends well before the events of 9/11, and predates the resurgence of the Orientalist framework of the "clash of civilizations" underlying the neoconservative regime's War on Terror. The "clash of cultures" trope is part of a deeper perception of cultural difference and the meaning of integration into the United States. For example, at a welcome program held at the school in fall, 2001, one of the teachers remarked to me that the South Asian students were smart, earnest, and diligent but had to "travel the farthest cultural distance" in adjusting to the school, especially the girls. This comment made me wonder: far from what? And where were they supposed to arrive? The comment rightly suggested that adjustment to a school, as to a society, is a process that is like a journey with many forks and turns in the road. It is also true that the South Asian students were from small towns and villages, rather than from urban centers in South Asia, and so had to grapple with the more conservative expectations of their families while fulfilling the "model minority" expectations of their teachers and peers. But the comment still assumes a certain destination, if one that allows for a distinct ethnic identity within a plurality of cultural groups.

This view of cultural centers and margins rests on a liberal multiculturalist discourse about difference that has shaped the popular culture practices of youth and has been consolidated in interesting ways after 9/11. The notion of multiculturalism was very apparent in the high school, where students were expected to display their ethnic identities in cultural performances, similar to the college shows they attended, and during ethnically specific "heritage" months. After I finished my research, I heard that Amin and Samir, two South Asian boys, had organized a successful South Asian culture show at the school for the first time, with music, dance, and skits similar to the other ethnic culture shows. The South Asian cultural performance became an annual event marking the presence of South Asian students within a multiculturalist politics of recognition (Taylor 1992).

These cultural performances certainly fostered a sense of community, especially for the immigrant students, and created social contexts in which the students could take an active role, so they were useful in creating a certain kind of space within the school. But it is also the case that they reinforced a multiculturalist approach to structuring social lives and cultural production, emphasizing ethnic identity as the basis for integration into the school, as a microcosm for the larger city and society. The school officially hosted various ethnic clubs, such as the Black Student Union, Asian Club, Haitian Club, Portuguese Club, and Spanish Club, which drew far more students than clubs related to political issues such as the Free Tibet Club, History/United Nations Club, and an antiwar student group.

These students certainly enjoyed the cultural performances of ethnic clubs, but they also defied the ethnic boundaries represented in the school's institutional structures—and in state-supported notions of ethnic groups that dominate U.S. society. Many of the South Asian immigrant students crossed over into other groups of youth. For instance, Ismail, an Indian Gujarati student, argued for a more expansive conception of community: "I hang out with different kids, but even I heard it from a lot of desis who say, 'Why you go with them?' They don't like it, but I say if you want to live in a different world, you have to exist with them . . . . your relationship is gonna be bigger, right. But if you're gonna live in the desi community, you're only going to know desi people, not the other people." One Bangladeshi girl told me she was involved with the Black Student Club and was helping organize their annual show, because she had friends in the club. It seemed that institutional multiculturalism in the school coexisted with what Paul Gilroy (2005, 120) calls a "multiculture," based on an everyday cosmopolitanism that emerges in "heterocultural" urban spaces. Gilroy suggests that in these metropolitan spaces, diverse racial and immigrant groups interact and produce an ordinary hybridity, or vernacular cosmopolitanism (67); however, this multiculture is still influenced by market-driven and state-produced ideas of diversity. Cross-ethnic affiliations among these immigrant youth coexisted with various degrees of contestation of ethnic authenticity and subcultural loyalty that in some ways echoed the tensions about interracial affiliations among college youth in New York, but were more muted given the dense multiculture of the high school. Yet there were indeed moments of interethnic tension among these different groups of youth in Wellford, as there are in any school or community, and that involved South Asian youth, especially in the post-9/11 moment.

The discourse of multiculturalism is absorbed by immigrants, students, and youth, for the United States uses education, the law, bureaucratic processes, media images, and official rhetoric to propagate and celebrate this official doctrine of inclusion. Affiliations with popular culture in immigrant communities need to be situated within this context of multiculturalism, an ideology that has been contested by conservatives and nativists since the 1980s, for it continues to provide one of the dominant frameworks for performing cultural representation in the United States. The "new managed" multiculturalism promotes an official rhetoric of racial inclusion and pluralism, but critics of multiculturalism observe that it highlights the idea of "diversity" in constructing groups of citizens as culturally "different" while evading discussions of political inequity. Multicultural citizenship is appealing to neoliberal states, for it encourages citizens to turn to a politics of representation rather than of systemic change, by fostering a cultural, rather than structural, analysis of social inequality. As Nancy Fraser points out, "pluralist multiculturalism" fails "to connect a cultural politics of identity and difference to a social politics of justice and equality . . . to link struggles for recognition to struggles for redistribution" (1997, 186).

South Asian immigrant youth expressed a vernacular multicultural citizenship based on everyday understandings of pluralism emerging from the social fabric of their relationships and their participation in multiculturalist performances. Yet their popular culture practices did not consistently fit into the domestic framework of multicultural inclusion, edging beyond the nation-state through transnational cultural consumption and affiliating with other groups of youth and subcultures that challenged mythologies of inclusion. Arguably youth subcultures, including hip-hop as an increasingly mainstream phenomenon, are absorbed by a multiculturalist doctrine of "diversity," which is used by neoliberal capitalism in its marketing of commodities to different segments of the population, so that multicultural citizenship is performed through the consumption of distinct products that mark racial or ethnic identification. There is an ongoing tension between these performances of multicultural and transnational citizenship that sometimes overlap and sometimes conflict, as expressed through the coexistence of different forms of cultural consumption among immigrant youth.

The liberal multiculturalist inclusion of South Asians was disrupted, to an extent, after 9/11 by the framing of Muslim South Asians and Arabs as potential "enemies" of the state, or at least as "aliens" whose values were presumably opposed to those of "Western civilization" and the American "way of life" (Grewal 2005). Arab Americans have historically been cast as not quite within the boundaries of U.S. cultural citizenship (Joseph 1999; Salaita 2006), but for many South Asians, this sudden and occasionally violent exclusion from the American fold was new, especially for upwardly mobile South Asians who had generally been considered "model minorities" within the nation. The War on Terrorism shifted the image of South Asians, particularly those identified as Muslim or Arab, from being "good" minorities—although with "foreign" cultural traditions—to potentially "bad" minorities who could be a threat to the nation.

The public anxiety and suspicion of the national allegiances of Muslim Americans made performances of ethnic and national identity a charged issue for many Muslim youth, as transnational affiliations increasingly came under scrutiny as linked to "anti-American" activities. The chilling effect of the surveillance, detentions, and deportations of Arab, Muslim, and South Asian Americans led to a cautiousness about public displays of ethnic and religious identification, particularly in the immediate aftermath of 9/11, and an often hyperpatriotic assertion of "American" identity. Some Muslim American women stopped wearing their headscarves and some Sikh American men took off their turbans, while others were afraid to attend community forums or religious gatherings. Multicultural citizenship came to be replaced by patriotic citizenship, but others chose to contest their exclusion and challenge U.S. policies. Many youth I spoke to did not shy away from expressing their views about the War on Terror and their opposition to the U.S. invasions of Afghanistan, at least in private. While the school's progressive climate supported their expressions of cultural and ethnic identity, and also provided them a public forum in which to share their experiences after 9/11, these students were often hesitant to speak publicly about political issues given the surveillance, detention, and deportation of Muslim Americans in the War on Terror.

Awareness of government informants in mosques and surveillance of Muslim communities has led to a shrinking of spaces for collective mobilization since 9/11 (Bayoumi 2006). This affects cultural consumption as well, for Muslims, Arabs, and South Asians became careful about which public events they attended and how they traversed public space. As I discussed earlier, these South Asian Muslim youth generally confined their cultural consumption to private spaces, but as the boundary between private and public spaces dissolved after 9/11, and FBI agents went to people's homes to interview them, the home also became part of the domain of public scrutiny. For example, I noticed that in Ismail's house there was an American flag displayed prominently in the living room, as if asserting "good Muslim" citizenship even inside their home or possibly anticipating an FBI interview.

The intensified fear of surveillance in the community is justifiable given cases such as that of Tashnuba Hyder, a sixteen-year old Bangladeshi American high school student in New York who was arrested and detained for seven weeks in a maximum-security juvenile detention center on suspicion of being a potential suicide bomber, the first terrorism case to involve minors (Bernstein 2005). FBI agents posing as youth counselors entered her bedroom, searched her schoolwork, and questioned her about a writing assignment on why religions oppose suicide bombing, after monitoring her online visits to an Internet chat room featuring a radical British Muslim cleric. The FBI was unable to produce any evidence linking her to a terrorist plot, but her family was pressured to take "voluntary departure" for immigration-related charges that were never revealed in a case that the government kept secret even after she and her mother were exiled to Bangladesh (Bernstein 2005). In a loose dramatization of the case in the film *Crossing Over*, an FBI agent points out that Hyder was not a "normal" American teenager because her room was bare and her essay proved that she wanted to be a suicide bomber; thus the commoditized features of a certain notion of youth culture are used to prejudge "normal" adolescence and discipline young people's belonging to the national security state.[4]

Conclusion

The popular culture practices of South Asian youth in the United States are intertwined with notions of national and transnational belonging shaped by the policies of the United States toward their communities at particular moments in time. After 9/11, the transnational connections of South Asian Muslim youth have come under public scrutiny, especially if linked to religious or political movements. The South Asian Muslim youth in Wellford, therefore, coexisted in an uneasy space between the celebratory multiculturalism of their liberal high school and the broader suspicion of Muslim immigrants as un-American, if not anti-American, in the public sphere of the city. Since these working-class youth confined their cultural consumption practices to the private sphere, due to restrictions of work, age, and generation, the school was in a sense the primary public space where they could perform ethnic or interethnic affiliations, even if within the parameters of multiculturalist politics, and express their political critique.

The second-generation Indian American youth in New York were able to revel in public performances of "desi" youth culture because of several factors: their class background, demographic concentration in New York, age, generational status, and the historical moment. The War on Terror has certainly had an impact on expressions of pan-South Asian identity as religious fissures have intensified and communities have been reshaped by surveillance and deportation policies; some Muslim immigrant communities, such as the Pakistani enclave in Coney Island, have dwindled considerably in size as men have disappeared and families have left the United States. In the larger cultural imaginary, however, there is a persistent interest in "Indian" culture and India has become an increasingly close ally of the United States in the War on Terror, while Pakistan remains a dubious friend that is viewed as a dangerous hotbed of "Islamic militancy."

The relationships of the United States to various South Asian nations profoundly shape popular perceptions of their national cultures; Indian culture continues to be seen as exotic, and now also as modern and hip, while Pakistan—or Bangladesh or Sri Lanka—are hardly ever included within the rubric of "Indo-chic." These demarcations are also reflected at the level of the communities themselves, for the events of 9/11 intensified already existing cleavages between Indian and Pakistani communities. Those preoccupied with the threat of "Muslim terrorism" wonder if there will be an Islamicization or radicalization of Muslim youth and how this will affect their popular culture practices. My research in Wellford suggests that the underlying public anxiety and suspicion that is reflected in the question itself definitely affects public performances of ethnic and religious identity. Furthermore, class and labor are issues that are not addressed enough when discussing the experiences of Muslim American youth as if they are outside of the sphere of class relations. As part-time, low-wage workers in the service sector, the popular culture consumption of these immigrant youth was limited more by class factors than by religious issues. Thus, comparing these two cases underscores that we need to think about the ways in which popular culture practices of youth are shaped by the policies of the state and labor market as well as by local context and historical events.

NOTES

1. I have changed the name of the location in order to try to protect the identities of the youth as much as possible.

2. The 2000 census reported 2,720 Indian immigrants (2.7 percent of the population), 125 Pakistanis, and 120 Bangladeshis in Wellford, a city that is 68.1 percent white American, 11.9 percent African American, 11.9 percent Asian American, and 7.4 percent Latino (U.S. Census Bureau 2000). This, of course, does not include undocumented immigrants. The "native" population is 74.1 percent and foreign-born is 25.9 percent; 17.7 percent are not citizens and 31.2 percent speak a language other than English. Wellford is of course skewed by the presence of the academic community; while 8.2 percent (3,108) of those enrolled in schools are in high school, fully 70.5 percent are in college or graduate school, and 38.5 percent of the population over twenty-five years old has a graduate or professional degree. The median household income in 1999 was $47,979, which is above the national median, but 12.9 percent of individuals lived below poverty level, slightly above the national level, which some explain due to the significant presence of students. In 2002–2003 there were about 400 foreign-born students in the high school; South Asians were the fourth largest group among them, after Haitians, Latinos, and Portuguese-speaking students from Brazil and Cape Verde, according to the director of the bilingual program and international student center.

3. The high school has approximately 2,000 students, of whom about 40 percent are white and the remaining 60 percent are students of color. African Americans are the largest group of students of color (about 25 percent), followed by Latinos (15 percent), and Asian Americans (about 7 percent). From 2000 to 2002, 33 percent of students had a first language other than English and 14 percent were in the bilingual program.

4. *Crossing Over*, directed by Wayne Kramer (New York: Weinstein Co., 2008). Despite its sympathetic portrayal of the story of Taslima Jahangir, the film has several problematic and Orientalist representations of Muslim and Middle Eastern families.

CHAPTER 6

The Intimate Circle

FINDING COMMON GROUND IN MARIACHI AND NORTEÑO MUSIC

Clifford R. Murphy

Stepping into Tijuana's from the cold of the New England seaport street, pushing in through the swinging doors into a warm and golden Mexican hacienda, we are greeted in Spanish by a petite woman with long black hair and a menu in her hand. She seats us next to a Latino family out for a Saturday night dinner; kids scramble on and off the laps of their parents and stop to take in the music as it passes by. It is, in all respects, an intimate setting—the small restaurant is tightly packed with families, each sitting at small tables piled with enchiladas, rice, beans, glasses of *horchata* and Dos Equis. A five-piece mariachi group squeezes between tables, and the customers shift their seats to get an equal view of the performers. The mariachis—in their sharp black matching outfits—form a hemicycle facing the customers, moving up close to them to form a full circle. The performance too is intimate; musicians stand close, and the trumpet, six-string bass *guitarrón*, six-string guitar, five-string *vihuela*, accordion, and vocal harmonies project a uniformity of sound and identity that is both directed at and inclusive of those customers in its embrace.

Looking around the restaurant at the Mexican décor, food, and musicians, and at what appears to be mostly Latino patrons with some African Americans and Euro-Americans intermixed, one could mistake this place for southwest Texas. Yet when stepping outside, taking in the damp ocean air hanging on the compact, colonial streetscape, it becomes unmistakably clear that this is a New England port city.

A mariachi ensemble in Massachusetts appears out of place at first, and yet on closer examination there is something even more incongruous at work here: Chelsea, Massachusetts, where this ranchera scene plays out on a nightly basis, has been a predominantly Latino city for nearly three decades. What is incongruous about this scene is not the mariachi in Massachusetts, but the act of unified ethnic solidarity and multiethnic sociability reenacted during its performance. Mariachi Estampa de América—one of several groups that play regularly in family-style restaurants and late-night bars throughout Chelsea—consists of performers from various Central, South, and North American Latino nationalities. Chelsea's early history as a Latino city was characterized by tension and open fighting between different Latino nationalities, and by a multiethnic resistance to Latino solidarity. Nevertheless, the ubiquitous nature of Mexican radio broadcasts of mariachi and norteño music throughout Latin America since the 1930s—and the repercussion of mariachi and norteño music such broadcasts have engendered in Central and South America, the Caribbean, Mexico, and the southwestern United States—has created important commonalities for music-making and musical sociability in Chelsea's Latino community. The mariachi, then, acts as an engine for multiethnic sociability in settings like Tijuana's and in turn further develops multiethnic Latino identity in places like Chelsea.

There is another incongruity in the instrumentation of the mariachi group, particularly in the use of the accordion. Traditionally, mariachi ensembles do not utilize the accordion in live performances, and they only occasionally use it on commercial recordings. Nevertheless, the accordion plays a central role, both musically and symbolically, in Mexican norteño music and in conjunto music (a regional variation of the same genre prominent in the southwestern American border region, particularly in San Antonio, Texas). Although mariachi, norteño, and conjunto music are derived from many similar folk and popular traditions, it is unusual for performing groups to attempt to bridge styles in live performance. Relative to the fairly conservative musicality of mariachis, norteño music—like American country music—is wildly popular as a contemporary pop form throughout Latin America, and it often incorporates electronic elements. While the appeal of mariachi music appears to span all generations and class backgrounds, norteño and conjunto are decidedly associated with the working class. Accordion player and Mariachi Estampa de América band leader Elías Interiano deliberately incorporates the accordion into the mariachi ensemble in order to appeal to a broader base of Latin American immigrants, including those with a working-class background. According to Javier Iraheta, a singer and guitarrón player in Mariachi Estampa de América,

> There's a lot of Central Americans in this area, and they *love* norteño music. Once we put the accordion together with the mariachi, it's like we're doing both things at the same time. We're playing the classical music—the mariachi music—and the norteño. We're covering both cycles of styles. That's one of the reasons we use the accordion. We can cover more of what the people want, what they request. (Iraheta and Interiano 2008)

The ubiquitous nature of both mariachi and norteño music back in Latin America is, according to Iraheta, what draws normally disparate peoples together:

> The thing is, Mexican music is very popular. It's not just in Mexico, it's in the whole Latin America, you know? So when we're in different bars and restaurants and things like that, it doesn't matter. It's just people. You're playing and people recognize what you're doing. They know what you're doing. They know the songs. They start enjoying it, they start screaming or whatever. That's the major thing, because they know the music and it doesn't matter where they're coming from. (Iraheta and Interiano 2008)

Passing through the swinging doors of Tijuana's is like stepping into a romanticized Mexican cantina. The stucco walls, adorned with cattle skulls, sombreros, and serapes, and the use of Spanish as the lingua franca of the wait staff, patrons, and musicians, reinforce a distinctly Mexican impression. Mariachis dressed in matching black *charro* (cowboy) outfits with silver medallions down the out seams of their pants visit each table, including single patrons, affectionate couples, and even large families, including them as equals, if but for a moment, in their circle of sound. The overwhelming feeling is one of Mexican solidarity; a uniform Mexican identity, from the name of the restaurant and the décor of the place to the dress of the musicians and the nationalistic identity they project.

Chelsea is the region's most Latino city and yet its most diverse Latino community. The multinational character of Latino Chelsea and its minority Mexican presence is represented in the makeup of Mariachi Estampa de América—with its Salvadoran, Guatemalan, Mexican, Colombian, and American-born members. Throughout the 1980s and 1990s such diversity was—according to both local musicians and interested sociologists—the source of significant conflict. Local strife and gang violence were especially acute in Latino Chelsea during the 1990s. Temporary migration—whereby individuals would live and work in Chelsea only to return to their home country after a few years—helped to perpetuate poor housing conditions for subsequent waves of Latino immigrants. Temporary settlements were in turn fostered by poor housing conditions. Interethnic tension and the temporary nature of immigrant settlements were significant obstacles to Latino solidarity in Chelsea—obstacles that community organizers deemed critical to overcome in order to improve living quality and stabilize the community. Multiethnic Latino sociability engendered and enacted by mariachis at Tijuana's indicates a shift toward a more cohesive Latino community.

During a set break, I strike up a conversation with the group's accordion player—Elías Interiano—and ask him about Mariachi Estampa de América. He explains that his group, like the audience, includes people from Central, South, and North American countries. The group's cohesion is achieved through the charro personae in the band and the musicians' shared background and interest in mariachi and norteño music. A sense of solidarity between the group and its audience is achieved through the use of the accordion to bridge mariachi and norteño styles and repertoires, and the manner in which the mariachi interacts with and includes the audience. Although most of the participants—both musicians and audience members—are not Mexican, the tone of the performance is decidedly centered on Mexico on account of the nationalistic symbolism and thematic content of the music. Phenomenologically, this symbolic unit is further reinforced by Tijuana's Mexican food and décor.

A Brief History of Latino Immigration in New England and Greater Boston

Spanish-speaking people comprise the second largest language group in New England—roughly one-twelfth the size of the English-speaking population and three times the size of both the French- and Portuguese-speaking populations (Zelinsky 2005). Yet New England remains a region rarely identified with Latinos, partly because in the popular and scholarly imaginations the region's self definition remains frozen and tied to the Colonial and Civil War eras, despite the multiethnic diversity that has characterized New England for nearly 150 years (Conforti 2001; Nissenbaum 1996). Perhaps, too, Latinos are not generally identified with New England because—relative to other ethnic groups of their size in the region—they represent a recent chapter in New England's long history as a destination for immigrant peoples. Latino immigration to New England began in earnest during World War II when Puerto Ricans arrived in large numbers to fill wartime vacancies in the agricultural labor force (Cooper 1997). According to the 1990 U.S. census, Puerto Ricans then comprised the largest proportion (42 percent) of Greater Boston's Latino population (Kala and Jones 2006). Significant numbers of immigrants from El Salvador, Colombia, the Dominican Republic, Guatemala, Honduras, Mexico, and other Central and South American and Caribbean countries began arriving here in the 1980s. As a result, the Latino community has swelled within a 100-mile radius of Boston, particularly in the Greater Boston regions of Jamaica Plain, Chelsea, Revere, Malden, Somerville, Cambridge, Roxbury, and East Boston, as well as in New England cities along the Connecticut River (Holyoke and Springfield, Massachusetts, and Hartford, Connecticut), the Blackstone River (Providence, Rhode Island; Pawtucket, Rhode Island; Worcester, Massachusetts), and the Merrimack River (the Massachusetts cities of Lawrence, Lowell, Haverhill, and Methuen and the New Hampshire cities of Nashua and Manchester) (Rodriguez 2001).

The Latino population of Boston and several of its neighboring cities (Chelsea, Revere, Malden, Cambridge, Everett, and Somerville) is differentiated from Massachusetts's other urban Latino centers (Greater Lawrence, Springfield, and Worcester) on account of its ethnic makeup: the vast majority of Latinos in Springfield (89 percent) and Worcester (70 percent) are of Puerto Rican origin, and Lawrence's Latino community is mostly Dominican (50 percent) and Puerto Rican (31 percent) (Kala 2006). While Puerto Ricans constitute Boston's largest Latino ethnic group (26 percent), the rest of the community is fairly well divided between those of Dominican (14 percent), Guatemalan (10 percent), Salvadoran (11 percent), Colombian (9 percent), and Mexican (5 percent) origin (Kala 2006). Likewise, the Latino community of Greater Boston is further differentiated from other urban centers in Massachusetts because nearly half of the Latinos in the greater Boston area are foreign born (46 percent), with Lawrence (36 percent) constituting the second largest foreign-born community and Worcester (18 percent) and Springfield (8 percent) falling a distant third and fourth (Kala 2006).

Chelsea—The Intimate City

The city of Chelsea is a working-class community situated in Boston Harbor, facing the city of Boston on the Mystic River. Geographically, Chelsea is the smallest city in the state of Massachusetts (1.8 square miles). With over 35,000 residents living within its small boundaries, Chelsea boasts a population density greater than the city of Boston, making its nickname—"The Intimate City"—well deserved (City of Chelsea 2008; Kopf 1974). Nearly half of Chelsea's residents (48 percent) are Latino, and in 2006, 31 percent of them were foreign-born (City of Chelsea 2008). Chelsea is one of the poorest cities in the state, and its history is marked by periods of intense immigration, instability, collapse, and rebirth.

Originally called Winnisimmet by the Massachusett Indians and settled by English immigrants in 1624, the town was founded in 1739. By the 1830s it had become an aristocratic suburb of Boston. By 1839 Winnisimmet was incorporated as the town of Chelsea, with a population of 2,390. Two decades later, in 1857, Chelsea was incorporated as a city when its population had grown to about 12,000. Most residents were immigrants from Ireland and French Canada (Cooper 1997, 7). By the end of the nineteenth century, Chelsea had become a destination for many more European immigrants, especially Irish, Italian, and Polish. In 1908 the Great Chelsea Fire destroyed one-third of the city, leaving 18,000 homeless and constituting the third largest urban fire in American history (8). Many of Chelsea's earliest families left the city at that time, and by 1915, 84 percent of the city consisted of first- or second-generation immigrants, mostly of Eastern European origin (Russian Jews and Poles). This brought about an influx of Yiddish, Polish, Italian, French, and Gaelic languages and heightened the presence of Judaism and international variations of Roman Catholicism (8–9).

Puerto Rican immigration to Chelsea began during World War II with the arrival of immigrants to fill the agricultural labor force (Cooper 1997, 9–10). After the war, many Puerto Ricans settled in Chelsea and worked in Greater Boston's then-healthy beer and shoe industries (Amy-Moreno 2005). The mix of Chelsea's older European immigrants with its World War II–era Puerto Rican arrivals is most famously illustrated by the music of jazz pianist Armondo "Chick" Corea, who was born in Chelsea in 1941. Corea's parents were first-generation Italian Americans (his father was a trumpet player in a Dixieland jazz band). He has credited the strong Puerto Rican presence in Chelsea for his interest in Latin-influenced jazz (Tomkins 2008).

In 1948 the state of Massachusetts built the Tobin Bridge and the Southeast Expressway through Chelsea's central neighborhoods—razing the heart of those neighborhoods to build a highway infrastructure—to the outcry of the local community. The interstate infrastructure—which remains today even after the Big Dig placed much of Greater Boston's interstate underground—cuts the city of Chelsea apart from itself while also passing over the community and raining considerable pollution down on its inhabitants (Cooper 1997, 9). By the 1990s, deindustrialization and demilitarization (the Charlestown Navy Yard borders Chelsea) had taken a toll on the economic base of the city. A large section known as the "rag shop" district, where large World War II–era salvage yards lay filled and abandoned, was zoned for urban renewal. In 1973 the salvage yards ignited and touched off the Second Great Chelsea Fire, which consumed eighteen city blocks, or one-half of the city. The large portion destroyed by fire was rebuilt to house a shopping center and light industry; it was not rezoned for affordable housing (Cooper 1997, 10). In the aftermath of the fire, an exodus of residents of European descent left Chelsea destabilized and impoverished.

This period was also characterized by the beginning of a second wave of Latino immigration to Chelsea. People fleeing war and economic devastation in Latin America arrived in Chelsea in large numbers in the 1980s. Immigrants and refugees from Central and South America and the Caribbean were drawn to the city's existing (Puerto Rican) Latino population, affordable (albeit decrepit) housing, and proximity to a wealth of service industry jobs in Greater Boston. Latino transiency was at a peak in the 1980s. The temporary nature of settlements further destabilized an already unstable local economy. By the end of the 1980s, Chelsea's school systems had failed. In 1989 management of the Chelsea public schools was taken over by Boston University. In 1991 criminal economic irresponsibility on the part of successive Chelsea mayors caused the city's economy to collapse entirely, and Chelsea became the first American city since the Great Depression placed into receivership by its home state (Cooper 1997, 11). Following a restructuring of local government, the city was awarded a new charter in 1995. Since then, Chelsea's numerous Latino civic organizations have played a significant role in rehabilitating social and economic infrastructure.

Chelsea's Latino Community

The Latino population of Chelsea is distinguished from its New England counterparts by its multiethnic diversity. Such a broad base of national origins has brought a rich tapestry of cultural influences to Chelsea, but this has not been without problems. In 1997 sociologist Eileen Cooper—a Chelsea native and local community activist—observed that Latinos in that city were resistant to multiethnic solidarity, preferring to be identified by their national origin and not as "Latino" or "Hispanic." Cooper identified resistance to Latino solidarity, low-paying jobs stemming from poor education, unaffordable housing conditions, and temporality as key reasons for continued economic and community instability. Writing in the 1970s, Cooper stated, "Many of Chelsea's Latinos are newcomers who view the United States only as a temporary home. This hampers efforts to build community and develop pan-ethnic solidarity among a diverse Latino population" (Cooper 1997, iii).

What Cooper called "resistance" to pan-ethnic solidarity could be better characterized as "indifference" to ethnic identification or simply a choice to identify with one's own nation of origin rather than as "Latino." Still, Chelsea in the early 1990s is remembered by its mariachi musicians as a place where interethnic tension spurred by underworld violence was a very real problem deterring multiethnic sociability and pan-ethnicity. Studies of Latino communities in Boston and Chelsea from the 1990s show that interethnic/national tensions deterred efforts to organize and mobilize Latinos (Puerto Rican, Dominican, Honduran, Salvadoran, and Guatemalan factions) to mobilize for affordable and humane housing conditions (Medoff and Sklar 1994; Meléndez and Uriarte-Gastón 1993). According to Cooper (1997, 2), "Unity among these Latinos [was] not a reality" and needed to be "deliberately nurtured."

Since the early 1990s, however, the work of community organizations in Chelsea—Latino and non-Latino—including the Centro Latino de Chelsea, Roca, the Chelsea Latino Coalition, and the Chelsea Neighborhood Housing Services (CNHS) appear to have encouraged Latino and broader Chelsea community solidarity. Traditionally a gateway community for Latino immigrants in New England, Chelsea witnessed a trend toward permanent Latino settlement during the mid-1990s; annual home sales in Chelsea doubled between 1992 and 1996, and the number of mortgage loans to Latinos tripled. Home-buyer assistance programs, improvements in city government and schools, and the collaboration of Latino civic organizations and local police to stem the growth of gang activity all helped stabilize the community and decrease transient settlements. The housing trends of the late 1990s, the significant growth in the Latino population, and the development of spaces for intergroup sociability (not only mariachi-oriented, but also after-school programs for Latino youth aimed at reducing gang involvement, as well as dance clubs catering to pan-ethnic youth) indicated a shift toward a pan-ethnic identity, showing a broader inclusiveness of multiple Latino ethnicities now evident in the names of civic organizations that shifted from "Puerto Rican" to "Hispanic" and finally to "Latino." The rise of multiethnic mariachi groups signifies that a more inclusive, cohesive, stable, and permanent Latino community is indeed growing in Chelsea. An important engine of multiethnic Latino sociability and a site of cohesion of pan-ethnic Latino identity have been the Mexican-themed cantinas and taquerias scattered throughout Chelsea and in neighboring Revere, where music sung by Mexican charros—mariachi, norteño, and cumbia—serves to create a symbol of Latino immigrant solidarity.

Mexican Music as Multiethnic Latino Working-Class Music

Mariachi and norteño music has become a source and symbol of multicultural Latino identity for Latinos in Chelsea who claim Mexican, Central and South American, American southwestern (Tejano/Chicano), and—to a lesser extent—Caribbean heritage (Sheehy 2006). Publicly, this music is generally performed at Mexican-themed taquerías, cantinas, and family-style restaurants, and to a lesser degree at folk and community festivals. Privately, mariachi music is performed regularly at house parties in Chelsea, Revere, and other heavily Latino Greater Boston area locations. The performed identity of mariachi groups is decidedly Mexican, a fact reinforced by distinctive artifacts—serapes, sombreros, neon signs for Mexican beers, cattle skulls, frescoes of haciendas, and Mexican flags—adorning the walls of public performance venues where mariachis play.

Mariachi music evolved out of the Jalisco region of Mexico in the nineteenth century and has undergone significant change over the past one hundred years, particularly in the mid-twentieth century, when it was transformed by Mexican radio, television, and movies into a popular, folkloristic, and nationalistic form. As it disseminated beyond Mexican borders, mariachi music has come to be associated with, and often incorporates, compatible folk/popular music from northern Central America and the American southwest, especially the *ranchera* tradition of northern Mexico. Ranchera tunes—what many Mexicans and Mexican Americans call "Mexican country music"—consist of two forms: *canción ranchera* (which has roots in indigenized Mexican folk variations on European Opera arias) and *corrido ranchero.* The *corrido* is a narrative folk ballad depicting anything from Tejano clashes with Texas Rangers to the hardships of immigrant workers, to contemporary epic accounts about (and commissioned by) Latino drug dealers (*narcocorridos*) (Simonett 2001). The *corrido* follows a set pattern, while the *canción* is a considerably more elastic form (Brunvand 1996). The ranchera and corrido forms also serve as the foundation of the norteño/conjunto tradition prevalent in the Mexican American border region. That tradition, popular in the American Southwest and northern Mexico, has been influenced by Eastern European (and urban American) polka and American country and western music.

Mariachi and norteño styles have proved a powerful influence in folk and popular music and culture in Mexico, the Mexican American border region, Colombia, El Salvador, Guatemala, and other parts of Central America and the Caribbean. Mariachi incorporates folk songs and dances from the Mexican state of Jalisco (where mariachi music is believed to have originated), waltzes, polkas, canciones rancheras, corridos rancheros, boleros, blues, and other styles existing along a Latino-European-American folk-popular continuum. Standard mariachi ensembles include multiple violins and horns in addition to guitar, guitarrón, and vihuela. Generally, norteño music is a twentieth-century hybrid of mariachi music, polka, blues, and country and western. The signature instrumental features of norteño music (and its Texas variation, conjunto, which uses accordion and *bajo sexto*, a twelve-string baritone guitar that originated in northern Mexico near the Texas border) make it easy to differentiate from mariachi music despite the reliance of each style (mariachi, norteño, and conjunto) on rancheras and polkas. In addition, unlike mariachi music, contemporary norteño music is often performed with electric instruments, saxophone, and drums. Norteño is, at times, a music that could be mistaken by the uninitiated for accordion-driven honky-tonk (with Spanish vocals) or the urban polka of Rust Belt Americans such as Eddie Blazonczyk or Frank Yankovic. Norteño music underscores the very real relationship between Mexican folk music and the social dance music of Europeans (influences brought by colonial powers and by immigrants of German, Czech, Slovakian, Slovenian, Polish, and Italian origin).

Professional music clubs and eating establishments in the Boston area that feature regular performances by mariachi and norteño groups are mostly located in Chelsea (Tijuana, Cinco de Mayo, Casa Mariachi, and El Rancho Grande), Melrose (Mexico Lindo), and Revere (Plaza Garibaldi and Club Lido). The name Plaza Garibaldi suggests the kind of ethnic succession that has taken place in Revere, Chelsea, and other neighboring cities where Italian neighborhoods have gradually become Latino ones. Plaza Garibaldi, however, derives its name from a popular square in Mexico City, where mariachis from Jalisco travel to hire out for local performances. Plaza Garibaldi in Mexico City is named after an Italian, Guiseppe Garibaldi—grandson of the Italian revolutionary and unifier of Italy—who was a volunteer in the Mexican Revolution and whose forces excelled in the battle that toppled the Díaz dictatorship (Turner 1967). The Chelsea club El Rancho Grande gets its name from a song by the same name—a ranchera from Mexico that spawned a similarly titled film in 1936. The *Rancho Grande* film is widely considered to have popularized ranchera and mariachi music as a Mexican trademark (*Mexican-American Border Music* 1994). Beginning in the 1930s, the Mexican radio producer Emilio Azcárraga intensely promoted mariachi music on Latino radio in Central, South, and North America, as well as in the Caribbean (Knights 2004). So successful was Azcárraga's promotion of mariachi music throughout the hemisphere that some popular and early scholarly histories attribute its invention to Azcárraga himself (Alisky 1955; Bensusan 1980; Ruiz 1988). Azcárraga's influence spread to television and films, and the subsequent association of mariachi music with Mexican charro films brought about an infusion of orchestral influences, via the film industry, on the standard mariachi ensemble. Mariachi ensembles in the music clubs and eating establishments of Chelsea tend to eschew the orchestral influences of charro films, often using one violin or excluding violins all together; they resort to larger orchestral ensembles only during large stage performances.

Mariachi Music in Greater Boston

Greater Boston has relied primarily on the creative efforts of a few mariachi and norteño bandleaders—José "Pepe" Gutiérrez (Mariachi Mexamérica, Mariachi Guadalajara),[1] Verónica Robles (Son de América), Javier and Lucy Iraheta (Cuerdas de Oro), Elías Interiano (Mariachi Estampa de América), José Luis Sicairos (Mariachi Chapala), and Carlos Alfredo (Mariachi Real de Jalisco) (Montero-Sieburth and Meléndez 2007, 69–70). Gutiérrez is considered the first mariachi in greater Boston, having assembled a band in the 1980s, Mariachi Mexamérica, to play in his restaurant Tacos el Charro in the Jamaica Plain section of Boston. Many of the players active in mariachi music in Massachusetts have passed through Gutiérrez's group at some point, including Elías Interiano, Juan Arias (violin, guitarrón), and Javier Iraheta (guitarrón, vihuela, guitar, bajo sexto).

Gutiérrez is a staple of regional folk festivals, but his critics attribute his lack of real prominence to the frequent turnover of players in his ensemble.

Education and urban policy scholars Martha Montero-Sieburth and Edwin Meléndez credit the arrival of entrepreneurial Mexican immigrants like Gutiérrez for the growth of a Mexican restaurant industry, the development of a Mexican immigrant community, the subsequent development of the Mexican food industry (tortilla manufacturers, Mexican food importers, and so on), and the arrival and growth of the mariachi scene in Greater Boston. According to Montero-Sieburth and Meléndez (2007), men like "Pepe" Gutiérrez created jobs for immigrants, giving their friends and family reason to settle in the area. In turn, those emerging settlements ushered in a market for Mexican food products, leading to the opening of more jobs. The Mexican-themed cantinas and taquerias that sprouted across the Boston area—first at Gutiérrez's Tacos el Charro in Jamaica Plain and then in Chelsea, Malden, Revere, Somerville, and beyond—offered numerous venues for mariachi performances.

Mariachi leaders Verónica Robles and her husband Wily López have been active members of the Chelsea community, participating on the staff of Centro Latino de Chelsea and the Chelsea Cultural Council. Robles and López recently launched a local cable access television program—*Órale!*—intended to offer a local alternative to international Spanish-speaking television programs. The focus of *Órale!* reflects Robles's mission to promote multiethnic identity and honor the diversity of traditions in the local Latin American community. As a musical performer, however, Robles centers her efforts on her Mexican heritage. Her performances feature a four- to ten-piece female mariachi ensemble augmented by folkloric dancers projecting Mexican authenticity (albeit atypically modified to include an all-female mariachi band) in music, dance, and rhetoric. That Robles the mariachi performer (as opposed to the community activist or television producer) aims to be a paragon of traditional Mexican authenticity is reflected in her nickname, "La Mera" ("The Real One").

Mariachi Estampa de América

Mariachi Estampa de América—the group discussed at the outset of this chapter—is ostensibly a mariachi band. It does perform as a large ensemble on special occasions and uses several violins and horns on such performances, and it plays songs typical of the mariachi repertoire. On the other hand, the group always incorporates accordion and norteño songs, either while performing in small venues, at house parties, or at festivals. Mariachi Estampa de América includes the sounds of guitar, guitarrón, vihuela, trumpet, violin (on occasion), and an accordion—central features of early mariachi ensembles (except for the accordion)—instead of the classic mariachi of the film era, and its repertoire includes songs from mariachi and norteño traditions. The group also includes a number of traditional cumbias (Afro-Amerindian folk tunes from Eastern Colombia that have become popular in many parts of Latin America and in Latino communities in the United States).

In this sense, Mariachi Estampa de América represents an emerging tradition combining forms found throughout the home countries of various ethnic groups in Massachusetts, synthesized through the idiom of the mariachi ensemble and augmented by the accordion. Elías Interiano, the group's founder and leader, states that this fusion is intentional; he uses the accordion to bridge three musical strands (mariachi, norteño, and cumbia) popular throughout Mexico, Central and South America, the Caribbean, and the American Southwest. According to both Javier Iraheta and Elías Interiano, the group's sound is shaped by the strong presence of Central Americans in Chelsea; it encompasses styles that reach beyond just Mexico. For this reason Interiano chose to call his group Mariachi Estampa de América (Sound of the Americas).

The use of the accordion by Mariachi Estampa de América is unusual in a mariachi group and significant as a symbol of Latino working-class identity. Anthropologist Manuel Peña has shown that upwardly mobile Latino musicians along the U.S.-Mexico border tend to discard the accordion as they move into the middle class. Middle-class orquesta music and elaborate mariachi productions (such as Boston-area mariachi groups led by Pepe Gutiérrez and Mariachi Guadalajara, and Verónica Robles and Mariachi Son de América) forgo the accordion entirely when performing stage concerts. By contrast, working-class Latino music like conjunto, norteño, and cumbia always feature the accordion prominently when performing at public and private working-class events (Peña 1985a, 1985b, 1999). Mariachi music appears to span all classes, but it is rare for any such ensemble to include an accordion player. Therefore, the inclusion of the accordion by Mariachi Estampa de América is strong evidence of its working-class leanings. Mariachi Estampa de América's audience consists almost entirely of multiethnic Latino workers. During performances musicians stand on an equal footing with the audience.

Before moving to the greater Boston area, Elías Interiano did not play accordion. He was born in rural El Salvador, where he and his brother, William, learned to play guitar for Catholic folk masses. The family migrated to the capital city when guerilla warfare threatened the safety of villagers. The Interiano family later migrated to Mexico, Texas, and Florida. In the 1990s, Elías and William traveled to Boston seeking employment. After observing a Salvadoran in Chelsea named Mariano playing the accordion, Interiano opted for the same instrument, taking lessons from Mariano before he returned to El Salvador.

Aside from being drawn to accordion music for its musical qualities, Interiano recognized the accordion's importance as an anchor of musical arrangement. The instrument can direct vocal harmony and horn and violin arrangements, give rhythmic direction to supporting instruments, and provide a bridge between mariachi and norteño music. "Sometimes you have to do crazy things in order to make the client happy," says Interiano. "We can do a little bit of both. Well, you can't *really* do real norteño with mariachi stuff. But, yeah, that's about the closest you're gonna get" (Iraheta and Interiano 2008). For reasons that are not entirely clear, mariachi ensembles are not difficult to find in New England, whereas local norteño groups are a rarity despite the great popularity of the genre among New England's working-class Latinos. As such, there is a demand for live norteño music, and as a band leader, Interiano is eager and capable of folding norteño music into the group's performances: his primary influences are mariachi and norteño groups from northern Mexico and the American border—Mariachi Vargas (California), Sol de México (Mexico), Tigres del Norte (Mexico), Vincente Fernández (Texas), and Antonio Aguilar (Mexico).

The ethnic affiliation of the performers Elías Interiano hires to fill his mariachi ensemble is reflective of his multinational mien; he hires men of Colombian, Salvadoran, Guatemalan, Mexican, American, and on occasion Puerto Rican and Dominican backgrounds. The first time I talked with Interiano about the makeup of his mariachi ensemble, he told me that night's performers were Mexican, Salvadoran, Colombian, and Tejano—what Interiano calls "Texican." "Even the white guy," Interiano said, pointing to trumpet player Tom Halter, "is from Argentina" (Murphy 2007).

Interiano's group has performed throughout his "home" communities of Greater Boston, working each week at Tijuana's for the past seven years. The group has also helped establish mariachi music in several other area venues, including Cinco de Mayo (across the street from Tijuana's), Rancho Grande, and Plaza Garibaldi. Their performances are interactive, and they ask individuals what songs they would like to hear. This interaction leads to a considerable number of bookings for house parties, weddings, sweet sixteen celebrations, and other secular and religious events. According to Interiano, private parties constitute the bulk of the group's performances (Iraheta and Interiano 2008).

The eating establishments where Interiano's group plays draw multiethnic audiences well beyond the Latino community. Although most patrons are Latino, the customers reflect a wide spectrum of Chelsea's (and Greater Boston's) working-class population, including European Americans and African Americans. Mariachi performances for white and black listeners tend to feature a different kind of engagement with the music, with listeners having difficulty making requests—musicians always ask listeners for requests—but paying rapt attention to the performances. Interiano believes the group's hybrid repertoire of mariachi and norteño music has a universal appeal that can transcend language barriers: "It doesn't matter where you're from. It's amazing how the music can bring peoples' attention from all over the world. No matter whether you're Chinese or Moroccan or whatever. It doesn't matter. A lot of people don't understand us. You know they don't understand—sometimes—the music but they still enjoy it."

In 2008 Javier Iraheta further attested to the coexistence of diversity and continuity in Mariachi Estampa de América, saying, "We all get along pretty good. Pretty much everybody that's playing right now in Massachusetts, they were doing this back in their country. And when they came here, they tried to integrate into whatever group was around. That's why I think we come together. We're trying to do the same thing we were doing before. And it doesn't matter where you came from so long as you get along with the other members of the group."

Nonetheless, language barriers can create different levels of understanding about the overt emotionalism and projected masculinity of the Mexican charro in the forefront, and the specifics of the lyrical content—its heartbreak, its pastoral nostalgia, and its tales of outlaws and national heroes—becoming obscured. The uniform appearance of the mariachis—their matching charro outfits working in concert with the Mexican-themed restaurant décor—can lead non-Latino listeners to presume that the mariachis are all Mexican. Non–Spanish-speaking black and white audiences tend to believe mistakenly that the members of Mariachi Estampa de América are all Mexican. Such misperception suggests that the mariachis effectively convey a unified impression, projecting a kind of Latino solidarity—albeit a specifically Mexican one. Part of the mariachi's performance purposefully aims at conveying such an integrated and authentic identity. It turns out that the "white guy" that Interiano identified as a man from Argentina was actually born and raised in Colorado before moving to Boston in his twenties. All the same, the collective impression projected by Mariachi Estampa de América is Mexico-centric.

Interestingly, when performing for Latino audiences in Chelsea, Mariachi Estampa de América uses both mariachi and norteño music to forge a unifying aspect of multiethnic Latino identity and experience, while the outfits of the Mexican charros convey a different type of uniform identity to non-Latino audiences. This latter form of solidarity comes to the forefront when audience members verbalize their perception of the mariachis as Mexicans at public concerts promoted by the arts community, including the Lowell Folk Festival (Lowell, Massachusetts), the Working Waterfront Festival (New Bedford, Massachusetts), the Somerville Arts Council's Union Square Festival (Somerville, Massachusetts), the El Salvadoran Independence Day Celebration (Revere, Massachusetts), and the Deerfield Fair (Deerfield, New Hampshire).

The Charro and the New England Country and Western Singer

Charro regalia empowers mariachis to adopt a strong public persona in a community in which they make up a significant and noticeable part of the laboring force. In a case typical of Anglo-Latino dynamics, former Massachusetts governor and 2008 presidential hopeful Mitt Romney was embroiled in scandal when he publicly denounced the use of illegal immigrant labor while personally employing a grounds crew of undocumented workers from Guatemala on his estate in Belmont, Massachusetts (Saltzmann, Cramer, and Paige 2006). Many of the Latinos who fill the Chelsea restaurants like Tijuana's work as landscapers or truck drivers, the modern, regionalized, urban equivalent to the cowboy (Murphy 2008). The charros in the mariachi ensemble make them visible and uplift their social standing. According to Elías Interiano, the charro persona comes "from people out of the city. From the *rinches* (ranches). The macho man typical thing. That's what, well that's the feeling I have." For Javier Iraheta, the charro is an even more empowering and ennobling public persona:

> The mariachi suit, you know, you have to wear it. Anytime you perform, you have to wear it. Because, one—it gives you security. You feel secure when you're wearing it, you know? It gives you respect from the audience. It's a different feeling when you play the same music and you don't have the suit on. It's a completely different feeling inside of you. And I think the people see it that way, too. If you don't have the suit and you're playing? It's like something is missing there. And once you put it on, you got the respect of the person in front of you. And you feel that inside of you, and you feel secure doing what you're doing. (Iraheta and Interiano 2008)

The use of the archetype of the charro by non-Mexican Latinos in Chelsea bears a direct correlation to country and western cowboy singing by European American immigrants in New England during the early to middle twentieth century (Murphy 2008). As such, a "Mexican" Chelsea charro provides an archetypal figure familiar to working-class New Englanders and their immigrant parents: that of the self-reliant, traditionalist cowboy singer.

The community organization Centro Latino de Chelsea lists on its Web site the strengths that characterize the Latino community: "strong work ethic and self-reliant attitude," as well as a "deep sense of community and commitment to family, especially extended family" (Worby 2008). These same themes characterize the lyrical motifs of the charro songs and the songs of country and western music as performed over the past seventy years by Greater Boston's earlier waves of immigrants (predominantly Italian, Portuguese, Irish, and French Canadian). Historically, New England country and western has been a multiethnic musical form dating back to times when European immigrants of differing nationalities were self-segregated in occupational, religious, and social spheres. It has been a music in which performers alternated between the "traditional" country and western repertoire and the tunes (and language) of their European immigrant community (Murphy 2008). The use of "cowboy," "cowgirl," or "western" stage names by the majority of southern and eastern European country and western musicians created an Americanized identity. Performers felt ennobled by cowboy costumes while subverting standard definitions of American identity combining cowboy iconography with songs in French, Italian, or Greek (Murphy 2008). New England country and western musicians held steadfastly to the "western" long after cowboy songs ceased to be commercially relevant. They continue to pair songs about community and family ("country") with songs of nomadic self-reliance (Murphy 2008).

The regional content of New England country and western songs tends to focus on lyrics about truck drivers, lumberjacks, family farming, and abandoned mills (Murphy 2008). Such themes of agrarian labor and self-reliance in the service of family and community are compatible with other forms of "country" and "western" music, such as mariachi and norteño songs, which focus on similar themes.

Likewise, the dedication of the performers to maintain immigrant traditions while performing music of a multiethnic origin suggests there is vast middle ground joining ostensibly disparate tastes.

Linguistic differences, however, make it difficult for fans of the two types of music to grasp their thematic similarities. The following story is an example: During a performance at the 2006 Lowell Folk Festival, an Italian American country and western performer who began his professional career in the early 1930s told the audience about his experience growing up in Charlestown and Boston's North End. As he intoned cowboy songs and traditional and popular Italian songs he learned from his father, the singer—also an accordion player—spoke with pride of his family's immigrant heritage and his involvement in "western" music. Then he noted bitterly that his father had come from Italy "the legal way," unlike, presumably, immigrants today. His remarks in the midst of a festival whose goal was to celebrate the cultural pluralism that characterizes American vernacular music was decidedly out of step with the spirit of the event. Yet it offered a glimpse into a frequently unspoken perception of Massachusetts's Latino community as an assortment of illegal (Mexican) immigrants.

Conclusion

The recent embrace of Chelsea's charro singers by non-Latino festival promoters from outside of the community has transformed the charro into an ambassador of sorts for Boston's rapidly growing Latino community. The presence of the charro outside of Latino Chelsea both reinforces misunderstandings of that community's "Mexican-ness" and provides insight to how and why mariachis and the Latino business owners who hire them have chosen to identify as Mexican. Large folk festivals, such as the one produced at Lowell, and even the smaller Working Waterfront Festival in heavily Latino New Bedford, Massachusetts, tend to offer traditional music associated with ethnic groups with ties to a readily identifiable geographic region and style, such as Cajun music, Mississippi Delta blues, Appalachian mountain music, conjunto music from the Texas-Mexican border, or American Rust Belt polkas. Such presentations underscore the belief that cultural pluralism and multiethnic American identity is an asset that strengthens the region and the nation. Nevertheless, the celebration of conservative vernacular music can create the unintended impression that, musically speaking, less intermingling is more authentic. As such, it is possible that the participation of a multiethnic group enacting an imagined Mexican identity, such as Mariachi Estampa de América at the Lowell festival, might enable that group to transcend questions of authenticity by creating the impression that its members are all Mexicans playing Mexican music.

The staging of multiethnic groups like Mariachi Estampa de América at public festivals aimed to benefit the general population (Latino or otherwise) presents a highly nuanced and confounding situation for the performance of ethnic solidarity. However, errors in perception present the mariachis with an opportunity to educate listeners about the diverse national origins of the local Latino community while letting them know that mariachi and norteño music are common parts of the Latin American experience. Says Iraheta of that type of encounter:

> They [Anglos, or "Americans"] make us feel like we're playing for Mexico. Yeah, sometimes it's really curious. They say, "What part of Mexico are you from?" And I'm like, "I'm not Mexican." And they're like, "How come you're doing this?" And it's like I just explained to you: the music isn't just Mexican, it's all over Latin America. So I grew up with this music. As a child [in El Salvador] I started listening to these songs, the older songs. That's how you start feeling the music, this typical style. That's how you start loving it. You can't stop doing it. It doesn't matter that you're not Mexican. So when anybody asks me, "Why [are] you doing this?" I don't feel offended or anything like that because I know it's hard to understand if you're from this country. But there's an explanation in the answer I just gave you: we grew up with this music, and we're lovin' it like any Mexican. It's the same thing. (Iraheta and Interiano 2008)

Anglo patrons at family-style restaurants featuring mariachi music are made to feel as if they are in Mexico, even when the performers are not necessarily from that country. And it is there, in the family-style setting, that the mariachis engender a performed multiethnic inclusiveness that is powerfully intimate and symbolically meaningful. It is at venues like Tijuana's that the mariachi welcomes listeners—Latino, Anglo, and African American—into the circle of their magical performance.

NOTE

1. Gutiérrez is also known as "El Tapatío," a nickname derived from the name of a hot sauce (Tapatío Hot Sauce) used in many Mexican restaurants.

CHAPTER 7

GenerAsians Learn Chinese

THE ASIAN AMERICAN YOUTH GENERATION AND NEW CLASS FORMATIONS

Deborah Wong

Today's Asian American youth generation is still haunted by the immigrant experience, and its material conditions continue to shape Asian American youth.[1] As George Lipsitz has argued, the ideological dominance of the nation-state in area studies (including American studies) has "poorly prepared us for the ways in which culture functions as a social force or the ways in which aesthetic forms draw their affective and ideological power from their social location" (2001, 17).

In this chapter I try to connect the late capitalist phenomenon of Pacific Rim popular culture to the emergence of Asian American youth who may move across borders in some ways but reconfirm the power of citizenship in others. Because the spatial placement of Asian Americans is pressured by fantasies of a globalized Pacific Rim, some American youth of Asian descent are willing to accept a class-driven consumption model of culture, while others turn to more challenging popular spheres of race-based interethnic exchange.

Immigrant arrivals have everything to do with the specific conditions of nation-state relationships. The immigrant experience is thus always particular even as it is folded into the sweeping gestures of statecraft and legislation. Generation is a theoretical concept that has had to change in order to keep up with the circumstances driving its upsets. The first-, second-, and third-generation configuration of immigrant experience suggests shared conditions that obscure significant differences *within* the same generation. Even the supposed clarity of Japanese American generations has been problematized by Asian American studies: the Issei-Nisei-Sansei monolith is less clear when Shin Issei (new Issei), such as Japanese war brides, and Nisei Kibei, who were schooled in Japan, are considered (Wong 2006). The classic ethnic studies model for relative generation—that is, the first generation emigrated to the United States, the second generation was born in the United States to immigrant parents, the third generation was the product of the U.S.-born second generation, and so forth—does not stand up well to the particularities of Asian American youth culture and the conditions of its emergence.

At the turn of the millennium, the North American youth generation of Asian descent locates itself within a globalized circuit of Pacific Rim exchange more than it does with the Asian American complex of the 1960s and 1970s.[2] I do not dismiss the importance of generation in relation to the experience and memory of immigration,[3] but different waves of Asian immigration from many countries over several centuries have resulted in a wide range of Asian American generational distinctions. For instance, a second-generation Japanese American born in the 1920s was subject to markedly different legal and political pressures than a second-generation Korean American born in the 1980s to parents who emigrated following the U.S. Immigration and Nationality Act of 1965.

David K. Yoo, the eminent historian of the Nisei (second-generation Japanese Americans) argues both for and against the second generation as a meaningful Asian American category. He notes that Nisei who "came of age in California in the second quarter of the twentieth century" grew up in diverse home environments: some were completely bilingual, some had only nominal fluency in Japanese, and some were sent to Japan for schooling (Yoo 2000, ix). This resulted in stronger Japanese than American cultural and language skills. Yoo, who is a second-generation Korean American scholar, writes, "As a child of immigrants, I often sensed an affinity with these older Nisei—an affinity that I attribute to some extent on a shared second-generation experience even while recognizing real differences" (xiii). For Asian Americans, then, second-generation identity is a dynamic category instantly subject to the vagaries of time and place even while inviting examination of how Asians become Asian Americans—and how Asians negotiate citizenship in the United States.

The watershed of 1965 looms large in American immigration studies. It Asianized the face of American immigration and forced new ways for thinking about generation.[4] American ethnic studies responded to the realities of post-1965 immigrant communities by theorizing the 1.5 generation as a discrete formation, applicable to any immigrant group but in fact particularly characteristic of many Asian immigrant communities in which young people born in Korea, India, Hong Kong, Taiwan, Vietnam, and beyond became impressively bicultural. Sandhya Shukla writes, "Diasporas simultaneously illumine and recreate vectors of time and space," and she shows how South Asian immigrant generation is located precisely in the environment of post-1965 American legislation and millennial globalization (2003, 213).[5]

Mass-mediated youth culture on the West Coast has generated a uniquely Asian American youth profile that is unabashedly upwardly mobile; generally speaking, this stands in marked contrast to the class consciousness of hip-hop culture. I address the "GenerAsian" concept by focusing on West Coast Asian Americans and, concomitantly, offer a close reading of Jin the emcee, the second-generation Chinese American hip-hop artist whose 2004 single "Learn Chinese" offers one line of response to early twenty-first-century (Asian) American pop culture.

In some ways, the old confusion between Asians and Asian Americans—the Asian American as eternal foreigner—is exacerbated by global corporate exchange.[6] Davé, Nishime, and Oren ask, "How do we address the Asian American presence within our hyperglobalized mainstream culture?" (2005, 1). A strong twenty-first-century Asian American youth culture is defined (at least partly) by its consumption of Asian popular culture. Indeed, I am fascinated by this generation's *enactment* of the globalized circuit of exchange. Sometimes this youth culture is marked by a hip, ironic reframing of materials that is powerfully agentive, but sometimes it reenacts the slippage between the Asian and the Asian American. Often it hinges on the fact of post-1965 Asian immigration to the United States and a stepped-up transnational movement between the first worlds of Hong Kong, Taiwan, Japan, Korea, and the United States. Aihwa Ong's influential work has modeled a dynamic set of relationships between subjects, nation-states, and political economies. She shifts analytical emphasis away from globalization per se and toward the ethnography of transnational practices and responses. She writes, "I prefer to use the term *transnationality. Trans* denotes both moving through space or across lines, as well as changing the nature of something. Besides suggesting new relations between nation-states and capital, transnationality also alludes to the *trans*versal, the *trans*actional, the *trans*lational, and the *trans*gressive aspects of contemporary behavior and imagination that are incited, enabled, and regulated by the changing logics of states and capitalism" (Ong 1999, 4).

The Asian American youth generation in question includes young people who move easily between the United States and an Asian home country, and others who are geospatially based in the United States but who consume Asian popular culture, American popular culture, *and* Asian-disseminated American popular culture. Ong's insistence on movement of many kinds, through different economies, varied desires, and across borders describes the ways that these youth negotiate and enjoy the embeddedness of lives that literally and figuratively move through interconnected cultural economies. I am thinking of my self-identified 2.0-generation Korean American undergraduate student Jessica who speaks to her parents in Korean, plays the *kayagum*,[7] speaks English with no trace of a Korean accent, spends summers in Seoul, reads *Rolling Stone* and the *Source* from cover to cover every week, and watches the current Korean soap operas at home in Los Angeles. I am thinking of my 1.5-generation Taiwanese American undergraduate student Bonnie, who has Pokémon charms dangling from her backpack and J-pop ringtones on her cell phone. I am thinking of my 1.5-generation undergraduate student Jin Hee, who asks to be called "Genie" and argues in Korean with her mother about having non-Korean friends, and who chooses to spend her free time tutoring at-risk Latino and African American elementary students in Riverside. I am thinking of Edmund, a second-generation Filipino (not "Filipino American") who parked his skateboard at my classroom door and gave his final presentation on game music, in which he displayed an encyclopedic knowledge of Japanese videogames, anime, and manga.

The successful, affluent, transpacific Asian American is also one of the newest targets of xenophobic anxiety. He (and I use this gendered pronoun deliberately) stands in marked contrast to the brown tide of workers (undocumented and otherwise) who enter the United States from Mexico and below (I also use this above/below, top/bottom metaphor deliberately). Indeed, racialized class-based fear is the problem behind both anxieties. Whereas nineteenth-century yellow peril hysteria and twenty-first-century worries about undocumented workers focus(ed) on the working-class base of the American economy, the updated version of the model minority is the upper-middle class, a successful, transnational Asian American subject who conjoins race and class in worrisome ways. This Asian American subject is not only getting the highest SAT scores but also is not even categorically American. Aihwa Ong considers the late twentieth-century class of mobile ethnic Chinese and notes that the "flexibility" of Pacific Rim globalized capital and citizenship is celebrated by those who are most likely to benefit from it, such as "elite Hong Kong executives" (1999, 20). Attending to the class formations created by Pacific Rim corporate commerce is as important as theorizing its effects on ideologies of race and the nation. As Ong writes:

> Among transnational Chinese subjects, those most able to benefit from their participation in global capitalism celebrate flexibility and mobility, which give rise to such figures as the multiple-passport holder; the multicultural manager with "flexible capital"; the "astronaut," shuttling across borders on business; "parachute kids," who can be dropped off in another country by parents on the trans-Pacific business commute; and so on. [. . .] Flexibility, migration, and relocations, instead of being coerced or resisted, have become practices to strive for rather than stability. (19)

Erika Lee and Naoko Shibusawa suggest some critical strategies for thinking about Asian Americans as transnational subjects:

> De-center the state, but do so without ignoring state power.
> Investigate migratory circuits and border crossings—not only across the Pacific but also across the Atlantic and within the Western hemisphere.
> Emphasize the mutual, interactive nature of cultural, institutional, and economic flows. In this respect, transnational histories are not merely comparative, looking at parallel developments across national borders. They seek as well to illuminate the connections that bind people and places to each other. (2005, x)

These critical handles address the mobile connections that inform, shape, obstruct, and construct Asian American identities and offer simple principles for theorizing Asian American presence in a less nation-bound and more connective manner. Any consideration of GenerAsian as a transnational youth culture will require these kinds of critical starting points.

Still, the rising Asian American upper-middle class has created new instabilities. Pensri Ho's research focuses on 1.5 and second-generation Chinese American and Korean American professionals in southern California (twenty-five to thirty-five years old in 1995–1998) and their troubled relationship with race.[8] Though some were eager to cite the model minority myth as the key to their success, they discovered that their Asianness was as likely to be held against them by non-Asian coworkers. The contradictions surrounding Asian American success thus highlight the deadly relationship between class and race in the United States: Asian Americans are a problem whether successfully working class or middle class. Ho writes that this professional class is the result of a complex set of conditions: many of the young professionals she interviewed had at least one professional parent, access to higher education, and had experienced transnational movement between the Asian home site and the United States. In Ho's analysis, this young professional class discovered that they represented the Asian model minority once they entered the white-collar workforce even though many had "trivialized, suppressed, or denied" their ethnicity when younger (2003, 151). She focused on their ability to draw on multiple identifications as a key cultural resource: "Their resultant transpacific racialized American experiences were paired with their lifelong exposure to American and Asian mass media portrayals of the Asian 'Other' to create an Americanized Asian 'Other' cultural identity, which they mimetically exploit and embody for personal and professional gain" (150). Ho argues that the model minority myth is essentially a way to encourage Asian Americans to accept the terms of white American middle-class success and the glass ceiling that maintains Asian American marginality in the American racial hierarchy. She further shows how it is a means to simultaneously reward and contain Chinese American and Korean American professionals. As a result, such young professionals shift uneasily between "celebration and rejection of the self as the Asian Other," simultaneously accepting and denying the terms of racial asymmetry (153).

Millennial second-generation Asian Americans have complex relationships with American racial regimes and globalization discourses. Yen Le Espiritu finds that second-generation middle class Filipinos in southern California negotiate assimilation and racism precisely because they are located at the intersection of race, class, and postcolonial self-awareness. American culture is familiar to them because they were born here *and* because their parents grew up with American cultural imperialism in the Philippines. They more likely live in white American suburbs than in Filipino ethnic "enclaves." They are unavoidably aware of their racial difference:

> The majority do not live in an ethnic neighborhood, attend school with other Filipino children, or belong to Filipino organizations. Thus, like later generation white ethnic groups, their ethnic behavior is largely symbolic, characterized by a nostalgic but unacquainted allegiance to an imagined past. However, there is a crucial difference; because Filipinos are dark-skinned, their ethnic/racial role is ascriptive rather than voluntary, and thus their ethnicity often

> is politicized rather than just a leisure-time activity. The intersection of their race, class, and ethnicity means that these Filipinos simultaneously conform to the forces of acculturation and assimilation, challenge the U.S. model of multiculturalism, and construct a distinct new culture that is not simply an extension of the "original" or of the mainstream "American" culture.
>
> (Espiritu 1992, 24)

The shaping force of race, class, transnational movement, and nation is thus pronounced even for a generation that has apparently assimilated. Similarly, Hung Cam Thai found that second-generation Vietnamese Americans between the ages of eighteen and twenty-seven described changing self-awareness between childhood and young adulthood. Most said that they had gone through a stage as children when they equated Americanness with whiteness and tried to act and view themselves as white American. One Vietnamese American interviewee referred to a process of "deprogramming the self" during her college years when she entered a period of ethnic "recovery" and "discovery" that was profoundly transformational (Thai 2001, 66). Most gravitated toward a stronger, explicit understanding of themselves as Vietnamese and as members of Vietnamese families; Thai refers to this as a "cultural ideology of collectivism" reinforced by trips to Vietnam (73–75). She argues that "ethnogenesis, or [a] 'collective identity shift,'" took place for her young interviewees as they entered young adulthood—as well as for second-generation Korean Americans and Chinese Americans, which she cites in related research (76).[9]

Mexican immigrants and their 1.5- and second-generation children stand in stark relief as an unruly labor class in relation to upwardly mobile, privileged transpacific Asian American youth. Contrast Ho's young Asian American professionals with the raucous Mexicans and Mexican Americans who protested against HR 4437 in the spring of 2006: Mexican flags were widely used in public protests for immigrant rights and were quickly replaced with American flags when the rhetoric of citizenship and allegiance was used against protesters. Yet young upwardly mobile Asian American professionals are just as likely to be cast as foreign, which challenges us to read class against race. My position is that neither generation nor "the immigrant experience" is generalizable and that the specific economic and legislative conditions of any given moment will fundamentally shape the specificities of generation—and especially the second generation. With this in mind, I turn to the matter of two early twenty-first century Asian American youth cultures.

GenerAsians, AZNs, and Other Self-Identifications

The current generation of twenty-something West Coast Asian Americans has a distinctive profile. Most of its members were born after 1985. It is hip, playful, often aware of Asian American history, and closely in touch with certain forms of East Asian mass mediated culture (especially Japanese anime and Hong Kong martial arts films). Some of its members are involved in the street racing scene focused on

Japanese import cars, hip-hop (especially clothes and slang), and skateboard culture.[10] It is marked by a blurring of generational formations: 1.5 and second-generation Asian Americans come together in some of its activities. It is often (though not always) decidedly middle class in its aspirations and access to disposable income.

Jennifer Lee and Min Zhou argue that "Asian American youth create and define an identity and culture of their own against the backdrop of contemporary immigration, continued racialization, and the rise of the new second generation (the U.S.-born of foreign-born parentage)" (Lee and Zhou 2004, 2). They also note that scholarly work on U.S. youth culture has almost entirely ignored the presence of young Asian Americans (9). Davé, Nishime, and Oren comment that Asian American popular culture—and the youth generation engaged with it—is only understandable if viewed in the context of "trans-Asian" contact, which is characterized by "counterflows" of culture and "porous boundaries between America and Asia" (2005, 4–5). They suggest that Asian American popular culture is not discretely *American* but is rather the result of inter–Asian American contact. This poses new theoretical problems even as it reactivates older ones. As Davé, Nishime, and Oren put it, "Paradoxically, this current visibility of global 'Asianness' renders the cultural presence of Asian Americans in mainstream American culture conceptually problematic: simultaneously hypervisible and out of sight" (1).[11]

Similarly, Sunaina Maira and Elisabeth Soep argue that youth cultures are shaped by the politics of globalization and transnationalism. Taking youth studies as a point of departure, they ask, "What might studying youth reveal about social identities being remade through transnational popular culture and new communication technologies in the context of debates about cultural authenticity, renewed nationalisms, and free-market relations?" (2005, xviii). Maira and Soep reposition youth as "key players" in the constitutive links between nation and globalization and note that the overlap between globalization studies and youth culture has long been critically "evaded" due to the historiographical and ideological assumptions driving each area (xix, xxi). They illuminate the disconnects, contradictions, and force between consumption and national identity, and the ways that youth emerge prominently in the very figuration of the nation-state, particularly the United States (xxiii–xxix). California emerges in their analysis as a site where many of these dynamics intersect due to intensified immigration into the state from both Asia and Latin America and to the "confluence of social, political, and economic factors" that have crystallized the cultural work done by youth (xxix).

The term "GenerAsian" is more and more widely used by members of this generation to self-identify. It was purportedly coined in 1998, when GenerAsian X was used to describe the target audience for *Shopping for Fangs* (1997), a low-budget independent film made by Quentin Lee and Justin Lin focused on Asian American post-college young people in southern California's Asian immigrant San Gabriel valley.[12] The *X* quickly vanished and GenerAsian was in general use by 1999–2000. GenerAsian is featured in Justin Lin's independent feature film *Better Luck Tomorrow* (2003), which follows several overachieving but deeply disaffected young Asian

American men through part of their senior year in a southern California high school. Since the release of *Better Luck Tomorrow* at the 2002 Sundance Festival, Lin has gone from Asian American independent filmmaking to directing Hollywood feature films.[13] In *Better Luck Tomorrow*, his depiction of amoral upper middle-class Asian Americans in Orange County who rob, do drugs, and cheat on high school tests created a ripple of discussion among Asian American audiences and critics because the film's characters, by and large, are depicted as having no interest or investment in Asian American identity politics. Indeed, the film is not about Asian American identity, and it does not have a clearly articulated Asian American message. In an interview for *Mother Jones*, journalist and critic Oliver Wang asked Lin about this absence:

> [OLIVER WANG]: What's striking about *Better Luck Tomorrow* is that it's not caught up in any "Who am I?" identity politics. The teens in the film might worry about their next heist but not existential questions about what it means to be Asian American.
>
> [JUSTIN LIN]: I was talking to a filmmaker—he made one of the early Asian American films—and he literally thought they were going to go bankrupt. He figured if they were going to do that, they were going to put as many messages as they could into that film. That's the feeling—when you have the opportunity to speak, you're eager to get all of your messages across. Hopefully, with this film, there is a maturity to it. People don't want to sit there to have you explain why you need to exist. You just do, and people have to come along with it.

Lin's film attracted attention not only because Asian Americans were not idealized as the model minority but especially because Lin did not make a message film about Asian Americanness. Or did he? For some audiences, watching a cast of characters who "happen" to be of Asian descent was satisfying in itself; certainly this kind of spectatorship aligns with mainstream ideologies of multiculturalism that allow audiences to believe race does not matter. In other ways, of course, Lin *was* making a film about Asian Americans, or perhaps he was even making an Asian American film, and his previous work confirms his own position as an Asian American filmmaker. *Better Luck Tomorrow* opened the way for a wholly new Asian American youth identity politics in which it was no longer necessary to have to argue for presence or even for the right to middle-class citizenship and success.[14]

Oliver Wang—to whom I refer more than once in this chapter, since his work on Asian American music, film, and popular culture is far-reaching and critically adept—writes that the "new second generation of Asian Americans" is the "unlikely, unknowing, and sometimes unwilling heirs to the legacy of the [Asian American] movement" and its nationalist assumptions (2001, 456). He reminds us that the construct of the Asian American is still so recent that it is bound to change and perhaps to be continuously redefined, and he argues that music is one of many sites of cultural production where that work will be done. We have already entered a different historical moment (a "postmovement" era, as Wang calls it) in which the political construct of Asian American pan-ethnicity is no longer the spark that ignites cultural production.[15] Wang writes, "In contrast to the previous generation, who made music 'for, by, and about' Asian Americans, many of the new artists seek to make music for an audience beyond their constituency. This doesn't equate to a *rejection* of an ethnic audience, but they're not seeking dialogue solely with that community. Their music is, as the cliché goes, 'for everyone'" (2001, 457).

GenerAsians are thus more focused on mainstream participation than on eking out a separate, nationalist foothold in North America. To summarize my argument at this point, GenerAsian youth have a distinctive profile for a host of reasons. Their generational distance from the 1960s era of the Asian American movement gives them a very different political profile. Their distance from the 1965 changes in immigration laws grants them a certain confidence in citizenship without cultural assimilation and a strong belief in the right to information technologies that grant them the ability to cut across geocultural space and to create virtual communities. GenerAsians are more apt to describe themselves as Chinese rather than Chinese American, and as Vietnamese rather than Vietnamese American, and they are also likely to view the Pacific Rim as an open arena of cultural exchange.

In short, there is a tight circuit of production between the *representation* of Asian American youth as beyond identity politics and the *construction* of a newly assertive postethnic identity for American youth of Asian descent. Some American Asians continue to assert ethnicity and race but—markedly—without the 1960s–1970s assertion of a pan–Asian American community. Rather, transnational movement, globalized economies, and the right to middle-class consumption mark this new kind of American Asian youth culture.

At this point, the term "GenerAsian" is in fairly wide circulation among young Asian Americans.[16] It is strongly marked for age and Asian ethnicity but not for gender, class, immigrant generation, or sexuality. It does not seem to be used more by some Asian ethnicities than others; that is, Asian American youth of Chinese, Japanese, Korean, Thai, Vietnamese, and Filipina/o heritage are equally apt to self-identify in this way. Use of the term usually indicates some awareness of ethnic heritage and the political identifications that compel historicized awareness. The term has been around for long enough so that it not only includes high school and college-aged youth but also sometimes extends beyond, into post-grad twenty-something professionals (who are perhaps not yet ready to let go of the implied hipness that accompanies the identification) and even into pre–high school youth—that is, its demographic composition may be in the process of widening. Yet many twenty-something Asian Americans may have a stronger and more specific connection to AZN than to GenerAsian identity.[17] Significantly, the term "GenerAsian" now has currency as a branding term. That is, the term is changing as corporations use it to identify emergent Asian-Pacific markets.[18] Although the GenerAsian sensibility was generated by North American Asian youth, it is now in the process of being exported to Asia through mass-mediated popular culture.

But what exactly is exportable? In its emphasis on mediated community and its pleasure in information technologies, the GenerAsian aesthetic is similar to that of the deracialized Gen X, but it also involves an awareness of Asianness as hip. That is, it draws on a specific form of Pacific Rim Asianness that is heavily based in J-cool popular culture and its widespread consumption through anime, Pokéman, Hello Kitty, and J-pop.

Yolk and *Giant Robot*

In 1994 two magazines focused on Asian American youth culture were founded, and each provided a certain view of GenerAsian political economy and aesthetics. I argue that, together, they emerged from and then synergistically generated the sustained terms for a GenerAsian transpacific youth culture.

Yolk magazine (1994–2003) was a formative site for GenerAsian style. It addressed Asian American culture from 1994 to 2000 and then underwent extensive redefinition in 2000.[19] It had always covered Asian as well as Asian American style, fashion, and popular culture, but after 2000 its Asian popular culture coverage was much broader. The magazine title was also revised as *Yolk: GenerAsian Next 2.0*, and it proclaimed that it had "its sights set on becoming the definitive Asian American entertainment, lifestyle, and pop culture magazine."[20] In short, its expanded Asian pop culture coverage and its self-proclaimed Asian American location were connected and simultaneous.

Most of the magazine's cover images between 2000 and its demise in 2003 (thirteen out of fifteen) featured Asian American women in skin-baring glamour poses; many articles were devoted to Asian films, food, and music. The layout was punchy, bright, and self-consciously cutting edge. In short, the GenerAsian profile defined by *Yolk* was deeply hip, and its hipness was substantively informed by Asian popular culture: the message was that GenerAsian was in North America but in touch with Asian popular culture, or that it was an exemplary Pacific Rim consumer.

Giant Robot magazine, on the other hand, focused on Asian pop culture from its very first issue in 1994. Its subtitle is *Asian Pop Culture and Beyond*, and its readers are "half-Asian and half-not."[21] Its Web site explains its purpose and focus as follows:

> From movie stars, musicians, and skateboarders to toys, technology, and history, Giant Robot magazine covers cool aspects of Asian and Asian-American pop culture. Paving the way for less knowledgeable media outlets, Giant Robot put the spotlight on Chow Yun Fat, Jackie Chan, and Jet Li years before they were in mainstream America's vocabulary.
>
> But Giant Robot is much more than idol worship. GR's spirited reviews of canned coffee drinks, instant ramen packs, Japanese candies, Asian frozen desserts, and marinated bugs have spawned numerous copycat articles in other publications. GR's historical pieces on the Yellow Power Movement, footbinding, Asian-American gangsters, and other savory topics have been cited by both academics and journalists. Other regular features include travel journals, art and design studies, and sex.

The magazine was founded in Los Angeles by two University of California–Los Angeles undergraduates, Eric Nakamura and Martin Wong, and was initially a stapled zine. Since then, it has expanded exponentially and includes stores in West Los Angeles, San Francisco, and New York that carry Asian popular culture such as toys, clothing, books, comics, candy, and accessories. The magazine, now glossy and sold at Barnes and Noble and Tower Records, does not have an articulated political position or agenda but has featured some edgy Asian American content (including a historic 1998 issue on Asian American and African American activism in the 1960s). The founders/editors have an anti-exploitation philosophy and argue for supporting "quality" Asian products. They have a somewhat cynical attitude about the American commodification of Asian popular culture even though they are clearly on the cutting edge of that process. They claim that the difference is their selectiveness and connoisseurship.

Together, *Yolk* and *Giant Robot* offered a new kind of Asian American panethnicity, modulated by an enthusiastic and sometimes ironically knowing consumption of globalized Asian popular culture.[22]

Hard on the heels of such stepped-up celebrations of Pacific Rim exchange, the term "AZN" has crept into common use among GenerAsian members, and it is often paired with "AZN pride" or "pryde."[23] Note the disappearance of "Asian American." "AZN" or "azn" emerged out of hip-hop culture (i.e., its free play of slang and Ebonics) and cell phone and Internet chat room abbreviations and slang. It is especially used by high school students (and some college students) and was apparently generated on the West Coast before spreading more widely.[24] The Internet Urban Dictionary offers a troubling snapshot of how the term and, by extension, AZN/GenerAsian members are regarded by non–Asian Americans. Like Wikipedia, this dictionary is a compilation of slang definitions gathered through open submission. Here are samples of some of the definitions, along with the thumbs-up/thumbs-down votes submitted by readers who indicated their approval or disapproval of each definition:[25]

AZN 1422 up, 666 down

retarded form of "asian."

immature children who's eyes have not been open to the world who claim "asian pride," usually high school/high school drop outs and under with bleached hair that spend their days at the local arcade playing DDR, also types "LyKe Dis On thE InTerNeTzZzZz"

Azn 598 up, 264 down

The younger asians or non asians that profess that they are better than everyone else (even though they are not). Signs of the "Asian retards" are:

(1) Typing in alternating CAPS and lowercase letters.

(2) Using words such as: dis, dat, sho, da, ETC.

(3) Claiming that Asians are the best even though they don't know shit about their own heritage.

(4) *sigh* I hoped it wouldn't come to this. The dreaded "Got Rice?" song . . .

AZN

383 up, 146 down

1.) Shortened form of Asian.

2.) Today, commonly used by non-Asians to identify themselves as Asians. This can be contributed to the fact that most self-respecting Asians would not be caught dead doing some of the actions "AzN's" perform on the internet.

*AzNpRyDe: MaI Hon*Da i2 FaSt!!!!11!!!

azn

251 up, 113 down

Asians (mainly from California) who shame their race by bleaching their hair blonde and trying to develop the personality of a "ghetto" negro. Ironically, these azn's do nerdy things such as hang out in arcades playing Tekken and DDR, but they still uphold their "ghetto" personna online in chat rooms and blogs/xanga accounts.

azn: look, my hair is blonde
white guy: you're not white
azn: yO nIgUh?
black guy: you ain't black
azn: got rice?
asian guy: you're not asian

azn

89 up, 72 down

Azn is another acronym for Asian. It's relation is usually related to young, mostly SouthEast Asian Americans, mainly from the hip hop generation.

In order to find their own identity, Azn youth often use upper and lower case letters in order to communicate in online-slang. While there are uneducated Azn out there acting up, there are those who are educated enough to identify Azn with their own pride and heritage.

Even though many of these youths are born in America and may not even speak their native tongue, using Azn slang to communicate is a way of finding their own identity in an American culture dominated by mainstream music such as hip hop, rap, pop, and rock.

I have a nephew embedded in this culture. You would not be able to tell by the way he types on line that he is an A student who excel in sports. Having this Azn attitude is simply a way to push out the steam of realizing that you are born a minority and trying to find your own identity.

AzN PrIdE !!
GOt rICe BiaTCh.

Clearly, the term "AZN" activates a range of responses, from pride to the most time-worn, stereotyped vilifications of Asians and Asian Americans. The posters' ethnicity is mostly unmarked, though more than a little apprehension over blackness is voiced, possibly by Asian Americans. If the term "AZN" is a site for Asian American identity work, then its location at the crossroads of interethnic media and information technology leaves it vulnerable to accusations of cultural inauthenticity (bleached blonde hair and "borrowed" African American culture), cultural arrogance and superiority, and socioeconomic privilege. The last entry above (last only here—there are many more entries on the Web site) offers a thoughtful, presumably "elder" Asian American perspective on the need for AZN identifications and the cultural work for which the term clears a way: the poster cites the absence of Asian Americans from mainstream American popular culture and the need to try out new, confrontational relationships—but relatively few readers "approved" this perspective.

That poster also refers to an online music video titled "Got Rice, Bitch?" by an artist named "AZN Pride" who swept the Internet in 2004.[26] The song pokes fun at AZNs "from within" and is satirically pro-Asian.[27] The lyrics assert that "we" got "brainz," "skillz," "carz," and "clothz"—that is, the lyrics play with Asian American stereotypes and trends:[28]

> It's the AZN better recognize
> Got rice bitch, got rice
> Got food, got soup, got spice
> Got brainz like us, got skillz like us
> Got carz, got clothz, got girlz like us
> Whats sup we the shit we kill yall foolz
> We got money in the banks from our family jewelz
> Can we help it if we rain and corrupt the schoolz
> It don't matta fuck the law shit we break the rules
> We jack carz fuck games yo we got the toolz
> Hoop it up break it down then we go shoot some pool
> Fuck with me you fuck with all of us don't think its kool
> 1 on 1 fuck that it's 3 on 1, no duels

The song went viral and found its way onto Asian joke sites as well as Asian American chat lists. At this point, it is nearly ubiquitous: the song has been endlessly reposted and its lyrics retranscribed, so I have been unable trace it to any starting point. Its point of origin is perhaps less important than the fact that it attracted a lot of attention. "Got Rice, Bitch?" was endlessly recirculated, and reposting is the highest compliment on the Internet.

Though the AZN configuration is fraught in certain ways, its valence as young and hip led to its use as the name for a cable station on air from 2005 to 2008, "AZN Television: The Network for Asian America." The station's Web site featured a set of statistics arguing in market terms for its existence: according to them, "the Asian American market" is 4.8 percent of the U.S. population (14 million people);

85 percent speak English fluently, have $397 billion in "buying power," have the "highest household income [and] education of any ethnic group in the U.S.," have a median income of $56,000, and have a median age of thirty-one.[29] In short, the station was not directed toward the youngest GenerAsian that created the AZN profile, but instead toward an affluent post-college Asian American demographic.

To summarize, the AZN pride sensibility emerged around 2000, is a specifically youth stance, and has been ridiculed and satirized as much as it has served as a site of identification for young Asian American men. A Wikipedia stub notes that the term "Asian pride worldwide" is also common "to express an identity which extends beyond national borders to all people of Asian descent."[30] The term thus serves double duty as a source of young masculinized Asian American confidence on the one hand and ridicule on the other, and its arrival in "Got Rice, Bitch?" outsourced its effectiveness right back into longstanding tropes of xenophobic fear over Asian dominance. Its appearance at the helm of the (ultimately unsuccessful) AZN Television network suggests that it has been appropriated by corporate concerns. Its demographic base, which is older every day and more settled into its socioeconomic niche, has not articulated its own political presence as clearly as the Asian American movement generation did in the 1960s and 1970s. Without a defined minoritarian politics, the AZN generation's reliance on ethnic pride leaves it wide open to model minority accusations. GenerAsian and AZN Pryde suggest a new youth bloc that emerged from the ground up and was then redefined by marketers and the media as an upper middle-class configuration.[31] The latter have little motivation to theorize the complex class bases of this demographic; indeed, GenerAsian has been reconstructed at least partly by marketers who focus on communities with disposable income. If the members of GenerAsian and AZN Pryde have been recast as privileged youth of color with access to the playground of transpacific capitalism, then clearly the work of asserting the diversity of Asian American communities is ongoing.

In contrast, the world of hip-hop addresses race and class all the time, and the presence of young Asian American men has always had the potential to create politicized interethnic configurations—but not without tension. The appearance of Jin the emcee suggests an alternative critical awareness to the GenerAsians, within the same age and ethnic group but with a working class awareness.

Jin in Your Face

In 2004, just a few months after Jin Au-Yeung released his hit single "Learn Chinese," I taught a course on Asian American musics and asked my students to compare three Asian American emcees: Jin, the Mountain Brothers, and praCh Ly. Many but not all of the thirty undergraduates were Asian or Asian American, mostly 1.5 or second generation. They eventually agreed that praCh Ly, a self-produced Cambodian American rapper from Long Beach, had a well-articulated and principled political message but the weakest musical skills and lo-fi production; that the Mountain Brothers were right in the middle, with a polished but decidedly "indie" sound, complex rhymes, and a now-you-see-it-now-you-don't Asian American sensibility; and that Jin was the most musically polished and highly produced but the least political.

I turn to Jin because he is a highly visible—and audible—second-generation Chinese American rapper whose hip-hop identifications offer important points of difference from GenerAsian practices. Jin is—famously, to date—the only Asian American rapper ever signed to a major recording label. The hip-hop world (from recording moguls to grassroots fans) presents real challenges and opportunities for non–African American participants, and Jin has developed rhetorical strategies for performing Chineseness. This second-generation child of Chinese immigrants has become a serious contender in conversations about race in interethnic environments. Jin is a mixture of denial, cooption, and assertive presence, and although I initially felt he had sold out, I have (in two short years) come to see him as a particularly effective figure who has managed to make it in the mainstream yet keep his message coming. Better still, he is young, so there is still much to come.

To my knowledge, Jin does not identify as "GenerAsian," "AZN," or even as Asian American. Over and over again he refers to himself as "Chinese" or "Asian" in his songs and interviews. Jin is increasingly involved in transpacific cultural production, though, from the perspective of the world of hip-hop. He focuses on how class, ethnicity, and talent are defined and positioned in that environment, and his career to date has contained seven events through which he has located his work in fascinating and sometimes contradictory ways: (1) his triumph over African American opponents as a freestyler (2002); (2) getting signed by a major recording label; (3) the release of his hit single "Learn Chinese" and first album, *The Rest Is History* (2004); (4) his response to "The Tsunami Song" (2005); (5) his decision to leave the Ruff Ryders recording label; (6) his reappearance as an independent artist and mentor in his second album, *The Emcee's Properganda* (2005); and (7) his album *ABC* (2007), which is mostly in Cantonese.

Jin Au-Yeung was born in Miami in 1982. His parents are Chinese immigrants who ran a less-than-successful Chinese restaurant during his childhood. Jin grew up in a working-class, interethnic environment in Miami and started freestyling with Latino and African American friends in middle school. He moved to New York City with his family in 2001 when he was nineteen and immediately got involved with the hip-hop scene, where he focused on freestyling. He hired a manager in 2001–2002 and got onto BET's "Freestyle Fridays" on *106 and Park* in early 2002, where he earned fame by winning a series of freestyling battles. In these one-on-one three-minute matches, always up against African American emcees,[32] Jin quickly became known not only for his improvisational rhyming skills but also for aggressively asserting his Chineseness rather than allowing opponents to use it against him as an insult (e.g., "Yeah I'm Chinese / Now you'll understand it / I'm the reason your little sis's eyes are slanted / If you make one more joke about Chinese food or karate / The NYPD will be searching Chinatown for your body."[33]

After winning seven matches in a row by March 2002, he was something of a legend not only in the hip-hop world generally but especially among Asian

American hip-hop fans.[34] When he was inducted into *106 and Park's* Hall of Fame, he announced that he had just signed with Ruff Ryders. As cultural critic Jeff Chang writes, "Across the country, Asian American teens traded CD-Rs of his TV battles and leaked tracks, lit up Internet boards, and downloaded his singles from AOL more than 500,000 times" (2005). From that point on, his career took off quickly. In 2003 he had a minor role as a mechanic in *2 Fast 2 Furious*, about the street racing scene in Miami. After much fanfare, his single "Learn Chinese" was produced by Wyclef Jean (formerly with The Fugees). *The Rest Is History* was finished in 2003, but Ruff Ryders delayed its release several times, and it eventually came out in November 2004.

Between 2002 and 2004, Jin's development was followed closely by Asian American hip-hop enthusiasts. As I have written elsewhere, Asian Americans have always found it difficult if not impossible to break into the American recording industry, and hip-hop poses special challenges due to the ways that Asianness is ambivalently positioned between whiteness and blackness (Wong 2004, 233–256). Asian American hip-hop artists are inevitably forced to make decisions and assertions about their racial position. At its best, the outcome is new, effective cross-ethnic formations. As Ellie Hisama (2004) notes, "Hip hop provides brilliant opportunities for musical crosscurrents and affinities between ethnic communities of color. American hip hop since 1990 offers compelling examples of interaction and exchange between African and Asian diasporic communities, and demonstrates the overwhelming political and aesthetic power of the polycultural."

While Hisama focuses on the points of possibility for interethnic connection, in practice Asian American emcees are frequently accused of being inauthentically black and few have been able to argue for an unmarked voice (where race does not matter), let alone for the value of an Asian American voice. A few have made their Asianness central to their message but—not coincidentally—have been unable to break into the industry and instead have become most well known on the college performance circuit.[35] Others have stayed within local environments, performing at live events within their ethnic community rather than trying to get signed.[36] On his DVD, Jin says, "But the key—the most important thing—is to remember where [hip-hop] started"—that is (presumably), to respect the urban African American roots of hip-hop.[37]

Jin somehow managed to push past these problems, partly by putting his ethnicity right out front and partly by being very, very good at battling. Jeff Chang, a noted hip-hop historian and critic of Asian American popular culture, pinpoints the effectiveness of Jin's cultural and aesthetic location, suggesting that he manages to work against prevailing expectations and to surprise at the same time:

> In fact, Jin does present something wholly new, not just in American but also global pop: an unapologetically working-class, second-generation kid flowing in Cantonese and New York-inflected Ebonics with the same fluency. He's no pricey Hong Kong import, no sexless high-kicking martial arts expert in yellowface. By simply rapping in a black tee with a diamond-encrusted Ruff

> Ryders pendant, he could have the most impact on the notion of an "authentic" Asian American masculinity since Bruce Lee. (Chang 2003)

Jin is decidedly *not* a GenerAsian in his orientation, but Chang identifies a key point of contact: for GenerAsians, Jin provides a politicized possibility that (at least then) was thoroughly embedded in the industry and the mainstream public sphere—a subject who is both authentically Asian American but not mired in the identity politics of the 1960s. As Chang writes, "For overeducated hip-hop-gen AZN cult-crits like me, Jin presents a subject worthy of our subjectivities, a voice that validates our own time in the wilderness" (2003). With this in mind, I turn to "Learn Chinese" to consider how things went a little wrong in 2003–2004.

"Learn Chinese"

Jin's most impressive skill is his ability to battle, and "Learn Chinese" is in the finest tradition of hip-hop braggadocio: it opens with the confrontational lines, "Yeah I'm Chinese, and what? / Yeah you know who this is, Jin, and let me just tell you this / The days of the pork fried rice and the chicken wings comin to your house by me is over." The chorus says it all:

> Ya'll gonna learn Chinese, ya'll gonna learn Chinese
> Ya'll gonna learn Chinese, when the pumps come out, you're gonna speak Chinese
> Ya'll gonna learn Chinese,
> Ya'll gonna be Chinese
> Ya'll gonna learn Chinese, when the pumps go off, ya'll gon' speak Chinese

In other words, "you" are going to come around to his way of thinking, being, and speaking—you are going to abide by his terms. Moreover, you are going to get there through fear and submission: the "pumps" are shotguns, and when they come out, you are going to be so frightened that you will spontaneously speak Chinese, no, *be* Chinese, because Jin is in charge. This chorus is heard three times in the course of the song. In footage taken from a live performance of the song in a New York City club, Jin performed on stage with three members of his crew, and the sight of him and these powerful-looking African American men—all taller than him, chanting his chorus in unison, arms raised, index fingers pointed at the audience—is an astonishing and convincing moment. You are going to *be* Chinese, whether you like it or not.

The recorded version of the song is a dense soundscape of Jin's voice alone, Jin's voice with his own voice layered over it, the three voices of his crew who chime in at the ends of many lines in unison with him, and a spare base line that includes a "Chinese-sounding" pentatonic melodic motive heard at the beginning of the song and then in each chorus. Along the way, the lyrics are constantly "interrupted," sometimes by Jin speaking Cantonese, sometimes by his crew responding in Cantonese, and sometimes by Wyclef. Wyclef mostly inserts shout-outs and promotional phrases; for example, he inserts the word "Refugees," referring simultaneously to The Fugees (the group popular during the mid-1990s) and to the clothing line he introduced in 2005. Ruff Ryders is referenced a number of times by name and once as "Double-R." At one point, a sexy woman's voice—breathy, girlish, perhaps imitating the sound of Japanese teenaged pop stars—sings an "Oriental" melody and then croons, "Mr. Jin, you are the sexiest man / Mr. Jin, I love the way you do your thing."

The lyrics are a mixture of bragging, sexist claims about women, gangsta talk about guns, thugs, and hooligans (for which Ruff Ryders is famous), and edgy race commentary. Jin refers to himself as the "original chinky eyed MC" in an age-old strategy of reclaiming injurious language—but he is also referencing the fact that other (non-Asian) rappers have called themselves "chinky-eyed" when describing what their eyes look like after getting high on weed, and he's saying he's more authentically chinky-eyed since he is an actual "chink," so the reclamation has several clever layers. References to Chinese food and Chinatown abound, but Jin knows his history and is all too aware that blackness, whiteness, and Asianness are interconstitutive. He raps, "We should ride the train for free, we built the railroads / I ain't your 50 cent, I ain't your Eminem, I ain't your Jigga Man, I'm a CHINA man," and yet the bottom line is that he's a Chinatown gangsta who will blow you away—"I wish you would come to CHINA TOWN / Get lost in town, end up in the lost and found."

The music video is both brilliant and dismaying, and it defeats any attempt to pinpoint a projected audience. Its intended viewer could be any hip-hop fan, or any Asian American, or any mainstream viewer. Certainly it can be watched in several ways. (Indeed, it opens with a scene that tells us it is about spectatorship.) It works off an all-too-predictable mix of Orientalist imagery, yet it also walks a tightrope, simultaneously reifying and challenging stereotypes. It is a relentless series of tropes drawn from Asian cult cinema, or film noir, or *Year of the Dragon*. The setting is a dark and dangerous Chinatown straight out of any Hollywood feature film, and Jin struts around as a gangster, decked out in a suit and eye patch, surrounded by Chinese goons, looking stereotypically grim and dangerous. Scenes of a karate class are intercut for no apparent reason—it's Asian, so it's there. You're in a Chinese restaurant kitchen. Everyone's Chinese except for some of the women, and many of them are African American, sexy, on display as manikins, dancing, gyrating, and draping themselves over Jin given half the chance. Somewhere in there is a narrative about a beautiful Asian woman being held hostage—she's tied to a couch, and Jin comes and rescues her. It's parody and it's serious, and it fulfills expectations even as it winks at those expectations. It ends with a chase scene as Jin races through the karate dojo and tries to get away from the gangster Jin, only to wind up in a face to face confrontation that ends with "To Be Continued."

The most interesting part of the music video is the opening sequence that literally provides a narrative frame for the Orientalist "story."[38] A late-model car pulls up outside a house and Jin steps out, dressed pretty much like himself, carrying a plastic delivery bag. He's delivering Chinese takeout. He rubs a speck of dirt off a side mirror and then swaggers up the path to the house. He's so full of attitude that you wonder—as you're supposed to—how long he's going to hold down this job. Cut to inside the house, where three African American guys are sitting around in a living room watching TV and talking. A big poster of Jin is on the wall, and one of the guys wears a Ruff Ryders sweatshirt. You're only several seconds into the sequence, but you already see that this is playfully ironic, and it's good. One of the guys says, "Have you heard about this new Ruff Ryders movie about the brothers Chin?" Another asks, "The one about the Chin Chin? Yeah, that's dope." The first answers, "I'm telling you, that Mr. Chin Chin is gangsta dope—hey, there goes that joint right there!" and points to the TV. The guys turn their attention to the TV set, where Jin has appeared—and we get sucked into it as the camera zooms into the TV and we're suddenly watching/hearing Jin outside, climbing the steps up onto the porch and swaggering up to the door as we hear his voice declare, "Yeah, I'm Chinese . . . and what?" There's fast intercutting between Jin outside knocking on the door and the guys inside watching him and carrying on a spirited (unheard) conversation about him; Jin pounds on the door, but no one answers. As he raps "the days of the pork fried rice and chicken wings coming to your house are over," he throws the bag of takeout food at the foot of the door in disgust and swaggers away. As he goes down the front walk, he turns to the camera and looks the spectator right in the eye as he says, "Ya'll gon learn Chinese." This is no kowtowing delivery boy.[39]

Then we're plunged into another world—out of the frame and into the song, where Jin is alternatively seen out on the street as "himself," surrounded by an urban nighttime crowd of young African American men, women, and sleek sports cars, and we then see him embedded in the other narrative about him as a high-level Chinatown gangster. A curious aspect of the video is the moment, about halfway through, when Jin as himself confronts Jin the gangster: he forces his way through the restaurant kitchen, past cooks and goons, and faces the gangster at his table in the fancy restaurant, where he is surrounded by a bevy of women. But the threat that he suggests is immediately and confusingly disarmed when the gangster directs his women to get up. They rise from the table en masse and surround Jin/himself, waving scarves suggestively and overcoming him (apparently) with their sexiness. It's a weird extended moment (that coincides with the "Mr. Jin, you are the sexist man" lines) that overlays a harem trope with the tired old adage of the Asian man who isn't masculine enough to stand up to women.

In short, for this Asian American viewer, the video is both a playful send-up of Asian stereotypes and a disturbing mélange of old-fashioned Orientalia plus old-fashioned hip-hop misogyny. For fans and critics with a stake in the Asian American public sphere, this is perplexing and frustrating: shouldn't race consciousness preclude sexism, homophobia, and other social illnesses? Oliver Wang offers a ruthless assessment of these issues:[40]

> The video for "Learn Chinese" is rife with problems. One of the biggest and most obvious is Jin's gender politics—women figure in this video like they

> figure in most rap videos: sex objects desired for nothing more than their bodies. Disappointing but generically so. The more complicated issue is how Jin positions a racialized class element—the second verse of his song is basically about how gangsta Chinese can be, especially in Chinatown and this is Jin's attempt at equating, if not outdoing, the trope of the Black Ghetto by offering Chinatown as an even more lurid competitor. He's glamorizing the ethnic enclave in the same way that African Americans have glorified the ghetto and projects, and Latinos talk about the barrio but Jin's approach to Chinatown is even less critical than these other examples.
>
> [. . .]
>
> Jin trades in one stack of stereotypes: kung fu fighters, take-out delivery men, etc. and just replaces them with another set of equally suspect images.

Wang's critique is dead on, but the one thing I wonder about is his attribution of Jin as the instigator and "author" of this narrative through these images. The interface between Jin's ideas, his efforts to sell his work, Wyclef Jean's role as producer, and Ruff Ryders's decisions about how to handle an Asian emcee in their constructed gangsta black world is an interstice where I suspect Jin lost control over his product. At that level, everyone is guilty, and in fact Jin decided to leave Ruff Ryders less than two years later, in 2005, due to dissatisfactions with the promotion of his album. *The Rest Is History* reportedly sold only about 100,000 copies. Further, the album release was repeatedly delayed and then suffered because of lack of promotion despite guest appearances on the album by Kanye West, Wyclef, and Double R crew member Styles P. Some argue that the album simply was not very good.[41] Whichever the case, Jin's relationship with Ruff Ryders changed in 2005. During the months leading up to the breakup, the tsunami hit South and Southeast Asia on December 2004, killing about 229,000 people, and a black-Asian controversy in New York showed a new side of Jin.

"The Tsunami Song" and *The Emcee's Properganda*

On January 18, 2005, three weeks after the Sumatra-Andaman earthquake, one of the most popular and successful hip-hop radio stations in New York City aired a parody song about the tsunami. Hot 97 WQHT-FM's show "Miss Jones in the Morning" played this song twice that morning, set to the melody of "We Are the World" but with a rather different message:

> There was a time, when the sun was shining bright
> So I went down to the beach to catch me a tan.
> Then the next thing I knew, a wave 20 feet high
> Came and washed your whole country away.
> And all at once, you can hear the screaming chinks.
> And no one was saved from the wave.
> There were Africans drowning, little Chinamen swept away.
> You can hear God laughing, "Swim you bitches swim."

[Chorus]
So now you're screwed. It's the tsunami,
You better run and kiss your ass away. Go find your mommy.
I just saw her float by, a tree went through her head.
And now your children will be sold. Child slavery.

Outrage ensued. The Asian American community mobilized, protests and demonstrations were mounted, and the radio station owner apologized and then suspended Miss Jones. On January 25, Jin released a rapped response that showed him at his best—in pure battle mode—but newly politicized.[42] He freestyled as follows:

and tell the rest of your staff that they need to clean up their act
fuck the tsunami song and whoever thought of it
matter fact, fuck the engineer that recorded it
and the brains behind the scenes that applauded it
anything for ratings huh?
this shit is corporate
that little bullshit statement has gotta be, the worlds most half ass apology
thousands are still getting discovered each day
how dare you compare a life to a weeks pay
[. . .]
and its rare that I'm even rapping pissed
jin is far from a human rights activist
so dont take this in a political fashion
nope its just a good old lyrical bashing
in fact I'm making it a mission of mine
wont stop till every last petition is signed
hip hop is designed to unify the masses
and we demand that you be denied the access
radio is whack, yo somebody gotta say this
same five songs on every single playlist (god)
[. . .]
im juss sayin
dont let it be your peoples that they dissin next time
making fun of they tragedies just for a cheap laugh
and you sittin there like what the fuck
know what I'm saying
so keep them emails going through
keep them complaint letters goin out
keep them phones calls goin into the radio stations and the sponsors
tellin 'em how you feel
and what a fucked up move they made
let 'em know
let 'em know its about the people

This blistering critique is markedly different from Jin's cocky participation in the Chinatown gangster tropes of "Learn Chinese." Jin locates himself as the member of the broader Asian community and zeroes in on the corporate decisions that allowed the broadcast of the song, noting that the very structure of hip-hop radio creates a narrow (and in this case racist) channel. Knowing his frustrations around the release of his album, it seems likely that he was already thinking about the ways that race and corporate decision-making are related, but putting it into fighting words marked a turning point for him. On May 18, 2005, he publicly announced that he was putting his career on hold, but he reemerged in a matter of months as The Emcee and released his second album, *The Emcee's Properganda*, on October 25, 2005, not through Ruff Ryders but through CraftyPlugz/Draft Records, an indie label. That is, he made the radical decision to side-step one of the most highly regarded recording labels in the hip-hop industry.

Many fans agree that *The Emcee's Properganda* has a distinctively indie/underground sound that is distinctively different from *The Rest Is History*, and most also agree that the second album is much, much better. It was produced by African American deejay The Golden Child, and it features Asian American emcee Yung Mac and Chinese American rapper L.S. Jeff Yang (2006) writes,

> The push to include, and the resistance against inclusion, could also be seen in the rise, fall and rebirth of Asian America's hip-hop hope, Jin Auyeung, who went from beating all comers in rap battles to being signed by Ruff Ryders and releasing a much-anticipated but underwhelming and long-delayed debut album, *The Rest Is History*. Criticism, both from within and without the Asian community, prompted Jin to announce his retirement in May (on his MySpace site, no less). A few months later, he reemerged sans label and hype. Now calling himself simply The Emcee, he took home 50 grand in the Power Summit's annual rap battle in the Bahamas, and released a thumping indie sophomore album, *The Properganda*, that made his first one look like, well, history.
>
> Though still officially under contract, Jin publicly accused Ruff Ryders of "not giving a damn" about him, or at least not knowing what to do with a playa from a different game.

Jin's transpacific presence has accelerated since 2004. A documentary, *No Sleep til Shanghai* (2005),[43] chronicles his eight-city tour of Asia (including Shanghai, Tokyo, Taipei, and Singapore), focusing on Jin's place in the transnational world of hip-hop. His 2007 album, *ABC* (i.e., American-born Chinese), was almost entirely in Cantonese and was marketed on both sides of the Pacific (released first in the United States and then in Hong Kong). As Jennifer Jay notes, "*ABC* serves up vivid images of daily life in the typical Chinese American family of eating, dating, living in America and Hong Kong. Jin brings into focus overlapping worlds in *ABC*, restaurant culture in America, the distant cultural and glamorous world of Hong Kong, and his love of the hip-hop world. In some ways Hong Kong television was an escape for him, and for his parents, and he integrated the two worlds with his rap lyrics in *ABC*" (2008, 388).

ABC closes the circuit in a way that could be construed as typical of GenerAsians, but in fact he creates an entirely new niche, offering testimony about the Chinese immigrant experience in Cantonese and about the 1997 handover of Hong Kong to China. In doing so, he challenges any simple construct of intended audience. He moved to Hong Kong in 2008 and has signed with the conglomerate Universal Music Group Hong Kong. He is emblematic of a new kind of transpacific 1.5/second-generation performer whose fan base is literally on two continents.[44]

It is far too soon to predict how Jin's career will proceed, but in a remarkably short time he has reformulated himself and his priorities. He has sharpened his approach to how race, the music industry, and emceeing interrelate. Jin does not use the term "Asian American" and is not trying to create Asian American community through his work. Rather, he has consistently worked in hip-hop environments that are interethnic and now transnational. He is still early in his career, but he has already gone from being a Chinese American interloper, to signing on with a major hip-hop label and releasing an album, to rejecting the industry and striking out on his own, to a new transpacific location. At the time of this writing, he is immersed in a deliberately multiethnic and sometimes transnational circle of emcees and deejays. His reach includes but is not limited to the GenerAsian mainstream, as it were—he is not primarily directed toward an Asian American audience, but it is certainly one audience among others. He is essentially doing the hard work of making it in hip-hop without downplaying his Asianness. He is matter-of-fact about his ethnicity. He *had* to be when freestyling: his opponents inevitably used it against him, so he developed an effective, strongly preemptive approach that sometimes plays into stereotypes of Asian superiority and insulated arrogance. Missing from his narratives is any trace of what Davé, Nishime, and Oren call "the familiar representation-based models that emphasize victimization and alienation" (2005, 3). To date, Jin's work has proceeded along two separate but interrelated channels. His work with a major recording label resulted in commanding work that was (perhaps inevitably) laced through with Orientalist commentary even as it insisted that the listener come around to his subjectivity. His political work since then has been increasingly independent and confident.[45] In a few short years he has moved restlessly between asserting his Chineseness and putting it right out front even while working in a matter-of-factly interethnic milieu in which he collaborates and supports Asian American and African American emcees. Yet his most recent album addresses the Chinese American experience in Cantonese. He also rapped in English in Taiwanese American pop singer/producer Lee-Hom Wang's "Heroes of Earth," a song and music video released in 2006 that has attracted immense interest in Taiwan and among 1.5 and second-generation Mandarin-speakers in diaspora. In short, Jin is part of a broader transpacific pop music phenomenon that is still in its early stages but is deeply linked to second-generation Asian American identity.

Conclusion

Asian American youth cultures are proliferating, and class has emerged as a particularly salient parameter in their dissemination. Some Asian American youth who participate in hip-hop culture become part of a broader interethnic conversation about class and social justice; this pan-minority configuration carries tremendous political promise. However, the transpacific culture of northeast Asian cool relies on the dangerous neoliberal rhetoric of an open Pacific Rim and folds its participants into its troubling logic. These two youth cultures—GenerAsians and hip-hop—are distinct but not hermetically sealed: they have points of contact and overlap but in many ways represent contrasting identifications, and they illuminate emergent class formations. Hip-hop is not consumed by only the working class, even though its habitus is wrought in that environment.[46] Its dissemination is neither uncontrolled nor innocent: the entertainment industry establishes the terms for appropriation as the form has moved out from its point of origin. What happens, or could happen, when GenerAsians listen to Jin? While no ethnic minority should have to apologize for upward mobility, the need for an articulated racial politics of socioeconomic success and transnational connection is more urgent than ever. The difference between transnational opportunity and opportunism is not always clearly marked, and First World imperialisms are both the driving force and assumed outcome to Pacific Rim connections.

The rise and fall of *Yolk* magazine and Jin's cometlike ascendance and then rejection of the hip-hop music industry suggest that new cultural formations are emerging that uneasily outline nascent ways for thinking about the Asian American generation. Indeed, my undergraduates in 2004, looking only at "Learn Chinese," felt that Jin was the least politicized of several Asian American emcees, though I am fairly certain they would now see him differently. Then again, "Learn Chinese" and "Got Rice, Bitch?" were both in their ears during 2004, so it was easy that year to get deafened by hip Orientalia.

As William Wei points out, college campuses remain the primary site for Asian American youth activism, but in different ways from the 1960s. Asian American youth are now more ethnically heterogeneous than they were in the 1960s and are more ready to accept the mainstream terms of social mobility. As Wei writes, "Indeed, they make no apologies for their middle-class aspirations and avidly pursue the so-called American dream" (2004, 310). This speaks to the deeper issue of how American race and class formations are linked. Some of these young people will discover that a glass ceiling is still solidly in place in American bureaucracies and corporations. As GenerAsians move into positions of greater power and responsibility, they will find that they need critical and political tools for addressing the carefully wrought links between race, class, nation, and capital. Those tools can be found in many places, from ethnic studies classes to Jin's asides. At a club in New York City, Jin raised his fist to an almost entirely Asian American crowd and shouted, "Where're my fuckin' Asians at?" and they shouted back, smiling, bobbing, dancing. My hopes lie in these moments when pleasure, consumption, and action converge in thinking subjects.

NOTES

I have learned much from Oliver Wang over the years. He generously provided detailed feedback on this chapter, which is really part of an ongoing conversation with him. My thanks to Scott Cook, Department of Chinese and Japanese, Grinnell College, who went out of his way to find a Web site for me that included translations of the Cantonese phrases in Jin's "Learn Chinese." I am grateful to Patricia Fernández-Kelly and Paul DiMaggio for inviting me to participate in their symposium at Princeton University, to Paul DiMaggio for extensive comments and suggestions, and to Cecelia Menjívar for offering a close reading as my discussant. The National Humanities Center provided the haven that allowed me to write this chapter.

1. In previous writings, I have used the term "Asian American" a bit too sweepingly to describe all Americans of Asian descent. Thinking about current Asian-based American youth culture has forced me to rethink this by attending more carefully to the specific historical conditions that created an Asian American sensibility to begin with. As will become clear in this chapter, I do not think that this sensibility is shared by all young American Asians.

2. I am referring to the Asian American movement that emerged alongside the Black Power movement, the Chicano movement, the American Indian movement, and the women's movement. The term "Asian American" was coined in the 1960s and was meant to (1) acknowledge the discrimination and racism experienced by many Americans of Asian descent and (2) reoperationalize the ways Asians have sometimes been regarded by other Americans as an undifferentiated racial group. Individuals who self-identify as Asian American (usually in addition to their specific ethnic heritage) are well aware of ethnic and national differences across Asian immigrant groups. Generally, Asian American self-identification signals a racialized understanding of the United States; it presupposes the shaping force of racism and its systemic effects on American society. My use of the term "Asian American" thus stems from a commitment to attend to difference by using the terminology and categories developed by scholars working in Asian American Studies and Ethnic Studies.

The Third World Strikes at San Francisco State University and the University of California, Berkeley, in 1968–1969 were formative sites for the Asian American movement. Key events since then have reinforced identifications across Asian American political concerns. The struggle for reparations for the World War II Japanese American internment camps was cast as an example of how anti-Asian xenophobia affects all Asian Americans. Similarly, the hate murder of Chinese American Vincent Chin in 1982 prompted organized responses by many different Asian American groups. In short, the political construct of the Asian American is meant to enable coalitions across different Asian ethnicities. William Wei (1993) is the authoritative source on the history of the Asian American movement.

3. The tight focus on relative generation that has traditionally served as a definitive model for ethnic studies reveals that discipline's roots in sociology.

4. According to Sucheng Chan, "The 1965 Immigration Act, which removed 'national origins' as the basis of American immigration legislation, has changed the pattern of immigration into the U.S. more profoundly than its architects ever expected. Until that year, the immigrant stream had been predominantly European, with sizable contributions from the western hemisphere, particularly Canada and Mexico, since the 1920s. But after the 1965 law went into effect, Asian immigration has increased so steadily that Asians now compose more than half of the total influx. While Mexico is the source of the largest number of immigrants, the next four most important sending countries are the Philippines, Korea, China (the People's Republic of China on the Asian mainland and the Republic of China in Taiwan each has its own quota), and Vietnam" (1991, 145). Pyong Gap Min (2002a, 2) notes that there were 1.5 million Asian Americans in 1970 and 11 million by 2000, and that the ethnic diversity of Asian Americans also expanded after 1965, including secondary immigration (e.g., Chinese and South Asian immigrants arriving in the United States from the Caribbean, Africa, and the United Kingdom).

5. I would argue that post-1965 immigration drove a number of changes, including the transformation of American studies from a field focused on (mostly) white American class-based history and culture into a vibrant interdisciplinary site that, by the 1980s, positioned

difference as central to American identity. See the first chapter of George Lipsitz's *American Studies at a Moment of Danger* (2001) for a much more nuanced historiographical argument for how American studies has gone through at least three stages of critical development, and how American studies scholarship in the 1980s–1990s was a response, broadly speaking, to the civil rights movement and related social movements of the 1960s. He cites immigration as a related impetus in his compelling overview of how the United States has become less white due to massive Asian and Latino immigration since 1965 (2001, 8–14). He argues that American studies has been responsive to these interrelated changes and that the "other" American studies has always been social movements that emerged from outside the academy. He writes, "The power of patriotism and patriarchy, of war and whiteness as cultural forces in the 1980s encouraged American studies scholars to see the price that previous movements for social change had paid by marginalizing issues of race, gender, and sexual identification" (25).

6. As Lisa Lowe puts it, "A national memory haunts the conception of the Asian American, persisting beyond the repeal of actual laws prohibiting Asians from actual citizenship and sustained by wars in Asia, in which the Asian is always seen as an immigrant, as the 'foreigner-within', even when born in the United States and the descendent of generations born here before" (1996, 5–6).

7. A traditional Korean instrument with twelve strings and a repertoire that is several centuries old and quite extensive.

8. Within Asian American studies, research has shifted toward 1.5 and second-generation issues and away from an earlier emphasis on the immigrant generation. Indeed, more than a few Asian American studies scholars are themselves from these two postimmigration generations (Min 2002a, 3).

9. This generation is consistently characterized by an intriguing mixture of political awareness and a certain blindness to its own class location(s). Arar Han and John Hsu's introduction to *Asian American X* (2004), a collection of writing by Asian American youth, is a case in point. The two editors, both undergraduates at the time of their writing, noted that the contributors were "primarily first- to third-generation Americans who are in college and hail from middle-class backgrounds. It is likely that these writers are a self-selecting sample of our generation of Asian Americans, since all are attending, have attended, or plan to attend college" (2004, 8). Han and Hsu cite their shared experiences, noting that "as the children of white-collar professionals in Silicon Valley, we grew up with the privileges of an upper-middle-class American lifestyle" (3). They argue for the continuing necessity of an Asian American political consciousness grounded in knowledge about Asian American history, but they rely on a liberal humanist argument that sets up Asian American "collective" experience against the trump card of the "individualistic" and an unencumbered search for the individualized self (3–4). In short, their awareness of class and the privileges of higher education is severely limited.

10. Soo Ah Kwon argues that, for instance, the import-car street-racing scene in California is marked by "new forms of pan-Asian identity among the current generation of Asian American youth," in which car racing teams consist of young Asian American men from different ethnic groups who come together via a rhetoric of "Asian pride." Kwon also notes that the cost of modifying cars means that the scene is dominated by middle- and upper-middle class youth (2004 10, 11–12). See also Namkung (2004) on import car racing, Asian youth identity, and masculinity.

11. Lee and Zhou's *Asian American Youth: Culture, Identity, and Ethnicity* (2004) and Davé, Nishime, and Oren's *East Main Street: Asian American Popular Culture* (2005) are foundational edited collections that laid the groundwork for studying Asian American youth culture. Both books explore the link between Asian American youth culture and mainstream U.S. popular culture, showing how youth culture upsets established understandings of race, nation, media, and mainstream versus oppositional cultures. Both posit that Asian ethnicity still matters but in new ways.

12. http://en.wikipedia.org/wiki/Generasian_X.

13. Including *Annapolis* (2006) and *The Fast and the Furious: Tokyo Drift* (2006).

14. *Harold and Kumar Go to White Castle* (2004) was in much the same vein: the film can be viewed as a comedy or as Asian American satire (though not written or directed by Asian Americans). Asian ethnicity does no apparent "work" for the plot.

15. The political and cultural concept of Asian American "pan-ethnicity" is from Yen Le Espiritu's influential book *Asian American Panethnicity: Bridging Institutions and Identities* (1992).

16. The Wellesley College Asian/Asian American magazine is titled *GenerAsians.* GenerAsians is a nonprofit, university-based organization that addresses Asian/non-Asian interactions in Canada. GenerAsians Together is a Toronto-based community-building organization for gay, lesbian, bisexual, and transgendered Asian Pacific Canadians.

17. My thanks to Oliver Wang for this point. See Wang (2007, 66–67n64) for more on the term "AZN" and its place in rap and the Internet.

18. In 1998 and again in 2000, for instance, the New GenerAsians Survey was commissioned by the Cartoon Network and conducted by ACNielsen. In 2000, 7,752 Asia Pacific youth ages seven to eighteen were surveyed, including their attitudes, opinions, and buying habits (with an emphasis on fast food and snack preferences). The survey included youth in Australia, China, Hong Kong, India, Indonesia, Japan, Malaysia, New Zealand, Philippines, Singapore, South Korea, Taiwan, Thailand, and Vietnam—in short, the term "GenerAsian" in this case did not include the North American Asian diaspora. I would argue that the term is being absorbed into the corporate logic of a globalized Pacific Rim. For more information, see http://www.acnielsen.co.nz/MRI_pages.asp?MRIID=14.

19. Despite these changes, *Yolk* folded in 2003. As journalist William Wan wrote (Wan 2003), "*Yolk*, a pop culture magazine for Asian Americans, has folded after 10 years of scrambling to stay alive. The editors tried everything during the magazine's 31-issue run. They tried humorous articles and serious pieces. And finally, hearing the death rattle, they tried sex, adopting the photo-laden formula of racy men's magazines such as *Maxim* and *FHM*." But the periodical never turned a profit, and now the Alhambra-based *Yolk* is the latest in a line of Asian American publications to fold. Like others before it, the magazine, which reached a circulation high of 50,000 in 2000, had trouble convincing advertisers about the worth of its readers: English-fluent, college-educated Asian Americans coming from vastly different cultures.

20. http://yolk.com/about.html.

21. http://www.giantrobot.com/whatsgr/whatsgrindex.html.

22. Oliver Wang offers a different assessment of the relationship between these two magazines. In a personal communication to me (May 2, 2006), he pointed out that *Yolk* positioned itself "as the younger, L.A. contrast to the slightly older (30-something), more affluent, New York–centric personality exuded by *A Magazine*," and that both magazines then had to contend with the "spectacular popularity" of *Giant Robot*. Also, as Wang put it, "*GR* was far more 'respected' in terms of cultural cache than either *Yolk* or *A*." He suggested that *Yolk* was also probably responding to the new paradigm of men's magazines established by *Maxim* in the late 1990s when it became one of the most successful magazines in the publishing world. He argued that *Yolk* (a) followed rather than defined trends, (b) had a primarily southern California presence, and (c) that "far more Asian American youth would simply have read *Maxim*, *Stuff*, *FHM* or any of the other so-called 'lad' magazines that sprouted on newsstands around 2000" than *Yolk*.

A comparative view of Asian American print media subscription bases is also revealing. In 2000, a reporter for *AsianWeek* offered these figures (Gardiner 2000):

> *Giant Robot* is a Los Angeles–based magazine that takes a pop culture approach to the Asian American community. Founded in 1994 at 240 copies, *Robot* now claims a circulation of 25,000. "Last year it was at 20,000. Our magazine incrementally grows every issue . . . thousands are added," said editor Eric Nakamura. Twenty-one years strong, *AsianWeek* has seen its circulation climb from 30,000 in 1997 to over 50,000 in 2000. Its offices now include Los Angeles as well as the San Francisco Bay Area.
>
> And A. Magazine, a lifestyle glossy based in New York City, touts a circulation increase of approximately 50 percent in just four years, from 125,000 to 180,000 readers between 1994 and 1998. According to former editor Angelo Regaza, the magazine, now enjoying its ten-year anniversary, has a circulation of 200,000.

23. "Pryde" (slang for "pride") is used exclusively by and for Asian Americans, as far as I know. Toronto-based D Pryde (born 1993), for instance, is a Spanish-Filipino emcee who self-identifies as Asian, comparing himself to Jin.

24. See http://www.hollafront.com/forum/archive/index.php/t-54687.html for a fascinating Internet discussion of "azn pryde." A poster named pinoy187joe asked,

> EVERY AZN TEEN IN DA STATES, (now also in Canada, United Kingdom, Australia) goes tru da AZN PRYDE STAGE in high school. suddenly he wants to have azn friends only, disses white boys, likes cars, go to azn party, build a website, post poems etc.
> BUT WHAT IS IT EXATCLY AND WHO CREATED IT?
> HOW DID IT STARTED?????

He received numerous responses, including one from xdlin22, who wrote,

> azn pride means knowing your roots, culture, not being ashame of your culture, its not about stupid songs like that, its about knowing about your own culture, recognizing it for its value, you dont even gotta know that much history bout your own culture, just as long as you recognize it. I cant stand those fuckin asians who scream asian pride n shit but they dont even know who vincent chin is.

Similarly, B-GeNeRaL wrote:

> I REP ASIAN PRIDE!!
> Cause i feel that more of us need to show pride in our roots . . . especially in the US there's different racial diversities; white, black, Hispanics . . . etc. Reppin' AP to me is basically reppin ya family, cause at some point of ya life different races and even ya own will insult ya fam and what you stand for. having AP doesn't mean that you're racist . . . you just proud of ya culture and heritage and you aint afriad to show it off, if anybody insults u, u won't be afraid to step up, cause you know you got ya fam behind ya back.

25. http://www.urbandictionary.com/define.php?term=azn.

26. Found at http://www.starterupsteve.com/swf/Asian.html, titled "AZN Pride," though it is now known more widely as "Got Rice, Bitch?"

27. My initial reading of this rap was that it was smugly anti-Asian, but Oliver Wang convinced me otherwise. He pointed out (pers. comm., May 2, 2006) that its bravado is a play on gangsta rap and that it was probably made by "a bunch of kids goofing around, half serious and half not."

28. The complete lyrics can be seen at http://www.asianjoke.com/pictures/got_rice.htm.

29. At http://azntv.com/docs/AZN_Network_Overview.pdf. The channel competed in certain markets with iaTV (ImaginAsian Television), launched in 2004, which is still on air at the time of this writing in 2009 (unlike AZN Television).

30. http://en.wikipedia.org/wiki/Asian_pride.

31. See Zhou et al. (2008) for a searching ethnographic examination of how 1.5 and second-generation Vietnamese, Chinese, and Mexicans in Los Angeles perceive and negotiate social mobility and how it is "attained, deterred, or denied" (55). They consider a wide range of socioeconomic success based on a number of factors. As they conclude, "National origin matters. The Chinese arrive in the United States with strong parental human capital and advantageous family situations in terms of a two-parent family, high educational expectations for children, and prioritized investment in children's education. Vietnamese arrive as refugees with relatively weak human capital, but this disadvantage is offset by their strong family situations and favorable state and public receptions" (55).

They identify a complex set of determinants for successful upward mobility, including legal/citizenship status, middle-class cultural capital brought from the home country, and family educational expectations. Addressing the same data, Zhou and Lee ask, "Is the way that we, as scholars, define *success* and *mobility* analogous to the way that members of the second generation define these concepts? Correlatively, if we were to reconceptualize our definitions and reframe our analyses accordingly, would we reach different conclusions about mobility" (2007, 194). They show that Filipino, Chinese, and Vietnamese children of immigrants demonstrate contrasting and uneven trajectories—including, sometimes, Filipino downward mobility between the first and second generations—and suggest that "successful" incorporation into U.S. society is complex and inevitably reflects a wide range of possibility across ethnic groups, including intra-Asian ethnicities. They critique the accepted wisdom that "convergence to the middle class" is "the only outcome that remains socially acceptable" (193).

32. As Paul DiMaggio wrote to me, triumphing over African American opponents as a freestyler is a mythic step for nonblack rappers, with *8 Mile* as the *Rocky* of this myth (pers. comm., July 9, 2006). In contrast, Jin grew up among Latinos and African Americans and has worked in markedly interethnic hip-hop environments since the beginning of his career, though he has also mentored a number of Asian American emcees.

33. In his "Biography" on http://jinsite.com.

34. I first heard about Jin in 2002, a few weeks after his repeated appearances and wins on *106 and Park*, when an Asian American undergraduate at Duke University told me I really ought to pay attention to him. Fan bases are inevitably hard to pin down, but it is clear that Jin's following includes Asian Americans and a broad non–Asian American listenership.

35. For instance, see the profile of Korean American rapper Jamez Chang (Ling 1999, 355–361).

36. For instance, see Oliver Wang's (2004) dissertation on Filipina/o American mobile crews in the Bay Area in the 1970s.

37. In the track titled "Hip Hop and Other Drops."

38. Similarly, Wang (2003) cites the promise of the frame sequence: "The opening is particularly interesting—the fact that the first image we see is of three Black men watching Jin's video (a video within a video) triggers me to want to think of what Laura Mulvey would say about this cross-racial, homo-social scopophilia but frankly, I don't want to bore you with cinematic psychoanalysis. What's interesting though is that I seem to think Jin is doing two things . . . he's both making a critique, i.e. 'this is how ignorant black people view us Asians' but it's also an attempt to connect with a BET audience by suggesting that if black folk in the video can dig on this video, the BET crowd can too. The black trio are strawmen, to be sure, but they actually help to validate Jin on some level too."

39. My thanks to Oliver Wang for this great line (pers. comm., May 2, 2006).

40. Posted to his Weblog on December 16, 2003, at http://www.o-dub.com/weblog/2003_12_14_archive.html#107166109401115293.

41. For instance, one online column by critic Brian Kayser stated:

> So Jin quit!!! One down, 25,000,000 more wack rappers to go. Granted, Jin didn't have it easy being an Asian MC, but he made wack career choices. He's not a Ruff Ryder. Why sign with a group that does nothing but rap about drugs and guns? If you're a battle MC, why sign? That's like Sage Francis signing to SwishaHouse. What is it that's so dope about Sage Francis? Seriously. Someone tell me. Jin damn man you gave up quick. I think like 150,000 people bought that crap album, and you're gonna quit after that. You even sold out Asian culture on "Bridging the Gap" and got away with it. I remember hearin' stories about how you would harass mad people at shows and Fat Beats when Percee P used to be there to buy your CD . . . I had mad respect for you . . . then you put out ass songs and killed your career. Honestly Jin, if I were you, stop taking people's advice and do you. If you're [*sic*] strengths are battling and punchlines, why you gonna make a video with you riding on top of a car? That shit is corny. "Senorita" and "Learn Chinese" killed your career. I guess no one's gonna buy that DVD "The Making of a Rap Star" now either. You ever see that shit in ads? Honestly Jin woulda been better on QN5. Damn Jin.
> (http://www.hiphopgame.com/index2.php3?page=column31)

42. The audio file of Jin's response was widely available on various Web sites (including his MySpace site) for quite a few months, but it is no longer posted anywhere, as far as I can tell.

43. *No Sleep til Shanghai* (2005), 70 mins., directed by Todd Angkasuwan, http://www.nosleeptilshanghai.com.

44. Jin's latest Web site, http://www.ayojin.com, focuses on his Hong Kong base. Jin's Internet presence has reflected different aspects of his career to date. His official Ruff Ryders Web site (http://www.jinsite.com, which stopped getting updates in December 2004) featured

public relations focused on *The Rest Is History*. For a few years, his emcee site (http://www.theemcee.com, no longer active) promoted his second album and then shifted toward his work as a mentor for younger hip-hop artists, several of them Asian American. At the time of this writing, his MySpace site (http://www.myspace.com/therealjin) is constantly updated and is self-consciously geared toward Jin's creation of an independent persona—and I mean that both in industry and performative terms. He also has an *ABC* page on MySpace.

45. For example, he has commented on Barack Obama's campaign, the Virginia Tech massacre, and Rosie O'Donnell's "ching chong" broadcast.

46. The hip-hop fan base of middle- and upper-middle class non–African American youth is well known.

CHAPTER 8

Unfinished Journey

MEXICAN MIGRATION THROUGH THE VISUAL ARTS

Gilberto Cárdenas

In this chapter I focus on the visual record surrounding Mexican immigration to the United States, including photographs, posters, drawings, paintings, prints, installations, and performances. I draw primarily on work produced in the United States by Mexican and Chicano artists to construct a comprehensive account of the unique experience of Mexican migrants over the last century. Two objectives frame my efforts: to discern how the visual record lines up with the written account and to assess what can be learned about Mexican migration from its visual history and art.

On the basis of available data I show how immigration as an artistic theme evolved slowly over the course of more than a century, in parallel fashion to the casting of an immigrant identity, which was gradually shaped by social interactions at the local level but also, more significantly, by government policies. Early representations of Mexicans in what is now American domain antedate the 1848 U.S.-Mexico War, a conflict that resulted in the annexation of nearly half of Mexico's territory under the James K. Polk administration. From images of that period it is almost impossible to distinguish between residents with historical roots that antecede the war and those who arrived later. Photographs, paintings, and posters do not readily show when an immigrant identity began to take shape or when immigration began to be perceived as a separate phenomenon.

Similarly, art produced in the early part of the twentieth century, whether by artists in Mexico or Mexican-origin artists in the United States, rarely focuses on the immigrant experience. That is even true about Mexican muralism, one of the world's great aesthetic movements of the period. For reasons described later in this chapter, it is only after 1965 that immigration emerges as a significant subject in

Mexican and Chicano art. In other words, the visual record offers an opportunity to investigate the way in which Mexican immigration emerged as an independent artistic theme and the manner in which that process was shaped by government actions.

Mexican Migration in a Historical Context

Mexican immigration to the United States has a long and distinctive history. Three factors set it apart from other flows: duration and varying modalities of entry; forced exit and state-induced return; and coexistence of temporary and circular flows.

Nowadays, politicians, pundits, and the media starkly contrast legal and illegal immigration, as if the difference were obvious. The reality is more complex and embedded in the long relationship between two neighboring countries with a shared history and deep economic relations (García 1981; Kreneck 1988). The U.S.-Mexico War of 1848 resulted in the blurring of national identity for Mexicans who had resided in the same lands for several generations but who were precipitously redefined as American citizens. Similarly, historical evidence shows an interconnection between legal immigration and prior undocumented residence in the United States in the early twentieth century (Gamio 2002). Overwhelming numbers of Mexicans lawfully admitted into this country previously resided in the United States without legal status. At least since the mid-1920s unauthorized and legal immigration have coexisted without interruption.

As a result, Mexicans have been the target of the longest and most intense policing in the history of the United States (Adams 1987; Anastos and French 1991; Chavez 1997). Congressional initiatives have often focused on Mexicans working in this country, criminalizing them and putting in place disincentives for their long-term settlement. Such initiatives have included measures to prevent them from benefiting from government-sponsored programs despite their contributions to U.S. society and economy.

Until recently, Mexican immigrants, many of them unauthorized, were able to cross the U.S.-Mexico border back and forth in response to labor demand. They worked seasonally in the fields of the American Southwest, and since the 1990s in urban service sectors, returning periodically to their homes south of the border. Starting in 1986, however, it became increasingly difficult for Mexican workers to engage in circular migration because of punitive measures like Operation Gatekeeper, Operation Hold the Line, and Operation Safeguard (Massey and Durand 2004). After the 9/11 attack on New York and Washington, anti-immigration measures reached a crescendo not seen since the 1940s, when approximately 110,000 Japanese Americans were held in internment camps. Hostility against immigrants has significantly heightened the costs of unauthorized crossings, and that in turn has had an unanticipated consequence—the expansion of the Hispanic population in the United States, including the number of undocumented immigrants, which is now estimated to surpass 12 million. Unwilling to face the risks of circular migration, more and more people are bringing their families to this country to settle down permanently without proper documentation.

Given its duration, types of entry, and negative reception in the host society, Mexican immigration has been fraught with hardships and exploitation that limit individual prospects for social mobility (Chavez 1997; Portes 2001). This is especially true in areas where groups in power have used the legal system to enforce discriminatory measures. Moreover, a wide range of informal practices discourage even eligible immigrants from participating in programs that would benefit them.

The causes of large-scale immigration from Mexico to the United States have been exhaustively investigated for nearly a century, but the impact of U.S. policies on that labor flow has not received as much attention.[1] Mexican immigrants have disproportionately included young, able-bodied, hard-working individuals with high rates of labor force participation who elicit top levels of satisfaction among employers. Yet documented and undocumented Mexicans have borne the brunt of smear campaigns and systematic efforts to oust them. Such measures are unique in terms of their frequency and persistence when compared to equivalent actions against Asian and some European immigrants. In the present, as in the past, more than 90 percent of immigration enforcement resources and manpower have been deployed to the U.S.-Mexico Border (Massey and Durand 2004).

Partly as a result of this singular history, the terms "illegal alien" and "Mexican" are now almost synonymous in the minds of many Americans and, especially, in the fear-mongering discourse of ideologues. Opportunistic politicians use the alleged burdens imposed by immigrants in American towns and cities to seek larger appropriations for publicly funded programs and services. Radio and television personalities portray unauthorized aliens as security risks, tax cheats, and undeserving freeloaders who should be deported. Undocumented workers are held responsible for their circumstances while attention focuses mostly on their assumed transgressions and not on the limitations of a broken immigration system.

Artists—Mexican, Latino, or otherwise—whose sensibilities are directly or indirectly informed by personal experience or by their appreciation of the Mexican saga have succeeded in revealing sociocultural realities that have yet to be fully understood by politicians, commentators, and the public at large. Whether originating in the Spanish tradition—with its broad range of conventional forms—or in more recent conceptual or abstract expressions, Mexican art in the United States cannot be properly comprehended without giving attention to immigration.

Early Evidence

When examining the visual record of Mexican immigration it is important to evaluate archival and preservation efforts (Samponaro and Vanderwood 1992; Sarber 1977). Artistic production is thin, but not absent, in archival and museum holdings, such as the National Archives and Record Service, the Archives of American Art (Smithsonian Institution), and the Library of Congress. It is stronger in photographs by comparison to illustrations and portraiture, and relatively weak with respect to the social relations surrounding Mexican migrants. There are vivid lithographs and illustrations, sometimes in color, in magazines and books showing Mexican life in the United States prior to 1900. Nevertheless, it is often hard to distinguish nonimmigrant residents from long-term immigrant settlers (Berumen and Delgado 2002). Artistic coverage of ranch, farm, and community life provides a romanticized, relatively static picture of a culturally rich community that endured despite the rapid transfer of land from Mexican to non-Mexican owners after the war of 1848 (Camarillo 2005). Illustrations and photographs from the nineteenth century provide graphic documentation of cultural life, types of housing, and work in various economic sectors: farms, ranches, mines, sheepherding, and railroads. Church participation is often represented. Portraiture is also common. Pictures related to law enforcement are plentiful, and occasionally there are images of conflict between U.S. authorities—like the Texas Rangers and the Bisbee Rangers—and Mexican trespassers, border bandits, refugees, and smugglers.

By comparison, the visual record of European migration is richer. The Irish Emigration Project and the German Emigration Project in Central Texas are proof of this, as is the plentiful imagery of immigrant and nonimmigrant prospectors and settlers who flooded the Southwest in large numbers during and after the Gold Rush. Displaced Mexicans were often forced to flee those settlements or to move out after losing their land to the unscrupulous dealings of thieves and railroad barons.

Mexican Migration in the Early Twentieth Century

The difficulties faced by European immigrants in the United States have been well documented in the specialized literature and in government hearings (Bankston and Hidalgo 2006; Barkan 1996). As a whole, and in contrast to the Mexican case, European migration can be largely understood as a variation of the legal-permanent paradigm—that is, the recruitment of foreign-born workers who subsequently were afforded legal means to become established residents and citizens. Most European arrivals were employed in an expanding industrial economy and faced few formal restrictions on their settlement and naturalization. By comparison, Mexican immigration is best understood from the perspective of labor control and inequality (Chavez 1997). Because of their humble character, Mexican workers were nearly invisible in the early part of the twentieth century, and there is almost no information about their lives in community and family settings.[2] There is also little evidence about their relations to employers or government authorities.[3] It is necessary to dig deep into archives to finally locate Congressional hearings on agricultural labor in the 1920s and 1930s that give any attention to Mexicans (U.S. Congress 1920, 1934). Even then, a discussion of their migration as a specific phenomenon is rare. In hearings held in the 1910s and 1920s several Congressmen voiced racist and restrictionist sentiments and others advocated for the utility of Mexican labor in U.S. labor markets. During World War II, large-scale hearings took place, but again the focus was entirely on labor, not on immigration per se (U.S. Congress 1941–42; Weisman 1986).

Mexico and countries in the Western Hemisphere were exempt from immigration quotas enacted in the early 1920s, but they were not immune to laws that established and deployed the Border Patrol in 1926. That measure was related to a new immigration policy that relied mainly on temporary workers and only secondarily on legal permanent admissions. It depended heavily on the management and administration of immigration flows, and included temporary importation programs, and regularization schemes. Such immigration policies also incorporated a wide array of bureaucratic measures to manage entries. During that period, Mexican flows took many forms, including temporary and circulating workers along the U.S.-Mexican border; longer-term migrants, seasonal as well as interstate; and an increasing number of long-term settlers.

The importation program of 1917 was a unilateral decision on the part of the U.S. government to invoke administrative discretion in the admission of large numbers of Mexican workers during World War I. In effect, this policy transformed immigration from small-scale drift flows to large-scale currents into labor markets that quickly became dependent on Mexican labor. This transformation brought about mutual dependency between sectors of the American economy and Mexican workers, as more and more of the latter crossed the border in pursuit of employment (Massey et al. 1990). Labor-market patterns created in the preceding years grew into formal mechanisms. Such mechanisms became the dominant feature of the emerging international system connecting labor markets in the United States with Mexican rural sectors.

The massive influx of immigrants who settled permanently in the United States was thus a byproduct of an initial group of temporary migrant workers, some 200,000 or more, who entered legally during the 1917 importation program in response to labor shortages resulting from World War I. Many reentered legally after the end of the program in 1921, but an overwhelming majority came back without proper authorization. By 1926 Mexico had become the leading source of immigrants to the United States. Legal flows were largely regulated by the State Department through administrative discretion in the issuance of visas. The same procedure was used later to curtail legal entries from Mexico after the fall of the stock market and the Great Depression.

Throughout that period, a significant body of visual evidence about the circumstances surrounding Mexicans in the United States begins to appear. It consists of photographs of daily life, border crossings, and dispersion and settlement throughout the United States. The photographic account goes no farther back than the beginning of the twentieth century, but it is rich by comparison to the preceding phase. Mexicans are shown, for example, in front of their homes, as individuals or with their families, in public places, or participating in social activities such as fiestas and religious processions (Martinez 1991, 1993; Mumma 1992).

Many photographs taken in the early 1900s along the border vibrantly capture the journey of Mexican refugees. The 1910 Mexican Revolution—the world's first popular uprising of the twentieth century—resulted in the death of an estimated two million and the displacement of tens of thousands. Many of those who fled the bloody confrontation ended up in American border towns (Camín, Meyer, and Fierro 1993). Reports from the period note the emergence of charitable organizations whose purpose was to attend to the needs of Mexican refugees. An example of the drama lived out by those escaping violence is a photograph taken by Robert Runyon of a man on crutches standing in front of a large crowd of Mexican children, probably in El Paso, Texas (Runyon 2008). Striking pictures also show Mexicans at crossing points, living in tent camps, some being welcomed, others either detained or enduring a hostile reception. The growing Mexican presence in American border towns required public responses, many of which, although well intentioned, resulted in differential treatment such as segregation in neighborhoods and schools (Ganz and Strobel 2004).

In a photograph taken between 1913 and 1916, Robert Runyon dramatically captures the return flight of Mexicans seeking sanctuary south of the border. The image is set at the international bridge in South Texas just prior to the 1917 importation program. According to Paul Vanderwood, the picture may depict the results of harassment by the Texas Rangers, an organization that began as a vigilante group during the Texas Revolution, and then grew to become a formal police agency when that state joined the Union. Vanderwood notes that vigilantes regularly participated with the Rangers in attempts to control the Mexican population in South Texas (Samponaro and Vanderwood 1992).

Cheryl R. Ganz and Margaret Strobel (2004) provide examples of artwork produced in the 1920s and 1930s by Mexican immigrants who settled in Chicago. Those immigrants could have well been the founders of the first *taller* (workshop) involving Mexican artists in the United States. The stained glass window they created for the St. Francis of Assisi Catholic Church is a masterful piece comprising thirty-six panels. The mural depicts various aspects of the migration experience—leaving home in the countryside, traveling long miles by train, settling in Chicago, with its industrial landscape as a backdrop, and finally finding the Catholic Church as a center of community life.

As early as the late 1910s immigrants from Mexico were fully incorporated into the U.S. economy, and employers in many parts of the country were relying on them as a permanent source of labor. By the early 1920s Mexican immigrants had settled permanently in these areas as well. The byline to a photograph taken during this period suggests that Mexicans were firmly incorporated in the economy and society of the United States. The byline makes a point that sympathetic observers have continuously argued:

> The Mexican has established himself firmly in the economic life of the United States. Vast areas of the country are dependent upon his labor. His children and his children's children will live here as American citizens. They will help to elect our presidents; they will help establish our moral, political, and religious ideals and practices. Our future is bound up with theirs. We must think about

them; we must come to know them; we must work with them in the constructive and worthwhile things of life.

(Vernon Monroe McCombs, Frontispiece, 1925)

Photos taken in this early stage, particularly those that found their way into publications, offer insights about Mexican immigration that cannot be gained from other printed accounts (Chagoya 1996). The majority were not intentionally produced for exhibition or aesthetic purposes, but they have considerable merit as works of art. This is true across the entire spectrum of photographers—from a casual amateur like Paul S. Taylor to acclaimed professionals like Dorothea Lange, Ansel Adams, and Russell Lee.

Ansel Adams is responsible for early photographs of Mexican immigrants working in the San Joaquin Valley. He described a magnificent shot of a Mexican worker profiled atop a wooden structure as one of many that he took in his first commissioned project.[4] The masterly image appeared as the leading piece in a 1931 issue of *Survey Graphic*, a magazine published by Paul Kellogg, under the title *Mexicans in Our Midst: Newest and Oldest Settlers of the Southwest.* One of the finest ever assembled on Mexicans in this country, the publication included contributions from noted writers like Mary Austin, Paul S. Taylor, D. H. Lawrence, J. Frank Dobie, Manuel Gamio, and Max Hundman, and images by distinguished artists like Diego Rivera, Jose Clemente Orozco, and Georgia O'Keeffe.

The very title of the issue recognizes the continuities between the pre-immigrant presence in California and the New Mexican immigration. At the same time, the phrase "Mexicans in Our Midst" reflects a pejorative outlook that defines "our" space as non-Mexican. The cover, drawn by Diego Rivera, shows two workers shaking hands across the international demarcation line between Mexico and the United States. This was extraordinary at a time when very few artists addressed immigration or borders. Rivera's drawing stands out as a poignant reflection and perhaps the first image of Mexican immigration on the cover of a U.S. publication.

Thanks to the photographs taken by Ansel Adams and others, we see the faces of Mexican immigrants clearly for the first time. Their carefully framed, precise shots were used by *Survey Graphic*, a magazine that aspired to stir awareness about the social realities of American life. We are left to ask, however, who were these workers shown proudly posing in their best light? Might we ever know what became of them and their offspring? Who among them were deported, died in World War II, dropped out of school or completed college and successfully pursued careers in the United States? We can ask such questions because of the strength of the imagery created by photographers like Ansel Adams, Dorothea Lange, Paul Shuster Taylor, and Russell Lee; they cared enough to leave behind a visual record of Mexican workers who otherwise would have been reduced to faceless abstractions, their identity subsumed in vacuous debates over legality and illegality (see also Taylor 1933).

Immigrant flows from Mexico during the 1920s can be characterized as preponderantly circular, temporary, and largely undocumented. Even between 1922 and

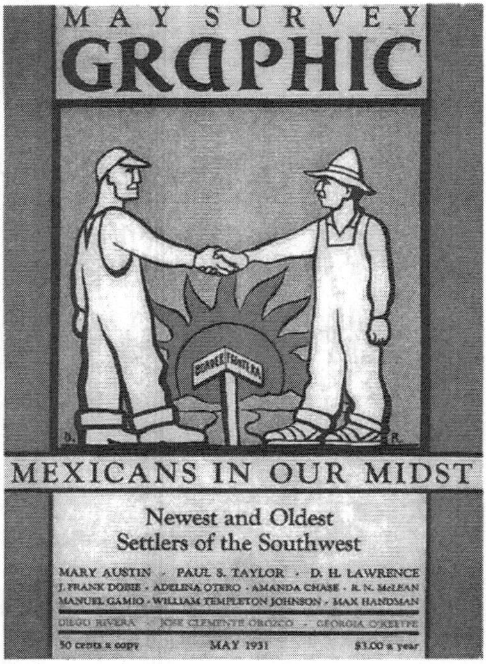

Figure 8.1. Diego Rivera, *Mexicans in Our Midst.* Cover of *Survey Graphic*, May 1931.

1927—a period of large-scale authorized admissions—legal migration was a by-product of temporary migration and illegal entries. Changes in the composition of the Mexican-origin population were dramatic. By 1930 foreign-born Mexicans constituted the largest component of the Mexican-origin population in the United States—a proportion not seen again until the beginning of the twenty-first century. In 1988 Luis Cancel, former director of the Bronx Museum of the Arts, curated a superb exhibit entitled The Latin American Spirit: Art and Artists in the United States, 1920–1970. The show, which opened at the Bronx Museum and toured the United States for several years, provided limited attention to Mexican immigration but offered important information about the work produced by Mexican artists living temporarily in the United States. A book about the exhibit was also published (Cancel 1988). Noted art historian Jacinto Quirarte's chapter on "Mexican and Mexican American Artists in the United States—1920–1970" is almost entirely devoted to Mexicans working on commissioned projects in the United States: Diego Rivera, Jose Clemente Orozco, David Alfredo Siquieros, Roberto Montenegro, and Rufino Tamayo. Those painters shared an acute awareness of social inequalities and overtly expressed political views. Their work almost completely overshadowed the production of Mexican counterparts who had migrated permanently to the United States: Emilio Amero, Antonio García, and Martín Ramírez. Quirarte's section on Mexican School Artists did include a few who resided in the United States for a significant part of their professional careers, such as Alfredo

Ramos Martínez, but for the most part the artists in his analysis were those temporarily in this country for exhibitions, commissions, and related activities (see also Lugo-Saavedra and Spray 1984).

Reverse Migration

The 1930s were a trying period for immigrant workers and their families. The Great Depression created a strong reaction against immigration in general and undocumented immigrants in particular (Aguilera-Hellweg 1995; Centro de Estudios 1983). Intensified law enforcement was used to round up and deport Mexicans and to disqualify them and their children from local, state, and federal benefit programs. Public and private repatriation were used to achieve the same ends. Mexico's government offered incentives for its nationals to return with their U.S.-born children who, under American law, were U.S. citizens. Leo Grebler and his colleagues estimated that more than a fifth of the Mexican population in the United States was rounded up and expelled in this period (Grebler, Moore, and Guzman 1970). Others returned to Mexico voluntarily to avoid retaliation. This remains one of the largest return flows for any one country in the history of immigration to the United States.

The photographic record of those events was primarily taken for documentary purposes, yet some images have great aesthetic value. A good example is a shot taken of Mexicans at the Los Angeles train station, seemingly bidding farewell to family and friends. The train stretches from the upper left corner of the frame to the right suggesting a departure to the south. Deportation is clear. The observer is left to ponder the future of these nameless people.

The visual record of immigration and its trials is strong in the 1930s for two reasons: First, the Work Progress Administration (WPA) launched a large-scale, government-sponsored photographic project targeting rural America; it employed nationally prominent photographers, including Dorothea Lange, Walter Evans, and Russell Lee among others. Second, a body of work was created by Mexican immigrant artists employed during the Great Depression by the WPA; among others, the Mexican artist Emilio Amero was included in that effort.

Amero, an accomplished photographer, illustrator, and printmaker, participated in the production of some of the first murals in Mexico. He arrived in New York in 1925, after several months in Havana, where he improved his skills as a lithographer (Axelrod 1987; Perisho 1989). In Cuba and New York, he worked with George C. Miller, meanwhile earning a living as an illustrator and commercial artist for companies like Saks Fifth Avenue and publications like *Theatre Magazine*, *New York Times*, *New Yorker*, and *Herald Tribune*. In 1930 he went back to Mexico and started the first print workshop at National Autonomous University of Mexico (UNAM), in the Academy of San Marcos. There he taught lithography to such prominent artists as Carlos Mérida, Alfredo Zalce, Jean Charlot, and Francisco Dosamantes. Documents in the U.S. National Archives show that Amero pursued his art in New York under the auspices of the Works Progress Administration.

Although his paintings do not address immigration specifically, he stands out as one of the first artists to systematically connect Mexican art to the emerging art of Mexicans in the United States. Before his death in 1976, he taught at various American universities and institutes, including the Florence Cane Art School in New York, the University of Washington, and the University of Oklahoma.

Temporary Worker Schemes and the Rise of Labor Circulation

By the mid-1940s the composition of the Mexican-origin population in the United States had changed again, with U.S.-born Mexicans now as the majority. Much of the visual record for the period 1940 to 1960 does not distinguish between the native-born and the foreign-born. It is worth noting that images of temporary and undocumented workers abound by comparison to those of legally admitted persons, although no major changes to immigration law were enacted throughout that phase. Migration caught the attention of artists and photographers, but on the whole it did not have the powerful impact of the 1930s. Dorothea Lange continued her documentary work on the rural sector, as did Russell Lee, in collaboration with University of Texas Professor George Sanchez. Photographers contributed the bulk of the visual record for this period—a record that explicitly criticizes unfair migration politics and is primarily seen in magazines and books, occasionally in union halls, and at times in community centers and faith-based organizations. Writers and scholars such as Carey McWilliams, Ernesto Galarza, Charles Loomis, Paul S. Taylor, and many more begin to shed light on immigration, sometimes criticizing the exploitation of and discrimination against Mexican workers.

The advent of World War II, and the labor shortages it caused, resulted in the establishment of the Bracero Program, a binational agreement with Mexico to allow for the importation of contract workers from that country mostly to the American Southwest. Extended several times, the program was formally supplemented by informal and discretionary administrative decisions that ensued in the admission of millions of Mexicans between 1942 and 1964. After the program ended in response to denunciations of human rights and labor violations, many Mexican workers who had earlier been admitted as braceros returned to the United States on their own but without permission. Again, illegal entries became a primary mode of arrival. During that stage, legal, permanent immigration was held to a very low level through administrative procedures. The Bracero Program was well documented photographically, but less so through drawings and paintings (Mraz and Vélez Storey 1996).

As in the mid-1920s, legal immigration from Mexico continued to be largely a by-product of unauthorized migration.[5] During the latter part of the Bracero Program (1955–1964), legal admissions from Mexico reached relatively high peaks, just as they had between 1925 and 1929, when they surpassed 15 percent. Held to a minimum from 1940 to 1954, the number of legal immigrants began to increase dramatically after 1955 because of the increasing pressure mounted by the labor movement and others opposed to the use of temporary bracero workers.

Nevertheless, the number of authorized workers and legally admitted immigrants from Mexico was outpaced by the flow of Mexicans entering the United States without proper documentation. Between 1956 and 1965 the number of unauthorized workers reportedly apprehended dropped and the number of those admitted under contract increased dramatically (Chavez 1997; Massey et al. 1990).

Post-Bracero Migration

The migration of Mexicans into the United States between 1965 and 2001 can best be characterized as a post-bracero phenomenon because it was that program that set into motion major processes, including the growth of municipalities along the border, commuter migration, temporary labor flows from the interior of Mexico (including its southern region), and the increase of legal entries—all phenomena that have continued to the present.

Greater incorporation into American society led to higher levels of political engagement among immigrant workers. Over the second half of the twentieth century, union-organizing efforts in the agricultural sector were strong and often militant, but they only came to fruition in 1964 when a new movement led by Cesar Chavez—the United Farm Workers Organizing Committee (UFWOC)—began to agitate in the grape fields of California and soon after launched the most successful secondary boycott in U.S. history. The UFWOC maintained a traditional stance that the labor movement as a whole had endorsed for decades but with a significant difference: immigrant workers played a prominent role in leadership and rank and file.[6]

The struggle of farmworkers converged with several other popular movements in the mid-1960s, including the civil rights movement and its by-products, the Black Power movement, the anti-Vietnam War movement, student power movements, an array of free-speech and counterculture movements, and the Chicano movement. Chicano art was born in 1965 when Cesar Chavez joined hands with theater director Luis Valdez to produce dramatic sketches, or *actos*, on the picket lines of the Delano fields in California's Central Valley. In other words, El Teatro Campesino was a byproduct of farmworker strikes, or *huelgas*, protesting the abuses of large agricultural interests (Reed 2005). Chicano art, which took elements from traditional Mexican culture and Beat and Dadaist currents, influenced major painters like Malaquias Montoya, Rupert García, Ester Hernández, and Antonio Bernal. Bernal's mural painted in 1968 on the wall of the offices of United Farm Workers/El Teatro Campesino Cultural Center "can be read as a kind of origin story of the Chicano movement" (Reed 2005, 107).

Chicano leaders bred a large-scale, spontaneous, and highly politicized narrative that articulated ideological positions based on notions of decolonization, militant consciousness, class struggle, cultural affirmation, and unity across racial, ethnic, and national boundaries. Artists and cultural workers also invoked principles of class solidarity to challenge dominant power structures in all arenas: political, educational, religious, economic, public, and private. In contradistinction to the

"Mexican-American generation" that had come of age between 1940 and 1964, the Chicano movement took an inclusive approach, embracing Mexican immigrants, both legal and undocumented, in its definition of Chicano (Griswold, McKenna, and Yarbro-Bejarano 1991; Ramírez and Estrada 1999). By contrast, the term "Mexican American" had derived from an exclusionary stance; it did not apply to Mexicans born abroad.

The new meanings spun by the Chicano movement soon found their way into the sphere of ideological revisionism and positive cultural affirmation. A highly politicized aesthetic emerged that vindicated the Mexican working class and simultaneously attacked dominant Anglo power. Chicano artists began to produce and distribute art filled with images protesting the mistreatment of immigrants and advocating for their rights in education, public spaces, workplaces, and the political process. Much of that production served as a tool for organizational efforts. Examples of that new trend are Chicano posters produced in the 1960s to gain support for causes that included the recruiting of union members and opposition to the war in Vietnam. Posters, as well, became means to preserve a culture that had been ignored by U.S. mainstream society. Chicano artists used Aztec gods, Mexican revolutionaries, immigrant farmworkers, and the lived experience of *la raza* (the people) to create a new populist aesthetic. Especially important as an iconographic element was the Virgin of Guadalupe, the religious image used in 1821 by Miguel Hidalgo y Costilla to unify Mexicans behind the War of Independence against Spain and used by Cesar Chavez, more than a century later, to bring farmworkers together in their fight against exploitation.

In 1972, the artist Leonard Castellanos produced the poster entitled *Rifa* as a manifesto of Chicano affirmation and vindication. Xavier Viramontes created the *Boycott Grapes* poster in 1973, one of the era's most famous images supporting the United Farm Workers Union. Both works portray Mexican icons, the agrarian revolutionary Emiliano Zapata in the first case and an Aztec warrior in the second instance, but the two posters recast those images to express a unique Chicano sensibility (Vallen 2008).

Worthy of attention during the early part of the Chicano movement (1970–1975) was the Centro Cultural de la Raza of San Diego, which was also founded as an artists' multidisciplinary collective, later becoming the center of *indigenismo* (indigenism), a current aiming to recover the rich indigenous legacy of Mexicans and Chicanos. The Centro cultivated contacts and cultural exchanges with Native American artists, performance groups in Mexico such as Mascarones and Concheros, and various Mexican and Mexican American Ballet Folklorico troupes. Such collaborations expanded Chicano art appreciation in the United States and other parts of the world. Victor Ochoa, cofounder of the Centro, was also a major figure in the formation of the Toltecas en Aztlán artists' collective. He contributed to the monumental mural campaign at Chicano Park in Barrio Logan, one of the poorest Mexican enclaves in San Diego (California Ethnic and Multicultural Archives 2008). Chicano Park is an astonishing assemblage of mural paintings combining autochthonous Mexican images and eclectic interpretations by Chicano artists.

Chicano art went beyond the bounds of ethnicity to engage national concerns. The poster *Vietnam Aztlán*, produced by artist Malaquias Montoya in 1972, gives voice to support for the antiwar movement. Chicanos, who had endured discrimination, police brutality, and poverty at home, were also dying in disproportionate numbers on the battlefields of Vietnam. Montoya's appeal for solidarity with the Vietnamese people was shared by many Chicano artists and also by significant numbers of people in the larger society.

In 1971 Congressman Peter Rodino, head of the House Sub-Committee and Immigration Committee of the Judiciary, introduced legislation to penalize employers for knowingly hiring undocumented immigrants. His legislative strategy unleashed a protracted debate about immigration and targeted the U.S.-Mexican border as a prime area of concern. The Rodino bill was the first in a series of legislative measures of an increasingly punitive character that have continued to this day. With the exception of the amnesty provisions in the 1986 Immigration Reform and Control Act (IRCA), the thrust of those legislative efforts has been to further criminalize immigrants, not to provide expedited, legal, and permanent admission for Mexicans wishing to work in the United States. Responses by Chicano artists left no doubt about their solidarity toward immigrants. Rupert García's classic serigraph, *Cesen deportación* (1972), combines graphics, bold colors and the rich iconographic meanings of barbed wire to make a bold statement against deportations. Barbed wire has been an important feature of Chicano imagery, used to convey a sense of the severity in the treatment of Mexican immigrants. Barbed wire is used to keep interlopers at bay, but it is also placed atop prison walls to prevent the escape of inmates. Its signifying intent could not be more vivid or raw.

Between 1971 and 1986 immigration, particularly undocumented migration, became a salient issue in the political arena.[7] A large number of strategies were launched to induce departures and make life and settlement harder for unauthorized workers and their families. Legislative and administrative actions were used to exclude undocumented immigrants and some categories of legally admitted aliens from receiving government benefits and to restrict their eligibility for

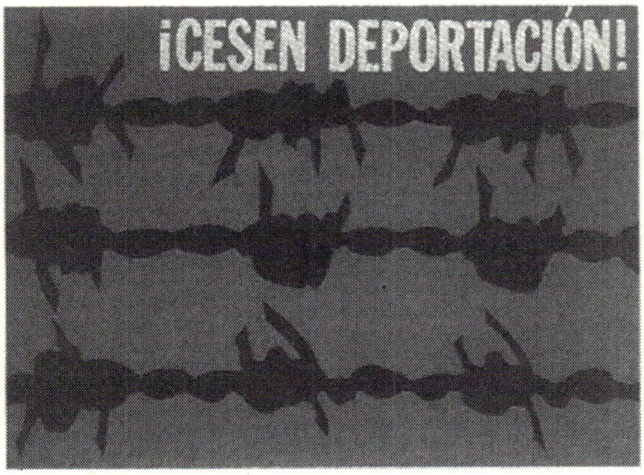

Figure 8.2. Rupert García, *Cesen deportación*, 1972. Courtesy of the artist.

educational, health, and service programs. In 1971 an anti-undocumented alien/anti-immigrant campaign was spearheaded by the Immigration and Naturalization Service (INS), working in concert with the House Judiciary Committee, as it had in earlier periods. In 1954, for example, the two entities had joined forces in an effort to bring public attention to unauthorized migration and to ready the public for extraordinary roundups and related enforcement operations. Members of Congress used the media to draw attention to the alien threat by releasing exaggerated estimates of the size and growth of the undocumented population and the adverse effects and costs it imposed.

Among the draconian steps taken against immigrants were legislative measures introduced in Texas in 1980 to exclude undocumented children—specifically, elementary and secondary school students—from receiving tuition-free public education. The Mexican American Legal Defense and Education Fund (MALDEF) fought such initiatives and in time succeeded in having the Supreme Court overturn them.[8] MALDEF and other organizations were also successful in challenging the passage of Proposition 187, a 1994 ballot initiative in California designed to deny unauthorized immigrants social services, health care, and public education. They were not as effective, however, in stopping English-only and anti–affirmative action laws in California, Arizona, Colorado, and several other states.

Attempts to disentitle immigrant workers and create barriers to their settlement prompted Chicano and Mexican artists in the United States to respond aggressively (Marin 2002; Noriega 2000; Perisho 1989). Mexican artists and Chicano cultural workers joined hands with civil rights organizations to produce and exhibit technically creative and emotionally stirring works showcasing the contributions of Mexican immigrants to American society and denouncing anti-immigrant actions. This was consistent with the Chicano movement's trajectory; even in its early days, artists did not portray Mexican workers in isolation. The idea of a single Mexican community, however incipient, was central in the production of Chicano artists and often focused on immigrants (Noriega 2000).[9] The anti-alien, anti-immigrant, anti-Mexican campaign that began in the 1970s sharpened consciousness even further.

The 200th anniversary of the drafting of the U.S. Constitution in 1987 did not fully capture the public's imagination, but it prompted a Mexican artist, José Antonio Aguirre, to create a stark representation of the immigrant experience. In one of his major etchings he revisited a gruesome event that year in which eighteen undocumented immigrants were found dead, after suffocating in a train boxcar outside El Paso, Texas. Aguirre used the *calaca*—a traditional Mexican image of a skull or skeleton associated with the marking of All Saints Day (*Día de los Muertos*)—along with the Statue of Liberty to signify the kind of "freedom" encountered by undocumented immigrants who attempt to cross the U.S.-Mexico border but whose final emancipation is death.

Similar artwork about the immigrant experience appears in the form of *ofrendas*, or home altars that, as in the case of Aguirre's etching, stress the connection between social justice and Mexican folk traditions of a personal, devotional, and family-based kind. Such forms are present prior to the 1980s, but it is since that decade that artists have made a concerted effort to display them not in homes but in public spaces, including museums (Tortolero 1988). The transfer of images meant to elicit private devotion in the public realm has attracted controversy. Some critics have interpreted the public display of devotional objects as a desecration of tradition and even as a betrayal of authenticity for base commercial ends (Brandes 2007).

Exhibiting Migration

I wish to underscore the importance of exhibitions about Mexican immigration that have included renderings of the immigrant experience. Relevant considerations in this effort are the strength of the works presented, various curatorial practices, the type of spaces selected for exhibition—national, regional, or local—and the audiences targeted. Issues of self-representation and interpretation—first-person voice or narrative versus less personal modalities—are also significant. Can we identify the first exhibition mounted to show the Mexican immigrant experience in public and in private spaces in the United States or Mexico? How many migration- and border-focused exhibitions have been presented and where, why, and for whom?

In 1984 the Fisher Gallery at the University of Southern California assembled an exhibit entitled Aquí: 27 Latin American Artists Living and Working in the United States, curated by Denise Lugo-Saavedra and John Spray. It included several Mexican artists, some of whom subsequently became identified with the Chicano art movement, like Carlos Almaraz, from Los Angeles, and Alejandro Romero, a Chicago resident. Yet the only artist who broached immigration directly was Cuban-born Luis Cruz Azaceta. Alejandro Romero's *Sol danzante* deals with immigration, but only as it relates to the social realities of Pilsen, one of Chicago's oldest residential areas where Mexicans reside (Lugo-Saavedra and Spray 1984).

The comparative absence of immigration as a theme in art exhibits and related materials is striking and not rare. An example is Eva Cockcroft's paper, "The United States and Socially Concerned Latin American Art" (Cancel 1988), which makes no mention of Mexican or Chicano artists in the United States. By contrast, the 1991 "Miracles of the Border" exhibit at the Valparaiso (Indiana) University Museum of Art was perhaps the first serious display devoted exclusively to the Mexican immigrant experience in the United States. It featured a large number of *retablos* painted by immigrants and collected by Jorge Durand and Douglas Massey (see chapter 11 in this volume). Retablos are small votive paintings to thank God, the Virgin Mary, or other Catholic saints for answering the prayers of individuals in need. In this case, the artworks express the gratitude of mostly undocumented Mexicans for miracles granted as they crossed the border or while they lived in the United States. The exhibit's accompanying book, *Miracles on the Border* (1995), offers insight about the meaning and functions of the paintings. Retablos may be considered as first-person narratives giving voice to a unique experience.

Galería Sin Fronteras, a commercial art gallery established in 1986, had as an explicit purpose to draw attention to the immigrant condition. Its founders expected, perhaps naively, that its art-viewing audience would include immigrants and their families. During the thirteen years that the gallery operated in Austin, Texas, it sponsored many shows, traveling exhibitions, publications in limited edition, fine art prints, and related projects. Shortly after its opening, Galería Sin Fronteras teamed up with Self Help Graphics, a Los Angeles–based arts organization, to produce a suite of etchings focusing on immigration. Privately funded, the portfolio contained ten works and four text sheets produced in handset type by the Lada Black firm. Entitled "The New Immigration," the portfolio featured five artists, three of whom—Jose Antonio Aguirre, Guillermo Bert, and Alejandro Romero—were born abroad and two of whom—Malaquias Montoya and Leo Limon—first saw the light in the United States. Their etchings have been viewed widely, and the portfolio has been incorporated into various collections in the United States and Mexico, including El Museo de la Estampa in Mexico City.

Several exhibitions organized by El Colegio de la Frontera Norte under the auspices of the Festival Internacional de la Raza were held at the Centro Cultural de Tijuana between 1984 and 1996. Those exhibitions were sponsored by the Consejo Nacional para la Cultura y Las Artes (Programa Cultural de las Fronteras) and toured various border localities and parts of Mexico. The exhibits featured contemporary works, most of them by artists from the greater border region. In 1992 Self Help Graphics and Galería sin Fronteras teamed up again to form a partnership with other print centers in the United States and Mexico. Their goal was to produce monoprints about border life and immigration. The resulting works were exhibited in several Mexican and U.S. cities, including Tijuana, Ciudad Juárez, Matamoros, Los Angeles, Austin, Chicago, and Mesa, Arizona. Some of them have been bought by private and public collectors like El Colegio de la Frontera Norte, the Cárdenas Collection, the Keller Collection, and the Mexican Fine Arts Center and Museum (see also Bowden 1996; Dear and Leclerc 2003; Henkes 1999).

Since 1998 several in-site exhibitions in San Diego have sought to address border-specific and broader transnational and global issues, including immigration. Collaborations across the U.S.-Mexico border, held in conjunction with artists from both countries, have fostered new art and exhibits. The Mexican Museum in San Francisco and the Mexican Fine Arts Center and Museum in Chicago have regularly presented the work of an impressive group that includes Guillermo Gómez Peña, a performance artist born and raised in Mexico City, who moved to Tijuana in the 1980s. There he began to collaborate with artists on both sides of the border, drawing attention to a wide range of issues pertaining to border life, U.S.-Mexico relations, identity, and cultural integrity. Gómez Peña and Coco Fusco, a Cuban-born artist, used dramaturgy to present political issues through expressive means. On one occasion they used music and movement to address the instability of the identities imposed on them as Hispanic Americans. Even more radically, in 1994

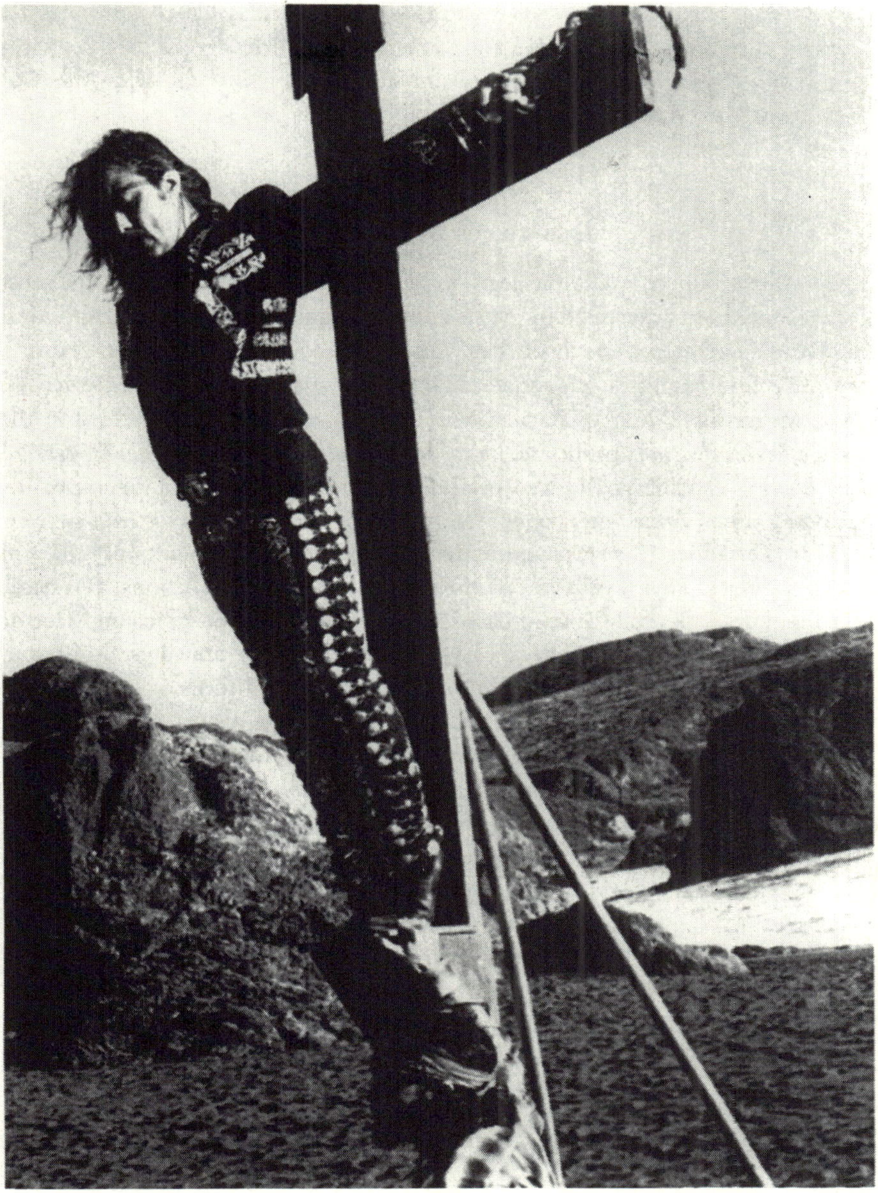

Figure 8.3. Guillermo Gómez Peña and Roberto Sifuentes, *Cruci-Fiction*, 1994. Courtesy of La Pocha Nostra Archives.

Gómez Peña used himself as part of a live *Cruci-Fiction*, a *tableau vivant*, enacted at Rodeo Beach, across from San Francisco's Golden Gate Bridge. Dressed in the traditional garb of the Mexican charro to signify a common stereotype of Mexican immigrants as banditos, he took the place of one of the two thieves said to have been crucified with Jesus (Gómez-Peña 1993, 1997).

Both Cusco and Gómez-Peña have achieved great success. Cusco continues her work as an interdisciplinary artist and writer in New York City. Gómez-Peña was awarded a prestigious MacArthur Foundation Fellowship in 1991—the first Mexican to earn that honor. He continues to address political concerns through his art.

Immigrant Sensibilities

By 1980 art produced under the aegis of the Chicano movement was for the most part secondary to art created by artists and photographers without overt political motives. Nevertheless, much of that work stemmed from a Chicano/Mexicano sensibility and was intimately connected to specific social and cultural experiences. Take, for example, Marcos Raya, a Mexican-born artist who has resided in the United States for most of his life, living and working in the Pilsen neighborhood near downtown Chicago. Raya's work reflects the daily struggles of inner-city life, including gangs, drugs, and alcohol (Noriega 2000). He portrays his own circumstances as an inner-city Mexican immigrant as well as the sociocultural milieu of his community. Raya works in paintings, found objects, installations, and occasionally murals. Several Chicago-based artists, including Rene Arceo and Hector Duarte, originally from Michoacán, have created paintings, drawings, prints, and murals, some of which address the immigrant experience directly.

David Avalos, a Chicano artist from the San Diego border area, created a national sensation when he distributed money from a National Endowment for the Arts grant to undocumented workers in transit to the United States. He also worked with Deborah Small to create an installation sharply criticizing the U.S. Bicentennial Exhibit at the San Diego Museum of Art. Guillermo Gómez Peña, Coco Fusco, David Avalos, and Deborah Small may not have been the first to use nontraditional approaches to address border and immigration issues, but they have been most effective in creating socially engaging artworks about the immigrant experience. Avalos, in particular, has produced provocative paintings and installations challenging beliefs about America's discovery, immigrant legality and illegality, and citizenship (Griswold, McKenna, and Yarbro-Bejarano 1991).

Historical accounts of art focusing on Mexican immigration have been limited but significant. In 2000 Jorge Durand and Patricia Arias published a very useful book, *La experiencia migrante—Iconografía de la migración México—Estados Unidos*, which offers a visual account of the Mexican journey, drawing primarily on photographs, some retablos, paintings, and posters. Durand and Arias discuss Martín Ramírez (1895–1963), a Mexican immigrant diagnosed as paranoid-schizophrenic in his thirties. A prolific artist, he produced nearly four hundred drawings of remarkable visual clarity and expressive power within the walls of DeWitt State Hospital in northern California, where he resided for the last fifteen years of his life (Davis Anderson 2007). In 1989 some of his works were included in the prestigious "Hispanic Art in the United States" exhibit, which featured thirty Latino artists, all of whom were alive at the time, except for Ramírez.[10]

The Taller de Gráfica Popular in Mexico City, founded in 1937, is the longest standing and most overtly political art collective in Mexico. It specialized in the production of *grabados* or prints—woodcuts, linocuts, and lithographs—making powerful statements about the circumstances of the Mexican working class, the Mexican government's service to special interests, and the oppressive nature of Mexico's class structure. Only rarely has the Taller de Gráfica Popular addressed the immigrant experience. That is typical; Mexicans rarely addressed immigration issues before the late 1980s. There were some exceptions, however; Alfredo Zalce and Francisco Mora captured the plight of braceros, and some Mexican artists who had settled in the United States or in Mexican border communities also focused directly on the immigrant experience (Mraz and Vélez Storey 1996).

Seattle-based artist Alfredo Arreguín is a good example. An accomplished and prolific artist-painter and printmaker, Arreguín combines his Mexican-origin experience with a long-time residence in the U.S. Northwest to create a hybrid art that is as Mexican as it is American. Others, like Mel Ramos, Rubén Ortíz, Cristina Cárdenas, Solomon Huerta, Roberto Gil de Montes, and Chicago-based artists Marcos Raya, Alejandro Romero, and Esperanza Gama, are among the Mexican-born artists who have settled in the United States and whose work reflects the immigrant experience in significant ways (see also Rodriguez 1988; Vida Nueva 2006).

Mexican-born artists Artemio Rodríguez and Silvia Capistrán have established a highly productive art center, La Mano Press, located in downtown Los Angeles. The facility serves as their studio, but it also sponsors classes and exhibitions, offering a mix of special events on and off site. La Mano Press allows Rodríguez and Capistrán to work with other artists, many of whom are also Mexican-born, in the production of linoleum, woodcut, lithograph, and silkscreen prints. Such collaborations have resulted in posters and banners used in large-scale demonstrations advocating immigrant rights and either supporting or opposing pending legislation in Washington, D.C. Their art is reminiscent of posters produced by Chicano art collectives of the late 1960s and 1970s. La Mano Press has also issued several limited-edition art books, including one, in 2006, that features a ten-year retrospective of Artemio Rodríguez's prints (Rodríguez 2006). Notre Dame's "Caras Vemos" exhibit featured a large-scale woodcut mural produced in limited edition by Rodríguez and his team and smaller artworks created solely by him.

Caras Vemos, Corazones no Sabemos: The Human Landscape of Mexican Migration to the United States

From September 3 to November 12, 2006, the Snite Museum of Art and the Institute for Latino Studies at the University of Notre Dame sponsored an exhibition entitled Caras Vemos, Corazones no Sabemos: The Human Landscape of Mexican Migration. The exhibition featured more than one hundred objects reflecting artistic sensibilities from the early 1970s to the present. According to guest curator, Amelia Malagamba (art historian at Arizona State University),

> Supporting visual materials are integrated into the narrative of the exhibition, including vintage photographs, first editions of early-published works on Mexican migration, and a series of ex-votos related to migration. Additionally, the exhibition utilizes unique soundtracks drawing on narrative experiences of Mexican immigrants and a variety of musical forms inspired by the phenomenon of migration throughout the galleries. More than a sound ambiance, this component becomes the audio narrative of the visual imagery. Much of the music selected reflects both the traditions and musical mestizaje resulting from the process of negotiating the realities produced by migration.
>
> (Malagamba 2006, 14)

Malagamba reports that the Caras Vemos, Corazones no Sabemos exhibit had a twofold purpose: to investigate the articulation of Mexican migration to the United States in Chicano and Mexican visual arts and to engage nontraditional audiences with artwork to stimulate discussion and educate the public about immigration from Mexico. The exhibit was both an artistic display and an educational effort. Its main themes were journeys, boundaries and barriers, urban landscapes and human geographies, negotiated identities, and constructed image repertories. Malagamba, the curator, has extensive knowledge as an artist, a *fronteriza* (border resident), and the former director of the Department of Cultural Studies at El Colegio de la Frontera Norte. In Caras Vemos she assembled contemporary artworks that effectively reflected the social realities of *mestizaje* drawing on artistic expressions that shape and are shaped by migration. The exhibit was an unprecedented event that finally synthesized the contributions of Mexican and Chicano art in relation to the unifying experience of migration.

Conclusion

The photographic record provides compelling imagery of the harsh treatment experienced by Mexicans in the United States. It also offers empirical evidence of the unintended consequences of temporary labor migration, undocumented migration, and legal immigration—that is, the formation of groups that eventually found means to reenter legally and those that were able to legalize their status and settle in the United States.

It is not surprising that an overwhelming majority of visual images reflect the unique character of Mexican migration history—there is an abundance of material on temporary and illegal labor flows and relatively little material pertaining to legal migration. Nevertheless, the photographic record documenting the Mexican experience in the United States during times of massive flows reveals impoverished yet culturally vibrant and tenacious communities throughout the country.

Whether produced in the United States or Mexico, artwork addressing immigration is relatively scarce until the mid-1960s and early 1970s. On the other hand, since the late 1960s Chicano and Mexican artists have addressed immigration directly, creating a significant body of work, the result of individual and collective efforts. Collaborations have produced impressive prints, murals, dramatic performances, and installations. Artists displaying their work in public and private venues have relied on strong, culturally based iconography to reflect on their own experiences, depict or reinterpret past events, or comment critically on current affairs and public policy. Many Chicano and Mexican artists have played an important role in civil rights and protest movements since the 1970s.

It is since the 1970s that we find a proliferation of artistic expressions directly addressing immigration issues or aspects of the immigrant experience by immigrants themselves, Mexican-origin artists, and sympathetic members of other groups. An important body of art now exists that addresses current immigration issues directly or indirectly. Artists have begun to ensure that the voids of the past will not be repeated in the future visual history of Mexican immigration.

NOTES

1. Massey et al. (1990) provide a useful summary.

2. In 1911 a select commission of the U.S. government issued some fifty-two volumes of reports on immigration. That commission, popularly known as the Dillingham Commission, did not give much attention to Mexican migration but issued a significant conclusion that would be realized in law and policy that "Mexicans were welcomed as laborers, but not as settlers."

3. This changed in the 1960s when the United Farm Workers' Union, led by Cesar Chavez, suddenly brought Mexican agricultural workers to the attention of the American public.

4. This work by Adams caught my attention many years ago in a conversation with Paul S. Taylor, a guest speaker at Notre Dame University in 1973.

5. The underground institutions that evolved during the 1910s were firmly established in the 1920s and fully operative during the Bracero Program.

6. The UFWOC favored the restriction of immigration in an attempt to prevent employers from using immigrant workers as strikebreakers.

7. The Immigration and Naturalization Service lobbied and received big increases in Congressional funding for enforcement efforts. The staffing of the Border Patrol increased from 2,580 in 1978 to 4,948 in 1992, supported by a funding increase from $78.1 million (1978) to $325.8 million in 1992 (Massey 2006).

8. *Plyer v. Doe*, 457 U.S. 202 (1982).

9. Chicano artists did not often use mural painting as a medium to address immigration. For a while that subject remained secondary to other issues and iconographic conventions derived from Mexican culture.

10. Victor Espinoza (Northwestern University) is conducting research on the life and work of Martin Ramírez, one of the most prolific of the relatively few Mexican artists living in the United States actively engaged in art production in the 1920s.

CHAPTER 9

Immigrant Art as Liminal Expression

THE CASE OF CENTRAL AMERICANS

Cecilia Menjívar

One of the first interviews I ever conducted with immigrants in the United States was with Rosario, a woman in her early twenties I met in San Francisco. She was born into a poor rural family in central El Salvador and started working as a housekeeper in San Salvador, the capital city, right after finishing sixth grade, from the time she was twelve years old. When we met, she seemed soft-spoken and pensive, and at first I was not sure whether we were going to be able to converse. As we talked, she struck me as thoughtful and cautious with her words; she would use similes and metaphors to express apprehensions, sadness, joy, and a plethora of emotions she had experienced since she had embarked on the journey north. Instead of simply recounting the difficulties and tribulations she had experienced in the United States, and how unattainable the American dream seemed to her, she said, "life in the United States is like a rose full of thorns because you can see it, and see that it's beautiful, but never get to touch it to enjoy it."[1] With time we got to know each other and she confided that she kept a small notebook in which she wrote her thoughts: "I don't know, like poems, you could say, but not poems, poems, like the ones poets write. I am not famous and what I write is mine." She smiled as she recounted that she often wrote late at night, after a back-breaking day of cleaning living rooms, kitchens, and toilets. When I asked her how she mustered the energy to do so, she said, "[Writing] serves me to console myself."

In turn, my conversations with Rosario made me realize that there was a vast realm of her "immigrant experience" that eluded my in-depth interviews and participant observation, the methods I have used to tap various aspects of immigrants' lives. Central American immigrant artists express this other realm vibrantly in poems, music, lyrics, performances, dance, and painting. The characters in their novels, pictures, films, and songs flesh out a violent history of displacement, a complex identity and status, a harsh adaptation to life in the United States, the uncertainty of Central Americans' legal status, the nostalgia that often accompanies their situation, and the vitality of still-unresolved events back home and in the United States. In this chapter I explore how Guatemalan and Salvadoran immigrants express aesthetically the emotional space of their still unresolved legal status. In my view, this uncertain legal status is so fundamental to these immigrants and their incorporation in U.S. society that it not only shapes the lives of the first generation but also seeps through to shape the identities, views, and dreams of subsequent generations. Thus, I examine how ambivalent legality is articulated in the art of first-generation Central Americans and how it emerges, in combination with other themes, in the work of these immigrants' children. Although ambiguous legal status is by no means the only theme that Central American artists capture in their work, it is a persistent one that surfaces forcefully, often in combination with its twin developments, civil war and political conflicts in Central America, even in the aesthetic expressions of artists who have lived in the United States all their lives. Thus, this examination allows us not only to reveal the multifaceted links between immigration and artistic production, but also to understand from a novel angle the profound and lasting effects of complex legal positions that affect the immigrants' lives and those of their children.

A handful of themes in Central American migration (particularly Guatemalan and Salvadoran) to the United States have captured scholarly attention. Early studies concentrated on resolving whether this migration was political, economic, or a combination of both (Hamilton and Chinchilla 1991; Jones 1989; Menjívar 1993; Stanley 1987); on the trauma and stress involved in this migration and on the effects the war had on these immigrants (Aron et al. 1991; Guarnaccia and Farias 1988); on their economic incorporation (Mahler 1995; Repak 1994); and on comparisons with Mexican immigrants (Chávez, Flores, and López-Garza 1989; Wallace 1989). More recently attention has been given to these immigrants' efforts to remain connected with their communities of origin (Baker-Cristales 2004; Hamilton and Chinchilla 2001; Landolt, Autler, and Baires 1999; Mahler 1999; Menjívar 2002; Rodriguez and Hagan 1992) and to the remittances that they send home (Funkhouser 1995; McKenzie and Menjívar n.d.; Menjívar et al. 1998). Scholars in the humanities have given attention to questions of identity, particularly among these immigrants' children (Arias 2001; Rodríguez 2005). Given the Central American immigrants' prolonged legal instability, there has been a concern with the effects that legal status has on their lives (Coutin 2000; Landolt and Da 2005; Menjívar 2006; Mountz et al. 2002; Rodriguez and Hagan 2004).

A focus on the artistic expressions of an immigrant group that is legally excluded or positioned only marginally opens up a window into immigrant worlds and meanings that sometimes elude our analytical gaze, worlds that often remain clandestine. Borrowing from Susan Coutin's (1999, 1) conceptualization, an examination of the artistic expressions of such immigrants allows us to enter nonspaces, "where actions are denied, relationships are discounted, identities assumed, and events do not officially happen." Central American immigrants turn to expressing their "in-between" position or "liminal legality" (see Menjívar 2006), and the views, feelings, and dreams that are associated with it, into lyrics, painting, verses, and prose regardless of their social position or length of time in the United States. As such, aesthetic expressions seem to be a critical means by which some immigrants, of different generations and walks of life, express the multiple emotions that accompany the temporariness of their legal (not social) existence.

Guatemalan and Salvadoran immigrants produce their art in a multiplicity of contexts and through a wide array of expressions. Thus, some expose their paintings in galleries, others publish novels and poems with well-known editorials and have literary agents, and still others belong to groups of artists and organize their production in "art worlds." There are many Central American artists, however, who produce their art outside the confines of organized artistic production; they record their own CDs and have no producers or distributors, others write poetry and publish it in home-based outfits, and still others do not share their writings or lyrics with the public but reserve them as intimate outlets that help them to assuage their anxiety and fears.

To be sure, the unstable legal position of Guatemalans and Salvadorans is not the only theme captured in the art of these immigrants. Other subjects include family life, landscapes, and works that convey women's position. For instance, Martivón Galindo, a Salvadoran architect by training who immigrated as an adult and has lived and worked in exile in the San Francisco Bay Area since 1981, writes poetry, paints, and works in a variety of visual art forms to expose feminist themes and particular experiences of immigrant women in light of the Salvadoran civil war. Her pastels, paintings, and drawings are infused with overt political messages and love of her homeland (Goldman 1994).[2] A gallery director in El Salvador, Galindo has continued to play an important role in linking artists and writers in the Salvadoran community, most notably through her work with the Cultural Documentation and Investigation Center of El Salvador. Similar themes of war and political terror also shape the work of Guatemalan novelist and screenplay writer Arturo Arias, two-time winner of the Casa de las Américas prize and cowriter of the screenplay for *El Norte.* Sometimes Central American artists focus their work on mainstream themes and thus it is no different than that of nonimmigrant, non-Latino artists, even if it is infused with styles and traditions of their homelands. Marta Ayala, a Salvadoran-born painter and muralist who grew up in San Francisco, works in the colorful tradition of primitive art, but her compositions express a wide variety of themes, including the lives of African American women. And Elba Rivera, another Salvadoran-born painter and muralist who grew up in the Mission District of San Francisco, relies on surrealist and abstract expressionist techniques to expose themes associated with humans' disregard for nature (Henkes 1999). Reflecting the struggles of their compatriots, often Central American artists make the subject of injustice and the resilience of the human spirit a central motif in their work (Goldman 1994).[3]

In this chapter I focus on the links that Central American artists make between an ambiguous legal position and the experiences and emotions it evokes in immigrants' everyday lives. Rather than focusing on a few aesthetic expressions in depth, I explore a variety of works that include poetry, novels, music, and performance in order to highlight the reach of the Central Americans' legal marginality in shaping their aesthetic production. In what follows I present the legal backdrop against which I discuss the artwork of first-generation artists and that of future generations. An important aspect of these immigrants' complex position is expressed in the language they use in their art. Most 1.5 generation artists, mainly poets, write in the English language, but so do some artists of the first generation (or they translate their work into English). Thus, while these artists' command of the English language conveys social membership and presence in the adopted country, the liminal legality they write about serves as a reminder that they do not fully belong. Thus, the use of English to write about legal exclusion highlights some of the contradictions of living legally marginal lives, which become particularly salient for these Central Americans, those "in-between" individuals whose very experiences encapsulate the gray areas of liminal legality.

Central American Liminal Legality

From the initial years of the massive U.S.-bound Central American migration that began in the early 1980s, the U.S. government took an inflexible stand against recognizing Central Americans as victims of geopolitical conflict in the Central American region, a position that has made them ineligible for different forms of legal protection. Although thousands of Salvadoran and Guatemalan immigrants fled the danger and devastation of their war-torn countries, they arrived in the United States to face a hostile reception: fewer than 3 percent of them were granted political asylum. Immigrants' rights groups lobbied on their behalf, and eventually Congress granted temporary protected status (TPS) from deportation to all Salvadorans who arrived prior to September 19, 1990, but Guatemalans were not considered deserving of this protection, although the U.S. State Department admitted the human rights toll of the political conflict in that country. TPS allowed Salvadorans to live and work legally in the United States for a period of eighteen months; the dispensation was extended a few times until it ended for good in September 1995. More recently El Salvador suffered two devastating earthquakes in early 2001 that aggravated many of the social, political, and economic problems left by years of civil war. Salvadorans who arrived after the earthquakes were originally granted TPS for nine months, a policy that was extended several times; the latest extension will remain in effect until September 9, 2010, for those who registered between August 21 and October 22, 2007. Once again, this is temporary, not permanent status, as has been made clear by the multiple deadlines for application and reregistration. Guatemala also endured the destruction of Hurricane Stan in late 2005, but Guatemalans who arrived after this disaster were not granted TPS.

In 1990, as a result of the settlement of a class action suit (*American Baptist Churches v. Thornburgh* [*ABC*] legislation) that alleged discrimination against Guatemalans and Salvadorans on the part of the Immigration and Naturalization Service, Salvadorans and Guatemalans were allowed to resubmit asylum applications. The success rate for Salvadoran applicants was 28 percent and 18 percent for Guatemalans (Immigration and Naturalization Service 1997). Provisions of the Immigration Reform and Control Act (IRCA) of 1986 were available to only a small percentage of Salvadorans and Guatemalans because most arrived after IRCA's January 1, 1982, deadline. To add further complexity to these immigrants' legal story, benefits of the 1997 Nicaraguan Adjustment and Central American Relief Act (NACARA) were extended only to Salvadorans who entered the country before September 19, 1990, and to Guatemalans who entered before October 1, 1990, and who had registered under the *ABC* settlement (or filed an asylum application before April 1, 1990). Successful Salvadoran and Guatemalan NACARA applicants were not treated like other nationals protected under this provision; those who already had been placed in deportation procedures had to appear before an immigration judge to request a cancellation of removal, and if approved they were given permanent resident status. Immigrant rights groups have lobbied Congress so that Salvadorans and Guatemalans—like Nicaraguans and other nationals included in NACARA—would have their status adjusted to permanent residence without hearings on a case-by-case basis, but since October 1998 Congress has refused to grant these immigrants this benefit.

Legal uncertainty among Guatemalan and Salvadoran immigrants has been further aggravated by a generalized restrictive immigration regime at the federal and local state levels. Most notably, the 1996 Illegal Immigration Reform and Immigrant Responsibility Act (IIRIRA) has facilitated the "removal" of hundreds of thousands of Central Americans for various criminal offenses (Rodriguez and Hagan 2004). Between 1997 and 2005, 42,862 Salvadorans and 54,250 Guatemalans were deported (U.S. Department of Homeland Security 2005; Immigration and Naturalization Service 2000). And although the 2000 U.S. census estimates that approximately one-quarter of Salvadorans and Guatemalans are now naturalized citizens, 73 percent of Salvadorans and 76 percent of Guatemalans are foreign-born (U.S. Bureau of the Census 2000), and the Immigration and Naturalization Service (1997) estimated that close to 60 percent of them are undocumented or protected only temporarily. Thus, a large proportion of these Central Americans has been and remains in the United States in an uncertain legal status with no resolution in sight and with the threat of deportation perpetually looming in the horizon. The Salvadorans' and Guatemalans' position vis-à-vis immigration law has meant living in "permanent temporariness" (Mountz et al. 2002) or "liminal legality" (Menjívar 2006) for a long time.

It is not simply an undocumented status that matters here but the long-term uncertainty inherent in Guatemalans' and Salvadorans' legal status, a situation that differs from being simply undocumented, because of the series of temporary permits, the ups and downs in the acceptance rates of asylum applications, and the lengthy adjudications of *ABC* and NACARA benefits, which have given them the illusion and hope that they will become permanent residents if only they wait a little longer. This complex position has left many of these immigrants living in uncertain terrain, in "nonspaces," as if they do not exist (Coutin 2005). They are physically and socially present in the United States but are often legally absent and living clandestine lives, a situation that leads to conflicts of membership (Coutin 2000, 2005).

With today's immigration regimes, however, Salvadorans and Guatemalans are not alone in their predicament. Indeed, immigration laws in major receiving countries have been "irregularizing" people by making it all but impossible to retain legal status over time (Calavita 1998, 2005), and current political and socio-historical conditions have led to a particular configuration of migrant illegality, under which immigrants are routinely constructed as "illegal" (De Genova 2002). The Central Americans' situation resembles that of the Mexican immigrants brought as small children to the United States who also find their lives dangling within gray spaces of legality. In many ways, therefore, the experiences of Salvadorans and Guatemalans can be thought of as the paradigmatic case of the consequences of new immigration regimes, akin to an "ideal type" in the Weberian sense, as their experiences vividly exemplify what it means to live in legal limbo indefinitely.

One New Jersey study finds that among Latin American–origin immigrants, Guatemalans rank at the bottom in a system of stratification based on legal status (Adler 2006). The same study found that the U.S. Immigration and Customs Enforcement (ICE) agents' raids disproportionately target Guatemalans, and therefore other Latinos often avoid being associated with them. In Dallas/Fort Worth a study found that when asked about important rights in the United States, Salvadorans gave priority to the right not to be harassed by "la migra" or the government (Brettell 2006, 86), as well as the right to work and have access to health care. As Salvadoran cultural critic Ana Patricia Rodríguez argues, Central American immigrants personify the (un)sung heroes of legendary border crossing (Rodríguez 2001, 387). Perhaps it is not surprising, therefore, that the legal conundrums that shape the lives of these Central American immigrants emerge forcefully in their aesthetic expressions as well. Their art reflects individual emotions as well as social experiences and as such captures vibrantly what it means to live legally ambiguous lives.

Central American Artistic Production in the United States

In *Odyssey to the North*, Salvadoran-born writer Mario Bencastro (1998) tells the story of Calixto, a Salvadoran who escapes the ravages of war in his country only to find that life in the United States is one of hardship, particularly for those who are undocumented or not fully documented. Through the technique of interpolated flashbacks, Bencastro recounts Calixto's decision to leave his country, the context of war, and the circumstances that led to it, as well as Calixto's life in the Washington, D.C., area. In the first pages of the book, Bencastro describes an incident in which a Central American worker who is cleaning the windows of a high-rise building in the Adams Morgan area falls to his death. "Spiderman," the man who died, is one of Calixto's coworkers. Calixto fears that he, along with the other spectators, might be blamed for the death if he testifies—which means he can end up in jail and then deported because of his undocumented status. After the paramedics take Spiderman's body in an ambulance, Calixto, who became unemployed the moment the accident occurred, decides to take a stroll at the national zoo, where he agonizes over whether he should return to his country, as the dead man had planned to do. He decides to stay and continue to look for the only kind of jobs he can get without legal status. Calixto's life parallels that of many Central Americans, including applying for political asylum and being denied, as well as living in fear but with a continuous longing to return to the country of origin. In the last pages of the book, Calixto toasts the New Year with a group of friends in Washington, D.C., and in the process captures the hopes and dreams of many of his compatriots, including obtaining the seemingly elusive permanent legal status:

> "Maybe the New Year will bring us better luck . . .
> Maybe things will get straightened out in El Salvador and we can go back.
> Cheers!
> Here's to you not washing so many dishes next year!
> Cheers!
> Here's to you not cleaning so many toilets!
> Cheers!
> Here's to you marrying a *gringa* and getting your green card![4]
> Cheers!

Similarly, the musical production of the Salvadoran group Lilo González y los de la Mt Pleasant recounts the experiences of Central American immigrants in the Washington, D.C., area, emphasizing the importance of their legal status. The lyrics of "Amor sin papeles" ("Love without documents" or "Undocumented love"), for instance, express the legal uncertainty in these immigrants' lives and the expectation of deportation at any moment:

> Si me deportan, te aseguro y te llevo en el alma de mi guitarra.
> Te aseguro, yo te quiero, como quiero a mi guitarra.
> Por eso quiero cantar, por eso quiero reir, por eso quiero llorar.
> Soy ilegal.
> Por eso yo quiero ser, como el agua y como el viento, para poderte querer, aunque sea por un momento.
> Por eso yo quiero ser, como el agua y como el viento, para poderte querer, sin pensar en documentos.
>
> [If I am deported, I assure you that I will take you in the soul of my guitar.
> I assure you that I love you like I love my own guitar.
> That's why I want to sing, that's why I want to laugh, that's why I want to cry.
> I'm illegal.

That's why I want to be like the water, like the wind; so that I can love you, even for just a moment.
That's why I want to be like the water, like the wind, so that I can love you without thinking about documents.] (my translation)

The songwriter, Lilo González, told me that it was the contradiction that he feels Salvadorans have had in their hearts—wanting to be back in their country but being unable to do so for fear they will not be able to return to the United States—that has led him to write his songs. He highlighted the uniqueness of the Salvadorans' circumstances. I asked him why he thought these immigrants' experience was any different from that of other immigrants, and he commented:

> Many are still stuck here without real documents to be able to go visit their family. If you look around at Christmastime and New Year's, you'll see how nostalgic Salvadorans get. They cry because these holidays are meant to be spent with family, but many can't go to be with them because they won't be able to come back. They have lived suspended lives for decades, with permits, temporary this and temporary that, and so they can't travel, as they wait and wait for a permanent adjustment. And they have to be here because they have to keep sending money, or else their families there don't eat.

Lilo's comment about the "suspended lives" he thinks Salvadorans have lived in the United States, and his references to "real papers" and the consequences of not having them, underscore the core of liminal legality among Central Americans. Even when these immigrants attain full legality and even citizenship (as in the case of Lilo), their early, liminal experiences continue to shape their views of their adopted country, as well as those of their natal land. Such experiences also filter down into their artistic expressions.

The theme of legality is never far from the minds of artists who infuse their work with socially aware messages. In a solo performance, Quique Avilés, a Salvadoran community activist, poet, and performance artist, plays Rosita, a hardworking, informal peddler of mangoes and an undocumented border crosser turned legal resident who sends remittances home (Rodríguez 2004). Rosita tells the story of her emigration and of her experiences in the United States. In Washington, D.C., she finds "sad and depressed" people who reflect back her pain, but whom she nurtures with humor and food (Rodríguez 2004), making for them, as she says, "illegal tamales, wetback tamales, legal resident pupusas and . . . citizen enchiladas" (Avilés in Rodríguez 2004).

The musical production that captures the troubles and tribulations of Central American immigrants has not been solely the purview of Central American artists in the United States.[5] For instance, one of the most famous interpreters of norteña music, Los Tigres del Norte, have written songs specifically depicting the Central American experience. In addition to their popular repertoire of *corridos* that portray immigrants' views and relationships with the United States, such as the songs on the CD *La jaula de oro* (The golden cage) or in the "Canción 187" (Song 187), they have written the corrido "Tres veces mojado," which narrates the story of a Salvadoran who crosses three borders: Guatemala, Mexico, and the United States:

> Cuando me vine de mi tierra El Salvador
> con la intención de llegar a Estados Unidos sabía que necesitaría más
>   que valor
> sabía que a lo mejor, quedaba en el camino
> [When I left my land, El Salvador
> With the intention of reaching the United States I knew I would need more
>   than courage
> I knew that perhaps I would be left stranded on the road] (my translation)

Another Los Tigres song, "El Centroamericano" (The Central American) tells the story of many undocumented Central Americans who find it easier to survive by adopting a Mexican accent and generally "passing" for Mexicans, so that when they are deported they are not sent all the way to their countries of origin and can try to cross back into the United States more easily. Interviewees in my research have described this strategy.

The socially aware production of Los Tigres (or Los Ídolos del Pueblo [The Idols of the People] or Jefes de Jefes [Bosses of Bosses], as they are also called), is composed of danceable music distributed widely through popular channels to a wide audience in the United States, Mexico, Central America, and beyond. Thus, Central Americans who live in the United States often listen to this music and see their lives reflected in it (Informe Sobre Desarrollo Humano 2005). In the same manner, Central Americans in their countries of origin also listen to this music at parties or at home, and through these corridos they become aware of the trials that their relatives and family members go through on their way north, as well as when they arrive in the United States. Youngsters in El Salvador whose parents have migrated to the United States, for instance, indicated in a recent survey that these corridos help them "to become familiar with the suffering that their loved ones have been through" and to learn what awaits someone who is contemplating undertaking the trip north (408–409). Thus, the long arm of legal instability among Central Americans reaches sending countries in multiple ways, eliciting responses in popular culture and artistic expressions in those locations. For instance, in El Salvador, Daniel Rucks wrote "La balada del deportado" (The ballad of the deportee), in which he tells the story of a "wetback" who begs a policeman to let him go because he does not want to go back to his homeland as a deportee and thus show that he has failed in the United States (409). When these artistic expressions are broadcast through radio and other media outlets, they can acquire transformative power.

The musical production of the Los Angeles-based group Los Jornaleros del Norte (The Day Laborers of the North) develops similar themes with a decidedly political stance and with a focus on the specific situation of day laborers. Los Jornaleros is a group composed of mostly Central American workers of different nationalities and a variety of backgrounds; they are united by the experiences at *la esquina* (the corner). As was the case for Chicano artists of previous generations, Los Jornaleros see their musical production as integral to their political work, and as a path to empowerment and social recognition. Gorodezky (1993) observes that Chicanos' quotidian experiences with U.S. racism have resulted in the production of literature and art that is characterized by its resistance and expressions of protest. Like Chicano art's powerful force in educating Chicanos about issues that affect their daily lives, Los Jornaleros seek to do the same. In this sense, Los Jornaleros not only draw from their own homelands' musical traditions and histories but also from Chicano artists' vision of conscientization and empowerment through art. Los Jornaleros's first CD, *Los Jornaleros del Norte*, includes ten compositions,[6] such as "The Ballad of Industry," "Prisoner USA," "Sí se puede," and "The Raids," which, according to the CD's cover text, the members view as songs "without borders that convey a message of hope and a true manifestation of struggle, organization, denunciation, education, and mobilization." In "The Raids" they describe the looming threat of deportation: "Raids are in style now / On all of the street corners / Immigration wants to get rid / of all the Latino people / They look for us everywhere / All afternoon and all morning." Indeed, the very origin of the group is related to an immigration raid. In March 1996, forty day laborers were waiting at a Kmart parking lot for their turn to have a medical examination at a Los Angeles County mobile clinic when immigration officers arrived in SUVs to apprehend them. Many of them ran away, but one decided to write the event into a song. They note that "from an experience of oppression, a practice of resistance and liberation was born. . . . Since then they have not stopped singing to the people" (*Los Jornaleros en Vivo*). An important goal of their musical production is to humanize immigration, particularly undocumented immigration, as well as immigration *perceived* as undocumented. According to their first CD cover, their music "puts a human face on the *esquineros*, [who are] always suspects of everything. So when you pass by groups of day laborers don't think only of the kind of work they do, the heavy and dirty work they do. Also think about the poet, the singer, the musician, the father, the son, the human being." By resorting to an art form infused with traditions from their homelands, day laborers seek to convey a more positive picture of immigrants, to transform the images of strangers and criminals into human beings, a particularly important act in a time of heightened anti-immigrant hostility and of immigrant criminalization. At the same time, through their art they transmit a decidedly political message of social justice, mobilization, struggle, and the importance of workers' rights.

In a conversation with the author, Salvadoran activist Pablo Alvarado, a founding member of Los Jornaleros and an internationally recognized organizer, cofounder of the Institute of Popular Education of Southern California, and executive director of the National Day Laborer Organizing Network, mentioned that he sees their music (as well as soccer) as an integral part of their mobilization efforts because it fosters coalition-building to create humane conditions for day laborers nationwide. Alvarado, also a main organizer of "La gran marcha," the Los Angeles pro-immigrant marches in spring 2006 in protest of congressional legislation HR

4437, said that they played their music at the march because for them it is a fundamental tool for mobilization and resistance. They have recorded their own CDs and do not have agents to promote their music. Their second CD was taped live at the rallies at the end of the spring protests. The National Day Laborer Organizing Network and its member organizations also organize day laborer cultural festivals, which bring together different art forms, including theater, poetry, music, and performances. When Alvarado received an award for his leadership in 2004, he declared that "there is no movement without culture."[7]

Specific events and individuals associated with immigration law enforcement that jeopardize the lives of Central Americans have inspired several artists. For instance, Saúl Linares, a Salvadoran factory worker and former day laborer living in Hempstead, New York, wrote a corrido, "The Ballad of Joe Arpaio," that captures his sentiments about the actions of Joe Arpaio, the Arizona sheriff known for his abusive tactics in implementing a controversial federal immigration program. Linares, who had never written a corrido in his life, penned the following ballad during a weekend retreat for immigrant-rights organizers while on a break from a "cultural night" of poems and songs:[8]

> Voy a cantarles un corrido a los presentes que le compuse a Joe Arpaio de Arizona.
> Un sinvergüenza, desgraciado, anti-inmigrante, que se ha ganado el repudio de la gente.
> Es un sheriff que está ganando mucha plata, mucho dinero que paga el contribuyente,
> Arpaio mete preso al inmmigrante porque el dice que son delincuentes pero tan sólo buscan un trabajo decente que en su país ellos no han encontrado.
> Y sin sentido y sin razón aparente por una calle encadenados los paseaba.
> Ya los latinos de Arpaio están cansados. Ya los latinos están muy organizados
> A Joe Arpaio le dicen y le repiten: sos criminal deberías estar preso
>
> [I will sing a corrido to all those who are present that I wrote for Joe Arpaio of Arizona, a shameless, disgraceful immigrant hater, who has earned the repudiation of the people.
> He is a sheriff making lots of money, lots of money at the expense of the taxpayer;
> Arpaio puts immigrants in jail because he says they are criminals, but they are only seeking a decent job, which they haven't found in their country.
> And without sense or apparent reason, he parades them in chains down the street.
> Latinos are tired of Arpaio; they tell Arpaio and then repeat, you are a criminal; you should be in jail] (Downes 2009)

A particularly critical aspect of the liminal legality in which many Central Americans live is long-term family separation. Many Central Americans left children, spouses, and parents in their home countries, a situation not uncommon among immigrants of all kinds. In the case of Central Americans, however, such separations are often unresolved and indefinite; no one in these families knows when (or if) they will see each other again. A Guatemalan day laborer in the San Francisco Bay Area spoke of a telephone conversation with his wife back in Guatemala: "I told my wife that I would definitely be home by Christmas," to which his wife responded: "Yes, but which Christmas?" (Worby n.d.). Separations without an expected outcome have a range of negative and complex consequences, from exacerbating already complicated relations between parents and children (Menjívar and Abrego 2009), to creating anxiety and instability among those who stay behind, particularly women (Menjívar and Agadjanian 2007). Even when not defined as abandonment or family dissolution (Menjívar 2006), such separations have critical repercussions for all involved, often representing a source of anxiety, sadness, and melancholy, states that are sometimes communicated through powerful artistic expressions.

In a solo performance in Los Angeles, the Salvadoran artist Carolina Rivera portrayed the role of a mother separated from her family. The artist depicts the mother's sacrifices on behalf of her children left back in El Salvador, including the poverty and dangerous living conditions in which she lives. The mother often feels lonely in the United States but finds courage and energy from knowing that her children are doing well in El Salvador. The pain of the separation is most evident when she receives photographs of her children and can no longer recognize them. Half the audience, made up of mostly of second-generation Central Americans, was in tears. Rivera's performance evoked the not uncommon emotional distress associated with indefinite family separation that many of the spectators have felt personally (Menjívar and Abrego 2009).

Similarly, Mr. Snoopy, who writes poetry (in English and Spanish) from juvenile hall, expresses the detrimental consequences he sees in his long-term separation from his parents. Mr. Snoopy is serving a twenty-five-year sentence for the shooting of a rival gang member. In a poem titled "Mi vida loca" (2000), he declares with poignant lucidity (and in line with scholarly analyses of his predicament) that a combination of having been left in the care of his grandmother in El Salvador when his parents migrated during the civil war, not having positive role models, and living in neighborhoods where gangs, drugs, and violence are rampant led him to his current situation. His writings capture vibrantly the larger frameworks that inform Central Americans' lives, conditions he interprets as shaped more by the political decisions that produce immigration law than by an individual's personal choices.

In the composition "Prisoner USA," Los Jornaleros del Norte also depict the pain of family separation linked to an unstable legal status. This song was written by a Honduran day laborer (an insert in the CD provides the English translation), but the lyrics could have been written by any other Central American or even a Mexican immigrant brought to the United States as a child.[9] "Prisoner USA" captures the detrimental consequences that "liminal legality" has for immigrants and for family members back home. The songwriter compares this state to being a prisoner in the United States, or as Lilo Gonzalez expressed earlier, as "being stuck in the United States."

> I am Honduran, I am Central American / And I'm dying to see my family
> One day I came from my country illegally / Or as a bracero, as they call us
> My brothers stayed behind / As well as my children
> And the woman I loved / One day I came to see what I could find
> It's been several years / Since I crossed the three borders
> And here I am still without papers / I ask the heavens that I might
> One day have the chance / To go back and see my loved ones
> But for the moment I must be patient / And remain a prisoner in the
> United States

Beyond the Immigrant Generation

The sociological study of generations can be traced to the seminal work on political generations of Karl Mannheim (1953). For Mannheim, individuals born at a particular time and space share experiences that have lifelong significance. Experiences shared during formative years mold a common frame of reference that can influence an entire generation. Building on the work of Mannehim, Eckstein (2004) notes that political generations should be not only understood as age-based experiences but also analyzed in terms of key historical events. In this conceptualization, social memory and selective interpretation shape how and whether generations evolve. This general conceptualization sheds light on how events in the homeland configure the experiences of various generations of immigrants. And at the receiving end we know that immigrant children and the children of immigrants have significantly different experiences from those of their parents and attach a distinct meaning to the same set of circumstances (Menjívar and Abrego 2009).

Scholars of immigration who have paid attention to the importance of generational analysis for the long-term prospects of immigrants (Fernández-Kelly and Konczal 2006; Fernández-Kelly and Schauffler 1994; Portes and Rumbaut 2001; Portes and Zhou 1993; Rumbaut and Portes 2001; Waters 1999) have noted the importance of different outlooks between immigrant parents and their children—a generation that has genealogical and demographic connotations (Rumbaut 2004). Rumbaut (2004) observes that the analytical task goes beyond that of measuring the generational remove. He notes that length of time in the United States does not only mean exposure to American life but also includes developmental stages and the context at the time of migration (Rumbaut 2004). From this research, as from Mannheim's early writings and Eckstein's work on immigrant generations, we learn that immigrant generational cohorts share significant experiences that shape their worldview and frame of reference. And although not everyone in a generational cohort will have the same understandings of their surroundings or react similarly to the same situations, the historical events and social circumstances to which they are exposed at both ends of the migration process, by virtue of their age and time of birth, give form to their experiences in particular ways and with dissimilar outcomes. Powerful developments, like legal instability, are felt beyond the first immigrant generation, but their meaning and expression will vary with the passage of time. Thus, artistic expressions that reflect marginal legality among Central Americans will take on distinctive nuances.

Salvadorans and Guatemalans, like many other immigrant children and children of immigrants, also deal with issues of identity, stereotypes, and preconceived notions about ethnicity, class, gender, race, legal status, sexual orientation, educational level, and occupation. Often experiences of isolation and exclusion lead them to create an imaginary home. Nevertheless, that home also excludes them, as they and the "home" have both changed. As Ana Patricia Rodríguez (2004) notes, the identity that 1.5 or second-generation Central Americans acquire is oftentimes a *second-hand* identity. To form an idea of homeland and have a sense of self, they must turn to what Rodríguez (n.d.) calls, "primary carriers of memory"—that is, the parents, older siblings, and relatives, as well as photographs, music, film, and other forms of material culture and information about their country. Diasporic generations then obtain filtered information mediated by the stories, memories, and texts transmitted by parents, relatives, friends, and texts of popular culture. And as is the case with the parent generation, an issue that reverberates through different aspects of the immigrant children's and the children of immigrants' existence is that of an unresolved legal status.

Central Americans born in countries of origin and raised in the United States (1.5 generation) often do not feel as if they belong in the United States, particularly when their own applications for permanent legal status are still pending after many years. The numerous deadlines, temporary permits, reapplications, inability to further their higher education, and the long waiting periods serve as strong reminders to young Central Americans that they are marked as outsiders in U.S. society, regardless of how familiar with the local culture and the English language they may be. Living in legal uncertainty is perhaps even more salient for them, as they often do not have memories of their countries of birth and have lived most of their lives in the United States. At the same time, they are often reminded that they are not full members of this society, a situation they share with other immigrants brought in as children who remain undocumented. A Salvadoran college student in Coutin's study who had obtained TPS and applied for political asylum under the terms of the *ABC* settlement explained what it feels like to live in liminal legality:

> Well, I can't say that I'm a resident, and I can't say that I'm not a resident. And then I have no memory [of El Salvador] . . . My family is real . . . As long as my family is with me, I have a home, you know? But other than that, there is nothing. There's nothing here, there's nothing there; it's a strange situation to be in. . . . Talking to people, I have no—it's like, for a minute you have no identity outside of your house. That's what it feels like sometimes. You're just walking around; you're like invisible to everything else. Everybody else is solid and you're not. (Coutin 2005, 18)

In the same vein, Baker-Cristales (2004) observes that those Salvadorans who have remained in the United States undocumented or in liminal legality do not feel at home in this country and continue to see their place of birth as home. Because of their legal uncertainty, however, they cannot travel there and thus hold on to memories and images of El Salvador as a place of belonging (2004). These Salvadorans create a "space-time dis-continuum" where images of their country of origin do not change regardless of how long they have been away. This allows them to construct an imaginary home so as to cope with issues of stress, belonging, and partial incorporation/inclusion into U.S. society (Baker-Cristales 2004). Because of a shared legal marginality, the situation is similar among Guatemalans. In her poem "Culture," Guatemalan-origin poet Leyda Garcia (a.k.a. Alma Chapina or Guatemalan Soul) writes,

Me duele el dolor de mi gente [My people's pain hurts me]
of the color line
the working-class line
the un-documented line
I choose to document Myself
to pay homage to my Mother's cracked skin
and aching back
I infuse my spirit / with her Oraciones [prayers]
a path She builds with words / that leads to Peace and Faith
Faith I need
for nothing matters
if I can't articulate the essence
holding me all together
Without essence
the pieces fit no mold . . .
the story has no ending
until I find a resting place
where Guate [Guatemala] lives
in me at peace
with ease
inside me.

(Garcia 2007, n.p.)

As Garcia's words reveal, maintaining a connection, though at times tenuous, or a "space-time dis-continuum," with the country of birth or origin as a place of belonging becomes central for those whose parents or themselves are living liminal lives. Taking a stand against the forces around her, through her writings she also chooses to "document" herself. Significantly, she does this in English, thus taking a stand to make herself socially (and politically) present in a world that attempts to erase her and keep many Guatemalans legally excluded.

Two pieces by Salvadoran-origin poets focus on the multifaceted feelings that arise out of an uncertain legal position and how this shapes the lives and incorporation of Central Americans of different generations. Born in El Salvador and raised in the United States, Jessica Grande captures the tribulations surrounding liminal legality in her work. Like Garcia above, she does so in English, thus reminding the reader of her social presence in the United States despite legal exclusion. In the "I.N.S. Series" she puts the bureaucratic aspect of these immigrants' liminal legality in a broader context, exposing the vivid experience of an encounter with the INS:

> Justice Department without grace
> sitting under marble-glass giant
> Babylon–apartheid–Central American 80s–Russian
> Hate Sentiment–Yellow Peril–Holocaust-Red
> Scare
> all under one roof trying to be residents
> brothers hold nervous sisters
> parents with extra rounded eyes
> and scarce wishes
> American Dreams turn to bitches
> perceptions of being fortunate in this country
> explode!
> Smithereens of frazzled faces
> cover the lawns of Beverly Hills Mansions
> clasping hands without rosary prayers
> counting fingertip lines to taste peace
> finger nail pieces swarm floor
> Officers pimping hopes
>
> The I.N.S. line
> go up to the front
> 20 bucks
> cheating for good news
> been here since 11:30 yesterday
> move on up
> sell the spot
>
> (Grande 2007, n.p.)[10]

Like Grande, Ana E. Miranda Maldonado was born in El Salvador and raised in New York and Los Angeles. A graduate of Stanford University School of Medicine, she says she writes to counterbalance her career as a physician. Professionally she works in medically underserved communities, and she chronicles her personal experiences through poetry. Her poem "I am that kind of Salvi" captures different facets of life permeated by uncertain legality, a life shaped by "documents," as well as the situation of those whose unresolved legal status keeps them from enjoying the benefits of society, including access to higher education.[11] She writes in English to make a point about her command of the normative language, which she juxtaposes to the obstacles facing those who live legally suspended lives,

I am that kind of Salvi / the kind that writes poems / about / El Salvador in
perfect English. / I can't recognize the melody to the Salvadoran national
anthem
but I can play the Star Spangled Banner / on the flute
and hell no / I'm not Americanized. / Estoy sin papeles [I am without
documents].
I'm without credentials, / I'm just missing my Latin American Studies degree,
my Central American Department minor, / my Chicano/Chicana Literature
transcript,
Sorry, I just have the documented proof / of my / Salvi / education . . .
my Salvadoran-ness / is undocumented. / I'm still writing my thesis:
"Seeking a Central American American identity." / I'm caught in
immigrant limbo
yes I have a green card, / yes I have a Passport, / reads: U.S. Citizen
but I'm a resident alien / in two worlds, / one commercialized / with
bling blings
and imperialist foreign policies / that I can't / afford / can't / support.
The other, / my country / from which I was torn / visions of war / in dreams
I cannot remember. / Yeah, / I'm one of those Salvis, / an enemy combatant
of the intelligencia, unlawful / resident of the / U.S.A. / United Salvi
Academy.
Hm, y que! / I'm undocumented / but I'm Salvi!

(Miranda Maldonado 2007, n.p.)

EpiCentroamerica: Central American Diasporic Art and Rumblings, a collective of young artists of Central American origin, define themselves as *epicentros*, or epicenters, a metaphor they use to convey the idea that they come from the center and extend outwardly in resonant ways through the work they produce. They define their group as "an organic literary collective straddling performance, spoken word and testimonial art forms composed of inter-generational community-minded cultural activists of Central American extraction that write to resurrect memory and inspire action. These Central American bodies in flux and immigrant voices rise from Hollywood bus stops, volcanic ashes, quetzal wings, peripheral MacArthur Park, Mission pupuserias (12) y mas."[12] Their poems, paintings, music, and performances often convey a sense of in-betweenness, of not fully belonging, but also of responsibility, as the second-generation Guatemalan-origin poet Maya Chinchilla explained to me: "Yes, the epicentros feel a sense of responsibility for being the first to do a lot of things here, and knowing at the same time that their parents have shielded them from all the stuff that happened back home. It's a lot to carry and some resort to writing poetry to express this position." In their work, the epicentros also feature themes related to their homelands' wars and civil conflicts that so fundamentally have shaped their lives.

Often the young Central Americans intersperse their prose with themes directly related to legal ambiguity as well as with other subjects that to them are Central American–specific, such as establishing an identity separate from a Mexican one or dispelling stereotypes about their group. Salvadoran-origin poet Ana Elisa Margarita Payes-Santacruz's (2000) poem "Who Am I?" captures this recurring theme, which she wrote in the English language,

> I may be brown, / But that doesn't mean I'm dirty . . .
> . . . I am an immigrant, / but that doesn't make me illegal
> I am from El Salvador, / but I won't be cleaning your house . . .
> . . . I'm a young Latina, / but I'm not gang banging or having babies left
> and right
> I speak Spanish, / but no, I'm not Mexican

Second-generation poet Raquel Gutierrez (2004) discusses what it means to be the child of Salvadoran immigrants when ties to the homeland are made even more tenuous by the scant information that "the primary carriers of memory," her parents, provide. Often parents try to protect the children from painful memories, and children are left with complex views of the homeland as a strange yet intimate place. Gutierrez's "El viento aventado," which she wrote half in Spanish and half in English, voices her feelings when her mother tells her stories about El Salvador during the times of the civil war:

> Y estos vientos de Octubre
> (And what about those October winds)
> pienso que es algo muy esotérico
> (I think it's something so esoteric)
> que se yo de algo tan Salvadoreño?
> (what do I know about something so Salvadoran?)
> Estar hablando de vientos y de papalotes
> (To be talking about winds and kites)
> Es algo muy extraño para mi
> (It's something very strange to me)
> Pero es que no dicen "papalotes"
> (But they don't call them "papalotes")
> Se dice "piscuchas"
> (They call them "piscuchas")
> Saber que sera eso, solo se
> (I don't know what that is, all I know is)
> Que en Ingles se dice "kite"
> (That in English it is called "kite")
> They fly kites in El Salvador?
> Like in the middle of the war and shit?
> That's what goes on in the mind of a daughter

Who looks at her mother like she's crazy . . .
But I don't even know the national anthem . . .

(Morales 2001, n.p.)

And then there are the experiences with identity formation of those second-generation Central Americans of mixed parentage. Sometimes they include in their work a mix of painful memories of the war and the legacy of liminal lives, but more important, their work reflects efforts to construct identities at the seams of the different parts that make up their selves. Their work tends to highlight common challenges faced by all second-generation immigrants, like making use of traditional expressions from their parents' homelands in their work. For instance, the poet and activist Anayvette Martinez, whose father is Salvadoran and mother is Nicaraguan, writes about her Central American heritage in contrast to a Mexican one through the use of colloquialisms and sayings that differ by country but that, according to her, make us all one, which is more beautiful than its parts. And the painter Dalila Mendez, who is half Salvadoran and half Guatemalan, resorts to vibrant colors and Mayan-inspired compositions and ancestral imaginary to depict aspects of her experience as well as that of those in similar positions. In her work Mendez accentuates the presence of a long line of strong women in her family, an experience she shares with other Central Americans, as women have figured prominently as pioneers in the migration.

Conclusion

In this chapter I have touched on different forms of Central American art in the United States and have focused on only one theme common to them. Although present in those aesthetic expressions and intertwined with the theme explored in this chapter, the subjects of the war and political dislocation were not discussed here. Similarly, I did not include an analysis of ethnic, gender, and other identities that also emerge in the art of Central Americans living in the United States. These limitations aside, I observe that the artistic production of Central American immigrants reveals in potent ways a history of displacement, disruption, and uncertainty. To use Meena Alexander's words, this is "art born of dislocation, art that enshrines disjunction" (1996, 152). These artists' work reenacts those aspects of their lives that would otherwise be invisible to others. Their poems, prose, lyrics, paintings, and performances create spaces that bring out important experiences about migration, some of which are Central American–specific. As in life, their art reflects the interconnections between an uncertain legal status, the civil wars, and political conflicts, but I focused only on the recurrent theme of legal instability and what it means to those who live it. Through their work, artists fuse this subject to other aspects of the context in which they live, including work, school, family separation, and the construction and affirmation of different identities. An examination of their art reveals that an ambiguous legality remains a defining force for the immigrant generation as well as for the generations raised or born in the United

States. As such, it will continue to shape these immigrants' views and aspirations and will become part of the cultural repertoire to which future generations of Central Americans will look as they shape their own identities.

Although immigrant children and children of immigrants also produce work inspired by the trials and hardships that accompany an unstable legal status, a concern with identity reaffirmation permeates their work as well. After all, these are children whose daily lives are punctuated by reminders of their ethnicity, of who they are (and who they are not), and thus they vividly capture in their art the ambiguities associated with these other aspects of their identity. The 1.5 generation of Central American writers and poets often write in the English language, in "perfect" English as some note, an act that underscores the contradictions in their lives. As such, this is perhaps one of the most telling features of their experience: while perfectly fluent in the English language after spending most of their lives in the United States, their legality remains uncertain; they are socially present but legally excluded (see Coutin 2000, 2005).

And the aesthetic expressions of Central Americans are not homogeneous. Some artists see their production as a shelter, a refuge, a space in which they can express their sentiments, joys, ups and downs, and desires. Others make their art part of their pursuit to change the world around them; for them, art becomes an instrument for social change and resistance. Still others see their art as bringing together communities and establishing a universal language through which they can communicate and understand one another. Furthermore, these artists produce and share their work in diverse forms, including galleries, protests, home-produced publications, and sometimes their work remains a private, intimate affair.

Day laborers, teachers, housecleaners, students, intellectuals, and those who produce aesthetic work for a living express themselves through art forms. Those who immigrated as adults, those who immigrated as children, and those who were born in the United States turn to art as a means to poetically inscribe their experiences. In any shape or form, artistic expression among Central Americans is framed in a world shaped by broader structures and multiple inequalities. Aesthetic manifestations are thus a product of social experiences and are outlined by the broader context in which they are produced. Indeed, the very act of producing their art is shaped by the forces that brought them to the United States as well as by those that keep them from realizing their dreams and aspirations—as Rosario, the woman at the beginning of this essay, eloquently explained to me years ago through her metaphors.

NOTES

I would like to express my gratitude to several individuals who graciously shared their views and provided me with excellent comments on this manuscript. Pablo Alvarado, Maya Chinchilla and Leisy Abrego deserve special recognition, as do the editors, Paul DiMaggio and Patricia Fernández-Kelly. None bears any responsibility for what I ultimately did.

1. Perhaps, as Raymond Williams would argue (O'Connor 2006), "poetic" language does not necessarily stand in opposition to ordinary language, as both are part of a wide range of

writing. More important than attempting to make that distinction is the special meaning that language possesses, as it can capture a multitude of feelings and express emergent aspects of social life.

2. For a thorough discussion of how the social and political conditions in Central America influences the work of artists there, see Goldman (1994). Goldman also includes detailed information about the work of Central American artists in exile in the region, such as Guatemalan-born artists and critics who work in Costa Rica.

3. This does not occur only in the United States. Back in their country, for instance, Salvadoran rappers also resort to popular music to expose social injustices. An admirer of Snoop Dogg and 50 Cent, Wilfredo Laínez, from his hometown in rural El Salvador, uses rap lyrics to denounce injustices to his community and his country (http://www.elfaro.net/secciones/podcasts/20080707/podcast.asp#podcast).

4. This book has been published in both English and Spanish.

5. Similarly, the Central American migration experience has been the basis of other works of art by non–Central American artists. For instance, the Houston Grand Opera "put the mirror of art" on the immigrant community of Houston with the production *The Refuge,* based on the life of a Salvadoran immigrant woman but written and interpreted by non-Salvadorans (Blumenthal 2007).

6. Their compositions are interpreted with catchy melodies in Spanish, but the insert on the CD has the English translation of the songs. I use these translations.

7. See http://leadershipforchange.org/awardees/.

8. Downes, the *New York Times* reporter who wrote about Linares's ballad, noted that at first Linares threw away the song but was then persuaded to retrieve it and save it. The next day, with guitarist Francisco Pacheco, they played it in a bathroom, for better acoustics, to record it on a portable recorder (Downes 2009).

9. Hondurans were granted TPS after Hurricane Mitch devastated large parts of their country in 1998; the status has been renewed a few times, and it is currently set to expire on July 5, 2010.

10. This is the layout of the poem in the original—the last paragraph is centered.

11. Short for "Salvadoran," "Salvi" is a term 1.5 and second-generation Salvadorans use to refer to themselves.

12. See http://epicentroamerica.blogspot.com.

CHAPTER 10

Negotiating Memories of War

ARTS IN VIETNAMESE AMERICAN COMMUNITIES

Yen Le Espiritu

By most accounts, Vietnam was the site of one of the most brutal and destructive wars between Western imperial powers and the people of Asia, Africa, and Latin America. Thirty years (1945–1975) of warfare destruction, coupled with another twenty years of postwar U.S. trade and aid economic embargo, cost Vietnam at least three million lives, shattered its economy and society, left the country among the poorest in the world, and scattered its people to different corners of the globe. And yet in the United States, public recollections of the Vietnam War—"the war with the difficult memory" (Sturken 1997, 122)—involve the highly organized and strategic forgetting of the Vietnamese people. As scholars, public historians, and the media have repeatedly documented, Vietnamese bodies, both during and after the war, have not been accorded the same humanity and dignity given to American bodies. The highly controversial Vietnam War Memorial, commissioned to commemorate and memorialize the U.S. soldiers who fought in Vietnam, provides a pointed example of this "forgetting." Framed within the nationalist context of the Washington Mall, the memorial must necessarily "forget" the Vietnamese and "remember" the American veterans as the primary victims of the war (Sturken 1997). Because the memorial is a key site where U.S. cultural memory of the Vietnam War is reproduced and debated, the Vietnamese become unmentionable in this context: "They are conspicuously absent in their roles as collaborators, victims, enemies, or simply the people in whose land and over whom (supposedly) this war was fought" (Sturken 1997, 62). Without creating an opening for a Vietnamese perspective of the war, these public commemorations of the Vietnam War refuse to remember Vietnam as a historical site, Vietnamese people as genuine subjects, and the Vietnam War as having any kind of integrity of its own (Desser 1991).

On the other hand, as a people fleeing from the only war that the United States had lost, Vietnamese have been subject to intense scholarly interest—an "overdocumented" population when compared to other U.S. immigrant groups. Indeed, the 1975 cohort, as state-sponsored refugees, may be the most studied arrival cohort in U.S. immigration history (Rumbaut 2000, 180). But as Ralph Ellison ([1952] 1981) reminds us, the highly visible can actually be a type of invisibility.[1] Conceptualizing the arrival of Vietnamese refugees primarily as a problem to be solved, most studies have fixated on their adjustment, with successful adjustment defined as the achievement of self-sufficiency (Espiritu 2006a). Scholars have also zealously documented the refugees' "damaged" psyche, portraying them as passive and pathetic, "incapacitated by grief and therefore in need of care" (DuBois 1993, 4–5). It is striking how the bulk of this literature locates the Vietnamese "problem" not in the violent legacy of decades of war and social upheaval, but within the bodies and minds of the Vietnamese themselves. This hyperfocus on the refugees' needs and neediness has made "un-visible" other important facets of Vietnamese personhood: their self-identity, their dreams for themselves, their hopes for their children, and their "ground of being." In short we know more about how scholars have constructed Vietnamese, but less about how Vietnamese have created their worlds and made meaning for themselves, including their own understanding of the Vietnam War and its aftermath.

Scholars of war memory have repeatedly shown that memory activities are never politically disinterested, but are always already mediated and shaped by relations of power (Fujitani, White, and Yoneyama 2001; Tai 2001). Elsewhere I have argued that the erasure of the war's costs borne by the Vietnamese constitutes an organized and strategic forgetting of a war that "went wrong," enabling "patriotic" Americans to push military intervention as key in America's self-appointed role as the world's protector of democracy, liberty, and equality (Espiritu 2006b). Casting Vietnamese as objects of rescue, immigration and refugee studies scholars have likewise refused to treat Vietnamese in the United States as genuine subjects, with their own history, culture, heritage, and political agendas (Espiritu 2006a). In this chapter, I move beyond a critique of this dominant knowledge to explore how Vietnamese American artists, through their critical memory work, have created alternative memories and epistemologies that unsettle and challenge the established public narratives of the Vietnam War and Vietnamese people. I am particularly interested in the strategic role of arts, broadly defined, in making social, public, and collective remembering possible, and in reforming sociopolitical realities (Fujitani, White, and Yoneyama 2001, 16). As a medium that gives us a record of the culture of a period, arts can be a means of reclaiming the past by making present other memories that have been pushed to the margins. As Lisa Lowe and others have argued, "Culture is a . . . mediation of history, the site through which the past returns and is remembered, however fragmented, imperfect, or disavowed" (Lowe 1996, x). This critical remembering is key to the formation of oppositional narratives and "to the imagination and rearticulation of new forms of political subjectivity, collectivity, and practice" (158).

Much of traditional Western art criticism has been deeply ambivalent about mixing art and politics, placing them in different realms of human endeavor (Selz 2006, 29). For racialized communities who have had to struggle for access to means of representation, "the question of aesthetic representation is always also a debate about political representation" (Lowe 1996, 4). As Elaine Kim (2003) suggests, many Asian American artists are committed to a cultural politics that challenges, resists, and hopes to transform U.S. nationalized memory and culture. War has been a major subject of Western art, with most representations of war glorifying and lionizing a nation's warriors for sacrificing their lives for their countries (Selz 2006, 35). However, since the devastating bombing of World War II, art protesting war, specifically the military slaughter of whole populations, has proliferated, reaching an unprecedented level of intensity with the Vietnam War (39). In recent years, Vietnamese American artists have begun to grapple with the war's disastrous consequences for Vietnam and its people, giving rise to oft-haunting artistic and cultural representations that imagine, remember, and trace the complex genealogies of war and forced displacements that precede and shape Vietnamese resettlement in the United States. As such, I am interested in Vietnamese American cultural forms for what they can reveal and expand on the tensions, irresolutions, and contradictions of Vietnamese American lives.

To take seriously Vietnamese standpoints on the war and its aftermath is to critically examine the relationship between history and memory, not as facts but as narratives. Like other communities in exile, Vietnamese in the United States feel keenly the urgency to forge unified histories, identities, and memories. Given the innumerable losses suffered by Vietnamese in the diaspora, and the ongoing erasure of South Vietnamese accounts of the war not only in the United States but also in Vietnam,[2] it is not surprising that Vietnamese American public retellings of their history often take the form of "anti-communism." Repeatedly we read media accounts of Vietnamese boycotting Vietnam-produced books, magazines, videos, and television broadcasts, waving American flags while shouting anticommunist slogans, denouncing human rights violations committed by the "corrupt" and "heartless rulers of Vietnam," and plotting the overthrow of the communist government.[3] In her ethnographic study of the San Diego's Vietnamese community, Thuy Vo Dang (2005) suggests that first-generation Vietnamese deploy the rhetoric of anticommunism in part to keep alive their history and memories of the war and of South Vietnam, lest it be further forgotten by the American public and/or the next generation of Vietnamese Americans. As Nguyen-Vo Thu-Huong (2005, 170) observes, "Vietnamese Americans as refugees occupy the position of self-mourners because no one else mourns us." At the same time, it is important to recognize that this "anticommunist" stance is also a narrative, adopted in part because it is the primary political language with which Vietnamese refugees, as objects of U.S. rescue fantasies, could tell their history and be understood from within the U.S. social and political landscape. Other political exiles, most notably Cuban Americans, have similarly adopted a vocal anticommunist position as a way to keep alive the memories of their losses (Grenier and Perez 2003).

At the same time, I am concerned that the media's hyperfocus on the Vietnamese "anticommunist" stance reduces the multifaceted histories of the Vietnam War and of Vietnamese lives into a single story about communist persecution. At this moment of reinvigorated U.S. imperialism, this anticommunist slant—that Vietnamese communists create refugees while Americans save them—has the potential to remake the case for the appropriateness of U.S. war in Vietnam and, by extension, its continued military interventionism in the world (Espiritu 2006b). As a counterpoint, I examine artworks that identify what has been removed from U.S. historical memory of the Vietnam War, that imagine alternatives to this dominant historical knowledge, and that give rise to new forms of Vietnamese American subjectivity and community. I have selected the artworks of three Vietnam-born artists who arrived in the United States as refugees at a relatively young age: visual artist Long Nguyen; spoken word artist Bao Phi; and writer lê thi diem thúy. Born in Vietnam but raised primarily in the United States, these artists' lives encapsulate the ambiguous but potentially productive state of "in-betweeness" inhabited by most Vietnamese refugees—of being between the old and the new, between languages, between homes, and between lives. Because these artworks refer repeatedly to history and politics, they demand that we confront the sad and violent history that exists between Vietnam and the United States, and the politics of translocated race, gender, and class that springs from this past.

All three artists featured in this chapter came to the United States as refugees: Bao Phi as part of the first wave who left Vietnam by plane just hours before and after the "fall of Saigon"; and Long Nguyen and lê thi diem thúy as part of the "boat people" exodus that took place from the end of 1975 to the beginning of the 1980s. Although the Vietnamese elites comprised the majority of the first wave, there were also many others with more modest means, like Phi's family, who were swept into this exodus.[4] In contrast, the largely poorer and less educated second-wave refugees fled Vietnam on crowded, leaky small fishing boats in a hazardous attempt to get to neighboring countries by sea.[5] The horrors of their flight captured the attention of the world: An estimated 10 to 50 percent died en route, victims of starvation, drowning, rape, and robbery (Freeman 1989; Viviani 1984). As survivors of war, all three artists' works are marked by emotionally charged recollections and at times (re)constructions of traumatic memories—of the visible tragedies as well as the hidden injuries that are part and parcel of war and flight. As countersites to U.S. national memory and culture, these artworks focus intently on fragmentation, loss, and dispersal brought about by war and displacement, but also on survival, critical re-membering, and the forging of complex relationships fashioned out of "peace" and resettlement.

"The Endings That Are Not Over": Long Nguyen on War Memories

Soon after the fall of Saigon in April 1975, U.S. media inundated the American public with images of desperate and frantic Vietnamese, wailing with pain, grief, and terror as they scrambled to escape "communist Vietnam" at any costs (Espiritu 2006b).[6] In particular, images of the boat people exodus—of Vietnamese on overcrowded rickety boats, attacked at sea by brutal pirates, and languishing in overflowing makeshift refugee camps—have become icons in the American consciousness, visually inscribing the refugees as only victims in the American imaginary. In a study of the representation of Southeast Asian refugees in academic and popular discourse, Thomas DuBois (1993, 5) notes in particular a fascination with refugee escape narratives, with "the events belonging to the escape itself presented in minute detail," while the events preceding or following the escape "are narratively telescoped into mere hints or allusion."[7] Refugee camp studies further bolster this crisis model, as researchers repeatedly portray refugees as abject figures who suffer not only the trauma of forced departure but also the boredom, uncertainty, despair, and helplessness induced by camp life (Chan and Loveridge 1987; Harding and Looney 1977; Kelly 1977; Tenhula 1991).

Viet Thanh Nguyen argues that Vietnamese bodies "have been the silent spectacle on which American historical writing has been staged"—a potential resolution to the unfinished U.S. debate over the "difficult memory" of the Vietnam War (1997, 607). In particular, the images of the spectacular suffering of the boat people visually and discursively transformed them from a body victimized by decades of U.S. warfare in Vietnam to one persecuted solely by the Vietnamese communist government. In numerous news accounts, reporters repositioned the United States as a valiant rescuer of fleeing Vietnamese, all the while ignoring its role in bringing about the "refugee crisis" in the first place (Espiritu 2006b). In the same way, refugee studies scholars often pair the construct of Vietnamese as passive objects of sympathy with a plea for the West to "assume an active role in caring, counseling, or intervening" (DuBois 1993, 4). An example of one such call to action: "The immediate moral responsibility of the Western world to relieve the increasing intensity of the sufferings of thousands of Indochinese refugees in transit camps in Hong Kong as well as those in the other major countries of first asylum in Southeast Asia, cannot be overexaggerated. Any further delay on the part of the western countries . . . will certainly allow an experience in transit to degenerate into one of 'no exit'" (Chan and Loveridge 1987, 757).

Such calls to action naturalize and buttress the United States' self-appointed role as rescuer, whose magnanimity promises swift deliverance from a bleak life of "no exit" to one of boundless possibilities. Not only does this construct represent the Vietnamese as only passive recipients of such generosity, it also precludes any critical examination of U.S. role in creating and sustaining the refugee "crisis" (Palumbo-Liu 1999, 235).

Dominant U.S. narratives also control dissonant memories of the Vietnam War by representing the war and its aftermath as being contained within a specific timeframe (and space)—and as being over and done with. Such an approach conceals the costs borne by the Vietnamese, both in Vietnam and in the diaspora, that linger long after the "ending" of the war in 1975. Against this dominant remembering of the fall of Saigon as the war's unambiguous conclusion, we need to ask: When does war end and who gets to decide? Through his paintings and sculptures that communicate the trauma of wartime refugee's life, visual artist Long Nguyen "remembers" an alternative temporality—one that emphasizes the war's irreconcilability and ongoingness, which has the effect of bringing to the fore the living effects of what seems to be over and done with. Born in Vietnam in 1958, Long Nguyen grew up in Nha Trang, a seaside resort in South Vietnam. Soon after the United States' last-ditch efforts to airlift Americans and Vietnamese allies out of Saigon in late April 1975, Long and his family, along with thousands of refugees, fled Vietnam in boats for neighboring Asian countries. After their boat's engine failed at sea—a small boat that was improbably crammed with four thousand passengers—a Danish vessel rescued and transported them to a refugee camp in Hong Kong. By late August 1975, Nguyen and his family were flown to Fort Chaffee, Arkansas, and eventually settled in Memphis, Tennessee, to join an aunt who had left Saigon with her husband prior to 1975. After graduating college with a degree in civil engineering and working for a stint as an engineer, Nguyen moved to San Jose to pursue his passion and talent for art. He earned his MFA in 1985 from San Jose State University's master of fine arts program, and has since shown his work throughout California and the United States.[8]

Much of Nguyen's paintings feature Vietnam in various stages of being scorched and blackened; the paintings also convey the senses of irrevocable loss and yearning that he felt for Vietnam. Central to his work are his childhood recollections of the war and his flight from Vietnam. In the early 1990s, as Nguyen began to address his actual life experience as a Vietnamese refugee, he switched to using water imagery prominently in his work, which symbolizes in part the danger of leaving Vietnam. Moreover, in Vietnamese the word for "water" and the word for "homeland," "country," and "nation" are the same: nu 'o'c (Huynh 1997, vii). In his 1991 *Homage to the Boat People* (fig. 10.1), Nguyen paints two panels in rich, mineral blue: the smaller left panel depicts a cyclone, a symbol of unmitigated destructive force; the right panel features three flayed, disembodied heads. The heads are transported on a vessel floating on a fiery river past flaming branches, "as though on a journey through purgatory" (Northrup 2003, 25).

In 1991 Nguyen began his remarkable "Tales of Yellow Skin" series. Nguyen names the series after a popular Vietnamese antiwar song, "Vietnamese Girl with Yellow Skin," written by Vietnam's beloved songwriter Trinh Cong Son, that tells the story of a village girl killed by a stray bullet, her blood flowing over her yellow skin. The young girl died before she ever experienced love. Inspired by the song, Nguyen began to work on a series of paintings in all shades of yellow. The series addresses the terrifying experiences of his past, alluding to destruction and fragmentation, incorporating organs, fragments of the body, and aspects of nature, most significantly water, fire, and cyclones (Northrup 2003, 13). In 1992 he produced a suite of four similarly composed paintings. *Tales of Yellow Skin #5–8* depict stacked body parts: heaps of hands on one (fig. 10.2), heads on another (fig. 10.3), and organs on yet another.

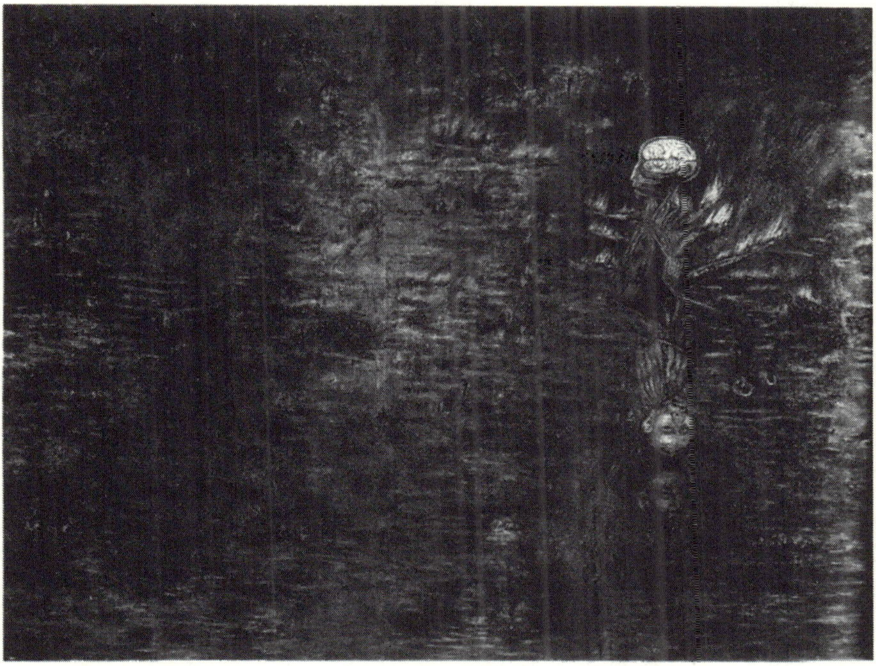

Figure 10.1. Long Nguyen, *Homage to the Boat People*, 1991. Courtesy of the artist.

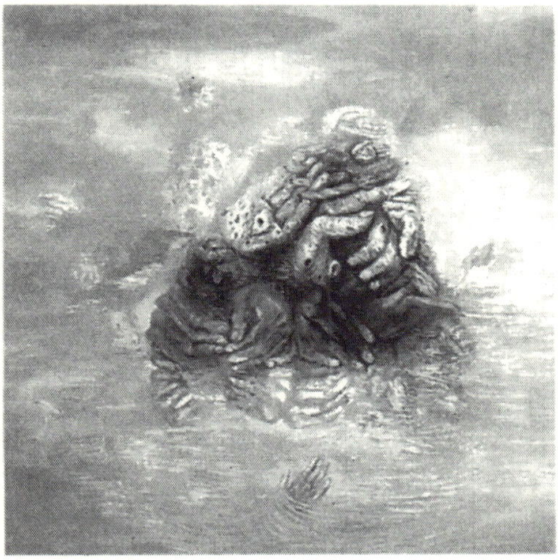

Figure 10.2. Long Nguyen, *Tales of Yellow Skin #6*, 1992. Courtesy of the artist.

Featuring bones, tendons, and intestinal coils, and tackling directly the recurring nightmares of a people that emerged from and out of the ruins of war, Nguyen's work rejects the "disappearing" of the Vietnamese war experiences, reminding us that violence cannot be easily resolved by the process of resettlement

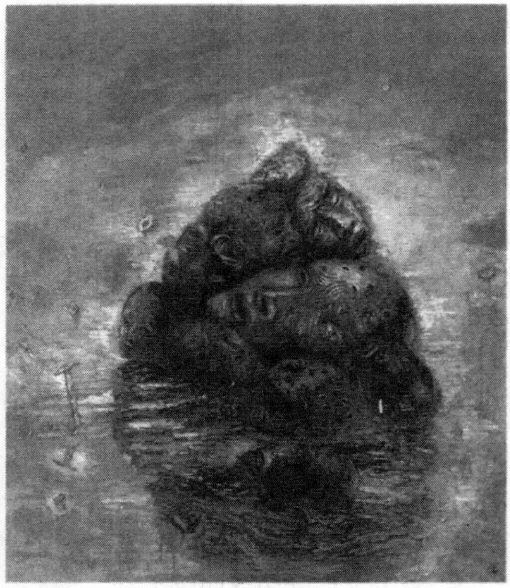

Figure 10.3. Long Nguyen, *Tales of Yellow Skin #7*, 1992. Courtesy of the artist.

or by the passage of time. The violence of that time and space spills onto the canvas, refusing to be contained—to be over and done with. These paintings, produced in the early 1990s, almost twenty years after the "end" of the Vietnam War, suggest that the war is indeed not over and that the memories continue to linger, haunting the lives of those who once inhabited that space and time. Unlike the scholarly literature that depicts Vietnamese refugees as pathetic subjects, Nguyen's paintings take on trauma in a more productive manner. Instead of featuring traumatized refugees, in which the refugees are conceptualized only in relation to pain, suffering, and distress, Nguyen's depiction of trauma disrupts the U.S. myth of "rescue and liberation" that narrates resettlement in the United States as the "happy ending" to the refugee story—a tale that "forgets" the U.S. role in generating the refugee flight in the first place (Espiritu 2006b). Although not overly political, Nguyen's gut-wrenching paintings prod the viewer to remember—and in that remembering to pay attention to what modern history has rendered ghostly, and to call into the being the seething presence of the things that appear to be not there (Gordon 1997).

"We Colored Boys": Bao Phi on Emerging Ties and Lives

In May 1975, soon after the arrival of the first wave of Vietnamese refugees, a Harris poll found that the majority of Americans did not welcome them: more than 50 percent of those polled felt that the refugees should be excluded; only 26 percent favored their entry (Rose 1985, 205). And yet, by the early 1980s scholars, along with the mass media and policymakers, began to praise the newly arrived Vietnamese as the desperate-turned-successful—that is, as the newest "model minority."[9] This model minority designation is misleading since the economic status of the majority of Vietnamese Americans, especially of the post-1978 arrivals, is characterized by low-status minimum-wage employment, dependence on public assistance, and participation in the unstable informal economy (Gold and Kibria 1993; Ong and Umemoto 1994; Zhou 2001). As a predominantly working-poor population with limited human capital and human resources, many second-wave Vietnamese refugees have resettled in low-income minority neighborhoods that have borne the brunt of governmental neglect, social isolation, and persistent poverty. Their location and isolation in these neighborhoods has spawned bitter conflicts but also promising affiliations with similarly marginalized peoples of color.

Since the 1960s scholars and policymakers have wielded the model minority concept as an ideological weapon to chastise and discipline poor black and brown communities for perceived persistent problems of poverty, unemployment, and crime.[10] More insidiously, some researchers suggest that the newly arrived Vietnamese refugees, especially those who live in underprivileged and underserved neighborhoods, succeed precisely because they refuse to adopt the wayward habits of their American neighbors, many of whom are people of color. As an example, Nathan Caplan, John Whitmore, and Marcella Choy (1989, 132) contend that "the refugees see not only the necessity to rely on their own cultural value system for guidance but also the need to insulate themselves from the behavioral and value standards of their nonrefugee neighbors." Freeman (1995, 73) concurs that Vietnamese refugees "try to insulate themselves from lower-class minorities, whom they associate with low education and poor paying jobs." In their study of second-generation youth living in a poor, biracial New Orleans neighborhood, Zhou and Bankston (1998) similarly conclude that the most successful Vietnamese youth are those who show "strong adherence to traditional family" and who are not influenced by their African American neighbors. Instead of critically interrogating interminority differentials and relations, these studies collectively represent Vietnamese Americans as "exemplars for other, culturally challenged minorities," thereby encouraging a Vietnamese American subjectivity formed in part through a competitive distancing from other groups of color (Kim 2000–2001, 35, 44). Moreover, the focus on interminority competition over scarce resources leaves uninterrogated the reasons for their blighted conditions in the first place.

Because Vietnamese Americans, and Asian Americans more generally, continue to be held up as the model for others to emulate, it is important that we understand how they are racialized relatively to yet differently from other groups of color. In a generative study of black-Korean conflict, Claire Kim (2000) argues that blacks, whites, and Koreans get positioned relative to each other, with blacks portrayed as the pathological underclass, Korean merchants as the hardworking minority, and whites as neutral enforcers of colorblind justice. In another example, Leland Saito (1998) shows how interethnic contacts shape the formation of individual groups; in this case, how Asian-Latino interactions help determine what it means to be "Asian American" and "Latino" in the San Gabriel Valley. Writing against the expectation of interminority conflict and competition, these scholars among others point to emerging "lines of affiliation, channels of communication, and spaces of transmission" among communities of color that have been forged out of their shared experiences with racialization and underclass stigmatization (Machida 2003, xv; Marquez 2004). In so doing, they explain how the conditions of Asian American lives are connected to and shaped by the condition of others' lives—and how this recognition of interconnectedness can birth new cross-racial communities. The focus on interminority connections thus challenges traditional assumptions of communities based on nationality, ethnicity, and familial ties and reveals that the processes of community formation are always socially situated and (re)constituted in relation to historical and material differences. In other words, communities are "constellations of social relations" that are "open, porous, invented and particularized as a product of interaction" (Massey 1999, 41).

Focusing on "lines of affiliation," spoken word artist Bao Phi's poetry eloquently calls for the forging of new ties and lives out of the ruins of America's "war zones"—both here and in Southeast Asia. In a shout-out to Phi, Ishle Park (2006) exclaims that Phi "is on a mission to keep us all knit tight, and to remind us how we are quilted together in this cold country."[11] Park's words nicely encapsulate Phi's raw and rough-edged but also tender and quiet poetry that mixes his fearless politics about race and class with resolute optimism in the power of love and community. Born in Vietnam, Phi fled Vietnam with his family in 1975 and resettled directly in Phillips, a poor Minneapolis neighborhood that was predominantly Native American and African American. As a student in an inner-city school dominated by students of color, Phi became cognizant of race and class privilege—a recurring theme in his poetry—when he met wealthier white students who were bused into his school for "integration": "[I] noticed that they sat around talking about the cars that their parents had just bought for them and all this other stuff while the rest of us were of lower income. I think that when you're a kid and you grow up around poor people of color, that's just kind of your life, and then when you meet other people whose lives are different, you're just like 'damn'" (Chen 2005).

Coming of age during the early 1990s, Phi—and subsequently his poetry—was also deeply affected by the interconnections between race, war, and violence as manifested in the first Persian Gulf War, the Rodney King beating, and the Los Angeles riots: "All of these things came to a point where I could either shut my eyes and not see what was going on or I could really ask why this was" (Chen 2005). A graduate of Macalester College, Phi has won the Minnesota Grand Poetry Slam twice and two poetry slams at the Nuyorican Poets Café in New York. He remains the only Vietnamese American man to have appeared on HBO's "Russell Simmons Presents Def Poetry" and to have placed at the National Poetry Slam Individual Finalists Stage, where he ranked sixth overall out of over 250 national slam poets.

In "For Colored Boys in Danger of Sudden Unexplained Nocturnal Death Syndrome and All the Rest for Whom Considering Suicide Is Not Enuf,"[12] a poem about growing up as a young man of color in Phillips, Phi furiously condemns the blighted conditions of his neglected neighborhood but also tenderly discloses the fierce love and loyalty that "we boys, colored boys" have developed for and with each other in this inner-city "war zone":

> We boys, colored boys, who ran through the streets
> with heads spinning, languages spilling into summer
> sticking into cracks on the sidewalks,
> pulling up weeds with our laughter

Growing up in poverty, largely unwanted and forgotten, trying to survive—these multilingual "colored boys" shielded each other against the raining batons of police brutality and the violence of meaningless and demeaning work:

> They told us the sky above our heads is the same
> but we knew this wasn't true
> the first time it rained
> batons
> we were the only ones getting wet.
> . . .
> We colored boys, who forged our IDs
> to lie about our age and work for minimum wage
> unpacking dirt kissed vegetables,
> rotating daily products,
> working to pay bills that misspelled our parents' names

It is this double move—of calling attention to both the racialized urban poverty and the emerging ties and lives—that keeps Phi's poetry from being read as a depoliticized celebration of multicultural America where people of all colors embrace each other as equals. Other working-class young men of color, such as second-generation Cubans and Arabs, have likewise chosen to reaffirm ties with other "colored boys" (Fernández-Kelly, this volume; Jamal, this volume).

Urban America has also rendered young men of color "ghostly"—leaving their seething presence un-visible and their violent death un-mourned. Phi penned "For Colored Boys in Danger" in part to expose this ghostliness: "how . . . being a young man of color meant . . . not being missed when you passed on":[13]

> I had a dream that we never woke up
> and the world didn't miss us
> the sons of fathers
> who died in their sleep
> hearts trying to keep up to the beating drum
> of a land that did not want them dancing

Living in a world that does not "want them dancing" and does not miss their passing, these young men of color, "who have all the heart to feel love and none of the words to say it," occupy the position of self-mourners, "hid[ing] each other in the maps of [their] memory." It is there in their memory that they hold fast to each other's fears and dreams, awaiting opportunities for public retellings that sometimes come in the form of suicide/murder as they insist on being "found":

> B____, the only way he could get close to the world
> was to jump down from a bridge
> to embrace it
> like a red winged angel
> no one came looking for him
> so he went to be found

Importantly, in "For Colored Boys in Danger," Phi connects the "war zone" of urban America to that of Southeast Asia, linking the death of "colored boys" in Phillips to that of Southeast Asian refugee men who succumb to sudden unexplained nocturnal death syndrome (SUNDS)—a medically unexplainable sudden death that has been associated with war trauma, survivor guilt, and relocation depression:

> I had a dream
> that we told our stories
> in sleep
> and the demons came
> to sleep on our chests
> before we could finish

This pairing—of the war in Southeast Asia and the war in urban America—makes visible the relationship between global and domestic structures of violence and inequality. In recent years, the best works in Asian American studies have placed the social and political formation of Asians in the United States in dialectical relation to international histories and locations (Lowe and Kim 1997; Nguyen 1997; Palumbo-Liu 1999). This innovative body of scholarship—by situating Asian American studies within an "international" frame—rejects the domestication of Asian American studies, displaces the United States as the sole nexus of historical change, and boldfaces the history of U.S. settler colonialism and imperialism in Asia and elsewhere. In connecting the colored boys' suicide to the war-induced SUNDS, Phi is suggesting that the U.S. wars in Southeast Asia, haphazard resettlement policies and practices, and neglect of urban neighborhoods are linked; and that it is this cumulative violence that has profoundly affected "colored boys" in urban America—both the living and the dead, as well as the living dead. Against these conditions of un-visibility, Phi implores us to ask, "What happened to their dreams?" for it is in the asking that we remember to retell their stories so that they would not be "lost to sleep."

"Structure of Feeling": lê thi diem thúy on Family Making

Most popular and scholarly writings on immigrant families tend to naturalize intergenerational tension, attributing it to the "culture clash" between "traditional" immigrant parents and their more Americanized children (Lowe 1996, 60–63). I examine intergenerational strain not as a private matter between Vietnamese immigrant parents and their children, but as a social, historical, and transnational affair that exposes multiple and interrelated forms of power relations. British cultural materialist Raymond Williams (1977) coined the concept "structure of feeling" to define social experiences that are often not "recognized as social but taken to be private, idiosyncratic, and even isolating" (132). As such, feelings, although "actively lived and felt," are "elusive, impalpable forms of social consciousness" and thus tend to disappear from social analysis altogether (Eagleton 1991, 48). Since the most common modes of social analysis define the social as the known and reduce it to fixed forms, they tend to miss the "complexities, the experienced tensions, shifts, and uncertainties, the intricate forms of unevenness and confusion" that constitute the living present (Williams 1977, 129). However, Williams argues that the alternative to these analytical reductions is not the silencing or disappearance of these complexities and tensions but "a kind of feeling and thinking which is indeed social and material" (131).

Told through the knowing eyes of a lonely and imaginative child, lê thi diem thúy's 2003 *The Gangster We Are All Looking For* is a quietly powerful account of a Vietnamese refugee family who is in America but not of it. Part memoir, part novel, it is among the first book-length fictional works to come from the boat people generation of the late 1970s and early 1980s. In 1978, six-year-old lê and her father fled their home village of Phan Thiet in southern Vietnam in a small fishing boat, leaving behind her mother and younger siblings. After a brief stay in a refugee camp in Singapore, they were resettled in Linda Vista, a racially diverse working-class community in San Diego. In 1980 lê's mother and younger sister, after a stint in a refugee camp in Malaysia, joined them in San Diego.[14] Growing up, lê sensed an implicit silence in her family about the Vietnam War: "When my dad got together with his friends, they would sing songs and tell stories about when they were schoolboys. But there was a way they leapt over the war and the aftermath of the war. There was no one for me to turn to with my questions: how did we get here? Why are we boat people? If my mom misses her parents, and our town, then why aren't we there?. . . . And because I had no one to ask those questions, I swallowed them inside myself" (*San Diego Reader* 2004). At the same time, she was bombarded with media images of the Vietnam War as a spectacle—and as an American tragedy: "In mainstream narrative about Vietnam, it's usually about the American GI, while the Vietnamese are part of the landscape. They rarely get particularized as characters" (Mehegan 2003). Lê wrote *The Gangster* in part to put on record what happened to the Vietnamese people, not just during the war but also before and after the war: "In this country . . . [t]he questions about what happened to Vietnamese people don't get brought up. . . . For America to grow in its consciousness, it needs to ask what happened to the Vietnamese" (*San Diego Reader* 2004).

In lyrical prose that reads like poetry, lê depicts the United States not as the land of opportunities but as the breaker of families—a place where family life will never be what it could or should have been. Haunting the narrator's family is the specter of her dead older brother, who drowned in Vietnam when he was just six years old—a death made more tragic by the absence of the father who was being held in a reeducation camp. The brother's death provides lê with a narrative device to move the story back and forth between Vietnam and California and to shift time, place, and viewpoint constantly throughout the novel. As lê interweaves memories of Vietnam with incidents in the United States, she melds the past and present, conveying the fluidity of time but also the unending-ness of the war's impact on Vietnamese lives. As she reminds us: "War has no beginning and no end. It crosses oceans like a splintered boat filled with people singing a sad song" (87). Unlike other immigrant accounts, lê's novel depicts the family's arrival in the United States not as the end but as the beginning of story, poignantly detailing the main characters' struggles with living a life not of their own design. The young narrator bemoans her parents' unfulfilled dreams and unfulfilling lives in America: "[Ma] worked as a seamstress, doing piecework at our kitchen table. [Ba] worked as a welder at a factory that made space heaters. Neither of them wanted to be doing it; Ma wanted to have a restaurant, and Ba wanted to have a garden" (43). She sees their poverty intensely, in the rusted gates of their small red apartment building, in her father's hopeless rage, and in her parents' "big fight[s] about nothing" and in the "awful quiet" that ensues (66–67).

Most poignant are the exquisite portraits of the haunted, brooding father "who cries in the garden every night" (27) and who is "sad and broken" (117). His loneliness, sadness, and brokenness—the result of years of devastating war, punishing reeducation camp, demeaning jobs, and crushing poverty—often turn into hopeless rage for a father's order: "He becomes prone to rages. He smashes television, VCRs, chases friends and family down the street, brandishing hammers and knives in broad daylight" (116). At night, once his rage has subsided, he sits motionless in the dark for hours, "his body absolutely still, his hands folded on his lap, penitent . . . straining toward things no one can see" (116). Mindful of the father's inner turmoil, the daughter's memories of him and their relationship contain a mixture of tender as well as terrifying moments:

> To protect myself, I tried to forget everything: that first night at the refugee camp in Singapore; those early morning walks after we arrived in America; the sound of his voice asking a question no one could answer; the shapes his fists left along a wall; the bruises that blossomed on the people around him; the smell of the fruit he brought home from the gardens he tended; the way the air seemed charged with memories of blood; the nets we fell through, faster and faster, year after year, dreaming of land. (117–118)

In the following scene that takes place in a runaway shelter, lê beautifully depicts the complexity of the father-daughter relationship, one that refuses to be privatized but calls into being the larger history and context of war, refugee resettlement, and chronic poverty:

> Before I had run away for good, my father once came to pick me up at a shelter. As we sat in a conference with two counselors, he was asked if there was

> anything he wanted to say. He shook his head. When pressed, he looked down at his hands. He apologized for what his hands had done. The counselors understood this to mean he was taking responsibility for his drunken rages. They nodded in approval. But then he drew his palms together and apologized for all that his hands had not been able to do. He spread his hands wide open, and said, in Vietnamese, to anyone who could understand, there were things he had lost grasp of. The room seemed to shrink in the face of his sorrow. Beside him the two counselors were like tight little shrubs no one had ever watered. I thought they had no right to frown at my father. I could not wait to get us out of there. I told the counselors that I was ready to go home. I remember crossing the parking lot, my hand in my father's hand, the two of us running to the car as though we were escaping together again. (118–119)

In this excerpt, lê denaturalizes domestic violence among poor refugee families by showing how it is intimately linked to the violence of war, of urban neglect, and of poverty. In so doing, she disrupts the widespread construction of patriarchy as particular to Asian culture, which freezes Asian immigrant men as always already "subjects-who-perpetrate-violence" and foregrounds the need to theorize and situate all forms of male violence (Mohanty 1991, 58). Stressing the intersection of race, gender, and class, she makes clear how gender differentiation and oppression is not a universal experience but is structured differently, depending on how it intersects with other inequalities such as race and class. Thus from their race and class vantage point, the two social service workers understand the gesture of the father as an apology for domestic violence—"for what his hands had done." In contrast, the marginalized father and daughter recognize that the apology is more for what "his hands had *not* been able to do" (emphasis added). More than a cultural misunderstanding, the scene evinces a power struggle in which the feminist values of the American counselors are deemed universal while those of the powerless refugees are misrecognized—though not entirely silenced. The novel thus exhorts us to acknowledge that economic and social discrimination have locked many working-class men of color into an unequal relationship with not only privileged white men but also privileged white women (Cheung 1990, 246; Kim 1990, 74).

Facing the overbearing and patronizing social service workers, the daughter abruptly and protectively took her father's hand and both fled—away from the oppressive state system that threatened to further humiliate a man who had just apologized for what "his hands had not been able to do." This scene encapsulates the parent-child role reversal common in immigrant families: the night they left Vietnam, it was the father who carried the daughter down to the beach and placed her on the fishing boat; but now in America, it was the English-speaking daughter who freed the father from the prying bureaucrats in the shelter. This act—"of escaping together again"—moves the story beyond the familiar trope of intergenerational conflict to one about joint lives. Although the daughter and father are divided by generation, culture, and language, they are connected by their shared histories. The crises that have shaped the father, while unknown to and unheard by the social service workers, are deeply felt and lived by the daughter who has witnessed and braved these misfortunes alongside her father. It is this witnessing that enables the daughter to see her father as one who is never utterly defeated: "His friends fell all around him . . . first during the war and then after the war, but somehow he alone managed to crawl here, on his hands and knees, to this life" (103). Avery Gordon (1997, 200) explains that a structure of feeling articulates "the tangled exchange of noisy silences and seething absences." There lies the contribution of lê's novel: it makes audible and visible the "noisy silences" and "seething absences" in Vietnamese life, exposing the material, cultural, and political circumstances that constrain the refugees' everyday life, their responses to and against these constraints, and the emotional tensions that result therein.

Conclusion

Dorinne Kondo has characterized the world of representation and aesthetics as "a site of struggle, where identities are created, where subjects are interpellated, where hegemonies can be challenged" (1997, 4). I have examined the politics and poetics of remembering the Vietnam War by focusing on Vietnamese American artworks that call attention to absences, that look for the things that are seemingly not there or barely there, and that imagine beyond the limits of what is already stated to be understandable. That is, arts that perform critical memory work that bring into being what is usually neglected or made invisible or thought by most to be dead and gone. Since memory activities—that is, the writing of history—are always mediated by relations of power and accompanied by elements of repression, we need to identify "what is at stake in remembering and forgetting past events in certain ways and not in others" (Yoneyama 1999, 33). As a consequence of U.S. history's erasure of Vietnamese, especially of South Vietnamese, accounts of the war, the most that we have are fragmented "flashes" of memory, of partial and imperfect recollections of what happened to the Vietnamese. At this moment of reinvigorated U.S. imperialism, this erasure makes un-visible the costs of the Vietnam War, making it more possible for the United States to build support for its military interventionism in the world. Earlier, in a different context, Toni Morrison instructs us to be mindful that "invisible things are not necessarily not-there" (1989). So instructed, Long Nguyen, Bao Phi, and lê thi diem thúy, through their brilliant work, have brought to life the war's costs borne by the Vietnamese—the lifelong costs that turn the 1975 fall of Saigon, the exodus from Vietnam, and the resettlement in the United States into "the endings that are not over." Even as they mourn the lives that could or would have been, these artists also offer rich and varied descriptions of the lives that did emerge from and out of this history, prodding us to remember that Vietnamese, refugees or otherwise, are always a "people larger than their situation" (lê 2003, 122).

NOTES

1. In his 1981 introduction to *Invisible Man*, Ellison laments that the hypervisibility of the black man in fact renders him "un-visible," enabling most whites to feign "moral blindness toward his predicament"—to see him as mere "background white noise" (xii).

2. Since the end of the Vietnam War in 1975, the current government of Vietnam has categorically refused to incorporate South Vietnamese perspectives on the war or to provide any critical evaluation of the war, particularly regarding the violence committed by northern troops on the people of South Vietnam. See Nguyen-Vo (2005).

3. Scott Martelle and Mai Tran, "Vietnam TV Broadcasts Anger Emigres," *Los Angeles Times*, April 27, 2000; "Protesters Urge Boycott of Vietnamese Media," *Los Angeles Times*, April 30, 2000; Bonnie Harris, "Ceremony to Remember Fall of Saigon Stirs Powerful Emotions," *Los Angeles Times*, May 1, 2000; Binh Ha Hong, "Scars of Vietnam Drive Hunger Strike," *Orange County Register*, May 1, 2000; Noelle Truong, "The Time's Not Right for Reconciliation," *Orange County Register*, May 14, 2000; Bonnie Harris, "Ceremony to Remember Fall of Saigon Stirs Powerful Emotions," *Los Angeles Times*, May 1, 2000.

4. Phi's family was able to leave because his father served in the South Vietnamese military.

5. Before 1977 a total of 130,000 refugees fled Vietnam. By 1979 an estimated 400,000 refugees escaped Vietnam in boats for nearby Asian countries (Zhou 2001). The 2000 census counted 1,122,528 Vietnamese in the United States, almost doubling the 1990 census count.

6. The phrase "the endings that are not over" is from Gordon (1997, 195). The "fall of Saigon" is a U.S.-specific term that denotes a contained singular event and that refuses to acknowledge either the *before* or *after* of that day. Vietnamese have other names for this day: "ngay giai phong" (Liberation Day) for Vietnamese in Vietnam and "ngay quoc han" (Day of National Resentment) and "ngay tuong niem" (Day of Commemoration) for Vietnamese in the diaspora.

7. Popular oral history collections that detail the refugees' traumatic escape, all done in the name of "helping" the refugees to "express themselves in their own terms," further reinscribe the refugees as only victims in the U.S. imaginary (Freeman 1989, 10).

8. The source of Nguyen's biography is Northrup (2003, 13–20).

9. Since World War II, social citizenship in the United States has been defined as "the civic duty of the individual to reduce his or her burden on society" (Ong 2003, 12). By the 1960s two racial categories had emerged—"model minority" and "underclass"—to refer to nonwhite groups who were deemed independent of or reliant on the state, respectively. In the midst of the civil rights movement and race rebellions in cities across the United States, the popular press and social scientists began to publicize the alleged economic success of Asian Americans in part to deligitimize black and brown demands for economic equity and formal political claims. In other words, Asian Americans who heretofore have been conspicuously absent from public racial discourse suddenly became highly visible as the model of successful ethnic assimilation—"as embodying the human capital of diligence, docility, self-sufficiency and productivity" (Ong 2003, 77). It is important to note that although Asian Americans are lauded for their alleged successes, they continue to face white racism in the political, economic, and social arenas as well as white resentment and violence for being "too successful." See Okihiro (1994, chap. 2).

10. As an example, researchers repeatedly pit Vietnamese accomplishments against those of other communities of color: "the Indochinese had already begun to move ahead of other minorities on a national basis" (Caplan, Whitmore, and Choy 1989, 75). By attributing Vietnamese students' achievements to their "emphasis on education and achievement through hard work and the willingness to delay immediate satisfaction for future gains," scholars imply that African Americans and Latinos fail because they do not possess these core values that are prerequisites for success (131).

11. Park is a Def Poetry Jam star and poet laureate of Queens, New York.

12. The title for this poem was inspired by Ntozake Shange's choreopoem, "For Colored Girls Who Have Considered Suicide."

13. From Bao Phi's "notes" on the poem. http://www.baophi.com/liner_notes.html.

14. Lê's biography is culled from David Mehegan (2003).

CHAPTER 11

Miracles on the Border

THE VOTIVE ART OF MEXICAN MIGRANTS TO THE UNITED STATES

Jorge Durand and Douglas S. Massey

In recent decades the volume of migration between Mexico and the United States has risen dramatically and transnational movement has emerged as a major force binding the two countries. Although Mexican immigration has been the subject of many statistical studies (see Durand and Massey 1992 and Massey et al. 1994 for reviews), it has been less common to examine it from the viewpoint of the migrants themselves. Nonetheless, a growing literature has sought to portray migration, especially migration without documents, from the perspective of its participants. Investigators have compiled oral histories to reveal the life course dynamics of international migration (Durand 1996; Gamio 1931); analyzed the content of popular Mexican songs about migration and border crossing (Fernandez 1983; Herrera-Sobek 1979); and assembled letters written by undocumented migrants to friends and family at home (Siems 1992). One study gave disposable cameras to immigrants and asked them to take pictures of features of their environments that to them appeared "American" and "Latino" (Massey and Sánchez 2007). Many studies have done participant observation and in-depth interviewing among migrants to appreciate the vagaries of life in the United States through their eyes (Chávez 1991; Durand 2002; González-López 2005; Hondagneu-Sotelo 1994, 2001). A few former undocumented migrants have even published memoirs (de la Torre 1988; Pérez 1991).

We add to this growing literature by undertaking a systematic analysis of votive paintings left by U.S. migrants and their families at religious shrines in western Mexico, the traditional heartland for migration to the United States (Durand 1988; Durand, Massey, and Zenteno 2001). Known popularly as *retablos*, from the Latin *retro-tabula* (behind the altar), these paintings are typically prepared or commissioned to offer thanks to a divine image for a miracle or favor received (Giffords 1974). They tell the story of a threatening event from which the subject has been miraculously delivered through divine intervention (Cousin 1982). Here we analyze a newly expanded sample of retablos dealing with Mexico-U.S. migration to update earlier work on this subject (see Durand and Massey 1995, 1997, 2001) and to discern the latest trends in the subjective meaning of migration from the viewpoint of those who actually live it.

Origins of Mexican Retablos

The word *retablo* originally referred to decorative or didactic paintings and sculpture placed behind the altar of Catholic churches in the early middle ages (Giffords 1974). Later it came to denote reliquary boxes placed at the rear of the altar (de la Maza 1950); and during the twelfth and thirteenth centuries it was generalized to refer to all painted altar panels and frontal pieces (Cousin 1982; Giffords 1991; Schroeder 1968). In the most literal sense, therefore, retablos include any paintings or objects placed around the altar.

The practice of leaving objects to thank or beseech a divine image has ancient roots, of course (Egan 1991). According to abundant archaeological evidence, the ancient Greeks, Romans, Etruscans, Iberians, and Gauls all possessed well-developed votive traditions (Decouflé 1964) in which it was common to acknowledge or pray for the restoration of health by leaving small figures of clay, wax, wood, or stone shaped like hands, eyes, arms, legs, feet, or vital organs. These traditions persisted into the Christian era, but during the fifteenth century these anatomical tokens gave way to a more elaborate display of supplication through painting.

Originating in the early Renaissance, the first votive paintings appeared in Italy at the end of the 1400s (Cousin 1982). The practice of votive painting spread rapidly throughout the Mediterranean and then diffused northward into the rest of Europe and ultimately the New World (Egan 1991). Votive practices entered Mexico more with Spanish soldiers than priests. Votive supplication has always been a popular folk tradition rather than a formal religious practice, and Egan (1991) relates that the Conquistador of Mexico himself, upon being bitten by a scorpion, prayed to the Virgin of Guadalupe for deliverance and promised to prepare a votive if he survived this misfortune. Cortez kept his promise and ordered the goldsmiths of Azcapotzalco to fashion a votive containing forty emeralds and two pearls set in a gold box that housed the remnants of the poisonous arthropod that dared to attack the conqueror of Mexico (Valle Arizpe 1941).

In transplanting votive traditions to Mexico, of course, the Spanish did not encounter a cultural vacuum. Indeed, archaeological evidence suggests that votive practices were well established in Mesoamerica long before the arrival of the Spanish (Montenegro 1950) and pre-Hispanic votive objects have been found in ruins throughout Mexico and Central America (Sánchez Lara 1990; Solís 1991;

Townsend 1992). Despite the existence of strong pre-Hispanic votive traditions, however, the practice of votive painting initially did not take hold among Mexico's indigenous populations after the conquest. Although popular religious expressions were tolerated by the evangelizing priests, they were not encouraged, and missionaries instead sought to insert European practices into the native spiritual milieu (Lafaye 1976).

As a result, votive painting first took root among American-born Spaniards, known as criollos (Giffords 1974, 119). As in Europe, the practice grew out of altar paintings of biblical scenes commissioned for didactic purposes (Montenegro 1950). Dating the earliest retablos in Mexico is difficult because they were usually executed on perishable media such as canvas or wood that did not survive. A series of engravings of the Virgin of Guadalupe done by the Belgian artist Stradanus between 1604 and 1622 suggest that retablos were present in Mexico by the early seventeenth century (Orendain 1948). The engravings show four painted retablos hanging to either side of the Virgin's altar, each containing an explanatory text recounting a miraculous happening (Genaro Cuadriello 1989; Sánchez Lara 1990).

As time went on, votive painting increasingly came to be associated with Mexico's mestizo population, people of mixed Spanish and Indian origins in whom pre-Columbian traditions were united with European styles in a way that did not threaten officials of the Catholic Church. The arrival of tin plate in the nineteenth century introduced a cheap and versatile medium that quickly displaced canvas and wood and opened retablo art to broader social participation (Giffords 1974, 1991). Over time, the origins of supplicants shifted from criollo to mestizo, and the geographic center of retablo painting shifted away from Mexico City and into the heavily mestizo west-central region of the country. By the 1920s, the production of votive art was concentrated in five key western states: Guanajuato, Jalisco, Michoacán, San Luis Potosí, and Zacatecas. Although votive practices continue to be expressed throughout Latin America, painted retablos achieved their fullest development and greatest expression in Mexico, and only there have they continued to function as a living artistic tradition (Durand and Massey 1995).

Aesthetics of Retablos

The classic Mexican retablo is painted on a piece of tin that has been reduced from a larger sheet by a progressive cutting into smaller sections (Giffords 1991). Most are rectangular in shape, with the largest being about 280 sq. in. (14 × 20 in.) and the smallest being around 18 sq. in. (3.5 × 5 in.). The most common sizes are 140 sq. in. (10 × 14 in.) and 70 sq. in. (7 × 10 in.) (Giffords 1974, 1991; Orendain 1948). In terms of composition, retablos typically incorporate three basic elements: a holy image, a graphic rendering of the miraculous event, and a text explaining what happened and expressing gratitude (Giffords 1974, 1991). The holy image is usually depicted suspended in clouds and located to one side of the composition.

Although the representation of the holy image must bear some relation to official iconography, the rules of interpretation are loose rather than rigid. In order to function effectively within the context of an ex-voto, a holy image need only convey identity in general terms. A variety of colors, styles, shapes, props, and levels of detail may be used to depict a holy image, as long as overall recognition is achieved. Strict reproduction of a holy image is not important because the action itself is the focus of the work. Moreover, because votive paintings are left at specific shrines, the identity of the image is usually clear from the context in which it is placed. Any doubts about the identity of an image are usually dispelled by the text, which mentions the image by name.

Textual material is generally found at the bottom of the painting. In addition to thanking the holy image, the text normally states the place of origin of the donor along with the date, place, and circumstances of the event, and it gives an account of the miraculous intervention by the holy image. Expressions of gratitude draw upon a standard vocabulary that has evolved over hundreds of years. Most begin with the words "doy gracias" (I give thanks) and express a heartfelt need to "hacer patente" (make known) the miraculous results of a divine intervention. In them, the supplicant states that at the moment of crisis, "me encomendé a la Virgen" (I entrusted myself to the Virgin) and tell how "me concedió el milagro" (she granted me the miracle). They often end with the simple statement that "por eso dedico el presente retablo" (for this I dedicate the present retablo).

The largest and most important part of the pictorial space in most retablos is given over to depicting the miraculous event itself. In rendering circumstances under which the divine intervention occurred, there are few strict protocols. According to Moyssén (1965, 26), "the imagination of the artist has ample scope to express the supernatural and divine intervention that is superimposed on logical reality and only is acceptable in terms of a blind and irrational faith." The principal desideratum is that artistic devices heighten the emotional intensity of the moment and emphasize the ongoing drama of events. Although the choice of materials, styles, and methods is open and flexible, over the years several techniques have become conventional (Durand and Massey 1995).

Mexican retablos typically rely on bold, bright colors to augment the emotional effect of the miraculous event. In order to convey the power of extreme circumstances, retablo painters make full use of the color spectrum, yielding luminous and vibrant works. Although scenes of family members gathered around a sickbed may occasionally be rendered in subdued tones, the colors are rarely dark. Actions and dramatic events are almost always presented in vivid colors. Background detail is frequently painted using divergent hues to add emotional power to the composition, and the actors themselves are often rendered in contrasting tones.

Mexican votive paintings also self-consciously manipulate space to underscore the dramatic nature of unfolding events. Scale and proportion are often skewed to intensify emotion; angles become sharper and perspective awkward in order to increase the dramatic power of a scene. Helplessness in the face of a dire situation is captured by juxtaposing tiny human figures with larger-than-life holy images (whereas in real life, sacred images tend to be small). The surreal nature of the moment is enhanced by a haphazard placement of figures, props, and background constructions.

Most votive paintings systematically segment and reorder time. Events that occurred sequentially are broken down into representative moments and shown simultaneously. Different stages in the progress of a miraculous event are arranged within a common pictorial frame. Supplicants shown in the throes of a dire circumstance in one part of a retablo are pictured offering thanks to the image in another. Actions occurring before, during, and after the miracle are shuffled and presented for maximum psychological effect.

At times, theater props and stage motifs are used to emphasize the drama of unfolding events. In such paintings, action takes place on crude stages erected magically in the picture space; curtains are pulled back to reveal figures in critical situations; lush and lustrous fabrics are draped over walls and furniture as if on a set; actors appear to perform before audiences of horrified onlookers; cinematic techniques such as the flashback and fast forward are employed to move about in time.

Finally, in the course of their evolution Mexican retablos have incorporated new materials and techniques to create collages that blend traditional painting with modern media. Photographs of family members are affixed to lend verisimilitude to painted scenes. Photocopies of documents are appended as proof of the divine intercession. A commercially printed image of the Virgin is glued to a spot specially prepared for the purpose. Unlike paintings of saints, therefore, Mexican ex-votos have not been threatened with extinction because of the advent of cheap, industrially produced products. Indeed, commercially printed images are simply incorporated into the composition. If anything, the range of techniques available to retablo artists has multiplied as the genre has continued to evolve.

From an aesthetic point of view, the artistic power of Mexican retablo painting comes from its economy of execution. According to Herrera (1983, 151), "the drawing is naively painstaking, the color choices are odd, the perspective is awkward, space is reduced to a rudimentary stage, and action is condensed to highlights. Adherence to appearances is less important than the dramatization of the ghastly event or the miraculous encounter between the victim and the resplendent holy image." In essence, retablos condense extreme human emotions such as fear, sorrow, apprehension, gratitude, relief, horror, and rage onto small sheets of tin painted in the most elemental of styles. Looking at people depicted in the throes of a circumstance that appears to have no earthly remedy, or imminently facing a crushing and painful loss, we not only share the intensity of the fear and sorrow, we also experience the relief of delivery. It is the rendering of such powerful and elemental human emotions in simple and unpretentious artistic terms that makes retablos so compelling as works of art. As the folklorist Frances Toor (1947, 67–68) has noted, "retablos—realistic pictures of super-realistic events—are painted with great sensitivity and profound recognition of a truth that makes a miracle of reality and of reality a miracle."

Analyzing Retablos

Our interest in migrants' retablos began in September of 1988, when we traveled to the sanctuary of San Juan de los Lagos to visit the Virgin of San Juan and inspect her votive paintings. As we perused the colorful pictures and dramatic texts, we noted several that dealt with migration to the United States. We began to look for more of these paintings, and within an hour we had located a dozen votive paintings left by U.S. migrants or their relatives. It quickly occurred to us that these paintings might shed a distinctive light on the topic of Mexico-U.S. migration, offering a rich source of historical and sociological data on a subject that has been notoriously resistant to study—undocumented migration. Because they depict salient events at the moment of their occurrence, moreover, they provide an immediate record of migrants' most pressing concerns. By scrutinizing these paintings, we thought, we might glimpse how illegal migration was perceived and understood by the people who experienced it.

In the ensuing years, we visited dozens of religious shrines known to support a votive tradition and scoured galleries and antique dealers on both sides of the border looking for retablos that dealt with the subject of U.S. migration. In religious sanctuaries throughout Mexico we have endeavored to take photographs and transcribe texts whenever we come upon a votive painting that deals in any way with migration to the United States, and in private galleries we have made it a point to purchase any such retablo. Together we currently own fifty-nine retablos painted or commissioned by U.S. migrants or their relatives, and we have made these available as a traveling exhibit that is regularly lent to museums and galleries throughout North America free of charge.

At the time of our book, *Miracles on the Border* (Durand and Massey 1995), we had located 124 retablos dealing with the topic of U.S. migration; we have since continued to compile texts and images, and the database now contains 166 retablo paintings. The scenes and texts contained in these works constitute the basic data for our study. In each case, we have a digitized photograph of the painting and a transcription of the text. Included in the database is any votive painting that we encountered and judged to have been prepared by a current or former migrant to the United States, or a member of his or her family. All of the retablos were executed on a durable medium—in most cases tin, but in a few cases cardboard, masonite, wood, or glass.

We chose to focus on durable media in order to control for the selective way that votive paintings survive. Although we can observe contemporary votive offerings on all sorts of perishable media, we can only observe works from the past that have survived. Thus, any view of migration reconstructed from earlier retablos is likely to be more highly selective than a view pieced together from votive materials encountered in the present. If certain sorts of themes are more likely than others to be rendered on perishable media, then the abundance of these sorts of themes would naturally increase as time progressed, irrespective of what migrants were actually concerned about at different points in time.

In order to hold constant the degree of selection over time, we focus on retablos that were executed on durable media that would be likely to persist over time. Although this approach controls somewhat for *one* source of selectivity, it by no means eliminates selection bias from our sample of retablos. We have no way of knowing, for example, whether certain kinds of migrants are more likely than others to produce retablos; and although tin is a relatively inexpensive medium, it could also be that migrants with more money and resources systematically choose to create retablos on durable rather than perishable media, thus lending the sample a potential class bias.

Finally, there are institutional factors that might determine the survivability of retablos, such as whether different parishes have different policies toward a religious tradition that is ultimately more popular and folkloric than Catholic or official. By far the most common icon in our database is the Virgin of San Juan de los Lagos, which accounts for 43 percent of all images in the database, followed by El Santo Niño de Atocha at 15 percent, and the related images of El Señor de la Conquista and San Miguel at 7 percent each. The latter two images are both located in the sanctuary of San Felipe Torres Mochas and in practical terms constitute a single pilgrimage site. These four sites, which together comprise nearly three quarters of the images, are all well-established places of pilgrimage with long traditions of displaying and preserving votive paintings on durable media such as tin, suggesting that institutional factors may not play a large role in determining what content has survived. However, well-established traditions are no guarantee of continuity in policies toward retablos, as we discovered at the sanctuary of El Señor de Villaseca in Guanajuato (which constitutes 5 percent of the images in the database). There a change in clerical administration brought in a priest who was adamantly opposed to folk traditions unsanctioned by Rome, and he arranged for all of the retablos to be removed from the sanctuary walls not long after we photographed them. Thus the potential selectivity of our sample of texts and images is a possibility that should always be born in mind in evaluating our findings.

Although migrants share many of the same problems as others who bring votive offerings before a sacred image, the experience of international migration yields distinct circumstances that distinguish them from other supplicants. A typology of retablos developed for general use, such as that of Creux (1979), is therefore of limited utility in attempting to comprehend and classify the range of problems experienced by Mexican immigrants. Although illness, catastrophe, war, fire, falling, work, and animal problems (Creux's categories) may befall migrants, the meaning of these problems is very different in a foreign context. In addition, Mexico-U.S. migrants face the pain of separation; the hazards of moving north; the risks of crossing the border; the fear of falling sick in a strange land; the threat of arrest and deportation; and the thorny, ever-present issue of documentation.

In view of these distinctive concerns, we developed our own typology of retablos that builds on the earlier efforts of Creux and others, but which takes into account the unusual situation of U.S. migrants. The scheme contains five major headings and fifteen detailed subcategories. The major headings follow the course of a migrant's journey to and from the United States. They include "Making the Trip," "Legal Problems," "Medical Problems," "Getting by in the U.S.," and "Homecoming." Under these broad rubrics, we define a variety of subcategories that address particular topics.

The Content of Migrants' Retablos

In order to carry out a detailed content analysis of retablos, we classified each ex-voto into one and only one of the fifteen subcategories. In cases where more than one subcategory could have applied, we classified the retablo according to the subject that, in our judgment, was dominant. The results of this operation are shown in table 11.1. As can be seen, the first general heading is "Making the Trip," and it considers three salient issues involved in moving from Mexico to the United States. Difficulties encountered while traveling north fall into the first subcategory, and those faced while crossing the border comprise the second; the third subcategory focuses on the special problems that women face in going north.

As the table indicates, around 17 percent of the retablos in our sample deal in some way with one of these themes. Some 2.4 percent of the pictures fall into the subcategory "Heading North." A good example under this rubric is the retablo left by a woman from León, Guanajuato, who was traveling north to the United States in October of 1946 when the roadway suddenly washed out and several of her companions were swept away. Fearing the worst, she called upon the Virgin of San Juan and entrusted them to her protection; later they miraculously turned up unharmed, a piece of good fortune that she credited to the divine powers of the Virgin.

Another 2 percent of the retablos come under the heading of "Women's Issues." One such painting, dated November 19, 1989, was left by María del Carmen Parra, who gives "thanks to the Holiest Virgin of San Juan de los Lagos for having granted that [my] daughter could marry in the United States." For many women, marriage to a migrant, a Chicano, or an Anglo-American (from the retablo it is not exactly clear who her daughter married) provides a path of potential mobility to a better life, one free from the strictures of poverty and patriarchy in Mexico, and one to which mothers frequently aspire on behalf of their daughters (see Goldring 1995; Hondagneu-Sotelo 1992; Espinosa 1998; Reichert 1982). In other cases, issues faced by women are more threatening, as when Concepción Zapata was heading north through Texas when a "Tejano" attempted to abduct her. She was able to escape by hiding behind a tree with her younger brother, for which she felt a debt of considerable gratitude to the Virgin of San Juan (Durand and Massey 1995).

By far the most frequent subject mentioned under the general heading of "Making the Trip" is "Crossing the Border," a subject that concerns 13 percent of the retablos in the sample. As this relatively high frequency indicates, the risks of border-crossing loom large in the minds of Mexican migrants who lack legal documents and must enter the United States surreptitiously. In addition to the risk of arrest and deportation, undocumented migrants also face the hazards of fraud,

TABLE 11.1

DISTRIBUTION OF RETABLOS BY SUBJECT

Subject	*N*	%
Making the trip	28	16.9
Heading north	4	2.4
Crossing the border	21	12.7
Women's issues	3	1.8
Legal problems	21	12.6
Arranging documents	11	6.6
Run-ins with the law	10	6.0
Medical problems	37	22.3
Getting sick	26	15.7
Having an operation	11	6.6
Getting by in the U.S.	48	28.9
Getting lost	1	0.6
War	14	8.4
Work accidents	8	4.8
Traffic accidents	16	9.6
Crime	2	1.2
Getting ahead	7	4.2
Homecoming	28	16.8
Grateful migrants	8	4.8
Thankful relatives	20	12.0
Unnamed miracles	4	2.4
Total retablos examined	166	100.0

injury, robbery, thirst, hunger, and drowning (see Massey, Durand, and Malone 2002). Those who make it through the gauntlet of border-crossing hazards naturally feel indebted to a holy image for watching over them, and for delivering them from danger (Durand and Massey 1995).

Angelina García Solís, for example, left a votive addressed to el Señor del Saucito "for the miracle that he granted me in the year 1949. Finding myself drowning in the waters of the Rio Grande in el Norte in the company of other friends, in the most desperate moment I invoked his help after I had given up hope. I give him a thousand and one thanks, and also to God, that through his mediation

He did me such an immense favor." Another anonymous votary thanked the Virgin of Talpa for saving "me from death on the 20th of September of 1948. Upon wishing to cross the Rio Grande, two friends were killed but I was able to save myself."

The second major heading is "Legal Problems," the subject of roughly 13 percent of the retablos in our sample. The problem of documentation looms large for Mexican migrants, since without a legal residence card or some other form of legal documentation, a person's tenure in the United States is insecure and can end at a moment's notice. As a result, undocumented migrants are vulnerable to exploitation and are confined to an underground economy of unstable, poorly paid jobs. Nearly 7 percent of the retablos we sampled concerned the issue of documentation. One of them was left by Luz Bravo Magaña, who on November 8, 1945, simply offered "thanks to the Virgin of San Juan de los Lagos for the miracle of having obtained without difficulty my passport from the American consulate" (anyone who has ever waited in line to get a visa at a U.S. embassy can appreciate how "miraculous" this event seemed). In 1989 another man left a retablo giving thanks to the Virgin of San Juan "for having acted on the petitions that I made to you for my brother to get his visa."

A second subcategory, comprising another 6 percent of the sample, focuses on encounters with law enforcement officials, the most feared of whom are immigration officers. Migrants occasionally run afoul of other authorities, however, and at times end up in jail. For such people, the usual problems of loneliness and fear are magnified by the fact that incarceration isolates them in a strange culture and prevents them from seeing loved ones who remain in Mexico. Thus, Juan Jaime Delgado addressed his retablo to the "Lord of Villaseca that is venerated in the Sanctuary of Mineral de Cata. I give infinite thanks for helping me get out of jail in the United States and for arriving safely in the city of Guanajuato in the year 1986." In his retablo, José Gutiérrez likewise gave "thanks to the Lord Saint Michael for having saved me from a sentence of 20 years in a prison in Chicago, U.S.A., releasing me after only 8 months."

A third general heading is "Medical Problems," perhaps the most common theme among retablos generally. Getting sick and experiencing accidents are risks of life that every human must face, but these events are especially terrifying when one has no friends or family nearby, when one does not speak the language, and when one lacks money or insurance to pay doctor bills. About 16 percent of the retablos we sampled mentioned getting sick in the United States. The gratitude that María de Jesús Torres felt after her daughter got well was such that she traveled all the way to Jalisco from her home in National City, California, to "offer infinite thanks to Our Lady of San Juan for having given health to my daughter, Teresa Torres, who suffered from asthma and epileptic attacks for several years." Facing an operation is also threatening when one cannot communicate effectively with the medical staff, or when one does not fully understand the medical system or its technology. About 7 percent of the retablos in our collection explicitly give thanks to an image for surviving a surgical procedure performed in the United States.

On January 3, 1962, in Santa Fe, New Mexico, for example, Concepción González Anderson underwent a surgical procedure in which "they did an examination to see if I had cancer. Thanks to the Holiest Virgin of San Juan, I was spared from this sickness for which I give infinite thanks for the miracle she gave me."

While living and working in the United States, Mexicans face a variety of additional issues related to well-being that are grouped under the fourth general heading, "Getting by in the U.S.," which comprises 29 percent of the retablos we assembled. Once a migrant has entered the United States, new difficulties arise. Getting lost in a strange setting is a problem treated in about 1 percent of the retablos. Often this misfortune befalls migrants from small towns who arrive in large U.S. cities, but it also occurs in the countryside, often in arid parts of California, Texas, or Arizona, where migrants travel for work. Ponciano Guzmán did not give details on his retablo of September 4, 1951; he just gave "thanks to the Virgin of Zapopan for having gotten us out of this desert without harm."

Unlike Mexico, the United States is a global power with many foreign commitments, and entering its armed forces carries the very real risk of having to go to war in a far-off place. Legal immigrants, as well as children of Mexicans born in the United States, are subject to the U.S. military draft (including the children of undocumented parents), and Mexican immigrants have fought in all major wars of the twentieth century, including the Persian Gulf, Iraq, and Afghanistan. Some undocumented migrants join the U.S. military as a means of legalizing their status. Among the 166 retablos we assembled, 8 percent thanked an image for a safe return from war. The oldest such retablo we found was prepared by the uncle of Angel Turburán and deposited in the Sanctuary of El Señor de Villaseca on July 19, 1917. Referring to his nephew's service in World War I, the text states that "having been mortally wounded in the war, his uncle Roberto Rodriguez, from . . . New Mexico, commended him to the Holiest Lord of Villaseca that he should not die. . . . Having cured him from his sickness he makes public this miracle."

Aside from the extreme case of warfare, Mexican migrants face other risks while abroad. One is accidents at work, mentioned in around 5 percent of the retablos. Migrants tend to be employed in agriculture, construction, the garment industry, and small-scale manufacturing, hazardous sectors where employers are under intense competitive pressure. In order to keep expenses low, companies invest little in safety devices or new equipment, thereby increasing the risk of work-related accidents. Some 4 percent of the retablos in our sample mention an accident at work. One such retablo was left by Manuel Reyes, who found himself picking cotton near Brawley, California, during the fall of 1954 when he got his hand caught in some machinery. At this moment, he invoked the image of San Miguel, who intervened to free him, "losing a finger but saving my life, and in proof of gratitude I dedicate the present retablo."

Another 10 percent of the retablos in the sample revolve around traffic accidents, a danger especially prevalent among migrants living in crowded urban areas and driving lonely country roads throughout the United States. In 1954 one grateful migrant gave "thanks to the Virgin of San Juan de los Lagos for having saved me from an automobile accident in which four persons were left dead and four injured that occurred in San Francisco, California." Another risk for migrants, especially in cities, is crime, which as the subject of 1 percent of the retablos, such as the one that alluded to a car-jacking experience that befell a migrant in Compton, California.

Of course, getting by in the United States is not simply a matter of surviving negative experiences such as crime and car accidents. Ubiquitous among the votive objects left in Mexican sanctuaries are tokens of some foreign success: a driver's license, a report card, a high school diploma, a college degree. Although it is less common to find retablos commemorating these events, some 4 percent of the offerings gave thanks for some personal achievement or advancement in the United States. One offered thanks to the Virgin of Zapopan for "having been able to obtain a nursing certificate in the U.S.A." Another, from a migrant in Los Angeles, simply thanked this Virgin for "a miracle obtained in the artistic world some years ago." Perhaps the most important part of getting ahead is finding a good job, for without work migrants cannot repay the expenses of the trip, support themselves, or send money back home to family members in Mexico (Durand 1988; Massey et al. 1997; Massey and Parrado 1994). One such retablo was left by J. Melquíades Murillo of Puerto de Loja, Guanajuato, who in 1961 gave "thanks to Holiest Mary of San Juan de los Lagos, because I prayed to Her that I might go and come across the border and that I might be hired."

The last phase of the migrant journey, "Homecoming," involves the return of migrants to the warmth of their families and familiar soil of their birth. Given the many hazards and difficulties faced in the course of a U.S. trip, migrants and their families are often overcome with gratitude when a long separation finally comes to an end. The strength of this emotion is such that a votive of thanks is commissioned and left at a local shrine. Roughly 17 percent of the retablos in our sample fell under the general heading "Homecoming," with 12 percent expressing the gratitude of family members and 5 percent offering thanks from the migrants themselves.

Typical of the grateful migrants was Tereso López, of Rancho de la Palma, near Silao, Guanajuato, who contributed a retablo on the occasion of his return to Mexico from the United States. He "gives thanks to the Holiest Virgin of San Juan. Finding himself in the United States and commending himself to the Virgin he asked that upon arriving on his soil he would go to visit her." Another retablo illustrates the relief felt by family members left behind when a loved one returns. Candelaria Arreola of El Grullo, Jalisco, was praying for her son's return in 1955 when he miraculously arrived. As she explains, "I give thanks to the holiest Virgin of Talpa for having brought my son home from the United States, where he stayed for a long time. I began to pray your novena and I hadn't even finished when he returned. Thank you my mother!"

Changes in Content over Time

A systematic analysis of the content of migrants' retablos thus provides a glimpse into the special problems and difficulties faced by Mexican immigrants. If we simply list those subcategories with relative frequencies of 5 percent or more, we see that crossing the border, arranging documents, and avoiding encounters with legal authorities are principal preoccupations of U.S. migrants, and that getting sick, having an operation, going to war, and experiencing traffic accidents are major risks of life in the United States. When they manage to overcome these problems and return home safely, migrants and their family members are filled with gratitude.

Additional insight can be gained by classifying the subject of migrants' retablos according to the period in which the trip took place, a task that is carried out in table 11.2. This analysis employs five temporal categories: 1900–1939 represents the early years of Mexico-U.S. migration; 1940–1964 corresponds to the Bracero era, when the U.S. government sponsored a temporary labor program that brought some 4.5 million Mexicans into the United States to work (see Craig 1971; Samora 1971); 1965–1985 is an era of rapidly growing Mexico-U.S. migration; and the modern period, which begins in 1986, marks when the United States embarked on a contradictory policy of lowering barriers to cross-border movements of goods, capital, information, services, commodities, and many classes of people while somehow rendering the frontier impermeable with respect to labor. A residual fifth category contains retablos whose date could not be firmly established.

The largest number of retablos (27 percent) come from the growth years between 1965 and 1985, followed by the modern era and the Bracero era (at 25 percent and 21 percent, respectively), whereas the least frequent period is the early

TABLE 11.2

DISTRIBUTION OF RETABLOS

	Period of migration				
	EARLY YEARS 1900–1939	BRACERO ERA 1940–1964	GROWTH YEARS 1965–1985	MODERN ERA 1980+	(UNDATED)
Subject (%)					
Making the trip	20.0	22.2	14.3	12.2	20.0
Legal problems	10.0	6.0	8.6	22.0	13.4
Medical problems	0.0	36.3	17.2	19.6	22.2
Getting by in U.S	50.0	33.3	34.3	22.0	24.4
Homecoming	20.0	3.0	22.9	19.5	17.8
Unnamed	0.0	0.0	2.9	4.9	2.2
N	10	34	45	42	45
% in period	6.0	20.5	27.1	25.3	27.1

years (around 6 percent of retablos). Roughly 27 percent of the retablos could not be dated with certainty. Given the limited number of retablos in our sample, we only examine temporal shifts in the main content categories.

Issues surrounding homecoming appear to be significant in all periods, with the exception of the Bracero era, when U.S. medical problems and the problems of getting by dominate. The problem of getting by in the United States is notably salient in the early and growth years of U.S. migration. Although this category is also prevalent during the Bracero era, it is underrepresented during the modern period. As transnational movement has become routine and institutionalized; therefore, issues relating to getting by have receded into the background, since, unlike their predecessors, migrants arriving after 1980 can count on a host of friends, relatives, and compatriots, as well as a range of formal and informal contacts, to facilitate their entry and employment within the United States (Massey, Goldring, and Durand 1994).

Perhaps the most striking trend over time is the increasing salience of legal problems, in particular those related to documentation. From the early to the modern era, the percentage of retablos dealing with legal problems increases from 10 percent to 22 percent; and after 1980 issues related to the acquisition of legal documents dominate all others. This trend reflects the fact that since the late 1970s U.S. law has become increasingly restrictive with respect to Mexican immigration.

In 1976 Mexico was placed under a quota of 20,000 immigrants for the first time, and in 1978 it was forced into a worldwide ceiling of 290,000 immigrants, which was subsequently reduced to 270,000 in 1980 (see Jasso and Rosenzweig 1990, 28–29). The 1990 Immigration Act reduced the number of visas accessible to legal resident aliens, and the 1996 Immigration Reform Act raised the household income threshold required to sponsor the entry of family members (Zolberg 2006). These changes have made fewer immigrant visas available to Mexican nationals, causing those who do manage to acquire papers to be very grateful when they get them.

Conclusion

In this analysis we have sought to follow a suggestion originally made by Gloria Giffords (1974, 124) in her seminal study of Mexican retablos, who argued that "an examination of all the ex-votos in any one shrine or church would produce a fascinating record of the people's hopes and fears, their thoughts, lives, and experiences, a record more honest than the fullest statistical study." Retablos provide a tangible and compelling view of the complex phenomenon of international migration, one that packs considerably more punch than mere statistics. Although we cannot reproduce them here, the forty color plates contained in Durand and Massey (1995) give a hint of the emotional power of retablos as compelling works of popular art. These works of popular art unambiguously reveal the degree to which U.S. migration has become a core part of the collective experience of the Mexican people. Working in the United States is now an institutionalized feature of that nation's culture and society. It has been interwoven into the rituals of daily religious life and has transformed those rituals. In western Mexico, seeing a retablo signed in Los Angeles, Dallas, or Chicago is as natural as seeing one from Guadalajara, Morelia, or León.

At present, hundreds of thousands of families in western Mexico have a member on "the other side" and know firsthand about the joys, privations, sorrows, and devotions of migratory life. Migrants customarily maintain close ties with their relatives at home, and while working abroad they dream of returning to build a house, open a store, buy land, or retire in luxury; and if these dreams remain elusive, at least they can look forward to making a visit to the local shrine to pay homage to a venerated image. Each year thousands make such a pilgrimage to appear before images of the Virgin located in Zapopan, Talpa, and San Juan, or to thank images of Christ in Mineral de Cata, San Luis Potosí, or San Felipe and the Holy Child in Plateros.

Retablos are important because they depict a side of migration usually not told in statistical reports or even in detailed interviews with migrants. Going north has become a rite of passage for young men, synonymous with adventure, excitement, and personal esteem (Kandel and Massey 2002). It represents a source of pride and satisfaction for those who return with goods and money; and success in the United States is a frequent subject of boasts and exaggerated stories (Reichert 1982). In this atmosphere, those who have not fared well are apt to remain silent. They do not want people to think they were lazy or afraid. Only to a sacred image can they tell the truth and reveal their true stories of sadness, fear, and apprehension.

Retablos testify to the feelings and experiences of people who migrate back and forth to work in a strange land. In Diego Rivera's (1979) words, they are "the one true . . . pictorial expression of the Mexican people," and they get at the heart of the matter in a way that academic reports never can. After looking at the pictures presented here, and seeing how deeply migration has become rooted in the popular culture of western Mexico, one intuitively grasps why simply passing a new law or changing a bureaucratic regulation will not easily end the ongoing flow of people across the border. For better or for worse, international migration is pulling Mexico and the United States closer together and blending their peoples and cultures in new and exciting ways. The process of binational union is now far too advanced to be easily controlled by the political and economic actors who originally set it in motion. Whatever one's feelings about it, the cultural synthesis embodied in these retablos is probably the way of the future.

CHAPTER 12

Visual Culture and Visual Piety in Little Haiti

THE SEA, THE TREE, AND THE REFUGEE

Terry Rey and Alex Stepick

Religious images, none more so than the Virgin Mary and Saint James the Greater, abound in Haiti and its diaspora. They constitute public expressions of one of the world's most original and vibrant national and now transnational artistic cultures. Whether in the mountains of Haiti or the streets of Miami's Little Haiti, however, their meanings vary and are contested among Haitian believers. For Catholics, the Virgin Mary and Saint James the Greater are, respectively, Christ's mother and one of his apostles. For practitioners of Vodou, they might represent instead Ezili and Ogun, originally African spirits. Meanwhile, for Protestants they might represent the idolatry (on the part of both Vodouists and Catholics) that Protestants perceive as the root cause of Haiti's many and grave social ills. For all religious Haitians, these images are deeply invested with meaning, however divergent their interpretations may be. In Miami, such "religious visual culture" must make newly arrived Haitian immigrants feel somewhat at home in a country that is very different from their homeland—welcome sights indeed. Such is the power of art and visual culture in Haiti and Little Haiti, for just as in the homeland the extraordinarily colorful and usually joyful art that surrounds them instills in Haitians a sense of cultural identity, pride, and brightness in the midst of abject poverty and political upheaval. Immigrant Haitian art—much like immigrant Haitian religion—serves to ground identity, inspire feelings of "worthiness," and provide refuge and solace, things that are especially welcome to black newcomers in Miami, the city that has seen more race riots since the 1960s than any other in the United States. Besides the Caribbean Marketplace, which is styled architecturally after the Iron Market in Port-au-Prince, there is nothing physical to Little Haiti's landscape—palm trees aside—that evokes Haiti. Yet the evocation of Haiti here is resounding, and it resides entirely in its people, their music, their language, their faith, and their art—art that appears virtually everywhere in this neighborhood that is the epicenter of Haitian life in Miami.

This chapter explores Little Haiti's "religious visual imagery," which makes connections "between the material and spiritual, between the past, present, and future of a culture, and between human beings" (Plate 2002, 16). As such, visual culture is indispensable to religion. To invoke the language of two of the most important recent theoretical discussions of religion, religious visual culture allows religion to be "a chain of memory" and a "crossing and dwelling." For Hervieu-Léger (1993, 82), religion promotes "consciousness, both individual and collective, of belonging to a particular chain of belief," while for Tweed (2006, 54) "religions are confluences of organic-cultural flows that intensify joy and confront suffering by drawing on human and superhuman forces to make homes and cross boundaries." A conflation of these definitions encapsulates quite well the meaning of Haitian religion in Miami, which is comprised fundamentally of "visual piety" (Morgan 2005, 6).

Haitian Art and Visual Culture

Haiti is a place of mesmerizing imagery and color. Baroquely framed caricatures of Rambo, Pele, and Jesus adorn the tap-taps—vibrant and usually overloaded taxi-buses fashioned from pickup trucks and minivans—that clog Haiti's urban streets, themselves adorned with the colorful facades of beauty salons and lottery booths, and flags flying over Vodou temples adjacent to splendid pastel gingerbread houses. Humble peasant dwellings, meanwhile, sometimes embody breathtaking architectural creativity, as do graves. As concerns "fine art," Haitian painting, renowned for its rich colors, symbolism, "primitivism," and originality, is prized by art collectors worldwide, as are "the best" sequin-embroidered Vodou flags, which symbolize the various *lwas* (spirits) of the Vodou pantheon. In Miami, meanwhile, the same joyous colors, symbols, and scenes enliven Miami's otherwise drab and blighted Little Haiti neighborhood.

Haitian art deeply enchanted French writers André Breton and André Malraux. For Breton, the crisp yet dreamy tonality of Haitian painting confirmed the surrealist ambition of a common human consciousness teeming with archetypes that subjugate reason itself, leading him to declare that Hyppolite's work "should revolutionize modern painting," being the "pure gift of happiness" of a "guardian of a secret," whose work is "entirely unalloyed, ringing as clearly as virgin metal." Breton delivered a Hyppolite painting to the 1947 UNESCO exhibition in Paris and extolled Haitian art in his 1945 book *Le surréalisme et la peinture*, while three years later New York's Museum of Modern Art added Haitian painter Jean-Enguerrand Gourgue's *Magic Table* to its permanent collection.[1] Malraux, for his part, felt that such art was more the product of gods than humans, and that "every Haitian is an artist, unlike any other country in the world." Some American writers also took notice; Truman Capote, for one, so admired Hyppolite's art "because there's nothing in it that has been slyly transposed; he is using what lives inside him: his country's spiritual history, its sayings, and worship" (Rodman 1988, 54). From New York to Paris, collectors soon began coveting Haitian art, such that by century's end a Hyppolite portrait on cardboard fetched $75,000 at Christie's in New York—a record price for any object of Haitian art.

Art critics, historians, and anthropologists alike have tried to answer the question of why Haiti. Why should this relatively small, poor, and tumultuous country possess what is arguably one of the world's most original and vibrant national artistic cultures? Selden Rodman (1988, 13) surmises that the answer has three "deep-rooted and complex" parts: (1) Pride in being the only successful national slave rebellion in world history; (2) "Haiti's growing pattern of peace and contentment"; and (3) "spiritual satisfaction from the African cult of vaudou." However premature and wildly inaccurate the second of these parts may be, disagreement with the first and especially the third is unimaginable. Karen McCarthy Brown (1995, 35) emphasizes the third, arguing bluntly (and perhaps with some measure of exaggeration) that "the Haitian aesthetic . . . is also necessarily a Vodou aesthetic." His own work deeply inspired by Vodou, leading contemporary Haitian artist Edouard Duval-Carrié adds that "every work of art from Haiti is either a chronicle of history or a very strong *statement about aspirations or frustrating aspirations*" (76, emphasis added).

Clearly Vodou inspires much Haitian art. Hyppolite, André Pierre, and others of their generation were Vodou priests. Vodou temples and ceremonies frequently feature *vèvès*, intricate symbols drawn on the ground with ashes, flour, coffee grinds, brick dust, or other powders. Among others, Hyppolite transports these images from earth onto canvas, using oils instead of powders with striking effect, while more recently Saincilus Ishmaël's dazzlingly vibrant and detailed work adds vèvès to the Virgin Mary's cloak. Brown feels that "the semantic field of crosses and circles" common to most vèvès, furthermore, provides something of a grid or structural apparatus for much Haitian painting at large (Brown 1995, 14, 35).

Vodou is a tremendously colorful religion, rich in iconography and ritual paraphernalia. This is in part the result of its syncretic, tolerant, and absorbent nature, and partially explains its inspiration for the extraordinary use of colors and sometimes dizzying array of imagery and symbolism that is often featured in Haitian painting. As Donald Cosentino argues, however, this has as much to do with material history as spiritual vision: "Commodities appear as if by magic, and then disappear with the same illogic. No wonder they are fetishized. First it was Catholic images and Masonic regalia abandoned by French slave masters. Now it is dolls found in dumps and sequins left behind by fleeing couriers. In an island stripped of forest and factory, imported items and ready-mades are perforce the raw material from which all art and religion are made" (Cosentino 1998, 42).

But not all Haitian art is religiously inspired, and less of it hangs on Vodou than most commentators would have us believe. Even as early as the 1940s, Haitian artists were painting quite secular scenes of everyday life—women doing the wash, *kombit* (people getting together to farm each other's land), and quotidian market scenes. For just as long, politics have seized the imagination of Haitian artists, as demonstrated by Philomé Obin's 1946 *Battle between the Cacos and the American Marines* and Hyppolite's celebrated 1947 portrait of President Florvil Hyppolite. More recently Stivenson Magloire, an artist whose politically progressive work has been exhibited in the United States and Canada, was beaten to death by political opponents in Port-au-Prince in 1994. *Botpipèl* (boat people) also feature in Haitian painting: Emmanuel Dostaly's *Cow without a Tail*, for example, is a bright landscape of a coastal fishing village where people appear to be going routinely about their daily chores. But in one corner a U.S. Coast Guard cutter at sea awaits a rickety boat boarding potential refugees.

Haitian painting is quite deservedly renowned, but so are Haitian artistic expressions in other media, like wood carvings, flat iron sculptures, and sequined flags, all so possessed of such boundless exuberance that Rodman (1988) entitled his influential and richly illustrated coffee-table oeuvre on Haitian art *Where Art Is Joy*. The paradox of course is that Haiti is a place of equally boundless suffering. As Francine Murat, director of the Haitian Center for Art, explained in the mid 1990s, "we have been living in turmoil for the last decade, and the only thing to hold us together was art. Art is important to our day-to-day life and has been our best ambassador abroad" (Stepick 1998, 97). And, just as their religion, language, foodways, and music accompany them as they cross the Straits of Florida to Miami, so too does Haiti's remarkable visual culture, much of it inspired by and infused with religion.

The Push of Haitian Religion

Besides the universal longings for a sense of meaning and for communion with the Sacred, it is to the existential needs rooted in enslavement and poverty that Haitian religion most forthrightly responds. Paramount among these is the need for a *bourad* (Creole for "a boost" or "a push"): to the next meal; to making a rent or tuition payment; to obtaining a visa or green card; to traversing a sea; or to placating a lover. It would be no exaggeration to call bourad one the most important forms of religious capital possessed—if not by all believers—by Haitians, be they Catholic, Vodouist, or Protestant. For most poor Haitians, whether in Haiti or abroad, religion is essentially not about high-flung cosmology but about supernatural assistance in tackling life's problems as best one can. Writing about Vodou's spirits in terms that could just as readily describe the function of saints for Haitian Catholics or the Holy Spirit for Haitian Protestant Pentecostals, Brown (1991, 254) explains that a lwa "is not a *deus ex machina* but a catalyst who mobilizes the will and energy of human beings."

Religion (Catholic, Protestant, Vodou, or any mix thereof) thus plays a central role both in shaping poor Haitians' understanding of suffering and in fortifying their struggle to survive and advance. Praying to Bondyè (God) and the Catholic saints, being baptized in the Holy Spirit, or serving the Vodou lwas, whether for protection, forgiveness, fullness of life, deliverance, or salvation, is done out of an unflinching faith that these spiritual beings can and do respond to humans' needs, and that religious practice elicits their response. Catholicism's greatest strengths in Haiti are thus its numerous saint cults, especially that (or those) of the Virgin Mary (Rey 1999). Saints watch over you on demand, and if they cannot pluck you from harm's way, they can certainly help you survive and recover. Likewise, Vodou "is a religion of survival, and it counsels what it must to ensure survival" (Brown 1991, 254). The impressive growth of Haitian Protestantism, furthermore, has also been attributed to such factors: "Protestantism [in Haiti] . . . exploits to the hilt a certain psychosis of fear, presenting itself as a refuge that offers a kind of security" (Romain 1986, 125). Furthermore, there is no greater force in contemporary Haitian religion than Pentecostalism, whose tremendous growth over the last fifty years, in both Protestant and Catholic forms, is largely explicable in terms of the quest for healing and spiritual strength (Conway 1980, 13; Rey 2005a), and in terms of the movement's "pneumacentrism" (Chesnut 2003, 5).

In rural Haiti, Vodou ceremonies draw together one's family, both immediate and extended, and help individuals negotiate the experiences of growing up, becoming ill, getting cured, and eventually (or suddenly) dying. The religion also offers prestige, an informal criminal justice system, and opportunities to participate in a multitude of communal rituals involving music, dance, theater, and crafts. Through Vodou, furthermore, those who behave improperly or immorally can be chastised and disciplined without a police force (Murray 1980). Vodou's cultural reach is so extensive that the Vodou temple (*ounfò*) in Haiti has been described as "sanctuary, clubhouse, dance hall, hospital, theater, chemist's shop, music hall, court and council chamber in one" (Jahn 1961). In the United States, Christian congregations accomplish all this and more by providing the social matrices of support to Haitians and other immigrants. When a Haitian immigrant is sick or in dire straits, for example, fellow churchgoers may gather at the person's house to pray. In addition, they may informally contribute money to help out, swing by the pharmacy to purchase medicine, or pick up her children from school. Churches formally help, too, by providing a wide range of social services.

Thus for Haitian immigrants, the function of religion is essentially the same in Miami as in the homeland, even as the kinds of struggles encountered in the "host" society may differ, sometimes radically, from those confronted in Haiti. Racist discrimination in the United States, for example, replaces the demoralizing classism that plagues their homeland. In response, Haitian immigrants recall with great pride that their country's history begins with world history's only successful national slave revolt; and that Haiti is the world's first politically independent black republic and the second independent nation in the Western Hemisphere. Because their ancestors' epic triumph over Napoleon's army drew tremendous strength from their religious faith (Mennesson-Riguaud 1958), moreover, and because religion has ever since been of preeminent importance in Haitian history and society, it is not surprising that today Haitians attend church as much or more frequently and in greater numbers than any other contemporary U.S. immigrant group (Stepick and Portes 1986). Richman (2005) asserts that for Haitians in Florida the church is the center of life, where they obtain not only "the goods of salvation" (Bourdieu 1971) and a bourad, but also forms of social capital that are likewise of critical importance to surviving and getting ahead in the United States.

Overall, the utilities and applications of religion among Haitian immigrants are consistent with those that predominate in the general history of immigrant religion in the United States. The social networks and organizational resources of religious organizations help immigrants not only define their identities but also combat prejudice and discrimination in their new society. The sermons and fellowship in Haitian congregations, for example, occasionally directly and almost always indirectly combat the extraordinary prejudice and discrimination that Haitians have faced in their journey and resettlement (Stepick 1998). Brodwin (2003) demonstrates how the appropriation of Pentecostalism by Haitian immigrants in Guadeloupe likewise defends them against denigrating stereotypes while also articulating sentiments of loss and remembrance of the Haitian homeland. This is not surprising, actually, as combating prejudice and discrimination in the "host" society is probably the most common form of civic engagement that is borne of immigrant religion in the United States (Stepick 2005).

By any measure, Haitians are extraordinarily religious. Nearly 75 percent of recent Haitian immigrants in South Florida reported in 1985 that they attended church at least weekly. Already by the mid 1980s, nearly 40 percent of then-recent Haitian refugees in South Florida were Protestants, more than double the percentage in their homeland (Stepick and Portes 1986). The best available demographic statistics indicate that in present-day Haiti roughly one in three persons is Protestant (Fontus 2003; Hurbon 2001; Woodson and Baro 1997). It is thus probable that a majority of Haitians in Miami in the first decade of the new millennium are Protestant.

Storefront Protestant churches abound in Little Haiti—nearly 100 in all—and a few Protestant churches have enjoyed tremendous growth. One Baptist congregation, Eglise Baptiste Emmanuel, for example, has converted a huge textile factory into the neighborhood's largest church edifice. Yet, in spite of the explosion of Protestant sects in Haitian Christianity, the most visible and important religious institution in Little Haiti is the Notre Dame d'Haiti Catholic Church and the adjoined Pierre Toussaint Haitian Catholic Center. A sprinkling of *botanicas* (stores that provide ritual paraphernalia, herbs, and various ritual services by Vodou priests and priestesses) round out Little Haiti's remarkable religioscape, to which our attention now turns.

Visual Expressions from Little Haiti's Triangle of Religious Forces

Because Little Haiti's religious visual culture is so rich as to effusively escape the confines of one essay, we limit our present analysis to only one example from each side of Haitian culture's "triangle of religious forces" (Woodson 1993): Catholicism,

Vodou, and Protestantism. On the Catholic side we focus upon a mural in the sanctuary of Notre Dame d'Haiti Catholic Church that depicts the exodus of Haitian botpipèl sailing under the maternal gaze of the Virgin Mary; on the Vodouist side we consider the vèvès that adorn Botanica Halouba, a religious goods store that houses Little Haiti's only public Vodou temple; and on the Protestant side we reflect upon a mural of a dove and a tree in the sanctuary of the Protestant storefront Mission Evangélique du Christanisme, which depicts the axis mundi of this transnational independent Haitian church. Far from being merely parts of Little Haiti's rich visual culture that collectively evoke the homeland and help Haitian immigrants feel a sense of *chez nous* in a foreign land, these are, to the believer, religious images. Moreover, the believer's seeing of these images is itself a form of "visual piety" (Morgan 2005, 6) that enables religion to function for the Haitian immigrant as bourad.

Notre Dame d'Haiti Catholic Church

Haitian refugees began arriving in South Florida in significant numbers in the early 1970s and by the end of that decade numbered around 50,000, most of them residing in Miami. In response, the Catholic Archdiocese of Miami arranged for the first Haitian Mass to be said in South Florida in 1973 at the Church of Corpus Christi in the Miami's Allapattah neighborhood. In 1977 the archdiocese established the Pierre Toussaint Haitian Catholic Center to serve its growing Haitian population, and in 1978 it assigned a recently ordained Polish American priest named Thomas Wenski to Corpus Christi. Shortly thereafter, Wenski was named director of archdiocesan Haitian Catholic Center, then housed at the Cathedral of St. Mary. The timing was uncanny, as in 1980 South Florida would receive a massive wave of Haitian immigrants who would forever change its cultural landscape.

To Father Wenski 1981 was a year of "divine providential timing" for the Haitian Catholic Mission in Miami.[2] May of that year witnessed the last graduating class of girls from Notre Dame Academy at the corner of Northeast 62nd Street and Northeast 2nd Avenue.[3] Then the school merged with Archbishop Curley High School because of dwindling enrollment, and the archdiocese decided to bequeath the Notre Dame campus to the Haitian Catholic Mission. Because more than ten thousand Haitian refugees had arrived in South Florida just the year prior, Wenski understandably perceived the hand of God behind the transfer of the school grounds to the Haitian apostolate. The Church of Notre Dame d'Haiti was thus established as a "quasi parish," with Wenski as its pastor.

The school cafeteria was transformed into the church, while the two stories of classrooms were used to house the multitude of social service programs offered by the Haitian Catholic Center, including English-as-a-second-language classes, job placement counseling, health screenings, and legal assistance. Almost immediately the center's service programs were drawing hundreds of beneficiaries of any religious persuasion, and in time—and to the present—more than one thousand people were coming to Notre Dame and the center each day. In this fashion did Notre Dame d'Haiti become the most important Haitian institution in Miami.

Though hardly ornate by Catholic standards, Notre Dame houses two striking examples of visual culture that powerfully reflect the Haitian botpipèl experience and the depths of faith of the Haitian people. Behind the altar, on the eastern wall, are several stained-glass windows, one of Pierre Toussaint, one of the Virgin Mary, and one of a boatload of Haitian refugees.[4] The architectural limitations of the former cafeteria are such that the Tabernacle, which normally is located in Catholic churches behind the altar and just off to the right, is found instead on the northern side wall. On this wall is a large mural depicting an overcrowded sailboat leaving Haiti, while in the sky are an Air d'Haiti jetliner, also leaving, and Our Lady of Perpetual Help, who is overseeing her children as Haiti's patron saint.

To Haitian immigrants in Miami, what does the image of an overcrowded wooden sailboat under the Virgin Mary's gaze in a Catholic church mean? To Catholics, it clearly reflects their belief that the Virgin Mary oversaw their arduous and often perilous journey to the United States. To Vodouists, it could very well be not so much an image of the Virgin Mary but of Ezili (or of some conflation of the two), the Vodou spirit with whom the Virgin is associated or identified, who is depicted in the mural as aiding botpipèl's passage. And to Protestants it might represent a folkloric or idolatrous misunderstanding among their Catholic and Vodouist compatriots that spiritual beings outside the Trinity distribute the grace that is only God's through Jesus Christ. These variations aside, it is inconceivable to us that any Haitian immigrant would respond to the image indifferently. Its greatest symbolic register is of course Catholic, as it depicts a Catholic saint and it adorns the wall of a Catholic church. These facts do not make the image any less

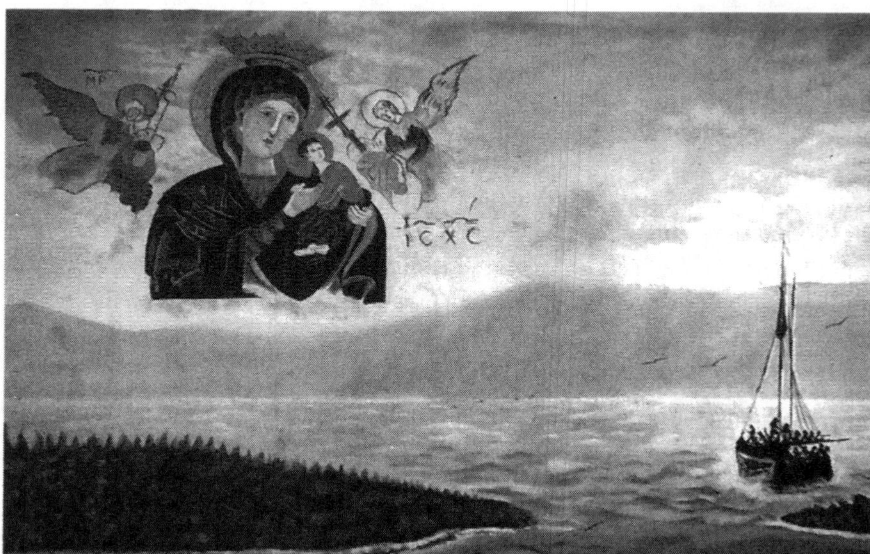

Figure 12.1. Our Lady of Perpetual Help, wall mural in Notre Dame d'Haiti Catholic Church. Photo by Terry Rey.

important to Vodouists, however, because most people who practice Vodou are also Catholic, and their viewing of Catholic images certainly constitutes that which Morgan (2005, 6) calls "visual piety," or "the constructive operation of seeing that looks for, makes room for, the transcendent in daily life."

People everywhere have long found water to be a powerful sacrament or symbol, thus making it essential to religion. Virtually half of Haitian Vodou's pantheon of lwas live in, under, or across water, as do ancestors (*zansèts*). Furthermore, everyone dies to pass a year and one day "at the bottom of a river or a lake" and sometimes then demands that the living ceremoniously extract them from under the water (Métraux [1959] 1972, 258). In Vodou, water is thus essential to cosmology, healing, pilgrimage, baptism, and purification, and is, along with blood, leaves, and stones, the religion's material lifeblood. Lwas and zansèts mostly derive from Africa, as do the distant ancestors whose descendants were enslaved and torn from Africa across the Atlantic. Given the paramount importance of ancestral spirituality in traditional African religion, the turbulence and trauma of such a disruption were and continue to be immeasurable for Haitian Vodouists. Because of this, aquatic symbolism in Vodou is invested deeply with pain, passage, and memory. What is more, the chain of African memory was so violently rattled by the experience of slavery that its clanging is still clearly audible in Haitian religion; a chain rattled fiercely yet again by the terrible poverty and suffering that has transformed tens of thousands of Haitians into botpipèl, who sometimes tragically wind up under the water as ancestors. The crossing of water is thus one of the master motifs of Haitian Vodou, and this resonates powerfully in the Notre Dame mural for Vodouist immigrants.

From a more "purely" Catholic standpoint, the Notre Dame mural is a reflection of the tremendous faith that Haitians have in the Virgin Mary, especially as Our Lady of Perpetual Help, Haiti's patron saint. Furthermore the items (spear, wine-soaked sponge, crown of thorns, cross, and nails) held by the Archangels Michael and Gabriel, who hover watchingly over the Madonna and the Christ child, reflect Christianity's central theological diptych: suffering and redemption, themes that resound quite powerfully for poor Haitians in general. That the child seems to be losing his sandal while longingly embracing his mother in the face of his tremendous future suffering is, furthermore, an invitation to all suffering people to turn to Our Lady of Perpetual Help.[5] It is thus unsurprising that Marian devotion predominates in Haitian Catholicism, and virtually every benevolent triumph in Haitian history is ultimately attributable to her motherly and unfailing oversight and grace. During the Haitian Revolution, for instance, a rebel prophet named Romaine-la-Prophétesse claimed to be the godson of the Virgin, who commanded him to raid plantations, slaughter whites, and aspire to be king of the island (Rey 1998). What's more, Polish soldiers in Napoleon's army deserted the French during the Revolution and fought on behalf of the revolting slaves under the banner of the patron saint of Poland, Our Lady of Czestochowa, whose cult remains among the most popular in Haitian religion. Perpetual Help and Czestochowa, at any rate, rank among the most popular religious symbols in Haiti.

Because, as noted above, most Haitian Catholics are also devoted to the lwas, the hagiography of Marian icons like Perpetual Help take on additional meanings to the more "orthodox" inscriptions that are read in them by *katolik fran* (literally, "frank Catholics," or Catholics who do not also practice Vodou). For one thing, most images of Mary in which the Christ Child also appears generally represent for Vodouists Ezili Dantò, the fiery manifestation of Vodou's leading feminine lwa in the religion's *petwo* rite (Brown 1995, 34). Perpetual Help's icon, moreover, includes not only the archangels Michael and Gabriel but a host of other symbols, like those mentioned above, making it especially fertile ground for Vodouist interpretation and syncretism. As Beauvoir-Dominique (1991, 131) explains, this icon "reveals a Virgin of somber color surrounded by two angels and Kabalistic signs, with the child Jesus on her knee holding a book. . . . What is this book? No doubt, this is his 'magic book,' wherein are recorded all of his ways, the source of his power, making this figure all the more formidable."

Of even greater importance to Haitian Marianism were the miraculous events of 1881–1882. Beginning in 1881 a smallpox epidemic ravaged Haitian cities so dreadfully that by March of the following year some 100,000 people had died of the disease. Having recently received a large icon of Our Lady of Perpetual Help as a gift, the curate of the cathedral in Port-au-Prince called for a procession and novena in the capital to implore the Virgin for healing. Although this icon of the Virgin Mary then was unknown and enjoyed no cult in Haiti, thousands came in despair over "the plague." "Halfway through this collective novena to Notre Dame du Perpétuel Secours, the skies opened and heavy rains brought an end to the unusually long drought" that had permitted the epidemic to reach such devastating proportions (Rey 1999, 166). This miracle solidified the Virgin's place in Haitian Catholic consciousness beyond measure, and sixty years later Our Lady of Perpetual Help was duly elevated to the status of patron saint of the Republic of Haiti (Rey 1999, 2002).

In light of Haiti's rich Marian history and deep Vodouist mythology, Little Haiti's Notre Dame mural symbolizes many things to most Haitians who see it: human origins and destiny; the maternal intercessionary powers of the Virgin Mary or Ezili; the structure of the universe; the spirits and the dead; the meaning of life and death; the pain inflicted by global economics; African rhythms and roots; and the desperate voyages of overcrowded rickety sailboats. To gaze upon this mural is, for Haitian Catholics and Vodouists, thus an act of visual piety par excellence.

Botanica Halouba

An overburdened cliché has it that "Haiti is 90% Catholic, 10% Protestant, and 100% Vodouist." In its wild statistical inaccuracy, this popular myth misrepresents the Haitian religious field entirely. For one thing, the community of Protestants in Haiti, who generally reject Vodou outright as diabolical, has blossomed in the last two decades to constitute roughly one-third of the entire population, as noted above. Also, "there are more *katolik fran* (Catholics who do not also wittingly practice Vodou) in Haiti than scholars have heretofore been willing to admit" (Rey 2004, 370). That being said, most people in Haiti still do practice Vodou, many others nominally and with varying frequency enter the religion for guidance and healing, and just about everyone's understanding of the universe and one's place in it is influenced in some way or another by the religion. Even among Haitian Pentecostals who demonize Vodou, there is no doubt that Vodou is real—that it effectively accesses and negotiates a supernatural reality that is objectively existent. Thus, like any national popular religion, Vodou's ethos spreads well beyond the confines of the personal and communal spiritual lives of its actual practitioners. Comparatively speaking, in Haitian society Vodou functions much like Calvinism does in the United States: although not all Americans are Calvinists, the Protestant work ethic, which is inspired in large part by Calvinist theology (Weber 1930), broadly influences how Americans of all ethnic and religious backgrounds understand life. And just as many American Christians can believe that money is the root of all evil while being nevertheless materialistically self-indulgent in good conscience, so too do some Haitian Pentecostals use their Bibles as amulets in ways that their Vodouist compatriots use a glass of water or a packet of leaves.

Vodou emerged as a religion among African and African-descended slaves in French-ruled Saint-Domingue (1697–1804), which at the time was the most lucrative European colony in the Caribbean. Despite the colony's formal prohibition against the practice of African religions, both on plantations and in maroon settlements these women and men extended and re-created ancestor and spirit cults from the mother continent, mixing in some Catholicism for good measure, and hence Vodou was born. Initially clandestine and variegated, Vodou has no founder, no unifying doctrine, and no formal organizational network. Neither any of these nor a Vodou scripture has ever developed.

Slaves brought to Saint-Domingue were baptized Catholic upon arrival and given minimal religious instruction by Dominican, Capuchin, and Jesuit missionaries. Syncretism immediately resulted, as slaves identified Catholic saints as new (to most of them) manifestations of African spirits, and they adopted crosses, holy water, and incense as powerful religious trinkets to be used in conjunction with the amulets that they reconstructed from African religious memory. The Catholic "pantheon"—with its single high creator God, Virgin Mary, and host of dead individuals (the saints) who intervene in the world of the living—lent itself quite fluently to assimilation with the traditional African community of spiritual beings, which likewise has a single distant creator God (called Bondyè or Granmèt in Vodou) and numerous spirits and ancestors, who, much like the Catholic saints, are perceived as accessible, and with whom the greatest amount of human/divine commerce, mostly through divination and spirit possession, transpires.

Because it was born as a persecuted faith in maroon communities and on slave plantations in colonial Hispaniola, and because it next endured formal and concerted persecution at the hands of the new and independent Haitian state until 1942, Vodou has long been accustomed to negotiating its existence underground. But, over the last twenty years the religion has become increasingly open in Haiti, where the 1987 constitution affords it "official religion" status along with Catholicism; where in 2003 President Jean-Bertrand Aristide granted legality to its baptisms and marriages; and where a few public Pentecostal-style "Vodou churches" have recently been opening in Port-au-Prince (Hurbon 2007). And once arriving in Miami with the first waves of Haitian refugees in the late 1970s and early 1980s, Vodou served Haitian immigrants as a familiar resource for empowerment in the face of tremendous difficulties and tumult, albeit more clandestinely than in the homeland.

We estimate that today some 25,000 Haitians in Miami, or 10 percent of the total Haitian population in Miami-Dade County, regularly practice Vodou, while many others occasionally consult with a *manbo* (priestess) or *oungan* (priest) for spiritual guidance, healing, or "luck" (*chans*).[6] Aside from the two or three small quasi-public temples in the city, Vodou in Miami is largely "underground," or home-based, with altars erected in practitioners' homes, where an oungan and/or a manbo might visit to preside over occasional ceremonies, usually either rites of passage or feasts for the lwas and the dead. Since the city is built on a swamp, there are no basements in Miami, which serve so well as temples for Vodouists in New York, where Vodou also thrives in the devotion of thousands of Haitian immigrants (Brown 1991).

Vodou's material and commercial lifeline in Miami is the botanica, or religious goods store, an originally Cuban American way of marketing African-derived religious products first in New York and later in Miami and elsewhere. Haitian versions of these enterprises generally are run by manbos or oungans and usually feature a small room in the back that serves as a divination chamber. The city's largest Haitian botanica, Botanica Halouba, actually has a temple inside. There are roughly two dozen Haitian botanicas in the city that cater to Hispanic clients in addition to Haitians. Meanwhile, there are more than 100 Cuban botanicas in Miami, which likewise offer similar divinations, rituals, and religious paraphernalia to practitioners of Santería, Vodou's Afro-Cuban sibling religion (Lammoglia 2001). For tourists these shops contribute to the city's "exotic" appeal, while locals see them as either sacred spaces or bastions of pagan superstition, depending on one's theological predilection.

Botanica Halouba is a large one-story yellow building decorated with vèvès for the rainbow-serpent lwa Danbala-wedo and Ezili Freda, among others. Vèvès are perhaps the most striking and original features in Vodou's intoxicatingly rich and eclectic symbology. Virtually each lwa has a personal vèvè that symbolizes her and her power, in much the same way that the cross symbolizes Jesus and his. The cross is of course a singular symbol, whereas the vèvè appears in as many varieties as there are lwas. Nevertheless, several vèvès would be recognizable to any Vodouist, regardless of the measure of devotion that she holds for the particular lwas that they represent. Ezili's heart-shaped vèvè, for example, evokes the divinity of motherhood; Agwe's boat evokes the sacred power of the sea; Mètkafou's cross speaks of the crossroads that all humans encounter on life's way—all Vodouists would readily recognize these and several other vèvès.

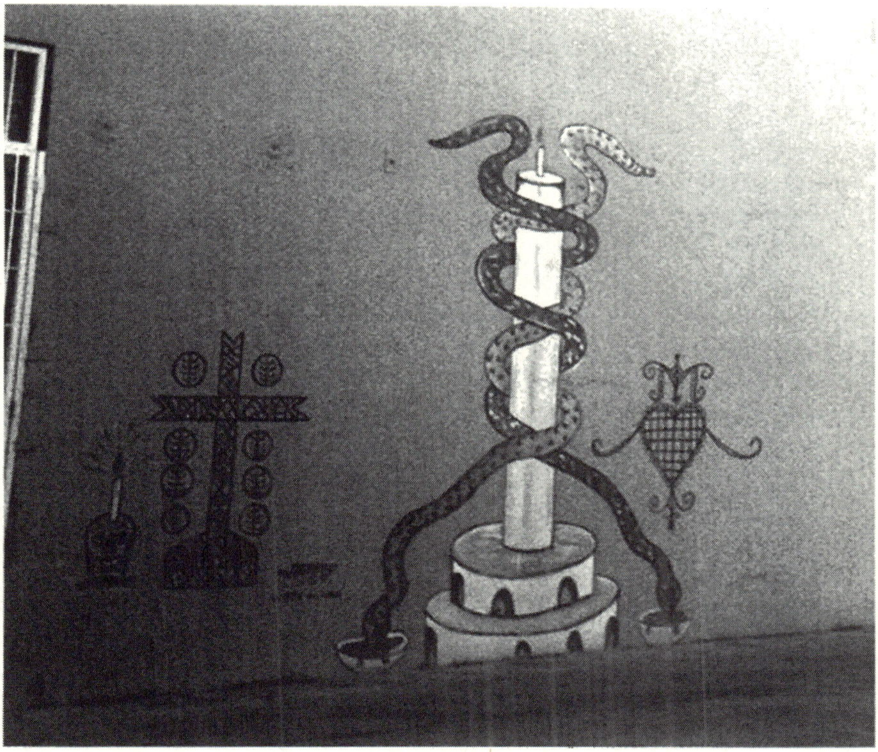

Figure 12.2. Vévé at the Botanica Halouba. Photo by Terry Rey.

It is quite reasonable for the vèvès of Danbala and Ezili, among a few others, to have been chosen from among hundreds of others to adorn the walls of Botanica Halouba, for they are two of the most important spirits in the Vodou pantheon. They share little in common hagiographically, though significantly each is associated with water, parenthood, and creativity. As explains Desmangles (1992, 125), "Vodouisants say that Damballah is an aged, noble father who assisted Bondye [God] when he created the universe. . . . (H)e is the father of the universe . . . the one who twines himself around the four pillars that support the universe." As such, we all depend ultimately on Danbala for our very existence, and he, like all lwa, can provide us with bourad should we engage him in a reciprocal relationship of devotion and service. In her various manifestations, meanwhile, Ezili is a protective mother and the religion's ultimate reflection of the divine feminine principle. More concretely, she also represents the quotidian realities that especially women (and transgendered men) face in the Haitian world. Brown (1979, 110) describes this function of Ezili and of all the lwas as "a very special sort of language": "In short, the gods provide the categories of thought that make people and the situations that arise between them thinkable." The very act of visual piety in which the Vodouist immigrant in Little Haiti sees the vèvès on the wall of Botanica Halouba, even if but in passing on the way to work on Northwest 54th Street, thus helps make existence in this new and often hostile world "thinkable."

Mission Evangelique du Christianisme

It is easy to think of Little Haiti as a religious marketplace. Some one hundred churches grace its five hundred square blocks; botanicas retailing Vodouist ritual paraphernalia and healing herbs abound; murals of Catholic saints adorn grocery stores; and on any given Sunday well-dressed, Bible-toting Christians shuffle about the neighborhood's streets. Its boundaries are unofficial and hence disputed, but generally U.S. Route 1 delineates its eastern border, Northwest 7th Avenue its western, the Design District its southern, and Miami's Catholic Cathedral of St. Mary its northern. Within these boundaries lies a roughly fifty-by-twelve-block swath of one of the poorest neighborhoods in Miami, which is America's poorest big city. About twenty years ago there were merely a dozen or so Haitian churches in the neighborhood (Vaughan 1983). In the interim this number has multiplied nearly tenfold, while the city's Haitian population has "only" tripled since then.

With so many churches, Little Haiti could well be one of the most religious inner-city neighborhoods in the United States. On Northeast Miami Avenue, for example, just two blocks north of Notre Dame d'Haiti Catholic Church, are aligned five other Haitian churches. Clustered within three blocks, they are all freestanding and hence not of the storefront variety: Grace United Methodist Church, l'Eglise de St. Paul et les Martyrs d'Haiti, l'Eglise du Christ de North Miami, the House of the Living God, and the First Haitian Free United Methodist Church. Fanning out a few blocks in any direction, one finds even more churches, most of them storefronts, an approach to physical church establishment that Haitians and other immigrants in the United States have inherited from African Americans.

By 1983 Haitians had established about a dozen Protestant churches in the neighborhood of Lemon City, which would soon be called "Little Haiti," most of them independent Baptist and Pentecostal storefronts. Gradually the number of churches increased, as more and more Haitians settled in the neighborhood upon successfully fleeing Haiti's perpetual economic and political crises. In the quarter century since the massive 1980 wave of Haitian refugees arrived in Miami, Little Haiti has witnessed an impressive proliferation of churches: to nearly one hundred in 2000. Of the eighty-four churches that we have identified in Little Haiti, independent storefronts of either Baptist (fifteen) or Pentecostal (fifty-one) persuasion predominate.[7]

Mission Evangélique du Christianisme (MEC) is one of the largest churches on Northwest 54th Street, Little Haiti's thriving east-west corridor, and one of the neighborhood's largest storefront churches. With some measure of pride, its leaders claim their church represents "the only truly indigenous form of Haitian Christianity."[8] Whereas all other Protestant churches in Haiti and in the Haitian diaspora are either parts of mainstream mission churches, offshoots of mission churches, or inspired by and/or modeled on North American forms of Pentecostal churches (Brodwin 2003, 86), MEC's origins lie in the mystical experiences and healing ministry of its remarkable Haitian founder, the missionary Salomon Sévère Joseph. His fascinating story is well worth summarizing here.[9]

Salomon Sévère Joseph was born on December 12, 1891, in Jonc-Daudin-d'Aquin on Haiti's southern coast about twenty miles east of Les Cayes, Haiti's third largest city. His father was a military officer and a devout Catholic, hence Salomon received a good formal education and was baptized and raised Catholic. One of twelve children, he was very pious and was a member of the choir of the local parish. In 1918 he began studying law, and in 1920 he founded an elementary school for peasant children in his hometown. He also married and soon fathered the first of his own twelve children.

His life changed radically when in 1930 he began to have tremendous mystical experiences, in particular receiving visions and hearing voices. The first vision was brief and occurred one day while Joseph was working the family fields with his father. He saw an angelic figure radiant and white and alerted his father, who saw nothing. A few nights later Joseph saw three similar figures approaching him. The youngest one said to him, "Do not fear, my child." The oldest one said nothing but kissed him three times on the cheek. The third one said to him: "And I will kiss you not three times but 3,399 times. And these kisses will be multiplied fourfold so that only the spirits will know the depth of our friendship." The tree beneath which Joseph received these initial visions is greatly revered by MEC members and is the site on which the first MEC church was constructed in 1934. A mural of this tree with a dove soaring above it graces the rear wall of the Miami MEC sanctuary.

Joseph's healing ministry began soon after these visions and continued for the remaining forty years of his life. In one sense, faith healing was a kind of supernatural offshoot of the de facto infirmary that his large and charitable family had established on their homestead. With no formal healthcare available in the area, "Lakou Joseph" (the Joseph homestead) attracted many sick peasants from the surrounding hills. In addition to providing free of charge whatever medicine the Joseph family had in stock, they also conducted communal prayers for healing, and employed the services of one family member who was a well respected *medsin fey* ("leaf doctor," or herbalist). In this milieu, "Sévè," as he was called locally, began healing the sick by laying his hands on them, exhorting them to repent, surrender to Jesus Christ, reject Vodou, and commit to fervent and regular prayer to the Lord. Any monetary donations that he and his family received were quickly turned over to the local Catholic parish—for a time, anyway. He even healed animals, which are of great economic importance to the Haitian peasantry.

Through his biblical studies and meditations Sévè reached the arresting conclusion that Catholicism was not true Christianity. As his conviction of the falsehood of his former church strengthened, and as his confidence as a healer grew, he incorporated the burning of Catholic icons and other ritual paraphernalia into his healing mission on the grounds that they were idolatrous. At one point, Sévè actually emptied the contents of a local Catholic church, placed them in a heap in the churchyard, and burned them. This act of divinely inspired vandalism led to the first of his three arrests, making him one of a number of Protestant religious leaders to be victimized by the antisuperstition campaigns that the Haitian Catholic Church, in collaboration with the state and the army, conducted to eradicate Vodou from Haitian society.

Over the ensuing decades, Sévè was credited with having performed countless miracles, usually in the form of healing sick humans and animals, including the resuscitation of his own dog, Mégarde, who followed the missionary wherever he went. Some attest that he even raised the human dead. People from throughout Haiti flocked to his church, and Sévè's mission flourished, even after his death in 1973. Eventually MEC would become not merely a transnational church but a well-organized international network of congregations. Besides its numerous branches in Haiti and the several congregations located in the United States, MEC also has churches in Canada, France, St. Martin, and French Guyana.

There are other features of MEC belief and practice that are also refreshingly original and hence appealing. For one, MEC members refer to themselves as *christianistes* (Christianists), as opposed to the usual term in French *chretiens* (Christians). And although born in part out of Sévè's anti-Catholic iconoclasm, the typical MEC service includes the peace greeting from the Catholic Mass, but instead of saying "peace be with you," the one to first offer her hand in a gesture of greeting proclaims "*l'humanité*" (humanity), to which the person receiving the greeting, upon shaking the greeter's hand, responds "*la foi*" (faith). This unique form of call and response, moreover, is enacted whenever anyone takes the microphone to address the congregation, with the speaker saying "*l'humanité*" (or sometimes repeating the greeting in the expanded form, now in Creole, of "*limanite na legliz la*" [humanity in this church]), with the congregation responding collectively "*la foi.*"

The MEC church edifice on Northwest 54th Street in Little Haiti was originally a warehouse or workshop, a location that the congregation has occupied since 1993. The Miami branch serves as the headquarters for Florida, which is home to four MEC churches, the others being located in Tampa Bay, Orlando, and Delray. Counting about three hundred members, many of whom are immigrants from the Aquin area in Haiti, the Miami MEC church is housed in a cavernous and square white concrete building, with an unpaved parking lot surrounded by a chain-link fence. The northwest corner lot is the parking area, which fills up regularly by at least fifteen minutes before the 11:00 A.M. Sunday worship service begins. An interesting variety of cars can be found here on any given Sunday, ranging from shiny new SUVs to much humbler beat-up jalopies. Especially conspicuous are the several yellow taxi cabs often in the lot that carry on their roofs colorful, racy advertisements for local strip clubs. This incongruity rather strikingly reflects Mircea Eliade's (1987, 25) notion that sacred and profane space are divided by a threshold—namely, in this case, the church door: "The threshold is the limit, the boundary the frontier that distinguishes and opposes two worlds—and at the same

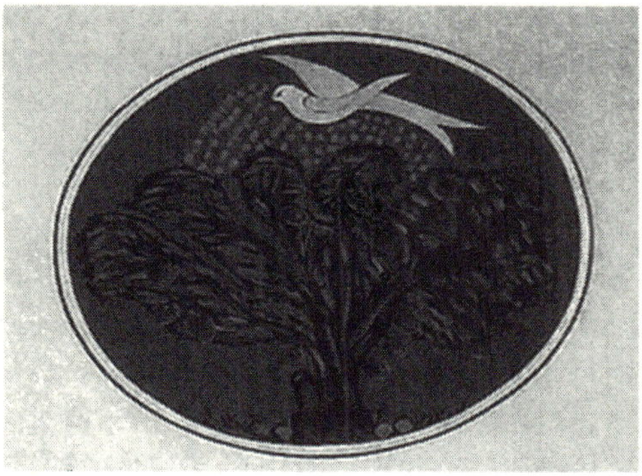

Figure 12.3. Dove as Blessing, wall mural in Mission Evangelique du Christianisme. Photo by Terry Rey.

time the paradoxical place where the worlds communicate, where passage from the profane to the sacred world becomes possible."

With the exception a small encircled mural of a dove gliding over a tree, the MEC sanctuary is devoid of religious imagery. For Haitian immigrants who attend this church, the mural is of tremendous importance because it depicts the tree in southern Haiti under which Salomon Sévère Joseph began his remarkable healing ministry over seventy years ago, the very place where MEC was founded. The dove symbolizes the Holy Spirit, who is portrayed here as radiating divine grace on the tree. A "translocative" and "transtemporal" image (Tweed 1997), for Miami's Haitian Christianists, seeing this painting is thus an act of visual piety that serves as a strong link in the "chain of memory" that their faith provides.

Trees are of great importance in Haitian religious culture. In Vodou, for instance, trees derive religious significance by providing the material for the sacramental drum, the stick to which the sacrificial animal is tied, and the gourd that, once transformed into a rattle, is the emblem par excellence of the religion's priesthood. More important, trees are widely believed in Haiti to be the residences of the lwas and "the preferred avenue of divine approach" (Deren [1953] 1991, 36). Furthermore, to the eyes of the Vodou practitioner there is no more sacred a natural landmark in the Haitian hills and plains than a mapou tree (*Ceiba petenda*) (Hurbon 1972; Rey 2005b). Not to be outdone, in popular Haitian Catholicism the three most important Marian apparitions in history all happened in treetops (Rey 1999). And in Sèvè's tree we find as close a thing as Protestantism would allow to a sacred tree. Effectively, trees can thus be found in the symbolic registry across all sides of Haiti's triangle of religious forces.

Sèvé's tree is a unifying symbol for MEC members, hearkening to Durkheim's notion of the totem as the communally adhesive heart of religion. For Durkheim ([1915] 1995, 100), the totem "serves to designate the clan collectively," to designate the individual as a member in the collectivity, and to distinguish it from other collectivities. To wit: "Everyone [i.e., all MEC members] knows about the calabash tree," explained Pastor Kersaint Joseph, president of the MEC Miami congregation.[10] Sèvé's ministry thus not only sacralized this particular calabash tree

(*Crescentia cujete*) in southern Haiti but, in the process, effectively provided the MEC with its axis mundi, its totem, and its taproot. It also provides MEC members with an essential link in their chain of memory and a source of pride in their uniquely Haitian Christian church.

The Tree and the Sea: Imagining a Conclusion

This chapter focuses on just one aspect of Haitian art, religious imagery, and is further limited to three subjects in one Miami neighborhood. Not much, really. Regrettably, we have ignored other forms of Haitian artistic expression entirely, like music and literature, which are no less impressive than Haitian visual arts and as undeniably deserving of scholarly attention as the truncated surface that we have attempted to scratch here. Haitian performing artists such as Wyclef Jean, the son of a Protestant reverend, and the Vodou-rock fusion groups Boukman Eksperyans and Ram have recently enjoyed great success and international acclaim. Most significant, in doing so they have helped to cause discernibly positive shifts in how Haitians in the United States are perceived and even in how diasporic Haitians view themselves.

When we consider that less than one hundred years ago U.S. Secretary of State William Jennings Bryan, upon learning a thing or two about Haitian culture five years into his country's first occupation of Haiti, exclaimed in racist disbelief, "Oh dear me! Just think of it! Niggers speaking French!" or when we consider that the U.S. Center for Disease Control in 1983 included Haitians among heroin addicts, hemophiliacs, and male homosexuals as groups at "high risk" for contracting and spreading HIV/AIDS, which effectively "identified for worried Americans the culprits" (Alcabes 2006, 5), it becomes glaringly apparent how socially and politically meaningful it is that Wyclef Jean has recently appeared on *Sesame Street*; that Ram's music features in a major Hollywood film, *Philadelphia*; and that the novels of Edwige Danticat have sold millions of copies in the United States and been featured on Oprah's Book Club. Such is the power of Haitian artistry. What's more, we suspect that these are key factors underlying a swelling of Haitian pride that we have witnessed in recent years, especially among Haitian youth, in Miami. It is heartening to further suggest that this could well contribute to a decline in the "cover up" phenomenon, wherein some young Haitians in the United States vehemently deny and mask their Haitian-ness and steadfastly—even obsessively—cultivate an African American identity, sometimes to tragic extremes (Stepick 1998, 1–3).

In this regard, Haitian art is proving to be quite a powerful agent in the struggle against discrimination, which is likewise an important function of Haitian immigrant religion. The admittedly limited scope of this chapter notwithstanding, we submit that religion, as much as (if not more than) anything else underlies and inspires Haitian creative expression in all media. Praise to the lwas are common in the lyrics of Boukman Eksperyans and Ram, Wyclef Jean's fourth album is entitled *Preacher's Son*, and Danticat's novels sometimes highlight Vodouist spirituality. This is all quite consistent with religion's unsurpassed importance to Haitians both at home and in the diaspora—a fact that is impressively reflected in the visual culture of Little Haiti. The neighborhood's religious imagery, such as Notre Dame d'Haiti's botpipèl mural, Botanica Halouba's vèvès, and MEC's mural of the tree and the dove, are powerful testimony to this.

In this vein, art and religion are united in their fundamental function for Haitian immigrants, for they both ultimately provide them with a sense of "worthiness" in a society that has generally believed and said that they are unworthy, that they have no proper place in the United States. Though nowhere concerned explicitly with the immigrant experience, Weber's focus on religious needs and their material influences presages the predominant theoretical discussions on immigrant religion in the growing scholarly literature. The notion that is most fundamental to Weber's theory (1963, 106), and most relevant to the interpretation of immigrant religion in the United States (or anywhere, for that matter), is that the religious practice of members of the "nonprivileged classes," to which most Haitian immigrants in the United States clearly belong, is driven in large part by "a hunger for a worthiness which has not fallen to their lot, they and the world being what it is."

Finally, the images studied in this chapter are indeed elemental to Haitian immigrants' "consciousness of belonging" (Hervieu-Léger 1993) to traditions that have both "crossed over" seas and obstacles to effect "homemaking" (Tweed 2006) in a new and strange world. To add yet one more trope, and to constructively counter one that we use above, we posit that, rather than a "religious marketplace," Little Haiti might be better viewed as a religious forest with roots in Haiti and branches in Little Haiti. This forest's branches bear the fruits that nourish the religious needs of the Haitian immigrant, needs that are conditioned or intensified by the struggle for acceptance in a racist society—needs to quell their "hunger for worthiness." That is a sociological explanation, of course. Its phenomenological equivalent would be "the praise of God" or "devotion to the spirits." Either way, it is the religious imagination and the religious imagery of Little Haiti that speaks this to us and, more important, to Haitian immigrants in the most resounding ways.

NOTES

1. Gourgue, whose mother was a Vodou priestess, painted this piece at the age of seventeen.
2. Bishop Thomas Wenski, interview with authors, September 26, 2000, Miami.
3. These streets are also named Martin Luther King Jr. Boulevard and Felix Morisseau LeRoy Boulevard, respectively, the latter after the great twentieth-century Haitian poet.
4. Pierre Toussaint (1766–1853) was born into slavery in Saint-Domingue and then brought to New York in 1787. He managed to purchase his freedom in 1807. Toussaint's deep Catholic piety and laudable philanthropic works have inspired a movement in the church promoting his canonization.
5. We are grateful to Patricia Fernández-Kelly for her insights into this hagiography.
6. Our estimation assumes similar religious demographics among Haitians as among Cubans in Miami and rests upon the clearer picture of Afro-Cuban religions in the city. As Lammoglia (2001) has demonstrated, there are roughly 100 Cuban botanicas in Miami that serve a community of 100,000 practitioners of Afro-Cuban religions, meaning 1,000 practitioners for each botanica. There are roughly 25 Haitian botanicas in Miami-Dade County; hence, if we grant that there are 1,000 Vodou practitioners per botanica, we arrive at the figure of 25,000. Doubtless, some will dispute this figure as either too high or too low, but much depends on

one's definition of "practitioner," by which we mean an individual who is initiated and/or regularly practices devotions to the lwas and ancestors *as their primary religion.*

7. There are certainly churches that we were unable to find, as many congregations meet in unmarked private spaces while others change location frequently. Thus, while we have located eighty-four churches in the neighborhood, there are easily more than one hundred.

8. Rev. Fandor Saint-Felix, interview with Terry Rey, March 21, 2004, Miami.

9. Details about the life of Joseph are entirely derived from Valéry (2000).

10. Rev. Kersaint Joseph, interview with Terry Rey, March 21, 2004, Miami.

References

Adams, Eddie. 1987. "Hiding in America: The Secret Misery of Illegal Aliens." *Parade Magazine*, January 11, cover.

Adler, Rachel. 2006. "'But They Claimed to Be Police, Not la Migra!' The Interaction of Residency Status, Class and Ethnicity in a (Post-PATRIOT Act) New Jersey Neighborhood." *American Behavioral Scientist* 50 (1): 48–69.

Aguilera-Hellweg, Max. 1995. *La frontera sin sonrisa*. El Paso, NM: El Paso Museum of Art.

Ahmed, Leila. 1992. *Women and Gender in Islam: Historical Roots of a Modern Debate*. New Haven: Yale University Press.

Ajrouch, Kristine. 1999. "Family and Ethnic Identity in an Arab-American Community." In *Arabs in America: Building a New Future*, ed. Michael Suleiman, 129–139. Philadelphia: Temple University Press.

Akram, Susan. 2002. "The Aftermath of September 11, 2001: The Targeting of Arabs and Muslims in America." *Arab Studies Quarterly* 24: 61–118.

Alcabes, Philip. 2005. "Heart of Darkness: AIDS, Africa, and Race." *Virginia Quarterly Review* (Winter): 5–9. http://www.vqonline.org/articles/2006/winter/Alcabes-heart-darkness/.

Alexander, Meena. 1996. *The Shock of Arrival: Reflections on Postcolonial Experience*. Boston: South End Press.

Alisky, Marvin. 1955. "Central American Radio." *Quarterly of Film Radio and Television* 10 (1): 51–63.

Allen, Ernest, Jr. 1996. "Making the Strong Survive: The Contours and Contradictions of Message Rap." In *Droppin' Science: Critical Essays on Rap Music and Hip Hop Culture*, ed. William E. Perkins, 159–191. Philadelphia: Temple University Press.

American Assembly. 1997. *The Arts and the Public Purpose*. Final report of the 92nd American Assembly. New York: Columbia University.

Amy-Moreno, Angel. 2005. "Latin Americans." In *The Encyclopedia of New England: The Culture and History of an American Region*, ed. B. Feintuch, D. H. Watters, and University of New Hampshire Center for the Humanities. New Haven: Yale University Press.

Anastos, Phillip, and Chris French. 1991. *Illegal: Seeking the American Dream*. New York: Rizzoli International Publications.

Appadurai, Arjun. 1996. *Modernity at Large: Cultural Dimensions of Globalization*. Minneapolis: University of Minnesota Press.

Arias, Arturo. 2001. "Central American-Americans: Invisibility, Power and Representation in the U.S. Latino World." *Latino Studies* 1: 168–187.

Aron, Adriane, Shawn Corne, Anthea Fursland, and Barbara Zelwer. 1991. "The Gender-Specific Terror of El Salvador and Guatemala." *Women's Studies International Forum* 14:37–47.

Asian Arts Initiative. 2008. http://www.asianartsinitiative.org/.

Axelrod, Alan. 1987. *Hispanic Art in the United States: Thirty Contemporary Painters and Sculptors.* New York: Abbeville Press.

Baker-Cristales, Beth. 2004. *Salvadoran Migration to Southern California: Redefining El Hermano Lejano.* Gainesville: University Press of Florida.

Bankston, Carl L., and Danielle Antoinette Hidalgo, eds. 2006. *Immigration in U.S. History.* Pasadena, CA: Salem Press.

Barkan, Elliott Robert. 1996. *And Still They Come: Immigrants and American Society, 1920* to the 1990s. Wheeling, IL: Harlan Davidson.

Baumol, William J., and William G. Bowen. 1966. *Performing Arts: The Economic Dilemma.* Cambridge, MA: MIT Press.

Baynes, Leonard M. 2009. "Race and Media: Several Key Proposals for the Next Administration." In *And Communications for All: A Policy Agenda for the New Administration*, ed. Amit M. Schejter, 301–324. New York: Rowman & Littlefield.

Bayoumi, Moustafa. 2006. "Arab America's September 11." *Nation* 283 (9): 22–26.

Bean, Frank D., and S. Bell-Rose, eds. 1999. *Immigration and Opportunity: Race, Ethnicity, and Employment in the United States.* New York: Russell Sage Foundation Press.

Bean, Frank D., and Jennifer Lee. 2007. "Reinventing the Color Line: Immigration and America's New Racial/Ethnic Divide." *Social Forces* 86 (2): 561–586.

Beauvoir-Dominique, Rachel. 1991. *L'Ancienne cathèdrale de Port-au-Prince: Perspectives d'un vestige de carrefours.* Port-au-Prince: Deshamps.

Becker, Howard S. 1974. "Art as Collective Action." *American Sociological Review* 39: 767–776.

———. 1984. *Art Worlds.* Berkeley: University of California Press.

Becker, Howard S., Robert R. Faulkner, and Barbara Kirshenblatt. 2006. *Art from Start to Finish: Jazz, Painting, Writing, and Other Improvisations.* Chicago: University of Chicago Press.

Bencastro, Mario. 1998. *Odyssey to the North.* Houston: Arte Público Press.

Benjamin, Walter. [1936] 1969. "The Work of Art in the Age of Mechanical Reproduction." In *Illuminations*, ed. Hanna Arendt, 219–253. New York: Random House.

Bensusan, Guy. 1980. Review of *Popular Music in Mexico* by Claes Geijerstam. *Latin American Research Review* 15 (1): 262–265.

Berger, John. 1990. *Ways of Seeing.* New York: Penguin.

Bernstein, Nina. 2005. "Questions, Bitterness and Exile for Queens Girl in Terror Case." *New York Times*, June 17, New York/region edition. http://www.nytimes.com/2005/06/17.

Berumen, Miguel Ángel, and Jesús Muñoz Delgado, eds. 2002. *La cara del tiempo: La fotografía en ciudad Juárez y El Paso (1870–1930).* Chihuahua: Cuadro por Cuadro Imagen y Palabra.

Bhattacharjee, Ananya. 1992. "The Habit of Ex-Nomination: Nation, Woman, and the Indian Immigrant Bourgeoisie." *Public Culture* 5 (1): 19–44.

Blumenthal, Ralph. 2007. "Not from Here: An Opera for Houston's Immigrants." *New York Times*, November 12. http://www.nytimes.com/2007/11/12/arts/music/12hous.html?th&emc=th.

Bosch, Lynette. 2004. *Cuban-American Art in Miami: Exile, Identity and the Neo-Baroque.* London: Lund Humphries.

Bourdieu, Pierre. 1971. "Genèse et structure du champ religieux." *Revue Française du sociologie* 12 (2): 294–334.

———. 1984. *Distinction: A Social Critique of the Judgement of Taste.* Trans. R. Nice. Cambridge: Harvard University Press.

Bowden, Charles. 1996. *Chihauhua: Pictures from the Edge.* Albuquerque: University of New Mexico Press.

Brandes, Stanley. 2007. *Skulls to the Living, Bread to the Dead: The Day of the Dead in Mexico and Beyond.* Boston: Wiley-Blackwell Publishers.

Breton, André. [1928] 1945. *Le surréalisme et la peinture: Genèse et perspectives artistiques de surréalisme et de fragments inédits.* New York, Brentanos.

Brettell, Caroline B. 2006. "Political Belonging and Cultural Belonging: Immigration Status, Citizenship, and Identity among Four Immigrant Populations in a Southwestern City." *American Behavioral Scientist* 50 (1): 70–99.

Broder, J., H. Dewey, J. Li, E. Mengers, and J. Tatum. 2008. "Creative Industries: Understanding Arts Based Development Potential in Philadelphia." Unpublished manuscript.

Brodwin, Paul. 2003. "Pentecostalism in Translation: Religion and the Production of Community in the Haitian Diaspora." *American Ethnologist* 30 (1): 85–101.

Brown, Karen McCarthy. 1979. "Olina and Ezili: A Woman and a Goddess in Haitian Vodou." *Anima* 5: 11–16.

———. 1991. *Mama Lola: A Haitian Vodou Priestess in Brooklyn.* Los Angeles: University of California Press.

———. 1995. *Tracing the Spirit: Ethnographic Essays on Haitian Art.* Davenport, IA: Davenport Museum of Art.

Brozensky, Jennifer, Esperanza Cabrera, and Kristi Collins. 1999. *Cuba and Its Music.* http://www2.cedarcrest.edu/academic/soc/ccameron/soc215/cuba/cuba.htm.

Brunvand, Jan Harold. 1996. *American Folklore: An Encyclopedia.* Vol. 1551, *Garland Reference Library of the Humanities.* New York: Garland.

Buhle, Paul. 2004. *From the Lower East Side to Hollywood: Jews in American Popular Culture.* Oxon, England: Verso Books.

Bushnaq, Inea. 2002. "Arab-Americans: Their Arts and New York City." In *A Community of Many Worlds,* ed. Kathleen Benson and Philip Kayal, 178–190. New York: Syracuse University Press.

Cadge, Wendy, and Sidhorn Sangdhanoo. 2005. "Thai Buddhism in America: An Historical and Contemporary Overview." *Contemporary Buddhism* 6: 7–35.

Calavita, Kitty. 1998. "Immigration, Law and Marginalization in a Global Economy: Notes from Spain." *Law and Society Review* 32 (3): 529–566.

———. 2005. *Immigrants at the Margins: Law, Race, and Exclusion in Southern Europe.* Cambridge: Cambridge University Press.

California Ethnic and Multicultural Archives. 2008. "Chicano Art: A Resource Guide." http://cemaweb.library.ucsb.edu/chicanoArt.html.

Camarillo, Albert. 2005. *Chicanos in a Changing Society: From Mexican Pueblos to American Barrios in Santa Barbara and Southern California, 1848–1930.* College Station: Texas A&M University Press.

Camín, Hector Aguilar, Lorenzo Meyer, and Luis Alberto Fierro. 1993. *In the Shadow of the Mexican Revolution: Contemporary Mexican History, 1910–1989.* Austin: University of Texas Press.

Cancel, Luis R. 1988. *The Latin American Spirit: Art and Artists in the United States, 1920–1970.* New York: Bronx Museum of the Arts.

Caplan, Nathan, John K. Whitmore, and Marcella H. Choy. 1989. *The Boat People and Achievement in America: A Study of Family Life, Hard Work, and Cultural Values.* Ann Arbor: University of Michigan Press.

Carpentier, Alejo, and Timothy Brennan. 2002. *Music in Cuba.* Minneapolis: University of Minnesota Press.

Centro de Estudios Económicos y Sociales del Tercer Mundo. 1983. *A través de la frontera.* Mexico City: Instituto de Investigaciones Esteticas U.N.A.M.

Centro Latino de Chelsea. 2008. *About Our Community.* http://www.centrolatino.org/community.php.

Chagoya, Enrique. 1996. "Beyond Boundaries." San Francisco: Galería de la Raza.

Chan, Sucheng. 1991. *Asian Americans: An Interpretive History.* New York: Twyne Publishers.

Chan, Kwok Bun, and David Loveridge. 1987. "Refugees in 'Transit': Vietnamese in a Refugee Camp in Hong Kong." *International Migration Review* 21 (3): 745–759.

Chang, Jeff. 2003. "Look at Me: Chinese American Rapper Jin Attacks Invisibility." *San Francisco Bay Guardian.* http://www.sfsb.com/39/03/art_music_jin.html.

Chang, Jeff, and D. J. Kool Herc. 2005. *Can't Stop Won't Stop: A History of the Hip Hop Generation.* New York: McMillan-Picador.

Chávez, Leo R. 1997. *Shadowed Lives: Undocumented Immigrants in American Society.* Belmont, CA: Wadsworth Publishing.

Chávez, Leo R., Esteban T. Flores, and Marta López-Garza. 1989. "Migrants and Settlers: A Comparison of Undocumented Mexicans and Central Americans in the United States." *Frontera, Norte* 1:49–75.

Chen, Elaine. 2005. "Straight Up with Poetry Slam Champion, Bao Phi." *Nha Magazine* http://news.newamericamedia.org/news/view_article.html?article_id=bcea018b9ead9819896a204a7ae0846f.

Cheung, King-Kok. 1990. "The Woman Warrior Versus the Chinaman Pacific: Must a Chinese American Critic Choose between Feminism and Heroism?" In *Conflicts in Feminism,* ed. M. Hirsch and E. F. Keller, 234–251. New York: Routledge.

Chesnut, R. Andrew. 2003. *Competitive Spirits: Latin America's New Religious Economy.* New York: Oxford University Press.

Chiswick, Barry, Y. L. Lee, and P. W. Miller. 2003. "Patterns of Immigrant Occupational Attainment in a Longitudinal Survey." *International Migration Review* 41 (4): 47–69.

City of Chelsea. 2008. *About the City of Chelsea: A Few Words about Chelsea* http://www.ci.chelsea.ma.us/Public_Documents/ChelseaMA_WebDocs/about.

Clarke, John, Stuart Hall, Tony Jefferson, and Brian Roberts. 1976. "Subcultures, Cultures, and Class." In *Resistance through Rituals: Youth Subcultures in Post-War Britain,* ed. Stuart Hall and Tony Jefferson, 9–74. London: Hutchinson / Centre for Contemporary Cultural Studies, University of Birmingham.

Cohen, Lizabeth. 2003. *A Consumer's Republic: The Politics of Mass Consumption in Postwar America.* New York: Knopf.

Collins, Randall. 2004. *Interaction Ritual Chains.* Princeton: Princeton University Press.

Conforti, Joseph A. 2001. *Imagining New England: Explorations of Regional Identity from the Pilgrims to the Mid-Twentieth Century.* Chapel Hill: University of North Carolina Press.

Conway, Frederick J. "Pentecostalism in Haiti: Healing and Hierarchy." In *Perspectives on Pentecostalism: Case Studies from the Caribbean and Latin America,* ed. Stephen D. Glazier, 7–26. Washington, DC: University Press of America, 1980.

Cooper, Eileen M. 1997. "La Ciudad Intima: Chelsea's Evolving Latino Community." Master's thesis, Harvard University, Cambridge.

Cosentino, Donald J. 1998. *Vodou Things: The Art of Pierrot Barra and Marie Cassaise.* Jackson: University Press of Mississippi.

Cousin, Bernard. 1982. *Le miracle et le quotidien: Les ex-votos provençaux, images d'une société.* Paris: Sociétés, Metalités, et Cultures.

Coutin, Susan. 1999. "Citizenship and Clandestinity among Salvadoran Immigrants." *Political and Legal Anthropological Review* 22 (2): 53–63.

———. 2000. *Legalizing Moves: Salvadoran Immigrants' Struggle for U.S. Residency*. Ann Arbor: University of Michigan Press.

———. 2005. "Contesting Criminality: Illegal Immigration and the Spatialization of Legality." *Theoretical Criminology* 9 (1): 5–33.

Craig, Richard B. 1971. *The Bracero Program: Interest Groups and Foreign Policy*. Austin: University of Texas Press.

Creux, René. 1979. *Les ex-voto racontent*. Geneva: Editions de Fontainnemore.

Davé, Shilpa, Leilani Nishime, and Tasha G. Oren, eds. 2005. *East Main Street: Asian American Popular Culture*. New York: New York University Press.

Davis Anderson, Brooke. 2007. "Found Art." *Los Angeles Times*, December 16.

Dear, Michael, and Gustavo Leclerc, eds. 2003. *Postborder City: Cultural Spaces of Bajalta California*. New York: Routledge.

Decouflé, Pierre. 1964. "La notion d'ex-voto anatomique chez les Etrusco-Romains." *Latomus—Revue d'etudes Latines* 72: 5–41.

De Genova, Nicholas P. 2002. "Migrant 'Illegality' and Deportability in Everyday Life." *Annual Review of Anthropology* 31: 419–447.

de la Cruz, G. Patricia, and Angela Brittingham. 2003. "The Arab Population: 2000." Census 2000 Brief, U.S. Department of Commerce, Economics and Statistics Administration, U.S. Census Bureau.

de la Maza, Francisco. 1950. "Los retablos dorados de nueva España." *Enciclopedia Mexicana del Arte*. Mexico City: Ediciones Mexicanas.

de la Torre, Nemesia. 1988. *Júzgenme: Sufrimientos y peripecias de una "Espalda Mojada" que terminó por ser una ciudadana Norteamericana*. Guadalajara: Impresos González.

Denny, Walter. 1984. "Contradiction and Consistency in Islamic Art." In *The Islamic Impact*, ed. Yvonne Haddad, Byron Haines, and Ellison Findly. Syracuse, NY: Syracuse University Press.

Deren, Maya. [1953] 1991. *The Divine Horsemen: Living Gods of Haiti*. New York: McPherson.

Desmangles, Leslie G. 1992. *The Faces of the Gods: Vodou and Roman Catholicism in Haiti*. Chapel Hill: University of North Carolina Press.

Desser, David. 1991. "'Charlie Don't Surf': Race and Culture in the Vietnam War Films." In *Inventing Vietnam: The War in Film and Television*, ed. Michael Anderegg, 81–102. Philadelphia: Temple University Press.

DiMaggio, Paul. 1987. "Nonprofit Organizations in the Production and Distribution of Culture." In *The Nonprofit Sector: A Research Handbook*, 1st ed., ed. Walter. W. Powell, 203–218. New Haven: Yale University Press.

———. 1991. "Social Structure, Institutions, and Cultural Goods: The Case of the United States." In *Social Theory for a Changing Society*, ed. Pierre Bourdieu and James S. Coleman, 133–155. Boulder: Westview Press.

———. 2006. "Nonprofit Organizations and the Intersectoral Division of Labor in the Arts." In *The Nonprofit Sector: A Research Handbook*, 2nd ed., ed. Walter W. Powell and Richard Steinberg, 433–461. New Haven: Yale University Press.

Dougherty, Jill. 2007. "Axis of Evil Inspires Laughs." *CNN*. http://www.cnn.com/2007/SHOWBIZ/TV/06/30/axis.comedy/index.html.

Douglas, Mary, and Baron Isherwood. 1979. *The World of Goods: Towards an Anthropology of Consumption*. Boston: Routledge & Kegan Paul.

Downes, Lawrence. 2009. "The Ballad of Joe Arpaio." *New York Times*, March 15. http://www.nytimes.com/2009/03/16/opinion/16mon4.html?emc=eta1.

DuBois, Thomas A. 1993. "Constructions Construed: The Representation of Southeast Asian Refugees in Academic, Popular, and Adolescent Discourse." *Amerasia Journal* 19 (3): 1–25.

Durand, Jorge. 1988. "Los migradólares: Cien años de inversión en el medio rural." *Argumentos* 5:7–21.

———. 1996. *El norte es como el mar: Entrevistas a trabajadores migrantes en Estados Unidos.* Guadalajara: Universidad de Guadalajara.

———. 2002. *Rostros y rastros: Entrevistas a trabajadores migrantes en Estados Unidos.* San Luis Potosí: Editorial El Colegio de San Luis.

Durand, Jorge, and Patricia Arias. 2000. *La experiencia migrante, iconografía de la migración México-Estados Unidos.* Guadalajara: La Nogalera.

Durand, Jorge, and Douglas S. Massey. 1992. "Mexican Migration to the United States: A Critical Review." *Latin American Research Review* 27: 3–43.

———. 1995. *Miracles on the Border: Retablos of Mexican Migrants to the United States.* Tucson: University of Arizona Press.

———. 1997. "The Retablo Art of Mexican Migrants to the United States." *Latino Review of Books* 3 (1–2): 22–24.

———. 2001. "Migrantes Agradecidos." *Artes de México* 53:74–80.

Durand, Jorge, Douglas S. Massey, and René Zenteno. 2001. "Mexican Immigration to the United States: Continuities and Changes." *Latin American Research Review* 36: 107–127.

Durkheim, Emile. [1915] 1995. *Elementary Forms of the Religious Life.* Trans. Karen E. Fields. New York: Free Press.

Eagleton, Terry. 1991. *Ideology: An Introduction.* New York: Verso.

Eckstein, Susan. 2004. "On Deconstructing Immigrant Generations: Cohorts and the Cuban Émigré Experience." Working Paper #97. Center for Comparative Immigration Studies, University of California, San Diego.

Egan, Martha. 1991. *Milagros: Votive Offerings from the Americas.* Santa Fe: Museum of New Mexico Press.

Eisenlohr, Charlene J. 1996. "Adolescent Arab Girls in an American High School." In *Family and Gender among American Muslims,* ed. Barbara Bilgé and Barbara Aswad, 250–270. Philadelphia: Temple University Press.

Eliade, Mircea. 1987. *The Sacred and the Profane: The Nature of Religion.* Magnolia, MA: Peter Smith Publisher.

Ellison, Ralph. [1952] 1981. *Invisible Man.* New York: Verso.

Espinosa, Victor M. 1988. *El dilema del retorno: Migración, género y pertenencia en un contexto. Transnacional.* Zapópan, Mexico: El Colegio de Jalisco.

Espiritu, Yen Le. 1992. *Asian American Panethnicity: Bridging Institutions and Identities.* Philadelphia: Temple University Press.

———. 2001. "Possibilities of a Multiracial Asian America." In *The Sum of Our Parts: Mixed-Heritage Asian Americans,* ed. Teresa Williams-León and Cynthia L. Nakashima, 25–34. Philadelphia: Temple University Press.

———. 2006a. "Toward a Critical Refugee Study: The Vietnamese Refugee Subject in U.S. Scholarship." *Journal of Vietnamese Studies* 1 (1): 920–1005.

———. 2006b. "The 'We-Win-Even-When-We-Lose' Syndrome: U.S. Press Coverage of the Twenty-Fifth Anniversary of the 'Fall of Saigon.'" *American Quarterly* 58 (2): 329–352.

Fernandez, Celestino. 1983. "The Mexican Immigration Experience and the Corrido Mexicano." *Journal of Studies in Latin American Popular Culture* 2: 115–130.

Fernández-Kelly, Patricia, and Lisa Konczal. 2006. "Murdering the Alphabet: Identity and Entrepreneurship among Second-Generation Cubans, West Indians, and Central Americans in the United States." *Ethnic and Racial Studies* 28 (6): 1153–1181.

Fernández, Kelly, and Richard Schauffler. 1994. "Divided Fates: Immigrant Children in a Restructured U.S. Economy." *International Migration Review* 28 (4): 662–689.

Fontus, Fritz. 2003. *Les églises protestantes en Haïti.* Paris: L'Harmattan.

Forman, Murray. 2002. *The 'Hood Comes First: Race, Space, and Place in Rap and Hip-Hop.* Middletown, CT: Wesleyan University Press.

Fraser, Nancy. 1997. *Justice Interruptus: Critical Reflections on the Postsocialist Condition.* New York: Routledge.

Fred, Morris, and Betty Farrell. 2008. "Diversifying the Arts: Bringing in Race and Ethnic Perspectives." In *Entering Cultural Communities: Diversity and Change in the Nonprofit Arts,* ed. Diane Grams and Betty Farrell, 143–170. New Brunswick, NJ: Rutgers University Press.

Freeman, Gary. 2004. "Immigrant Incorporation in Western Democracies." *International Migration Review* 38 (3): 945–969.

Freeman, James. 1989. *Hearts of Sorrow: Vietnamese-American Lives.* Stanford, CA: Stanford University Press.

———. 1995. *Changing Identities: Vietnamese Americans 1975–1995.* Boston: Allyn and Bacon.

Freud, Sigmund. 1930. *Civilization and Its Discontents.* New York: W. W. Norton.

Fujitani, T., Geoffrey M. White, and Lisa Yoneyama. 2001. "Introduction." In *Perilous Memories: The Asia-Pacific War(s),* ed. T. Fujitani, Geoffrey M. White, and Lisa Yoneyama. Durham, NC: Duke University Press.

Funkhouser, Edward. 1995. "Remittances from International Migration: A Comparison of El Salvador and Nicaragua." *Review of Economics and Statistics* 77: 137–146.

Gabler, Neal. 1989. *An Empire of Their Own: How the Jews Invented Hollywood.* New York: Anchor.

Gamio, Manuel. 1931. *The Mexican Immigrant: His Life Story.* Chicago: University of Chicago Press.

———. 2002. *El inmigrante Mexicano: La historia de su vida-Entrevistas Completas, 1926–1927.* Ed. Miguel Ángel Porrúa. Los Angeles: Regents of the University of California and Centro de Investigaciones y Estudios Superiores en Antropología Social (CIESAS).

Ganz, Cheryl R., and Margaret Strobel, eds. 2004. *Pots of Promise: Mexican and Pottery at Hull House, 1920–40.* Chicago: University of Illinois Press.

Garcia, Leyda. 2007. "Alma Chapina." In *Desde el Epicentro: An Anthology of U.S. Central American Poetry,* ed. Maya Chinchilla and Karina Oliva-Alvarado. Los Angeles: Epicentro.

García, Mario T. 1981. *Desert Immigrants: The Mexican of El Paso, 1880–1920.* New Haven: Yale University Press.

Geertz, Clifford. 1973. "Thick Description: Toward an Interpretative Theory of Culture." In *The Interpretation of Cultures,* 3–32. New York: Basic Books.

Gelder, Ken. 1997. "Introduction to Part Three." In *The Subcultures Reader,* ed. Ken Gelder and Sarah Thornton, 145–148. New York: Routledge.

Genaro Cuadriello, Jaime. 1989. *Maravilla Americana: Variantes de la Iconografía Guadalupana.* Guadalajara: Patrimonio Cultural del Occidente.

George, Nelson. 1998. *Hip Hop America.* New York: Penguin.

Gerges, Fawaz. 2003. "Islam and Muslims in the Mind of America." *Annals of the American Academy of Political and Social Science* 588 (July): 68–80.

Giddens, A. 1976. *New Rules of Sociological Method: A Positive Critique of Interpretative Sociologies.* New York: Basic Books.

Giffords, Gloria K. 1974. *Mexican Folk Retablos: Masterpieces on Tin.* Tucson: University of Arizona Press.

———. 1991. "The Art of Private Devotion: Retablo Painting of Mexico." In *Catalogue to the Exhibit the Art of Private Devotion: Retablo Painting of Mexico*, 33–63. Dallas: InterCultural Institute and the Meadows Museum.

Glover, Nicola. 2005. *Psychoanalytic Aesthetics: The British School.* http://www.human-nature.com/free-associations/glover/index.html.

Gold, Steve, and Nazli Kibria. 1993. "Vietnamese Refugees and Blocked Mobility." *Asian and Pacific Migration Review* 2: 27–56.

Goldberg, David Theo. 2002. *The Racial State.* Oxford: Blackwell.

Goldman, Shifra M. 1994. *Dimensions of the Americas: Art and Social Change in Latin America and the United States.* Chicago: University of Chicago Press.

Goldring, Luin P. 1995. "Gendered Memory: Reconstructions of Rurality among Mexican Transnational Migrants." In *Creating the Countryside: The Politics of Rural and Environmental Discourse*, ed. E. Melanie DuPuis and Peter Vandergeest, 303–329. Philadelphia: Temple University Press.

Gómez-Peña, Guillermo. 1993. *Warrior for Gringostroika.* St. Paul, MN: Graywolf Press.

———. 1997. "The Cruci-Fiction Project." *Drama Review* 41 (1): 147–151.

González-López, Gloria. 2005. *Erotic Journeys: Mexican Immigrants and Their Sex Lives.* Berkeley: University of California Press.

Goode, Judith G., Karen Curtis, and Janet Theophano. 1984. "Meal Formats, Meal Cycles and Menu Negotiation in the Maintenance of an Italian-American Community." In *Food in the Social Order: Studies of Food and Festivities in Three American Communities*, ed. Mary Douglas, 143–218. New York: Russell Sage Foundation.

Gordon, Avery. 1997. *Ghostly Matters: Haunting and the Sociological Imagination.* Minneapolis: University of Minnesota Press.

Gorodezky, Sylvia. 1993. *Arte Chicano como cultura de protesta.* Mexico City: Universidad Nacional Autónoma de México.

Grande, Jessica. 2007. "I.N.S. Series." In *Desde el Epicentro: An Anthology of U.S. Centra American Poetry*, ed. Maya Chinchilla and Karina Oliva-Alvarado. Los Angeles: Epicentro.

Grasmuck, Sherry, and Patricia Pessar. 1991. *Between Two Islands: Dominican International Migration.* Berkeley: University of California Press.

Greater Philadelphia Cultural Alliance. 2006. *2006 Portfolio.* Philadelphia: Greater Philadelphia Cultural Alliance.

Grebler Leo, Joan W. Moore, and Ralph C. Guzman. 1970. *The Mexican-American People: The Nation's Second Largest Minority.* New York: Free Press.

Grenier, Guillermo J., and Lisandro Perez. 2003. *The Legacy of Exile: Cubans in the United States.* Boston: Allyn and Bacon.

Grewal, Inderpal. 2005. *Transnational America: Feminisms, Diasporas, Neoliberalisms.* Durham, NC: Duke University Press.

Griswold, Richard del Castillo, Teresa McKenna, and Yvonne Yarbro-Bejarano, eds. 1991. *Chicano Art: Resistance and Affirmation, 1965–1985.* Los Angeles: Wight Art Gallery, University of California.

Griswold, Wendy. 1987. "A Methodological Framework for the Sociology of Culture." *Sociological Methodology* 17: 1–35.

Guarnaccia, Peter, and Pablo Farias. 1988. "The Social Meanings of Nervios: A Case Study of a Central American Woman." *Social Science Medicine* 26: 1223–1231.

Hamilton, Nora, and Norma Stoltz Chinchilla. 1991. Central American Migration: A Framework for Analysis. *Latin American Research Review* 26 (1): 75–110.

———. 2001. *Seeking Community in a Global City: Guatemalans and Salvadorans in Los Angeles.* Philadelphia: Temple University Press.

Han, Arar, and John Hsu. 2004. *Asian American X: An Intersection of Twenty-first Century Asian American Voices.* Ann Arbor: University of Michigan Press.

Harding, Richard, and John Looney. 1977. "Problems of Southeast Asian Children in a Refugee Camp." *American Journal of Psychiatry* 134: 407–411.

Hayward, Philip, ed. 1999. *Widening the Horizon: Exoticism in Post-War Popular Music.* Bloomington: University of Indiana Press.

Henkes, Robert. 1999. *Latin American Women Artists of the United States: The Works of 33 Twentieth-Century Women.* Jefferson, NC: McFarland & Co.

Herrera, Hayden. 1983. *Frida: A Biography of Frida Kahlo.* New York: Harper and Row.

Herrera-Sobek, María. 1979. *The Bracero Experience: Elitelore vs. Folklore.* Washington, DC: University of California, Los Angeles, Latin American Center.

Hervieu-Léger, Danièle. 1993. *Religion as a Chain of Memory.* Trans. Simon Lee. New Brunswick, NJ: Rutgers University Press.

Hisama, Ellie. 2004. "Afro-Asian Crosscurrents in Contemporary Hip-Hop." *Anarchist People of Color*, December 5, 2004. http://www.illegalvoices.org/knowledge/general_articles/afro-asian_crosscurrents_in_contemporary_hip_hop.html.

Ho, Pensri. 2003. "Performing the 'Oriental': Professionals and the Asian Model Minority Myth." *Journal of Asian American Studies* 6 (2): 149–175.

Hondagneu-Sotelo, Pierette. 1992. "Overcoming Patriarchal Constraints: The Reconstruction of Gender Relations among Mexican Immigrant Women and Men." *Gender and Society* 6: 393–415.

———. 1994. *Gendered Transitions: Mexican Experiences of Immigration.* Berkeley: University of California Press.

———. 2001. *Doméstica: Immigrant Workers Cleaning and Caring in the Shadows of Affluence.* Berkeley: University of California Press.

Howell, Sally. 2000. "Cultural Interventions: Arab American Aesthetics between the Transnational and the Ethnic." *Diaspora* 9 (1): 59–82.

Hurbon, Laënnec. 1972. *Dieu dans le vaudou haïtien.* Paris, Payot.

———. 2001. "Pentecostalism and Transnationalism in the Caribbean." In *Between Babel and Pentecost: Transnational Pentecostalism in Africa and Latin America*, ed. André Corten and Ruth Marshall Fratani, 124–141. Bloomington: Indiana University Press.

———. 2007. "Haitian Vodou in the Context of Globalization." In *Orisha Devotion as World Religion: Globalized Yorùbá Religious Culture*, ed. Jacob K. Olupona and Terry Rey, 263–267. Madison: University of Wisconsin Press.

Huynh, Sanh Thong. 1997. "Live by Water, Die for Water." In *Watermark: Vietnamese American Poetry and Prose*, ed. Barbara Tran, Monique T. D. Truong, and Luu Truong Khoi, vi–vii. New York: Asian American Writers' Workshop.

Immigration and Naturalization Service. 1997. "INS Releases Updated Estimates of U.S. Illegal Population." U.S. Department of Justice, News Release, February 7.

———. 2000. *Statistical Yearbook. 2000.* Washington, DC: U.S. Government Publishing Office.

Informe Sobre Desarrollo Humano. 2005. Una mirada al nuevo nosotros: El impacto de las migraciones. Programa de Naciones Unidas para el Desarrollo (PNUD). San Salvador, El Salvador: PNUD.

Innovation Philadelphia. 2008. *Creative Footprint: The Economic Impact of the Philadelphia Region's for-Profit Creative Economy.* http://www.innovationphiladelphia.com/publications/.

Iraheta, Javier, and Elías Interiano. 2008. "Interview with Javier Iraheta and Elías Interiano by Clifford Murphy." Massachusetts Traditional Arts Archives, Cultural Council, Boston.

Jahn, Janheinz. 1961. *Muntu: An Outline of the New African Culture.* New York: Grove Press.

Jasso, Guillermina,and Mark R. Rosenzweig. 1990. *The New Chosen People: Immigrants in the United States.* New York: Russell Sage Foundation.

Jay, Jennifer W. 2008. "Rapper Jin and ABC: Acquiring Spoken Cantonese and Transnational Identity through Restaurant Culture and Hong Kong TV." In *Proceedings of the 20th North American Conference on Chinese Linguistics (NACCL-20)*, vol. 1, ed. Marjorie K. M. Chan and Hana Kang, 379–389. Columbus: Ohio State University. http://chinalinks.osu.edu/naccl-20/proceedings/20_jay-j.pdf.

Jones, Richard C. 1989. "Causes of Salvadoran Migration to the United States." *Geographical Review* 79: 183–194.

Joseph, Suad. 1999. "Against the Grain of the Nation—The Arab." In *Arabs in America: Building a New Future*, ed. Michael Suleiman, 257–271. Philadelphia: Temple University Press.

Kala, Mandira, and Charles Jones. 2006. *Boston: Demographic Information on Latinos in Massachusetts using the American Community Survey.* Boston: Mauricio Gaston Institute for Latino Community Development and Public Policy.

Kandel, William, and Douglas S. Massey. 2002. "The Culture of Mexican Migration: A Theoretical and Empirical Analysis." *Social Forces* 80:981–1004.

Kant, Immanuel. [1790] 1987. *Critique of Judgment.* Indianapolis: Hacket.

Kelley, Robin D.G. 1997. *Yo' Mama's Disfunktional! Fighting the Culture Wars in Urban America.* Boston: Beacon Press.

Kelley, Ron, Jonathan Frielander, and Anita Colby, eds. 1993. *Irangeles: Iranians in Los Angeles.* Berkeley: University of California Press.

Kelly, Gail Paradise. 1977. *From Vietnam to America: A Chronicle of the Vietnamese Immigration to the United States.* Boulder: Westview Press.

Kemal, Salim. 1991. *Kant's Aesthetic Theory: An Introduction.* New York: St. Martin's Press.

Kibria, Nazli. 2002. *Becoming Asian American: Second-Generation Chinese and Korean American Identities.* Baltimore: Johns Hopkins University Press.

Kim, Claire. 2000. *Bitter Fruit: The Politics of Black/Korean Conflict in New York.* New Haven: Yale University Press.

———. 2000–2001. "Playing the Racial Trump Card: Asian Americans in Contemporary U.S. Politics." *Amerasia Journal* 26 (3): 51–60.

Kim, Elaine. 1990. "'Such Opposite Creatures': Men and Women in Asian American Literature." *Michigan Quarterly Review* 29: 68–93.

———. 2003. "Introduction: Interstitial Subjects—Asian American Visual Art as a Site for New Cultural Conversations." In *Fresh Talk, Daring Gazes: Conversations on Asian American Art*, ed. Elaine H. Kim, Margo Machida, and Sharon Mizota, 1–50. Berkeley: University of California Press.

Kitwana, Bakari. 2002. *The Hip Hop Generation: Young Blacks and the Crisis in African-American Culture.* New York: Perseus Books.

Knights, Vanessa. 2004. "Songs of Creole Identities: The Bolero in the Hispanic Caribbean." *Forum for Modern Language Studies* 40 (4): 389–400.

Kolko, Beth, Lisa Nakamura, and Gilbert Rodman, eds. 2000. *Race in Cyberspace.* New York: Routledge.

Kopf, Edward J. 1974. "The Intimate City: A Study of Urban Social Order, Chelsea, Massachusetts." Ph.D. diss., Brandies, Waltham, MA.

Kondo, Dorrine. 1997. *About Face: Performing Race in Fashion and Theater.* New York: Routledge.

Kreidler, John. 1996. "Leverage Lost: The Nonprofit Arts in the Post-Ford Era." *Journal of Arts Management, Law, and Society* 26 (2): 79–100.

Kreneck, Thomas H. 1988. *Del Pueblo: A Pictorial History of Houston's Hispanic Community.* Houston: Houston International University.

Kwon, Soo Ah. 2004. "Autoexoticizing: Asian American Youth and the Import Car Scene." *Journal of Asian American Studies* 7 (1): 1–26.

Lafaye, Jacques. 1976. *Quetzalcóatl and Guadalupe: The Formation of Mexican National Consciousness.* Chicago: University of Chicago Press.

Lammoglia, José A. 2001. "Botanicas: Absence in Cuba, Proliferation in the United States." Master's thesis, Florida International University.

Landolt, Patricia, Lilian Autler, and Sonia Baires. 1999. "From Hermano Lejano to Hermano Mayor: The Dialectics of Salvadoran Transnationalism." *Ethnic and Racial Studies* 22: 290–315.

Landolt, Patricia, and Wei Wei Da. 2005. "The Spatially Ruptured Practices of Migrant Families: A Comparison of Immigrants from El Salvador and the People's Republic of China." *Current Sociology* 53 (4): 625–653.

lê, thi diem thúy. 2003. *The Gangster We Are All Looking For.* New York: Knopf.

Lee, Erika, and Naoko Shibusawa. 2005. "Guest Editors' Introduction: What Is Transnational Asian American History? Recent Trends and Challenges." *Journal of Asian American Studies* 8 (3): vii–xvii.

Lee, Jennifer, and Min Zhou. 2004. "Introduction: The Making of Culture, Identity, and Ethnicity among Asian American Youth." In *Asian American Youth: Culture, Identity, and Ethnicity,* ed. Jennifer Lee and Min Zhou, 1–30. New York: Routledge.

Lee, Rachel, and Sau-ling C. Wong. 2000. "Introduction." In *AsianAmerica.Net: Ethnicity, Nationalism, and Cyberspace,* xiii–xxxv. New York: Routledge.

Lee, Robert G. 2005. "Foreword." In *East Main Street: Asian American Popular Culture,* ed. Shilpa Davé, Leilani Nishime, and Tasha G. Oren, x–xv. New York: New York University Press.

Libby, Gary R., and Juan A. Martinez. 2006. *Cuba: A History in Art.* New York: Museum of Arts and Sciences.

Light, Ivan, and Carolyn Rosenstein. 1995. *Race, Ethnicity, and Entrepreneurship in Urban America.* New York: Aldine de Gruyter.

Ling, Amy. 1999. *Yellow Light: The Flowering of Asian American Arts.* Philadelphia: Temple University Press.

Lipsitz, George. 2001. *American Studies in a Moment of Danger.* Minneapolis: University of Minnesota Press.

———. 2005. "Midnight's Children: Youth Culture in the Age of Globalization." In *Youthscapes: The Popular, the National, the Global,* ed. Sunaina Maira and Elisabeth Soep, vii–xiv. Philadelphia: University of Pennsylvania Press.

Lockman, Zachary. 2004. *Contending Visions of the Middle East: The History and Politics of Orientalism.* Cambridge: Cambridge University Press.

Lowe, Lisa. 1996. *Immigrant Acts: On Asian American Cultural Politics.* Durham: Duke University Press.

Lowe, Lisa, and Elaine Kim. 1997. "Guest Editors' Introduction." *Positions* 5 (2): v–xiv.

Lugo-Saavedra, Denise, and John Spray. 1984. *Aquí: 27 Latin American Artists Living and Working in the United States.* Los Angeles: University of Southern California Press.

Machida, Margo. 2003. "Visual Art and the Imagining of Asian America: An Editorial View." In *Fresh Talk, Daring Gazes: Conversations on Asian American Art,* ed. Elaine H. Kim, Margo Machida, and Sharon Mizota, xi–xv. Berkeley: University of California Press.

Mahler, Sarah J. 1995. *Salvadorans in Suburbia: Symbiosis and Conflict.* Boston: Allyn and Bacon.

———. 1999. "Engendering Transnational Migration: A Case Study of Salvadorans." *American Behavioral Scientist* 42: 690–719.

Maira, Sunaina. 1999. "Identity Dub: The Paradoxes of an Indian American Youth Subculture (New York Mix)." *Cultural Anthropology* 14 (1): 29–60.

———. 2000. "Henna and Hip Hop: The Politics of Cultural Production and the Work of Cultural Studies." *Journal of Asian American Studies* 3 (3): 329–369.

———. 2002. *Desis in the House: Indian American Youth Culture in New York City.* Philadelphia: Temple University Press.

———. 2005. "Youth Culture Studies, Empire and Globalization." In *Comparative Studies of South Asia, Africa, and the Middle East* 24 (1): 219–231, special issue edited by Louise Cainkar.

Maira, Sunaina, and Elisabeth Soep. 2005. "Introduction." In *Youthscapes: The Popular, the National, the Global,* ed. Sunaina Maira and Elisabeth Soep, xv–xxxv. Philadelphia: University of Pennsylvania Press.

Malagamba Ansótegui, Amelia, ed. 2006. *Caras vemos, corazones no sabemos: Faces Seen, Hearts Unknown, The Human Landscape of Mexican Migration.* Notre Dame: Snite Museum of Art.

Malagamba Ansótegui, Amelia Cárdenas, and Gilberto Cárdenas. 1992. *Images of the Border: Monoprint Workshop.* Austin: Galería Sin Fronteras.

Mandel, Daniel. 2001. "Muslims on the Silver Screen." *Middle East Quarterly* 8 (2): 19–30.

Mannheim, Karl. 1953. *Essays on Sociology and Social Psychology.* Ed. Paul Kecskemeti. New York: Oxford University Press.

Marcuse, Herbert. [1958] 1974. *Eros and Civilization.* Boston: Beacon Press.

Marin, Cheech. 2002. *Chicano Visions: American Painters on the Verge.* New York: Bulfinch Press.

Marquez, John. 2004. "Black and Gold and Brown Lives: Racial Violence, Memory, and Collective Resistance in Baytown, Texas." Ph.D. diss., University of California, San Diego.

Martin Alonso, Sandra. 1993. *Alicia Alonso: First Lady of the Ballet.* New York: Walker and Co.

Martínez, Elizabeth, ed. 1991. *500 Years of Chicano History in Pictures.* Albuquerque: SouthWest Organizing Project.

Martinez, Natasha Bonilla, ed. 1993. *La Frontera/The Border: Art about the Mexico/United States Border Experience.* San Diego: Centro Cultural De La Raza and Museum of Contemporary Art.

Marx, Karl. [1844] 1959. *Economic and Philosophical Manuscripts.* Moscow: Progress Publishers.

———. [1845] 1998. *The German Ideology.* Amherst, MA: Prometheus Books.

Massey, Doreen. 1999. "Imagining Globalization: Power-Geometries of Time-Space." In *Global Futures: Migration, Environment, and Globalization,* ed. Avtar Brah, Mary J. Hickman, and Mairtin Macan Ghaill. New York: St. Martin's Press.

Massey, Douglas S., Rafael Alarcón, Jorge Durand, and Humberto González. 1990. *Return to Aztlan: The Social Process of International Migration from Western Mexico*: Berkeley: University of California Press.

Massey, Douglas S., Joaquin Arango, Graeme Hugo, Ali Kouaouci, Adela Pellegrino, and J. Edward Taylor. 1994. "An Evaluation of International Migration Theory: The North American Case." *Population and Development Review* 20: 699–752.

Massey, Douglas S., and Jorge Durand. 2004. *Crossing the Border: Research from the Mexican Migration Project.* New York: Russell Sage Foundation Press.

Massey, Douglas S., Jorge Durand, and Nolane J. Malone. 2002. *Beyond Smoke and Mirrors: Mexican Immigration in an Era of Economic Integration.* New York: Russell Sage Foundation.

Massey, Douglas S., Luin P. Goldring, and Jorge Durand. 1994. "Continuities in Transnational Migration: An Analysis of 19 Mexican Communities." *American Journal of Sociology* 99: 1492–1533.

Massey, Douglas S., and Emilio Parrado. 1994. "Migradollars: The Remittances and Savings of Mexican Migrants to the United States." *Population Research and Policy Review* 13: 3–30.

Massey, Douglas S., and R. Magaly Sánchez. 2007. "Latino and American Identities as Perceived by Immigrants." *Qualitative Sociology* 30:81–108.

McAlister, Melani. 2005. *Epic Encounters: Culture, Media, and U.S. Interests in the Middle East since 1945.* Berkeley: University of California Press.

McCarthy, K. F., Arthur Brooks, Julia F. Lowell, and Laura Zakaras. 2001. *The Performing Arts in a New Era.* Santa Monica: RAND Corporation.

McKenzie, Sean, and Cecilia Menjívar. N.d. "The Meanings of Migration, Remittances, and Gifts: Views of Honduran Women Who Stay." Albuquerque: Arizona State University.

Medoff, Peter, and Holly Sklar. 1994. *Streets of Hope: The Fall and Rise of an Urban Neighborhood.* Boston: South End Press.

Mehegan, David. 2003. "Refuge in Her Writing." *Boston Globe,* June 2, B7. http://faculty.washington.edu/kendo/thuymehegan.html.

Meléndez, Edwin, and Miren Uriarte-Gastón. 1993. *Latino Poverty and Economic Development in Massachusetts.* Boston: Mauricio Gastón Institute for Latino Community Development and Public Policy and University of Massachusetts Press.

Menjívar, Cecilia. 1993. "History, Economy, and Politics: Macro and Micro-Level Factors in Recent Salvadorean Migration to the United States." *Journal of Refugee Studies* 6: 350–371.

———. 2006. "Liminal Legality: Salvadoran and Guatemalan Immigrants' Lives in the United States." *American Journal of Sociology* 111 (4): 999–1037.

Menjívar, Cecilia, and Leisy Abrego. 2009. "Parents and Children across Borders: Legal Instability and Intergenerational Relations in Guatemalan and Salvadoran Families." In *Across Generations: Immigrant Families in America,* ed. Nancy Foner, 160–189. New York: New York University Press.

Menjívar, Cecilia, and Victor Agadjanian. 2007. "Men's Migration and Women's Lives: Views from Rural Armenia and Guatemala." *Social Science Quarterly* 88 (5): 1243–1262.

Menjívar, Cecilia, Julie Davanzo, Lisa Greenwell, and R. Burciaga Valdez. 1998. "Remittance Behavior of Filipino and Salvadoran Immigrants in Los Angeles." *International Migration Review* 32:99–128.

Mennesson-Rigaud, Odette. 1958. "Le rôle du vaudou dans la guerre d'indépendance d'Haïti." *Présence Africaine* 18/19:43–67.

Mernissi, Fatima. 1991. *The Veil and the Male Elite: A Feminist Interpretation of Women's Rights in Islam.* Reading, MA: Addison-Wesley.

Métraux, Alfred. [1959] 1972. *Voodoo in Haiti.* Trans. Hugo Charteris. New York, Schocken.

Mexican-American Border Music. 1994. Vol. 1: *An Introduction—Pioneer Recording Artists, 1928–1958.* Arhoolie Folklyric CD7001.

Min, Pyong Gap. 2002a. "Introduction." In *The Second Generation: Ethnic Identity among Asian Americans,* ed. Pyong Gap Min, 1–17. Lanham, MD: Altamira Press.

———. 2002b. *Mass Migration to the United States.* New York: Altamira Press.

Mink, Gwendolyn. 1995. *The Wages of Motherhood.* Ithaca, NY: Cornell University Press.

Miranda Maldonado, Ana E. 2007. "I Am That Kind of Salvi." In *Desde el Epicentro: An Anthology of U.S. Central American Poetry,* ed. Maya Chinchilla and Karina Oliva-Alvarado. Los Angeles: Epicentro.

Mr. Snoopy. 2000. "Mi Vida Loca." In *Izote Vos,* ed. K. C. Kim and A. Serrano F. San Francisco: Pacific News Service.

Mohanty, Chandra. 1991. "Under Western Eyes: Feminist Scholarship and Colonial Discourse." In *Third World Women and the Politics of Feminism*, ed. Chandra Talpade Mohanty, Ann Russo, and Lourdes Torres, 51–80. Bloomington: Indiana University Press.

Montenegro, Roberto. 1950. *Retablos de México/Mexican Votive Paintings*. Mexico City: Ediciones Mexicanas.

Montero-Sieburth, Martha, and Edwin Meléndez. 2007. *Latinos in a Changing Society*. Westport, CT: Praeger.

Moore, Robin. 2006. *Music and Revolution: Cultural Change in Socialist Cuba*. Berkeley: University of California Press.

Mora, G. Cristina. 2011. "Regulating Immigrant Media and Instituting New Boundaries: The FCC and Spanish-Language Television, 1960–1990." *Latino Studies* 19(1–2).

Morales, Marlon I. 2001. *A Tease: Selections from Turning Tricks: Poems*. Los Angeles: Izote Press.

Morgan, David. 2005. *The Sacred Gaze: Religious Visual Culture in Theory Practice*. Berkeley: University of California Press.

Moriarty, Pia. 2004. *Immigrant Participatory Arts: An Insight into Community-Building in Silicon Valley*. San Jose: Cultural Initiatives Silicon Valley.

Morrison, Toni. 1989. "Unspeakable Things Unspoken: The Afro-American Presence in American Literature." *Michigan Quarterly Review* 28 (1): 1–34.

Morton, T. B. 2006. "Artists in Exile Exhibition." http://www.folkloreproject.org/programs/exhibits/exile/index.cfm.

Mountz, Alison, Richard Wright, Ines Miyares, and Adrian J. Bailey. 2002. "Lives in Limbo: Temporary Protected Status and Immigrant Identities." *Global Networks* 2 (4): 335–356.

Moyssén, Xavier. 1965. "La Pintura Popular y Costumbrista del Siglo XIX." *Artes de México* 61 (13): 22–28.

Mumma, Phil. 1992. *Between Two Worlds: The People of the Border*. Oakland, CA: Oakland Museum.

Mraz, John, and Jaime Vélez Storey. 1996. *Uprooted: Braceros in the Hermanos Mayo Lens*. Houston: Arte Público Press.

Murphy, Clifford R. 2007. "Fieldnotes on Visit with Mariachi Estampa de America (Chelsea, MA)." In *Massachusetts Traditional Arts Archives*, 1–5. Boston: Massachusetts Cultural Council.

———. 2008. "New England Country and Western Music: Self-Reliance, Community Expression, and Regional Resistance on the New England Frontier." Ph.D. diss., Brown University, Providence, RI.

Murray, Gerald. 1980. "Population Pressure, Land Tenure and Voodoo: The Economics of Haitian Peasant Ritual." In *Beyond the Myths of Culture: Essays in Cultural Materialism*, ed. Eric B. Ross, 295–321. New York: Academic Press.

Naff, Alexa. 1993. *Becoming American: The Early Arab Immigrant Experience*. Carbondale: Southern Illinois University Press.

Nakamura, Lisa. 2002. *Cybertypes: Race, Ethnicity, and Identity on the Internet*. New York: Routledge.

Namkung, Victoria. 2004. "Reinventing the Wheel: Import Car Racing in Southern California." In *Asian American Youth: Culture, Identity, and Ethnicity*, ed. Jennifer Lee and Min Zhou, 159–175. New York: Routledge.

Nelson, Alondra, and Thuy L. Tu, eds. 2001. *Technicolor: Race, Technology, and Everyday Life*. New York: New York University Press.

Ngozi-Brown, A. T. 1997. "'To Bring Grandeur Back to Blackness': Arthur Hall's Afro-American Dance Ensemble in the Historical Continuum of African Dance Performance in the United States." Master's thesis, Cornell University, Ithaca.

Nguyen, Viet Thanh. 1997. "Representing Reconciliation: Le Ly Hayslip and the Victimized Body." *Positions* 5 (2): 605–642.

Nguyen-Vo, Thu-Huong. 2005. "Forking Paths: How Shall We Mourn the Dead?" *Amerasia Journal* 31 (2): 157–175.

Nissenbaum, Stephen. 1996. "New England as Region and Nation." In *All Over the Map: Rethinking American Regions*, ed. E. L. Ayers, 38–61. Baltimore: Johns Hopkins University Press.

Noriega, Chon A. 2000. "East of the River: Chicano Art Collectors Anonymous." Santa Monica: Santa Monica Museum of Art.

Norris Square Neighborhood Project. 2008. "Grupo Motivos." http://www.nsnp.com/gm.html.

Northrup, Joanne. 2003. *Tales of Yellow Skin: The Art of Long Nguyen*. San Jose: San Jose Museum of Art.

O'Connor, Alan. 2006. *Raymond Williams*. Lanham, MD: Rowman and Littlefield.

Okihiro, Gary. 1994. *Margins and Mainstreams: Asians in American History and Culture*. Seattle: University of Washington Press.

Ong, Aihwa. 1996. "Cultural Citizenship as Subject-Making: Immigrants Negotiate Racial and Cultural Boundaries in the United States." *Current Anthropology* 37 (5): 737–762.

———. 1999. *Flexible Citizenship: The Cultural Logics of Transnationality*. Durham: Duke University Press.

———. 2003. *Buddha Is Hiding: Refugees, Citizenship, the New America*. Berkeley: University of California Press.

Ong, Paul, and Karen Umemoto. 1994. "Life and Work in the Inner-City." In *The State of Asian Pacific America: Economic Diversity, Issues, and Policies*, ed. Paul Ong, 87–112. Los Angeles: LEAP Asian Pacific American Public Policy Institute and University of California.

Orendain, Leopoldo. 1984. "Exvotos." In *Cuarto Centenario de la Fundación del Obispado de Guadalajara, 1548–1948*, 279–290. Guadalajara: Artes Gráficas.

Otto, Rudolf. [1917] 1958. *The Idea of the Holy*. Oxford: Oxford University Press.

Padgett, John, and Christopher Ansell. 1993. "Robust Action and the Rise of the Medici, 1400–1434." *American Journal of Sociology* 98: 1259–1319.

Palumbo-Liu, David. 1999. *Asian/American: Historical Crossings of a Racial Frontier*. Palo Alto, CA: Stanford University Press.

Park, Ishle Yi. 2006. SAAAC Forum, http://cgi.stanford.edu/group/saaac/cgibin/yabb/YaBB.pl?board=outside;action=display;num=1119243196.

Park, Jane C. H. 2005. "Cibo Matto's Stereotype A: Articulating Asian American Hip Pop." In *East Main Street: Asian American Popular Culture*, ed. Shilpa Davé, Leilani Nishime, and Tasha G. Oren, 292–312. New York: New York University Press.

Park, Robert. 1928. "Human Migration and the Marginal Man." *American Journal of Sociology* 33: 881–893.

Payes-Santacruz, Ana E. M. 2000. "Who Am I?" in *Izote Vos*, ed. K. C. Kim and A. Serrano F. San Francisco: Pacific News Service.

Peña, Manuel. 1985a. "From Ranchero to Jaiton: Ethnicity and Class in Texas-Mexican Music (Two Styles in the Form of a Pair)." *Ethnomusicology* 29 (1): 29–55.

———. 1985b. *The Texas-Mexican Conjunto: History of a Working-Class Music*. Mexican American Monographs, no. 9. Austin: University of Texas Press.

———. 1999. *The Mexican American Orquesta: Music, Culture, and the Dialectic of Conflict*. 1st ed. Austin: University of Texas Press.

Pérez, Ramón. 1991. *Diary of an Undocumented Immigrant*. Houston: Arte Publico Press.

Perisho, Sally. 1989. Sin Fronteras: Crossing Borders—Mexican American Artists in the Southwest. Exhibit at Gallery of Contemporary Art, University of Colorado, Colorado Springs.

Perkins, William E. 1996. "The Rap Attack." In *Droppin' Science: Critical Essays on Rap Music and Hip Hop Culture*, ed. William E. Perkins, 1–45. Philadelphia: Temple University Press.

Philadelphia Folklore Project. 2006. "Odunde Exhibition." http://www.folkloreproject.org/programs/exhibits/odunde/index.cfm.

———. 2008. "Artists." http://www.folkloreproject.org/folkarts/artists/.

Pierpont, Claudia Roth. 2006. "The Great Enemy: Philip Roth's New Novel." *New Yorker*, May 1, 82.

Plate, S. Brent. 2002. "Introduction." In *Religion, Art, and Visual Culture: A Cross-Cultural Reader*, ed. S. Brent Plate, 1–18. New York, Palgrave.

Poniewozik, James. 2007. "Stand Up Diplomacy." *Time Magazine*, March 8. http://www.time.com/time/magazine/article/0,9171,1597524,00.html.

Portes, Alejandro, and Bryan R. Roberts. 2005. "The Free-Market City: Latin American Urbanization in the Years of the Neoliberal Experiment." *Studies in Comparative International Development* 40 (1): 43–82.

Portes, Alejandro, and Rubén G. Rumbaut. 1996. *Immigrant America: A Portrait.* Berkeley: University of California Press.

———. 2001. *Legacies: The Store of the Immigrant Second Generation.* Berkeley: University of California Press.

Portes, Alejandro, and Rubén G. Rumbaut, with Patricia Fernández-Kelly and William Haller. 2006. "Religion: The Enduring Presence." In *Immigrant America*, 3rd ed., chap. 9. Berkeley: University of California Press.

Portes, Alejandro, and Julia Sensenbrenner. 1993. "Embeddedness and Immigration: Notes on the Social Determinants of Economic Action." *American Journal of Sociology* 98 (May): 1320–1350.

Portes, Alejandro, and Alex Stepick. 1994. *City on the Edge: The Transformation of Miami.* Berkeley: University of California Press.

Portes, Alejandro, and Min Zhou. 1993. "The New Second Generation: Segmented Assimilation and Its Variants among Post-1965 Immigrant Youth." *Annals of the American Academy of Political and Social Science* 530: 74–98.

———. 1996. "Self-Employment and the Earnings of Immigrants." *American Sociological Review* 61:219–230.

———. 1999. "Entrepreneurship and Economic Progress in the 1990s." In *Immigration and Opportunity: Race, Ethnicity, and Employment in the United States*, ed. Frank D. Bean and S. Bell-Rose, 143–171. New York: Russell Sage Foundation Press.

Prashad, Vijay. 1996. "Desh: The Contradictions of 'Homeland.'" In *Contours of the Heart: South Asians Map North America*, ed. Sunaina Maira and Rajini Srikanth, 225–236. New York: Asian American Writers' Workshop and Rutgers University Press.

———. 2000. *The Karma of Brown Folk.* Minneapolis: University of Minnesota.

Ramírez, Yasmin, and Henry C. Estrada. 1999. Pressing the Point: Parallel Expressions in the Graphic Arts of the Chicano and Puerto Rican Movements. Exhibit at El Museo del Barrio, New York.

Reed, Thomas Vernon. 2005. *The Art of Protest: Culture and Activism from the Civil Rights Movement to the Streets of Seattle.* Minneapolis: University of Minnesota Press.

Reichert, Joshua S. 1982. "A Town Divided: Economic Stratification and Social Relations in a Mexican Migrant Community." *Social Problems* 29: 411–423.

Repak, Terry. 1994. "Labor Market Incorporation of Central American Immigrants in Washington, DC." *Social Problems* 41: 114–128.

Rey, Terry. 1998. "The Virgin Mary and Revolution in Saint-Domingue: The Charisma of Romaine-la-Prophétesse." *Journal of Historical Sociology* 11 (3): 341–369.

———. 1999. *Our Lady of Class Struggle: The Cult of the Virgin Mary in Haiti.* Trenton: Africa World Press.

———. 2002. "Sending *Maji* and Money across Waters: Transnational Streams of Haitian Religious Culture." Paper presented at the Allen Morris Conference on the History of Florida and the Atlantic World, Florida State University, Tallahassee, February 2.

———. 2004. "Marian Devotion at a Haitian Catholic Parish in Miami: The Feast Day of Our Lady of Perpetual Help." *Journal of Contemporary Religion* 19 (3): 353–374.

———. 2005a. "*'Lavyèj Mari pa sou zafè kawotchou ankò.'* Le renouveau charismatique catholique en Haïti." *Journal of Haitian Studies* 11 (2): 34–47.

———. 2005b. "Trees in Haitian Vodou." In *Encyclopedia of Religion and Nature*, ed. Bron R. Taylor, 1658–1659. London: Continuum.

Richman, Karen. 2005. "The Protestant Ethic and the Dis-Spirit of Vodou. Religious Conversion, Labor Incorporation, and Transnationalism among Haitians in South Florida." In *Immigrant Faiths: Transforming Religious Life in America*, ed. Karen I. Leonard, Alex Stepick, Manuel A. Vásquez, and Jennifer Holdaway, 165–188. Lanham, MD: AltaMira Press.

Rieff, David. 1994. *The Exile: Cuba in the Heart of Miami.* New York: Touchstone Publishers.

Rivera, Diego. 1979. *Arte y Política.* Mexico City: Editorial Grijalba.

Roca, Octavio. 1984. *Alicia Alonso: A Passionate Life of Dance.* New York: Atheneum.

———. 2003. Interview with Alicia Alonso. http://alocubano.com/alicia_alonso.htm

Rodman, Selden. 1988. *Where Art Is Joy: Haitian Art: The First Forty Years.* New York: Ruggles de Latour.

Rodríguez, Ana Patricia. 2001. "Refugees of the South: Central Americans in the U.S. Latino Imagery." *American Literature* 73 (2): 387–412.

———. 2004. "Second Hand Identities: The Autoethnographic Performances of Quique Avilés and Leticia Hernández-Linares." *Revista Istmo* http://collaborations.denison.edu/istmo/no8/articulos/second.html.

———. 2005. "Departamento 15: Cultural Narratives of Salvadoran Transnational Migration." *Latino Studies* 3:19–41.

———. n.d. "Mozote Homeland: Diasporic Memories of the Salvadoran Civil War in Testimonial and Filmic Narratives." http://collaborations.denison.edu/istmo/n13/articulos/mozote.html.

Rodríguez, Artemio. 2006. *American Dream: Ten Years of Prints, Books and Drawings—Diez Años de Grabados, Libros y Dibujos.* Los Angeles: La Mano Press.

Rodríguez, Félix V. Matos. 2001. "The 'Browncoats' Are Coming": Latino Public History in Boston. *Public Historian* 23 (4): 15–28.

Rodríguez, Nestor P., and Jacqueline M. Hagan. 1992. "Apartment Reconstructuring and Latino Immigrants: A Case Study." *Comparative Urban and Community Research* 4: 164–180.

———. 2004. "Fractured Families and Communities: Effects of Immigration Reform in Texas, Mexico, and El Salvador." *Latino Studies* 2 (3): 328–351.

Rodriguez, Richard. 1988. "Introduction." In *To the Promised Land*, by Ken Light. New York: Aperture and the California Historical Society.

Romain, Charles-Poisset. 1986. *Le protestantisme dans la societé haïtienne: Contribution à l'étude sociologique d'une religion.* Port-au-Prince: Deschamps.

Rose, Peter. 1985. "Asian Americans: From Pariahs to Paragons." In *Clamor at the Gates: The New Immigration*, ed. Nathan Glazer, 181–212. San Francisco: Institute of Contemporary Studies.

Rothstein, Edward. 2005. "A Mosaic of Arab Culture at Home in America." *New York Times*, October 24.

Ruggles, Steven, Matthew Sobek, Trent Alexander, Catherine A. Fitch, Ronald Goeken, Patricia Kelly Hall, Miriam King, and Chad Ronnander. 2008. Integrated Public Use Microdata Series: Version 4.0 [machine-readable database]. Produced and distributed by Minnesota Population Center, Minneapolis.

Ruíz, Enrique E. Sánchez. 1988. "Los medios de difusión masiva y la centralización en México." *Mexican Studies / Estudios Mexicanos* 4 (1): 25–54.

Rumbaut, Rubén G. 1994. "The Crucible Within: Ethnic Identity, Self-Esteem, and Segmented Assimilation among Children of Immigrants." *International Migration Review* 8 (4): 748–793.

———. 2000. "Vietnamese, Laotian, and Cambodian Americans." In *Contemporary Asian America: A Multidisciplinary Reader*, ed. Min Zhou and James Gatewood, 175–206. New York: New York University Press.

———. 2004. "Ages, Life Stages, and Generational Cohorts: Decomposing the First and Second Generations in the United States." *International Migration Review* 38 (3): 1160–1205.

Rumbaut, Rubén, and Alejandro Portes. 2001. *Ethnicities: Children of Immigrants in America*. Berkeley: University of California Press and Russell Sage Foundation Press.

Runyon, Robert. 2008. "The South Texas Border, 1900–1920: Photographs from the Robert Runyon Collection." Austin: University of Texas. http://runyon.lib.utexas.edu/.

Saada, Leila. 2005. "Proud Icon." *Al-Ahram Weekly*, May 11.

Said, Edward. 1979. *Orientalism*. New York: Random House Publishers.

Saito, Leland. 1998. *Race and Politics: Asian Americans, Latinos, and Whites in a Los Angeles Suburb*. Urbana: University of Illinois Press.

Salaita, Steven. 2006. *Anti-Arab Racism: Where It Comes from and What It Means for Politics Today*. London: Pluto.

Saltzmann, Jonathan, Maria Cramer, Connie Paige. 2006. "Illegal Immigrants Toiled for Governor: Guatemalans Say Firm Hired Them." *Boston Globe*, December 1, p. 3.

Samora, Julian. 1971. *Los Mojados: The Wetback Story*. Notre Dame, IN: University of Notre Dame Press.

Samponaro, Frank N., and Paul J. Vanderwood. 1992. *War Scare on the Rio Grande: Robert Runyon's Photographs of the Border Conflict, 1913–1916*. Austin: Texas State Historical Association.

Sánchez Lara, Rosa María. 1990. *Los Retablos Populares: Exvotos Pintados*. Mexico City: Universidad Nacional Autónoma de México, Instituto de Investigaciones.

San Diego Reader. 2004. "Art Is Slow: Interview with lê thi diem thúy." February 5. Estéticas.

Sarber, Mary A. 1977. *Photographs from the Border: The Otis A. Aultman Collection*. El Paso: El Paso Public Library Association.

Sarroub, Loukia. 2001. "The Sojourner Experience of Yemeni American High School Students: An Ethnographic Portrait." *Harvard Educational Review* 71 (3): 390–415.

Sassen, Saskia. 2006. *Cities in a World Economy*. 3rd ed. Thousand Oaks, CA: Pine Forge Press.

Sattar, Muntasir. 2006. "Assimilate or Integrate? A Closer Look at South Asian Muslim Youth in New York City." *South Asian Magazine for Action and Reflection (SAMAR)*. htttp://www.samarmagazine.org.

Schroeder, Francisco Arturo. 1968. "Plateresco." *Retablos Mexicanos: Artes de México* 106 (15).

Selz, Peter. 2006. *Art of Engagement: Visual Politics in California and Beyond.* Berkeley: University of California Press.

Shaheen, Jack. 2002. "Hollywood's Muslim Arabs." In *A Community of Many Worlds*, ed. Kathleen Benson and Philip Kayal, 191–212. New York: Syracuse University Press.

———. 2003. "Bad Arabs: How Hollywood Vilifies a People." *Annals of the American Academy of Political and Social Science* (July): 171–193.

Shalal-Esa, Andrea. 2003. "Arab-American Writers Identify with Communities of Color." *Aljadid: A Review and Recode of Arab Culture and Arts* 9 (Winter/Spring): 24–26.

Sheehy, Daniel Edward. 2006. *Mariachi Music in America: Experiencing Music, Expressing Culture.* Global Music series. New York: Oxford University Press.

Shukla, Sandhya. 2003. *India Abroad: Diasporic Cultures of Postwar America and England.* Princeton: Princeton University Press.

Siegel, Beatrice. 1979. *Alicia Alonso: The Story of a Ballerina.* New York: Frederick Warne Publishers.

Siems, Larry, ed. 1992. *Between the Lines: Letters between Undocumented Mexican and Central American Immigrants and Their Families and Friends.* Hopewell, NJ: Ecco Press.

Simonett, Helena. 2001. "Narcocorridos: An Emerging Micromusic of Nuevo L. A." *Ethnomusicology* 45 (2): 315–337.

Smith, Christopher Holmes. 1997. "Method in the Madness: Exploring the Boundaries of Identity in Hip-Hop Performativity." *Social Identities: Journal for the Study of Race, Nation and Culture* 3 (3): 345–374.

Smith, Tammy. 2007. "Narrative Boundaries and the Dynamics of Ethnic Conflict and Conciliation." *Poetics* 35:22–46.

Social Impact of the Arts Project (SIAP). 2008. Cultural Assets Database, Metropolitan Philadelphia. University of Pennsylvania, Philadelphia.

Solís, Felipe. 1991. *Tesoros Artísticos del Museo Nacional de Antropología.* Mexico City: Editorial Aguilar.

Stanley, William. 1987. "Economic Migrants or Refugees from Violence? A Time-Series Analysis of Salvadoran Migration to the United States." *Latin American Research Review* 22:132–154.

Stephenson, Kye. 2005. "Wyclef Officially Launches Refugee by DIA Clothing." *All HipHop News*, June 29. http://www.allhiphop.com/hiphopnews/?ID=4561.

Stepick, Alex. 1998. *Pride against Prejudice: Haitians in the United States.* Boston: Allyn and Bacon.

———. 2005. "God Is Apparently Not Dead. The Obvious, the Emergent, and the Unknown in Immigration and Religion." In *Immigrant Faiths: Transforming Religious Life in America*, ed. Karen I. Leonard, Alex Stepick, Manuel Vásquez, and Ann Holdaway, 11–37. Lanham, MD: Alta Mira Press.

Stepick, Alex, and Alejandro Portes. 1986. "Flight into Despair: A Profile of Recent Haitian Refugees in South Florida." *International Migration Review* 20 (2): 329–350.

Stern, Mark J., and Susan C. Seifert. 2005a. *The Dynamics of Cultural Participation: Metropolitan Philadelphia, 1996–2004.* Philadelphia: University of Pennsylvania, Social Impact of the Arts Project.

———. 2005b. *"Natural" Cultural Districts: Arts Agglomerations in Metropolitan Philadelphia and Implications for Cultural District Planning.* Philadelphia: University of Pennsylvania, Social Impact of the Arts Project.

———. 2005c. *Philadelphia and Camden Cultural Participation Benchmark Project: Final Report.* Philadelphia: University of Pennsylvania, Social Impact of the Arts Project.

———. 2006. *Assessment of the Community Partners in Arts Access Initiative for the Knight Foundation: Interim Report.* Philadelphia: University of Pennsylvania, Social Impact of the Arts Project.

Stern, Mark J., Susan C. Seifert, and Mehreen Zaman. 2005. *Gauging the Informal Arts Sector, Metropolitan Philadelphia 2004.* Philadelphia: University of Pennsylvania, Social Impact of the Arts Project.

Sterne, Jonathan. 2000. "The Computer Race Goes to Class: How Computers in School Helped Shape the Racial Topography of the Internet." In *Race in Cyberspace,* ed. Beth Kolko, Lisa Nakamura, and Gilbert Rodman, 191–212. New York: Routledge.

Stolick, Matt. 2000. "From the Fringe: The Hip Hop Culture and Ethnic Relations." *Popular Culture Review* 11 (Summer): 121–127.

Sturken, Marita. 1997. *Tangled Memories: The Vietnam War, the AIDS Epidemic, and the Politics of Remembering.* Berkeley: University of California Press.

Suárez-Orozco, Carola, and Marcelo Suárez-Orozco. 2001. *Children of Immigration.* Cambridge, MA: Harvard University Press.

Sublette, Ned. 2004. *Cuba and Its Music: From the First Drums to the Mambo.* Chicago: Chicago Review Press.

Suleiman, Michael. 1999. "The Arab Immigrant Experience." In *Arabs in America: Building a New Future,* ed. Michael Suleiman, 1–24. Philadelphia: Temple University Press.

———. 2002. "Stereotypes, Public Opinion and Foreign Policy: The Impact on American Arab Relations." *Journal of Arab Affairs* 1 (April): 147–166.

Swidler, Ann. 1986. "Culture in Action: Symbols and Strategies." *American Sociological Review* 51:273–86.

Szwed, John. 2005. *Crossovers: Essays on Race, Music, and American Culture.* Philadelphia: University of Pennsylvania Press.

Tai, Hue-Tam Ho, ed. 2001. *The Country of Memory: Remaking the Past in Socialist Vietnam.* Berkeley: University of California Press.

Tannock, Stuart. 2001. *Youth at Work: The Unionized Fast-Food and Grocery Workplace.* Philadelphia: Temple University Press.

Taylor, Charles. 1992. *Multiculturalism and the Politics of Recognition: An Essay with a Commentary by Amy Gutmann.* Ed. Amy Gutmann. Princeton, NJ: Princeton University Press.

Taylor, Paul S. 1933. *A Spanish-Mexican Peasant Community: Arandas in Jalisco, Mexico.* Berkeley: University of California Press.

Tenhula, John. 1991. *Voices from Southeast Asia: The Refugee Experience in the United States* New York: Holmes and Meier Publishers.

Terry, Walter. 1981. *Alicia and Her Ballet Nacional de Cuba: An Illustrated Biography of Alicia Alonso.* New York: Anchor Books.

Tessler, Mark, and Dan Corstange. 2002. "How Should Americans Understand Arab Political Attitudes: Combating Stereotypes with Public Opinion Data from the Middle East." *Journal of Social Affairs* 19 (Winter): 175–181.

Thai, Hung Cam. 2001. "Formation of Ethnic Identity among Second-Generation Vietnamese Americans." In *The Second Generation: Ethnic Identity among Asian Americans,* ed. Pyong Gap Min, 53–83. Lanham, MD: Altamira Press.

Thornton, Sarah. 1996. *Club Cultures.* Cambridge, UK: Polity Press.

Tomkins, Les. 2008. *Chick Corea: Return to Forever—Talking to Les Tomkins in 1972.* http://www.jazzprofessional.com/interviews/Chick%20Corea_1.htm.

Toor, Frances. 1947. *A Treasury of Mexican Folkways.* New York: Crown Publishers.

Tortolero, Carlos. 1988. "Dia De Los Muertos (Day of the Dead)." Chicago: Mexican Fine Arts Center.

Townsend, Richard F. 1992. *The Ancient Americas: Art from Sacred Landscapes.* Munich: Prestel Verlag.

Turner, Frederick C. 1967. Anti-Americanism in Mexico, 1910–1913. *Hispanic American Historical Review* 47 (4): 502–518.

Tweed, Thomas A. 1997. *Our Lady of the Exile: Diasporic Religion at a Cuban Catholic Shrine in Miami.* New York: Oxford University Press.

———. 2006. *Crossing and Dwelling: A Theory of Religion.* Cambridge, MA: Harvard University Press.

United Nations. 2006. "Trends in the Total Migrant Stock: The 2005 Revision." http://esa.un.org/migration/index.asp?panel=4.

U.S. Bureau of the Census. 2000. *Public Use Micro-Data.* Washington, DC.

U.S. Congress. House. 1934. *Hearings before a Subcommittee of the Special Committee on UnAmerican Activities.* 73rd Cong., 2nd sess.

U.S. Congress. Senate. 1920. Committee on Immigration. *Hearings on Admission of Mexican Agricultura Laborers.* 66th Cong., 2nd sess.

———. 1941–1942. *Hearings before a Subcommitteeof the Committee on Immigration.* 77th Cong., 2nd sess.

U.S. Department of Commerce, Bureau of the Census, and Inter-university Consortium for Political and Social Research. 2004. Census of Population and Housing, 2000 (United States): Selected Subsets from Summary File 3 [computer file]. ICPSR13402-v2. Ann Arbor, MI: Inter-university Consortium for Political and Social Research.

U.S. Department of Homeland Security. 2005. "Table 41: Aliens Removed by Criminal Status and Region and Country of Nationality, Fiscal Years 1998 to 2005." In *Statistical Yearbook.* Washington, DC: U.S. Government Publishing Office.

———. 2007. *Yearbook of Immigration Statistics.* http://www.dhs.gov/ximgtn/statistics/publications/LPR07.shtm.

———. 2008. *Yearbook of Immigration Statistics: 2007.* Washington, DC: U.S. Department of Homeland Security, office of Immigration Statistics.

Valéry, Jude. 2000. *Manifestation du Saint Esprit dans le ministère du Rév. Salomon Severe Joseph (1891–1973).* Port-au-Prince: Fardin.

Valle Arizpe, Artemio. 1941. "El exvoto." *Notas de platería.* Mexico City: Editorial Polis.

Vallen, Mark. 2008. "Just Another Poster?—Chicano Graphic Arts in California." http://www.art-for-a-change.com/Chicano/chicano.htm.

Vaughan, Chris. 1983. "Churches Vie for the Soul of Little Haiti." *Miami Herald,* April 16.

Vida Nueva. 2006. "Somos América" (Tidings Corporation), May.

Vitiello, Domenic. 2000. "En marcha por el norte: Identity and Direction in a Rustbelt Ghetto." *Projections* 1 (1): 96–110.

Viviani, Nancy. 1984. *The Long Journey: Vietnamese Migration and Settlement in Australia.* Carlton, Victoria: Melbourne University Press.

Vo Dang, Thuy. 2005. "The Cultural Work of Anticommunism in the San Diego Vietnamese American Community." *Amerasia Journal* 31 (2): 65–86.

Waldinger, R., and M. I. Lichter. 2003. *How the Other Half Works: Immigration and the Social Organization of Labor.* Berkeley: University of California Press.

Wali, Alaka, Rebecca Severson, and Mario Longoni. 2002. *Informal Arts: Finding Cohesion, Capacity and Other Cultural Benefits in Unexpected Places.* Chicago: Columbia College, Center for Arts Policy.

Wali, Alaka, Nosir Contractor, and Rebecca Severson et al. 2007. *Creative Networks: Mexican Immigrant Assets in Chicago.* Chicago: Field Museum.

Wallace, Steven P. 1989. "The New Urban Latinos: Central Americans in a Mexican Immigrant Environment." *Urban Affairs Quarterly* 25: 239–263.

Wan, William. 2003. "Pop Culture Asian American Magazine Falters." *Los Angeles Times*, December 8. http://articles.latimes.com/2003/dec/08/business/fi-yolk8.

Wang, Oliver. 2001. "Between the Notes: Finding Asian America in Popular Music." *American Music* 19 (4): 439–465.

———. 2002. "The Sundance Kid." Interview with Justin Lin. *Mother Jones*, September/October. http://www.motherjones.com/arts/qa/2002/09/ma_114_01.html.

———. 2003. "Jin Wants You to 'Learn Chinese.'" http://www.o-dub.com/weblog/2003_12_14_archive.html.

———. 2004. "Spinning Identities: A Social History of Filipino American DJs in the San Francisco Bay Area (1975–1995)." Ph.D. diss., University of California, Berkeley.

———. 2007. "Rapping and Repping Asian: Race, Authenticity, and the Asian American MC." In *Alien Encounters: Popular Culture in Asian America*, ed. Mimi Thi Nguyen and Thuy Linh Nguyen Tu, 35–68. Durham: Duke University Press.

Waters, Mary C. 1999. *Black Identities: West Indian Immigrant Dreams and American Realities.* New York: Russell Sage Foundation.

Weber, Max. [1905] 1930. *The Protestant Ethic and the Spirit of Capitalism.* Trans. Talcott Parsons. London: Allen and Unwin.

———. [1922] 1963. *The Sociology of Religion.* Trans. Ephiram Fischoff. Boston: Beacon Press.

———. [1925] 1946. "Class, Status, and Party." In *From Max Weber: Essays in Sociology*, ed. and trans. Hans Gerth and C. Wright Mills, 180–195. New York: Oxford University Press.

———. [1925] 1978. "Ethnic Groups." In *Economy and Society*, part 2, chap. 5. Berkeley: University of California Press.

Wei, Li. 1994. *Three Generations, Two Languages, One Family: Language Choice and Language Shift in a Chinese Community in Britain.* Clevedon, UK: Multilingual Matters.

Wei, William. 1993. *The Asian American Movement.* Philadelphia: Temple University Press.

———. 2004. "Commentary on Young Asian American Activists from the 1960s to the Present." In *Asian American Youth: Culture, Identity, and Ethnicity*, ed. Jennifer Lee and Min Zhou, 299–312. New York: Routledge.

Weisman, Alan. 1986. *Frontera: The United States Border with Mexico.* New York: Harcourt Brace Jovanovich.

Whalen, Carmen. 2001. *From Puerto Rico to Philadelphia.* Philadelphia: Temple University Press.

Williams, Raymond. 1977. *Marxism and Literature.* New York: Oxford University Press.

Wong, Deborah Anne. 1994. *Speak It Louder: Asian-Americans Making Music.* New York: Routledge.

———. 2006. "Asian/American Improvisation in Chicago: Tatsu Aoki and the 'New' Japanese American Taiko." *Critical Studies in Improvisation/Études Critiques en Improvisation*, 1 (3). http://www.criticalimprov.com.

Woodson, Drexel G. 1993. Review of *Haiti: The Breached Citadel*, by Patrick Bellegarde-Smith. *New West Indian Guide/Nieuwe West-Indische Gids* 67 (1).

Woodson, Drexel G., and Mamadou A. Baro. 1997. *A Baseline Study of Livelihood Security in the Department of the Artibonite, Center, North, Northeast, and West, Republic of Haiti.* Tucson: Bureau of Applied Research in Anthropology, University of Arizona.

Worby, Paula. 2006. "Phoning Home: Family Separation Faced by Mexican and Central American Day Laborers and Strategies to Maintain Mental Well-Being." Paper presented at the 26th LASA International Congress, March 15–18, San Juan, Puerto Rico.

———. 2008. "About Our Community." *CentroLatino.org.* http://www.centrolatino.org/community.php.

Yang, Jeff. 2005. "Asian Pop/AZN, R.I.P." *SF Gate*, December 8. http://www.sfgate.com/cgi-bin/article.cgi?file=/gate/archive/2005/12/08/apop.DTL.

———. 2006. "Asian Pop: Chickening Out." *SF Gate*, January 26. http://www.sfgate.com/cgi-bin/article.cgi?file=/gate/archive/2006/01/26/apop.DTL.

Yoneyama, Lisa. 1999. *Hiroshima Traces: Time, Space, and the Dialectics of Memory*. Berkeley: University of California.

Yoo, David K. 2000. *Growing Up Nisei: Race, Generation, and Culture among Japanese Americans of California, 1924–49*. Urbana: University of Illinois Press.

Zelinsky, Wilbur. 2005. "Language Patterns." In *The Encyclopedia of New England: The Culture and History of an American Region*, ed. B. Feintuch, D. H. Watters, and University of New Hampshire Center for the Humanities. New Haven: Yale University Press.

Zhou, Min. 2001. "Straddling Different Worlds: The Acculturation of Vietnamese Refugee Children." In *Ethnicities: Children of Immigrants in America*, ed. Rubén G. Rumbaut and Alejandro Portes, 187–227. Berkeley: University of California Press.

Zhou, Min, and Carl L. Bankston. 1998. *Growing Up American: How Vietnamese Children Adapt to Life in the United States*. New York: Russell Sage Foundation Press.

Zhou, Min, and Jennifer Lee. 2007. "Becoming Ethnic or Becoming American? Reflecting on the Divergent Pathways to Social Mobility and Assimilation among the New Second Generation." *Du Bois Review* 4 (1): 189–205.

Zhou, Min, Jennifer Lee, Jody Agius Vallejo, Rosaura Tafoya-Estrada, and Yang Sao Xiong. 2008. "Success Attained, Deterred, and Denied: Divergent Pathways to Social Mobility in Los Angeles's New Second Generation." *Annals of the American Academy of Political and Social Science* 620 (1): 37–61.

Zolberg, Aristide R. 2006. *A Nation by Design: Immigration Policy in the Fashioning of America*. New York: Russell Sage Foundation.

Zukin, Sharon. 1982. *Loft Living: Culture and Capital in Urban Change*. Baltimore: Johns Hopkins University Press.

———. 1995. *The Culture of Cities*. Cambridge, MA: Blackwell.

Notes on Contributors

GILBERTO CÁRDENAS is the Julián Samora Chair in Latino Studies, assistant provost, and the director of the Institute for Latino Studies and the Inter-University Program for Latino Research at the University of Notre Dame. He has written on international migration, border studies, and Latino art and politics.

PAUL DIMAGGIO is the A. Barton Hepburn Professor of Sociology and Public Affairs at Princeton University, where he directs the Center for the Study of Social Organization. He is also the research director of Princeton's Center for Arts and Cultural Policy Studies and has written extensively about participation in the arts and about nonprofit arts organizations. He is the editor of *Nonprofit Enterprise in the Arts* and coauthor (with Francie Ostrower) of *Race, Ethnicity, and Participation in the Arts.*

JORGE DURAND is a research professor of anthropology at the University of Guadalajara, Mexico. With Douglas S. Massey, he spearheaded the Mexican Migration Project, an ambitious longitudinal study that has tracked Mexican migrants to the United States in places of origin and destination for more than two decades. With Massey he is the author of *Crossing the Border* and *Beyond Smoke and Mirrors: Mexican Immigration in an Era of Economic Integration.*

YEN LE ESPIRITU is a professor of ethnic studies at the University of California, San Diego. Her current research projects explore public and private "rememoration" of the Vietnam War and Vietnamese and Vietnamese American transnational lives.

PATRICIA FERNÁNDEZ-KELLY holds a joint position in the Department of Sociology and Office of Population Research at Princeton University. She writes on economic development and globalization, gender, and international migration. With Alejandro Portes she is the editor of *Exceptional Outcomes: Achievement in Education and Employment among the Children of Immigrants (Annals of the American Academy of Political and Social Science).*

AMANEY JAMAL is an assistant professor of politics at Princeton University. Her research focuses on democratization and the politics of civic engagement in the Arab world. She is the author of *Barriers to Democracy: The Other Side of Social Capital in Palestine and the Arab World*, which won the Best Book Award in Comparative Democratization from the American Political Science Association in 2008.

SUNAINA MAIRA is an associate professor of Asian American studies at the University of California, Davis. She is the author of *Missing: Youth, Citizenship, and Empire after 9/11*.

DOUGLAS S. MASSEY is the Henry G. Bryant Professor of Sociology and Public Affairs at the Woodrow Wilson School, Princeton University, and a former president of the American Sociological Association. He is recognized as a topmost authority on Mexican immigration to the United States. He has written extensively on a variety of subjects, including residential segregation, race and ethnicity, and international development.

CECILIA MENJÍVAR is Cowden Distinguished Professor of Sociology in the School of Social and Family Dynamics at Arizona State University. Her research interests focus on the effects of adverse social, economic, political, and legal contexts on diverse aspects of individuals' lives, including family dynamics, religious participation, and links to other social institutions.

CLIFFORD R. MURPHY is the Folklorist at the Maryland State Arts Council, where he codirects Maryland Traditions, a program of the Maryland State Arts Council. Maryland Traditions aims to document folk and traditional arts in Maryland and to share that documentation through public programs, events, and archives.

TERRY REY is an associate professor and chair of the Department of Religion at Temple University. His recent publications include *Bourdieu on Religion: Imposing Faith and Legitimacy*. Currently he is researching religion and violence in Haiti and the Congo.

SUSAN C. SEIFERT is a city planner and director of the Social Impact of the Arts Project at the University of Pennsylvania. Her research focuses on community cultural development, migrants and the creative economy, and the role of the arts and culture in neighborhood revitalization.

ALEX STEPICK is the director of the Immigration and Ethnicity Institute and a professor of global and sociocultural studies at Florida International University. He is also a professor of sociology and the director of the Center for Health and Social Inequality Research at Portland State University. His most recent book is *Churches and Charity in the Immigrant City: Religion, Immigration, and Civic Engagement in Miami*, coedited with Terry Rey and Sarah Mahler.

MARK J. STERN is a professor of social welfare and history and codirector of the Urban Studies Program at the University of Pennsylvania. His scholarship focuses on U.S. social history, inequality and social welfare policy, and the social impact of the arts. His most recent book (coauthored with Michael B. Katz) is *One Nation Divisible: What America Was and What It Is Becoming.*

DOMENIC VITIELLO is assistant professor of city planning and urban studies at the University of Pennsylvania, where his research and teaching focus on migration, community development, and urban agriculture.

DEBORAH WONG teaches at the University of California, Riverside, and is an ethnomusicologist. She is the author of *Sounding the Center: History and Aesthetics in Thai Buddhist Ritual* and *Speak It Louder: Asian Americans Making Music.*

Index

Italicized page numbers refer to figures and tables. Bolded page numbers indicate authors of selections.